CRUDE STRATEGY

CRUDE STRATEGY

RETHINKING THE US MILITARY COMMITMENT TO DEFEND PERSIAN GULF OIL

Charles L. Glaser and
Rosemary A. Kelanic, Editors

GEORGETOWN UNIVERSITY PRESS | WASHINGTON, DC

Library of Congress Cataloging-in-Publication Data

Names: Glaser, Charles L. (Charles Louis), 1954– editor. | Kelanic, Rosemary A., editor
Title: Crude strategy : rethinking the US military commitment to defend Persian Gulf oil / Charles L. Glaser and Rosemary A. Kelanic, editors.
Description: Washington, DC : Georgetown University Press, 2016. | Includes bibliographical references and index.
Identifiers: LCCN 2015040461 | ISBN 9781626163348 (hc : alk. paper) | ISBN 9781626163355 (pb : alk. paper) | ISBN 9781626163362 (eb)
Subjects: LCSH: Persian Gulf Region—Strategic aspects. | Petroleum industry and trade—Political aspects—Persian Gulf Region. | United States—Military relations—Persian Gulf Region. | Persian Gulf Region—Military relations—United States. | United States—Foreign relations—Persian Gulf Region. | Persian Gulf Region—Foreign relations—United States.
Classification: LCC UA832 .C78 2016 | DDC 355/.0330536—dc23
LC record available at http://lccn.loc.gov/2015040461

♾ This book is printed on acid-free paper meeting the requirements of the American National Standard for Permanence in Paper for Printed Library Materials.

17 16   9 8 7 6 5 4 3 2 First printing

Printed in the United States of America

Cover design by Faceout Studio, Charles Brock. Cover image by Thinkstock.

CONTENTS

List of Illustrations   vii

Acknowledgments   ix

Introduction   1
Charles L. Glaser and Rosemary A. Kelanic

Part I. *Background*

1 The United States and the Persian Gulf: 1941 to the Present   21
Salim Yaqub

2 Assessing Current US Policies and Goals in the Persian Gulf   49
Daniel Byman

Part II. *Key Questions*

3 The Economic Costs of Persian Gulf Oil Supply Disruptions   79
Kenneth R. Vincent

4 Saudi Arabian Oil and US Interests   113
Thomas W. Lippman

5 After America: The Flow of Persian Gulf Oil in the
Absence of US Military Force   141
Joshua Rovner

6 US Spending on Its Military Commitments to the Persian Gulf   167
Eugene Gholz

7 Resilience by Other Means: The Potential Benefits of Alternative
Government Investments in US Energy Security   197
John S. Duffield

Part III. *Conclusions and Policy Options*

8   Should the United States Stay in the Gulf?   233
    Charles L. Glaser and Rosemary A. Kelanic

9   The Future of US Force Posture in the Gulf:
    The Case for a Residual Forward Presence   251
    Caitlin Talmadge

List of Contributors   281
Index   287

ILLUSTRATIONS

Figures

3.1. US Oil Consumption by Sector, 2014   83

3.2. US Power Sector's Petroleum Consumption, 1970–2014   84

3.3. Proved World Oil Reserves by Region, 2014   86

3.4. Real Oil Prices and US Recessions, 1974–2012   89

Map

2.1. Major US Military Bases in the Middle East, January 2015   62

Tables

3.1. Persian Gulf Oil Output Volumes, 2014   86

3.2. Major Historical Oil Supply Disruptions   90

3.3. Estimates of the Economic Losses from a Major Oil Supply Disruption (Billion US$)   103

4.1. Oil and Budget Projections, 2005–30   116

7.1. Summary of Possible Measures and Potential Benefits   200

7.2. Summary of Possible Demand-Side Solutions   219

9.1. Summary of Threats to the Free Flow of Oil from the Gulf   254

9.2. Comparing the Underlying Assumptions of Different Postures   256

9.3. US Air Force Assets on the Arabian Peninsula   265

9.4. Typical Carrier Air Wing   269

ACKNOWLEDGMENTS

This book is truly a collective endeavor, and many people helped along the way toward its completion. First and foremost, we would like to thank the authors of this volume, not just for contributing excellent chapters, but also for offering helpful feedback on all sections of the manuscript that greatly improved the final product.

For detailed comments on early drafts that were presented at our authors' workshop, we would like to thank Steve Fetter, Greg Gause, Marc Lynch, Michael O'Hanlon, and Rob Weiner, as well as participants in the Energy Security Working Group at the Institute for Security and Conflict Studies in the Elliott School of International Affairs at George Washington University. Dan Jacobs provided excellent research assistance on issues that cut across chapters, and Catherine Silvey offered invaluable administrative support.

We are deeply grateful to an anonymous donor to the Elliott School, whose generous support made this volume possible. We also thank Don Jacobs and his team at Georgetown University Press for their expert editorial guidance, as well as the anonymous reviewers for their insightful input. Last but not least, we thank our families for their unwavering support.

Introduction

Charles L. Glaser and Rosemary A. Kelanic

America has long defined the free flow of Persian Gulf oil as a key component of its grand strategy. Since the late 1970s US military force has increasingly become the instrument for achieving this end. The 1979 Iranian Revolution spurred plans to bolster American military power in the region, and the mission took on new urgency when the Soviet Union invaded Afghanistan by the end of the year. In the wake of Moscow's surprising move, President Jimmy Carter warned in January 1980 that the flow of Persian Gulf oil was a vital US interest and that Washington would use "any means necessary, including military force," to protect it. The statement became known as the Carter Doctrine, and in one form or another, it has underpinned US policy ever since. The Rapid Deployment Joint Task Force created in March 1980 enabled the United States to quickly project power into the region. Three years later the United States created Central Command as a unified, multiservice command responsible for South Asia and the Middle East. To support its military requirements in the Persian Gulf, the United States built up significant sealift and airlift capabilities, prepositioned matériel in the region, negotiated access to regional facilities, and improved its major military base at Diego Garcia in the Indian Ocean. The United States fought the Gulf War of 1991 to ensure that Iraq's invasion of Kuwait was not the first step toward Saddam Hussein dominating the region's oil supplies. US capabilities deployed in the region increased further following that war. The Iraq War of 2003, although not directly related to US oil interests, would likely not have occurred but for the long-standing oil-driven involvement of the United States in the region.[1]

The American objective of protecting Persian Gulf oil has generated little controversy among scholars and policymakers since the Gulf became a focus of US military deployments in 1980. The Persian Gulf has kept its central role in US grand strategy primarily because it accounts for a large fraction of global oil exports and proven reserves. This unquestioned focus on protecting Persian Gulf oil may seem unsurprising given the widely appreciated importance of oil to the American economy. The United States consumes roughly 19 million barrels of petroleum daily, accounting for nearly 20 percent of global consumption.[2] Petroleum is the single largest source of energy in the United States, accounting for 36 percent of all US primary energy consumption, and it plays a special role in transportation, which relies on oil for 92 percent of its fuel.[3] More broadly oil plays a critical role in the health of the global economy, which in turn influences the US economy.

Nevertheless, the US military commitment to the Gulf should be revisited. Since the United States established its commitment, quite dramatic changes have occurred in the regional balance of power, the nature of threats to US security, and global energy trends—all of which bear directly on US interests. This opens up the possibility that the United States should significantly revise its policy toward the Persian Gulf both in terms of how it defines its strategic interests in the region and in the means it uses to pursue them.

Motivated by these observations, this book analyzes two questions. First, and most basic, *should the United States continue to rely on military capabilities to preserve the flow of Persian Gulf oil?* To answer this question, we examine the key rationales driving current US policies, lay out the assumptions and conditions upon which they depend, and assess how strong the case for American involvement really is. If the threats to Persian Gulf oil have diminished, or if oil disruptions themselves have become less dangerous to the United States, an American security commitment to the region may no longer make sense. Yet even if the old assumptions hold and the United States should remain strategically engaged in the Gulf, questions remain about whether the current US military posture in the Gulf is the right one.

This observation naturally segues to our second question: *If a US security commitment remains strategically sound, what military posture would be most appropriate for protecting Gulf oil from likely threats?* For the past few decades, the United States has relied upon a forward-deployed military presence to support its regional strategy. Yet given political change in the region, whether this posture still suits US interests is unclear. Depending on the nature and severity of threats to Persian Gulf oil, the United States may wish to adopt an over-the-horizon stance that reduces the American military's footprint in the Persian Gulf while preserving its ability to perform key missions.

Admittedly US interests in the Persian Gulf extend beyond oil to include preventing nuclear proliferation, fighting terrorism, and spreading democracy. Yet although our analysis of US policy for protecting the flow of oil constitutes a partial analysis of American strategy in the region, the potential implications are far reaching. Oil has been widely recognized as a critical driving force behind US policy in the Gulf since the Second World War. The presence of oil elevates the strategic importance of the entire region, raising the stakes across all US interests there. While the United States cares about nonproliferation, counterterrorism, and democracy promotion across many regions, such issues take on special significance in the Persian Gulf because of their potential ramifications for maintaining a steady flow of petroleum.

Why Reevaluate Now?

Many distinct factors suggest that a full reevaluation of the US strategic relationship to the Persian Gulf is necessary. One is simply that the American security role has gone unexamined for so long that it is practically taken for granted. Even scholarly analyses of US grand strategy that have challenged the justifications for the country's key alliances in Europe and Asia have called for the United States to retain its strategic ties to the Gulf. In this regard the Gulf is unique: It is the only major US commitment that has gone virtually unchallenged since the end of the Cold War. Many strands of the grand strategy debate favor American involvement in the traditional regions of Europe, Northeast Asia, and the Persian Gulf.[4] In contrast, neo-isolationist scholars have powerfully argued for ending US commitments in Europe and Asia, maintaining, even before the collapse of the Soviet Union, that these areas could protect themselves.[5] Moreover, they worried that if for some reason a conflict did break out, US alliance commitments would draw the United States into conflicts that were both dangerous and unnecessary for protecting its security. Unlike these sharply divergent positions on America's key major-power allies, there has been virtually no disagreement over US policy regarding the Gulf. In line with US policy and with so-called selective engagers, neo-isolationists have called for retaining the US commitment to the Persian Gulf.

Second, and related to the grand strategy debate, dramatic geopolitical events have altered the potential threats to Persian Gulf oil and changed the American relationship with the region. During the Cold War, the possibility that the Soviet Union could gain control of Persian Gulf oil posed a security threat to the United States, because denying access to oil could undermine the US ability to fight in Europe. As the Cold War wound down, the key threat became the possibility that a single regional power might gain control of the Gulf's oil and thus jeopardize American prosperity. Such a regional hegemon would then control a sufficiently large portion of global oil supply to manipulate prices and to coerce the United States by damaging its economy. Iraq's 1990 invasion of Kuwait provoked an American military response for precisely this reason.

Today, well after the 2003 Iraq War deposed Saddam Hussein and destroyed the Iraqi military, a more fluid and ambiguous security environment characterizes the region. In 2014–15 the Islamic State captured significant chunks of territory in Syria and Iraq, prompting the United States to redeploy American military advisers and launch air strikes on Islamic State strongholds. US forces stationed in the region remain in flux, reflecting these developments as well as delays in withdrawing combat forces from Afghanistan. Russian military intervention in the fall of 2015 to support the Bashar al-Assad government widened the crisis over the Syrian civil war. Meanwhile, the United States, its negotiating partners, and Iran have reached a nuclear deal that promises to greatly reduce Iran's ability to acquire nuclear weapons for fifteen years. However, not all US allies in the region are confident that the nuclear agreement will increase their security (and Israel has strongly opposed the deal). Finally, in the wake of the Arab Spring and the growing reach of the Islamic State, doubts remain about the stability of local regimes—especially Saudi Arabia, the linchpin to reliable Persian Gulf oil.[6]

Third, recent developments in the oil market further muddy the strategic picture in the Gulf. Globally, driven in large part by the rapid growth of developing countries, the center of gravity of oil consumption is shifting from the United States to Asia. While oil consumption by member countries of the Organization for Economic Cooperation and Development (OECD) is predicted to decline by almost 25 percent through 2040, growth in non-OECD consumption by more than 50 percent will more than offset it, with China and India accounting for more than half of this increase. By 2035 China is expected to surpass the United States as the world's largest petroleum consumer.[7] Especially striking, the country's imports of Persian Gulf oil are set to quintuple by 2030.[8]

In tandem with its thirst for oil, China has deepened its economic ties to the Persian Gulf, particularly with Saudi Arabia, and now imports about half of its petroleum from the region. China recently surpassed the United States as the largest purchaser of Saudi petroleum for the first time, prompting Khalid A. al-Falih, president and CEO of Saudi Aramco, to remark: "China is the growth market for petroleum."[9] In January 2012 the two countries agreed to cooperate in developing Saudi Arabia's civilian nuclear energy program and announced a joint venture to refine Saudi Arabian crude for the Chinese market in the Red Sea town of Yanbu, bypassing the Strait of Hormuz.[10] Arguably, on the one hand, China's growing involvement in the region makes achieving American goals more difficult. For instance, as efforts to stop Iran's nuclear program were intensifying, some faulted Beijing for providing "diplomatic cover" to Iran, a major source of Chinese oil, by resisting international sanctions designed to punish Tehran.[11] On the other hand, shared interests in the stability of global markets could pave the way for Sino-American cooperation in the Gulf and beyond.[12]

Finally, reevaluating the US commitment to the Persian Gulf is also necessary in light of the changed political climate for government spending. The Budget Control Act of 2011, designed to rein in the federal deficit, required the Pentagon to cut its budget five years in a row. While the defense budget increased in fiscal year 2016, political pressure to reduce government spending continues, raising questions about whether the United States can afford to maintain its foreign policy commitments and defense priorities. Some proposals have called for significantly cutting the size of the US Army, reducing it to a level not seen since before World War II.[13] Moreover, responding to China's continuing economic and military growth, the United States has decided to pivot, or "rebalance," toward Asia. The combination of uncertain defense budgets and the increased priority on Asia may require the United States to trim some of its historical priorities. All of these factors indicate that a reevaluation of US policy is in order.

What about the North American Oil Resurgence?

Yet another important development is under way in the Western Hemisphere that some believe could influence US foreign policy. Booming unconventional oil output has upended the long-held wisdom about the future of petroleum production in the United States and North America at large, prompting speculation that the United States may lose strategic interest in the Gulf.[14] According to the US Energy Information Administration (EIA), increased domestic "tight oil" production will keep US output steady at about 10 million barrels per day (mb/d) through 2040—a number that would have been considered unthinkable a few years ago.[15] Combined with fuel efficiency gains that reduce petroleum demand, these figures suggest that net US oil imports will drop nearly 50 percent over the same period.[16] More remarkably the International Energy Agency (IEA) projects a near doubling in Canadian oil output from 4.0 mb/d in 2013 to 7.4 mb/d in 2040, thanks to the country's vast resources of oil sands. Driven in large part by the Canadian boom, the IEA predicts that North America will emerge as a net oil *exporter* by 2020 and continue as such through 2040.[17] Already the United States relies less heavily on Persian Gulf oil than it did in the past, with its total imports from the region decreasing from 27 percent in 1993 to only 18 percent in 2010. Although the recent drop in oil prices, if it lasts, could undercut US unconventional oil production, analysts believe the industry will remain viable unless oil falls below $40 per barrel for a sustained period, and its resilience in the face of lower prices suggests the threshold could be even lower.[18]

Despite these dramatic changes, North American oil production does not diminish the importance of Persian Gulf oil to US prosperity. This essential point has frequently been lost in the American public debate, which remains mired in the flawed notion of "energy independence." That argument asserts that reliance on foreign oil undermines US security because foreign suppliers could hold the US economy hostage by threatening to turn off the tap. The solution is to produce more oil at home, thus removing this potential source of political leverage. The more independent the United States is in production, the argument goes, the more independent its policies can be of foreign influence.

This argument fundamentally misunderstands the functioning of global oil markets. Contrary to popular belief, the global nature of petroleum trade renders energy independence a largely meaningless concept when it comes to a fungible commodity like oil. Oil is sold on a global market; therefore, the price of oil in the United States is intimately related to its price everywhere else. Economists often explain this connection by likening the global oil market to a bathtub with many spigots (producers) and many drains (consumers). It does not matter how much oil from a particular spigot flows into a particular drain. What is important is the global oil price, which depends on the quantity of oil available in the tub and the size of worldwide demand. Any disruption that sharply reduces supply lowers the level of oil in the bathtub and hurts all consumers drawing from the tub. Thus, as long as the United States is integrated into the global economy, it will be affected by disruptions in the Persian Gulf or elsewhere that influence the global oil price, even if US oil imports from the Gulf fall to zero.

Other oil realities reinforce this central point. First, the North American unconventional oil boom, as remarkable as it may be, is unlikely to be so large relative to world production to fundamentally alter the global supply picture. For this reason Persian Gulf resources will remain crucial for future global production. North American proven oil reserves, while substantial, amount to roughly 233 billion barrels, or 14 percent of global oil reserves. By contrast, the big six oil producers of the Persian Gulf region—Iran, Iraq, Qatar, United Arab Emirates (UAE), Kuwait, and Saudi Arabia—have an estimated 800 billion barrels of proven reserves, or nearly half the world's total.[19] Clearly Gulf oil will still play the major role in meeting future oil demand.

Second, domestic controversy over hydraulic fracturing, or "fracking"—the method used to extract petroleum from oil sands, shale, and tar—makes full exploitation of North American unconventional reserves uncertain. At issue are two factors: the known environmental impacts of fracking, which are worse than those associated with conventional oil production, and the effects on human health, which are unclear but potentially negative. Extraction often requires massive amounts of freshwater, which the process transforms into toxic wastewater. Some evidence even suggests that fracking may contribute to earthquakes.[20] Concerns over these issues have elicited a public push to limit the practice, with mixed results. While states such as Pennsylvania and North Dakota have barreled ahead with the technology, New York has announced a statewide ban on fracking, and cities such as Los Angeles are considering similar measures.[21] In sum, increased US production neither changes the fundamental global dependence on Gulf petroleum for future oil consumption nor isolates the United States from supply interruptions that could increase the price of oil.

Analyzing the Oil Logic of the US Commitment to the Gulf

To analyze the US military commitment to protect the reliable flow of Gulf oil, we need to start with a clear understanding of the US interests at stake. The paramount US interest now is economic prosperity. The rationale underpinning the US commitment to the Gulf is that an interruption of Gulf oil will increase the global price of oil, and that increase will in turn harm the US economy in two ways—directly by raising oil prices in the United States and indirectly by damaging the economies of countries that are economically interdependent with the United States.

This differs importantly from the Cold War, when the possibility of the Soviet Union's gaining control of Persian Gulf oil posed a direct security threat to the United States. American leaders worried then that the Red Army might launch an invasion to seize control of the region's petroleum and deny the United States access, which might have weakened the Western alliance or, in the worst case, undermined the ability of the United States to fight a long war in Europe. The US commitment to maintaining the free flow of Gulf oil was partly born of these fears, yet the demise of the Soviet Union has not prompted a full reevaluation of the US military commitment to the region.[22] No threat comparable to the danger of Soviet intervention exists today; nothing has the potential to jeopardize the US military's capability to protect the homeland, its allies, and its vital interests.[23]

Importantly the end of the Soviet Union did more than simply lessen the threat to American interests in the Gulf; it changed the very nature of the danger, converting a threat to American security into a potential threat to its prosperity, and led to important ramifications for the criteria American leaders should use to evaluate US strategy in the Gulf. With prosperity motives ascendant, the issue of whether American military involvement constitutes a good investment of resources looms larger than it would if security were the sole concern. Moreover, recognizing that US policy in the Gulf is motivated "only" by economic concerns should change the risk calculus involved. When it comes to national security issues, the United States has historically been extremely risk averse and willing to expend tremendous resources for even small gains in national security. Risks to prosperity may be more tolerable in comparison, especially when we consider that the resources not allocated to the current military commitment could be devoted to other valuable purposes.

Any analysis of the US strategy to protect Persian Gulf oil must answer four key questions. For the reasons sketched previously, we expect that today's answers to these questions could differ markedly from the days of the Cold War, when the American commitment was first established. The first two questions measure the "value added" of an American security commitment by examining the counterfactual scenario of a world where the United States had no military engagement in the Gulf. First, *how much would a substantial disruption of Persian Gulf oil harm the American economy, assuming the United States does not intervene with military force to restore the flow of oil?* The larger the economic costs of a disruption would be, the more the United States should be willing to invest in military forces, and the more willing it should be to incur the cost of fighting, to avoid a disruption. The economic impact of a disruption depends on a wide range of factors, including its size and duration; the amount of spare capacity in the market; the price increase generated by the disruption; and, in turn, the damage inflicted on the US and global economy by this price increase. Because the Persian Gulf provides such a large percentage of global oil, a massive disruption is possible. Evaluating the impact on economic growth of disruptions of various sizes requires understanding both the relationship between oil supply and demand and the mechanisms through which oil price increases ripple through the US economy.

The second question is, *absent an American military commitment to the region, how likely are significant disruptions of the flow of Persian Gulf oil?* The expected consequences of a disruption depend not only on the economic damage it would inflict but also on its probability. If the likelihood of disruption is small, the overall risk to the American economy could remain small even if the potential costs of a major disruption loom large.

Persian Gulf security politics enter the picture here. In broad brush, the potential causes of disruption today fall into two basic categories—domestic political unrest and international conflict in the region. First, internal instability and cyber attacks in major oil-exporting nations could interfere with production, removing millions of barrels per day from the global market. Although several Persian Gulf nations could be vulnerable to this risk, a disruption of Saudi output represents the nightmare scenario. Saudi Arabia is especially important, both because it produces such a large share of global oil—about 11.5 mb/d—and because it possesses spare capacity that can be used to offset disruptions elsewhere.[24]

Second, disturbances to Persian Gulf oil could arise from international political dynamics. The most commonly identified dangers in this category are (1) the rise of a hegemonic regional power that controls such a large percentage of Gulf oil that it can manipulate global prices and use its position to punish or coerce the United States and its allies; (2) a large war between regional powers that interrupts the flow of oil by damaging oil infrastructure or making transport too dangerous; and (3) the closing of the Strait of Hormuz, through which most Gulf oil passes, by a hostile state, with Iran foreseen as the likely culprit. For the dangers in both the domestic and the international categories, we analyze how much the US military commitment to the Gulf reduces them. If the dangers are large but the United States can do little to reduce them, then the benefit of the US military commitment is small. Similarly, if the dangers are small to begin with, then the benefits are also small.

The remaining two questions consider the options available to the United States for reducing the possible economic costs of a disruption and the investment required to pursue these options. Our third key question for analysis is, *how much does the United States invest to sustain its military commitment to defend Persian Gulf oil?* The most direct investment involves the spending on the military forces required to perform necessary military missions in the Gulf. For decades the Persian Gulf has been one of the major theaters of operation for US forces. How much smaller and different could US forces be if the United States were to end its Gulf commitment? How much would these changes enable the United States to reduce its defense budget? Analyzing this third key question is complicated, as many US forces committed to Persian Gulf contingencies are also committed to other contingencies. Furthermore, the US investment in the Gulf is not limited to military forces. It includes the potential costs of military operations designed to protect the flow of oil, and they depend not only on the probability of these conflicts and their material costs but also on the human toll they inflict on the US military.

Finally, a full analysis of US policy needs to consider other, nonmilitary means of reducing US economic vulnerability to oil disruptions. If alternative approaches could provide a comparable reduction in the economic risk with a smaller investment of resources, the United States should shift from military to alternative means. Consequently, we need to know the answer to our fourth question: *How effective and expensive are alternative approaches to protecting the US economy from oil disruptions?* The variety of potential alternatives is large, including increasing the US strategic petroleum reserve, boosting the fuel efficiency of the US transportation fleet, substituting biofuels for gasoline, encouraging the electrification of the US transportation fleet, imposing a tax on carbon emissions, and cooperating with other countries to increase their resilience to oil shocks. The combined impact of these alternatives competes with, and potentially complements, US military policies.

Answers to these four questions provide the foundation for developing conclusions about the US military commitment to protect the flow of Persian Gulf oil. For example, if the cost and/or probability of disruptions are low, or if US military commitments cannot significantly reduce disruptions, then the case for current US military policies is significantly weakened. In contrast, if the economic costs of a disruption are high and its probability likely, and if the US military commitment to the Persian Gulf can significantly reduce its probability or duration, then the case for the US investment in and commitment of military forces is much stronger. However, even in this case, the effectiveness of military means must be compared to the potential of alternative investments that could reduce US economic sensitivity to disruptions. The alternatives could be a still better investment.

Structure of the Book

The chapters in part 1, "Background," set the stage for a thorough analysis of US oil-related policy in the Persian Gulf by reviewing the history and current status of the US commitment to the region. In chapter 1, "The United States and the Persian Gulf: 1941 to the Present," Salim Yaqub presents a history of American strategic engagement in the Gulf, from its origins during the Second World War to the present day. He chronicles how US interests in the Gulf evolved in response to changing threats and explains the security policies that American leaders adopted to further the primary goal of maintaining steady access to the region's petroleum resources. Yaqub identifies three major eras in US policy. First, from 1941 to 1971, the United States relied upon its ally, Great Britain, to preserve stability in the Gulf and counter Moscow's influence. Second, after economic woes forced the British to retreat from "east of Suez" in 1971, American leaders enlisted local proxies such as Iran and Iraq to preserve the regional balance of power. This approach lasted until an erstwhile US security partner, Saddam Hussein, upset the order by conquering Kuwait in 1990. Finally, Yaqub characterizes the period from the Gulf War until today as one in which the United States has assumed direct responsibility as a regional security guarantor and, consequently, has established a sizable military footprint.

In chapter 2, "Assessing Current US Policies and Goals in the Persian Gulf," Daniel Byman outlines present-day US interests in the region—including those beyond oil—and analyzes whether current American military commitments are well matched to these interests. Byman identifies four strategic objectives: ensuring the free flow of oil, combating terrorism, preventing regional nuclear proliferation, and encouraging democratization. After surveying the key threats to each, he sketches out the US military's footprint in the region and evaluates whether the US presence in its current form furthers—or potentially hinders—the attainment of these objectives. An important emphasis of Byman's work is the need to consider trade-offs, as US policy to meet one of its interests (e.g., oil security) may conflict with efforts to achieve others (counterterrorism). Finally, working under the assumption that US forces stay forward deployed in the region, Byman assesses three options for fine-tuning current policies: deepening the US commitment, supporting local political reform, and shrinking the American military footprint without lifting it completely.

Each of the chapters in part 2, "Key Questions," addresses a piece of the fundamental grand strategy issue: Should the United States continue to rely on military force to preserve the flow of Persian Gulf oil? As sketched earlier, answers to four questions provide the analytical foundation for grappling with the overarching grand strategy problem. In chapter 3, "The Economic Costs of Persian Gulf Oil Supply Disruptions," Kenneth R. Vincent examines the first question: *How much would a Persian Gulf oil shock damage American prosperity?* Most political observers take for granted that a Gulf supply disruption would wreak havoc on national incomes, but Vincent reveals a significant degree of disagreement among economists as to whether oil shocks truly cripple growth, and if they do so, when, why, and by how much. Although Vincent concludes with confidence that a sizable Gulf oil shock would significantly hurt the US economy, he argues that considerable uncertainty among analysts on basic points such as the price elasticity of oil supply and of GDP makes it impossible to measure the economic costs with any precision. Instead, he offers a range of damage estimates that provide "ballpark" economic costs for the purposes of our grand strategic analysis. At the center of the range for an enormous disruption—one, for example, that halves the flow of oil from the Persian Gulf—Vincent finds that we can expect US GDP to be reduced by approximately $500 billion, which is close to 3 percent of US GDP.

Chapters 4 and 5 address the second question: *If the United States ended its military commitment to protecting the flow of Persian Gulf oil, how much would the threat of disruption increase?* Threats to petroleum exports could arise from internal or external sources. In chapter 4, "Saudi Arabian Oil and US Interests," Thomas W. Lippman takes on the internal instability problem by challenging one of the most commonly cited rationales for stationing American troops in the Gulf—that is, the need to buttress the Saudi regime from domestic threats that could jeopardize the nation's petroleum exports. He argues that the potential danger is overblown. To determine whether the US military presence enhances domestic stability in Saudi Arabia, Lippman first analyzes how vulnerable oil production would be if the United States no longer pledged to guard Saudi Arabia's security. Lippman identifies five plausible scenarios that could harm Saudi oil exports: High rates of domestic oil consumption, coupled with depleted reserves, could undermine Saudi Arabia's ability to export in the latter half of this century; a cyber attack could disable petroleum company mainframes, suspending production; dissident groups could disrupt output through guerrilla attacks on Saudi oil infrastructure; an anti-US regime could come to power and withhold petroleum exports to punish the West; and civil war could ravage the country, causing collateral damage to Saudi oil facilities. Lippman concludes that the only scenario that constitutes a serious threat—that is, domestic oil consumption overwhelming Saudi production, leaving no surplus for future export—has no US military solution.

Joshua Rovner, in chapter 5, "After America: The Flow of Persian Gulf Oil in the Absence of US Military Force," examines how much the external threats to Persian Gulf oil exports might increase if the United States withdrew its regional security commitments. Rovner considers each of the three main threat scenarios: A local hegemon could consolidate the region's petroleum resources and, so doing, gain leverage over world oil prices; a major war in the Gulf could physically disrupt oil exports; and Iran might be more willing and able to interfere with oil traffic through the Strait of Hormuz. He argues that the first two dangers are unrealistic because the Gulf's leading powers—Iran, Iraq, and Saudi Arabia—are too preoccupied with domestic problems to make a run at hegemony or to initiate a regional war. Moreover, even if they wanted to pick a fight, they lack the necessary power projection capabilities to do so effectively. However, Rovner finds that if the United States removed its security umbrella entirely, Iran would be better positioned to close the Strait.

In chapter 6, "US Spending on Its Military Commitments to the Persian Gulf," Eugene Gholz tackles the third question and by extension answers the question, *how much could the United States reduce defense spending by ending this role?* Previous studies significantly overestimate US defense spending on the Gulf commitment, Gholz argues, because they inadequately account for sunk costs, the full range of expenditures, or the general-purpose nature of American military forces. Because US force planning is driven by the policy of preparing for two near-simultaneous major regional contingencies (MRCs), which are "generic" in the sense that they are not assigned to specific theaters, Gholz projects that the United States could only save $5 billion annually in force posture and acquisition costs unless it downsized its planning guidelines to one-and-a-half MRCs or one MRC. This saving is paltry compared to the total defense budget. However, the $5 billion figure represents the military's "overhead" costs of maintaining its commitment to the Gulf but does not include its operational expenses—that is, the costs of fighting future wars to defend Gulf oil exports. If instead the United States shifted to a strategy using one-and-a-half or one MRC, then the reduction in US defense spending could be much larger and reach on the order of $75 billion a year, or roughly 15 percent of the US defense budget.

This brings us to the fourth key question in our analysis: *Could alternative, nonmilitary investments comparably reduce US economic vulnerability to oil shocks at an equal or lesser cost than the military commitment?* John Duffield examines such possibilities in chapter 7, "Resilience by Other Means: The Potential Benefits of Alternative Government Investments in US Energy Security." Whereas the strategy of stationing US forces in the Gulf seeks to prevent supply disruptions from occurring in the first place, the policies that Duffield evaluates represent a different strategy to protect American prosperity—that is, improving the country's economic resilience in case oil price shocks do occur. Duffield categorizes alternative measures according to whether they engage the supply or demand side of the market. Supply-related initiatives include encouraging the development of unconventional US oil resources and increasing the size of the Strategic Petroleum Reserve. Demand-oriented policies consist of efforts to discourage American petroleum consumption, for instance, by raising taxes on gasoline or investing in alternative fuels or flex-fuel technology. Duffield contends that combined investment in these alternative strategies could nearly eliminate the direct damage of an oil shock to the US economy, though this effort could take decades. Even still the United States could sustain indirect damage caused by the harm done to countries with which the US is economically interdependent.

The two chapters in part 3, "Conclusions and Policy Options," explore the alternatives for reorienting US strategy toward the Persian Gulf. In chapter 8, "Should the United States Stay in the Gulf?," Charles L. Glaser and Rosemary A. Kelanic pull together the key findings from the chapters in part 2 to answer the basic grand strategy question: *Should the United States continue to rely on military force to preserve the flow of Persian Gulf oil?* We conclude that the case for maintaining a US military commitment is weaker than commonly assumed and certainly more tenuous than it was in the past. Geopolitical changes have eliminated some of the key possible routes to major disruptions. In addition, US policies have reduced the country's vulnerability to oil disruptions that do occur, and options exist for further reducing its vulnerability. Had the United States not pursued policies to protect itself, a major disruption of Persian Gulf oil could have cost its economy dearly, as Vincent makes clear in chapter 3. However, the petroleum reserves held by the United States and other IEA members, and increasingly by China, have the potential to greatly reduce, if not eliminate, the economic costs of all but the worst-case scenarios—for example, an extended and complete closing of the Strait of Hormuz. Unfortunately, we cannot exclude the possibility of a severe disruption. Although overall chapters 4 and 5 are optimistic about the threats facing the United States, looking a couple of decades forward one plausible threat—an Iranian attempt to close the Strait of Hormuz—continues to exist and would likely increase if the US deterrent were withdrawn. The 2015 nuclear deal with Iran should provide greater certainty for ten to fifteen years that Iran does not have nuclear weapons, thereby making the regional dynamics somewhat more predictable. Given the region's recent turmoil and instability and its sheer complexity, however, any projections a decade or more into the future must acknowledge the possibility of unforeseeable threats to the flow of oil.

Fortunately, approaches for coming close to solving the Hormuz problem over the next decade appear to exist. Building oil pipelines that bypass the Strait, thereby enabling oil to get to market even if the Strait is closed, could eliminate much of the danger. In addition, as Duffield lays out in chapter 7, the United States has a variety of nonmilitary alternatives—ranging from taxes on gasoline to increased subsidies for existing technologies and to increased investments in research and development—that could reduce its economic sensitivity to price shocks. The combination of these measures has the potential to so greatly reduce the economic risks of oil disruptions that the US investment in military capabilities would no longer be warranted. As summarized above, chapter 6 explains that if the US decision to leave the Gulf were accompanied by a shift to a one-MRC planning strategy, the United States could greatly reduce its defense spending. With the dangers of a severe oil disruption greatly reduced, US resources would be better directed to other valuable purposes. Moreover, while the probability of having to fight future wars in the Gulf is hard to predict, leaving the Gulf would enable the United States to avoid the potentially large operational costs, including human losses, of fighting these wars.

Given all of this analysis, we recommend that the United States lay the groundwork over the next decade or so for ending its military commitment to the Gulf. The United States should work to convince the Gulf states, especially Saudi Arabia, to increase the capacity of their bypass pipelines, and it should invest in further reducing US sensitivity to large oil disruptions. Once these improvements are achieved, the United States should revisit the question of leaving the Gulf.

Unless changes in the region have made major disruptions significantly more likely, the best option for the United States then would likely be to end its military commitment to the Persian Gulf.

Because the United States should not terminate its military commitment to the Gulf immediately, it remains important to consider US policy while the United States stays militarily committed to the Gulf. Moreover, even if leaving the Gulf is eventually the US government's optimal foreign policy option, the domestic political barriers to adopting such a radical shift in grand strategy could be prohibitive. For both reasons, in chapter 9, the volume's closing chapter, "The Future of US Force Posture in the Gulf: The Case for a Residual Forward Presence," Caitlin Talmadge answers the remaining question: *If the United States remains committed to preserving the flow of Gulf oil, should it adopt a significantly different force posture?* She presents an in-depth overview of the US military footprint in the region, one that she characterizes as a "heavy forward presence," and assesses its effectiveness in deterring and responding to oil-related contingencies. Talmadge compares the posture with two alternatives: an over-the-horizon approach, which would move the forces responsible for Persian Gulf security out of the region, and a residual forward presence, which is a new posture that she develops. Talmadge constructs a comprehensive framework that evaluates the merits of each strategy according to its underpinning assumptions. Ultimately she concludes that the best option would be to adopt a residual forward presence, which would maintain forward deployment in the Gulf but minimize the visibility of the US military's footprint both ashore and afloat.

Conclusion

Several factors, when combined, place the United States at a critical juncture for reevaluating its long-standing role as the military guarantor of Persian Gulf security. The explicit US commitment to protecting Gulf oil dates to the late 1970s, when the region and the globe looked very different than they do today. Across the intervening decades, a succession of geopolitical shifts reshuffled the threats. During the Cold War, the Soviet Union posed the greatest danger to American interests in the region—interests that included both US economic prosperity as well as US national security that required unimpeded access to Persian Gulf oil in the event of a conventional conflict in Europe. While the dissolution of the Soviet Union removed the direct security threat to US military power, prosperity threats remained. The Gulf War of 1991 greatly reduced the threat posed by Saddam Hussein's Iraq; the US invasion of 2003 eliminated whatever Iraqi threat may have remained. The years since then have seen the region plagued by civil wars and insurgencies that have cast a shadow over the region's ability to reliably produce oil. Volatile defense budgets also suggest that a reappraisal of US strategy may be necessary. The United States faces trade-offs between maintaining historical military commitments, including the protection of Persian Gulf oil, and adapting to new strategic priorities such as the challenges posed by a rising China—and all in a climate of fiscal uncertainty.

The current situation demands new analysis to determine whether a US military commitment to the region is still warranted and, if so, what military posture would be most appropriate. In this book we argue that four key questions must be addressed to evaluate US policy. First, how much damage would a Persian Gulf supply shock inflict on the American economy? The greater the damage, the more the United States should be willing to invest to lessen the risk of shocks through military or other means. Second, by how much would the risk of disruption increase if the United States terminated its military commitment? If the departure of American forces would significantly raise the likelihood of a shock occurring or make such a contingency more difficult to reverse, the United States might gain the most by staying put. Third, how much does the United States spend to meet its military commitments in the Gulf? Holding all else equal and assuming US forces actually do reduce the probability of disruptions, the lower the military price, the more inclined the United States should be to pay it. Finally, could nonmilitary investments offer better protection to the US economy for an equal or lesser investment than military forces? If government policies—including those that would increase transportation fuel efficiency, support alternative fuels, and enlarge the strategic petroleum reserve—can substantially increase US resilience to oil disruptions, nonmilitary options may represent a better strategy than continued reliance on US military power to tamp down potential threats to the flow of Persian Gulf oil.

The following chapters offer fresh perspectives on these questions. Based upon these analyses, we conclude that a major change to US grand strategy is much closer to being desirable than the widely accepted conventional wisdom suggests.

Notes

1. John S. Duffield, *Over a Barrel: The Costs of U.S. Foreign Oil Dependence* (Stanford: Stanford University Press, 2008), chap. 6; Michael T. Klare, *Resource Wars: The New Landscape of Global Conflict* (New York: Henry Holt, 2001), 58–78; and Charles A. Kupchan, *The Persian Gulf and the West: The Dilemmas of Security* (Boston: Allen and Unwin, 1987).

2. BP, *BP Statistical Review of World Energy, June 2015*, 9, https://www.bp.com/content

/dam/bp/pdf/energy-economics/statistical-review-2015/bp-statistical-review-of
-world-energy-2015-full-report.pdf.

3. Ibid., 41. Natural gas, the second-largest source, provides 30 percent of all energy consumed in the United States. The third-largest source, coal, provides 20 percent. Stacy C. Davis, Susan W. Diegel, and Robert G. Boundy, *Transportation Energy Data Book: Edition 33* (Oak Ridge TN: Oak Ridge National Laboratory, 2014), 2–4, table 2.2.

4. For a classic analysis of the immediate post–Cold War grand strategy debate, see Barry R. Posen and Andrew L. Ross, "Competing Visions for U.S. Grand Strategy," *International Security* 21, no. 3 (1996/1997). More recently see Barry R. Posen, "Pull Back: The Case for a Less Activist Foreign Policy," *Foreign Affairs* 92, no. 1 (2013); and Stephen G. Brooks, G. John Ikenberry, and William C. Wohlforth, "Lean Forward: In Defense of American Engagement," *Foreign Affairs* 92, no. 1 (2013).

5. Eugene Gholz, Daryl G. Press, and Harvey M. Sapolsky, "Come Home, America: The Strategy of Restraint in the Face of Temptation," *International Security* 21, no. 4 (Spring 1997): 25–29. For a more differentiated assessment of threats to the flow of Persian Gulf oil that continues to call for a US military commitment to the Gulf, see Eugene Gholz and Daryl Press, "Protecting 'The Prize': Oil and the U.S. National Interest," *Security Studies* 19, no. 3 (2010): 453–83.

6. For example, see Bruce Riedel, "Revolution in Riyadh," in *Big Bets and Black Swans: A Presidential Briefing Book,* ed. Martin Indyk, Tanvi Madan, and Thomas Wright (Washington DC: Brookings, 2013).

7. International Energy Agency (IEA), *World Energy Outlook, 2014* (London: IEA, 2014), 96. China's recent economic slowdown, however, has increased uncertainty about its rate of consumption growth.

8. Emile Hokayem, "Looking East: A Gulf Vision or a Reality?," in *China and the Persian Gulf: Implications for the United States,* ed. Bryce Wakefield and Susan L. Levenstein (Washington DC: Woodrow Wilson International Center for Scholars, 2011), 39; and Jad Mouawad, "China's Rapid Growth Shifts the Geopolitics of Oil," *New York Times,* March 20, 2010.

9. Mouawad, "China's Rapid Growth."

10. "Iranian Threats on Agenda of Upcoming Saudi-Chinese Summit Talks," *BBC Monitoring Middle East,* January 12, 2012; and Summer Said, "Saudi Arabia, China Sign Nuclear Cooperation Pact," *Wall Street Journal,* January 16, 2012.

11. John Lee, "China's Geostrategic Search for Oil," *Washington Quarterly* 35, no. 3 (2012): 87.

12. Jon B. Alterman, "The Vital Triangle," in Wakefield and Levenstein, *China and the Persian Gulf.*

13. Thom Shanker and Helene Cooper, "Pentagon Plans to Shrink Army to Pre–World War II Level," *New York Times,* February 24, 2014, 1.

14. Brian Scheid, "U.S. Oil Boom Fuels Security Fears in the Middle East," *Platts Oilgram News,* January 14, 2013; and "German Intelligence Report Examines Global Impact of U.S. Energy Independence," *BBC Monitoring Europe,* January 18, 2013. Such concerns

prompted the Obama administration to reassure its allies that the United States still places a high priority on Gulf security. Herman Wang, "Obama Adviser Says Oil Boom, Asia Focus Won't Scuttle U.S. Ties to the Middle East," *Platts Inside Energy with Federal Lands*, March 18, 2013. For debate over whether the United States should revise its Persian Gulf policy in light of the oil boom, see Stephen R. Kelly, "Oil under Our Noses," *New York Times*, March 21, 2012. For a rebuttal to this argument, see Michael A. Levi, "The False Promise of Energy Independence," *New York Times*, December 21, 2012.

15. US Energy Information Administration, *Annual Energy Outlook, 2015* (Washington DC: Department of Energy, 2015), 18. The recent, unexpected decline in oil prices has introduced greater uncertainty about future oil prices, affecting predictions of future US production.

16. Ibid.

17. IEA, *World Energy Outlook*, 98, 124.

18. Chris Tomlinson, "This Is What Energy Security Looks Like," *Houston Chronicle*, December 16, 2014.

19. BP, *BP Statistical Review*, 6.

20. Henry Fountain, "Ohio Looks at Whether Fracking Led to 2 Quakes," *New York Times*, March 11, 2014.

21. "New York to Ban Fracking; Environmentalists Cheer," *New York Times*, December 17, 2014; and Christine Mai-Duc, "Carson Imposes Moratorium on Oil Drilling over Fear of Fracking," *Los Angeles Times*, March 19, 2014.

22. For a critique of these arguments that explores both the Soviet ability to launch an attack and the purposes for doing so, see Robert H. Johnson, "The Persian Gulf in U.S. Strategy: A Skeptical View," *International Security* 14, no. 1 (Summer 1989): esp. 133–40.

23. There are, however, indirect national security threats—that is, scenarios in which US efforts to restore the flow of oil require using military force and risk escalation to large wars. The foundation of these dangers is prosperity, not national security. For more on this issue, see Charles L. Glaser, "How Oil Influences U.S. National Security: Reframing Energy Security," *International Security* 38, no. 2 (Fall 2013): 112–46.

24. BP, *BP Statistical Review*, 8.

PART I

Background

CHAPTER 1

The United States and the Persian Gulf: 1941 to the Present

Salim Yaqub

This chapter examines US policy toward the Persian Gulf since late 1941, the moment at which the United States first became concerned about that region's physical security and geopolitical orientation. After establishing America's strategic and economic interests in the Gulf, the chapter traces US policy over three chronological phases: 1941–71, when the United States supported Britain's position as the dominant outside power in the Gulf; 1972–90, when Washington relied on local powers to ensure Western access to the region's oil reserves and strategic positions; and the years since 1990, during which the United States has policed the area with its own forces. The chapter closes by briefly surveying the contemporary situation in the Gulf and assessing prospects for future US involvement there.

Since the 1830s, the US government has interacted with the societies girding the Persian Gulf. For longer than a century, it eschewed power politics and concentrated on facilitating American commerce and missionary activity in that region. Upon entering World War II, however, Washington began actively shaping the geopolitical destiny of the Gulf region, and it continued to do so into the postwar decades. US policymakers cared about the Gulf because its strategic positions and vast oil reserves were vital to the sustenance of America's allies and to the functioning of the global economy. Preserving Western access to the Gulf and preventing hostile forces from dominating it became basic and enduring US objectives.

For most of the postwar period, however, the United States was not the direct guardian of Western interests in the Persian Gulf; it relied on others to play this role. Britain, which had dominated the region since the Victorian era, continued to do so for a quarter century after World War II. For most of the 1970s, Mohammed Reza Shah Pahlavi, the ruler of Iran, served as the US-approved hegemon in the area, assisted by the government of Saudi Arabia. The supplanting of the shah's regime by the Islamic Republic of Iran in early 1979, followed by the Soviet Union's invasion of neighboring Afghanistan at the end of that year, deeply alarmed Washington, which proclaimed its readiness to use its own forces to protect the Gulf region. But the United States did not immediately act on this declaration. Instead, it enabled another local actor, Iraq under Saddam Hussein, to prevent America's new foe, the Islamic Republic, from dominating the area. By 1990 Iraq had also become an adversary, and the era of American proxies came to an end. Since then, the United States has policed the Gulf region directly, an approach featuring its own share of pitfalls.

Geostrategically, two broad and chronologically overlapping objectives have marked the US approach to Gulf security since 1941. The first has been to prevent any hostile power, external or indigenous, from dominating the Gulf region. This policy was directed against the Axis powers during World War II, against the Soviet Union during the Cold War, and against the indigenous actors Iran and Iraq in the 1980s and very early 1990s. The second objective has been to meet a cluster of threats falling short of domination—efforts by local actors, state and non-state alike, to disrupt US policy in the area, to menace US allies, or to attack US forces or civilians. Local threats of this sort became a significant concern in the 1980s and the primary one after 1991 as, on the one hand, the prospect of hostile domination of the Gulf receded and, on the other, the issues of terrorism and weapons of mass destruction (WMD) drew to the fore.

For most of the post-1941 period, the United States has pursued these objectives preventively, seeking to deter or eliminate potential threats well before they have had a chance to materialize. From the dominant perspective in Washington, such actions have reflected a reasonable—indeed, a necessary—abundance of caution. This stance has of course been more justifiable in some instances than in others. In the case of the Cold War, it is impossible to disprove that a less robust US posture might have tempted the Soviet Union to act more assertively in the Gulf region. All we can say is that after 1946 Moscow did not mobilize military forces to threaten the territorial integrity of any state abutting the Persian Gulf. In the case of Iraq in the early 2000s, by contrast, the US government clearly exaggerated the threat posed by Baghdad and responded to it in ways that proved more reckless than prudent. Realistic or not, imaginative threat assessment has been integral to US Gulf strategy.

The United States and the Persian Gulf before 1941

Prior to the 1940s, the United States remained aloof from the geopolitics of the Persian Gulf region and concerned itself instead with facilitating American citizens' commercial and missionary activities there. Geopolitically, the primary outside actor in the Gulf was Britain, which had dominated the area since the mid-nineteenth century. Initially, Britain prized the Gulf as a position from which to guard the approaches to its colony in India. The discovery of major oil reserves early in the twentieth century, however, gave the Gulf immense strategic and economic value in its own right. By the interwar period American oil companies, sometimes with official US government support, were actively prospecting in the Gulf region. In 1938 an American company discovered extensive reserves in eastern Saudi Arabia.[1]

Working with Britain, 1941–71

After 1941 the United States joined Britain in seeking to secure the Gulf's oil resources and strategic positions, first against the threat posed by the Axis powers and then against possible encroachment by the Soviet Union or disruption by local actors. Over the quarter century following World War II, Britain's power in the Gulf region waned as the US position grew more dominant. In terms of operational military forces, Britain's presence always dwarfed that of the United States. But the American role becomes more conspicuous when one considers the expanding arsenals and training missions that American arms manufacturers and the US military extended to Persian Gulf countries, and the infrastructural support provided by American oil companies. In the early 1970s an exhausted Britain departed the Gulf, forcing Washington to seek new security arrangements.

With its entry into World War II in late 1941, the United States became, for the first time, concerned about the physical security and geopolitical orientation of the Persian Gulf area. The Axis powers, seeking to fuel their war machine, coveted the region's vast oil reserves. The Allies were determined, therefore, to keep these resources out of enemy hands. The Gulf and its surrounding territory also gained importance as a transit route for providing war supplies to the Soviet Union, a member of the anti-Axis coalition. During the war, the United States played only a minor role in defending the Gulf from threatened Axis encroachment; that task fell mainly to British and Soviet forces.[2] The United States was, however, heavily involved in supplying the Soviet Union. From 1941 to 1945, Washington provided Moscow more than $11 billion in Lend-Lease assistance. One of the main conduits for such aid was the "Persian Corridor," whose warm climate made it usable at all times of year. War matériel was shipped through the Persian Gulf to Iranian ports and then transported northward to the Soviet Union. To secure this corridor, in early 1942 the United States sent thousands of troops and civilian personnel to Iran, joining an Anglo-Soviet occupation that had begun the previous year.[3]

At its wartime peak, the US contingent in Iran numbered thirty thousand soldiers and an equal number of civilians. Its primary duties were to help secure the country and to oversee the transport of military aid to the Soviet Union. Iran itself became a recipient of Lend-Lease assistance (consisting mainly of foodstuffs), and US military officers trained and advised Iranian military and internal police forces.[4] So began an intimate relationship between the US and Iranian governments that would continue for more than three and a half decades.

During the war, the United States also drew closer to Saudi Arabia in recognition of that country's recently discovered oil reserves and influential position in Arab and Islamic affairs. The US government established a diplomatic legation in Saudi Arabia and extended Lend-Lease assistance. Much of that aid took the form of direct cash payments to the Saudi government, as one of its main sources of revenue, pilgrim traffic to Mecca, had been disrupted by the war. The United States also provided military trucks, medical supplies, and agricultural, radio, and desalinization equipment. In 1945 the Saudi government permitted the US Air Force to construct an airfield in Dhahran, in eastern Saudi Arabia (in the vicinity of major oil fields), though the facility did not become operational until after the war.[5]

The rapid expansion of US activities in the Persian Gulf area caused friction with Britain, which saw a threat to its dominant position in the region. London was rankled by Washington's insistence that the Allies pledge to withdraw from Iran and fully respect its sovereignty once the Axis had been defeated, though both Britain and the Soviet Union accepted this condition to avoid alienating the United States. In 1944 the British proposed that they and the Americans jointly supervise the training and financing of the Iranian military, but Washington rebuffed the suggestion, preferring to undertake these tasks alone. In 1945 the United States did agree that its own monetary assistance to Saudi Arabia would not exceed Britain's, but American oil companies continued to dominate oil production in the kingdom, whose share of world production was rapidly rising. Nevertheless, one should not exaggerate the Americans' ascendancy. Throughout the Gulf region as a whole, Britain was still, by a large measure, the most powerful and influential outside force at war's end.[6]

Following the Allied victory, the United States remained concerned about the security of the Persian Gulf area, primarily on account of the region's enormous oil reserves. In the immediate postwar years, very little of the oil that Americans consumed domestically came from the Middle East, but US naval forces in the Mediterranean and the western Pacific relied heavily on Persian Gulf oil. More important, the economic recovery of Western Europe and Japan, in which the United States had a vital stake, was predicated on continued access to Gulf reserves. After 1945 the United States and Britain still feared hostile encroach-ment on the Gulf region, though the source of that threat had shifted from Nazi Germany to the Soviet Union. Indeed, one of the first Cold War crises occurred in Iran in early 1946, after the Soviet Union refused to withdraw its troops from the country, as Britain and the United States had already done. A combination of Anglo-US firmness and nimble diplomacy by the Iranian government persuaded the Soviets to pull out after all, but the episode seemed to underscore the vulner-ability of the Western position in the Gulf.[7]

Thus, in the early postwar years, the United States modestly strengthened its ties to the region. It continued to support Iran and Saudi Arabia, offering the latter a security guarantee in 1950. Two years earlier the United States had established a permanent naval presence in the Persian Gulf. Based in Bahrain, the fleet's three to five ships were negligible compared with Britain's naval forces, but the Middle East Force (MIDEASTFOR) symbolized America's growing inter-est in the region. Meanwhile, the US and British military establishments devised plans to defend Persian Gulf oil fields in case of war. Within both commands, there was considerable pessimism regarding the ability of Anglo-US forces to repel a determined Soviet offensive to seize this strategic prize. Following its withdrawal from Iran in 1946, however, Moscow made no serious effort to men-ace the Gulf militarily.[8]

In a 1950 deal brokered by the US State Department, the Arabian American Oil Company (Aramco), a consortium of American companies, agreed to share half of its oil revenues with the Saudi government. (The Treasury Department permitted Aramco to deduct much of this royalty from its US tax burden.) Over the ensuing two decades, Aramco cooperated with the Saudi Arabian govern-ment in developing the kingdom's infrastructure. It helped build oil drilling sta-tions, refineries, pipelines, and facilities that went well beyond the extraction and export of oil to undergird a more general modernization project: roads, rail lines, ports, schools, hospitals, disease eradication programs.[9] Though largely located in the private sector, these activities dovetailed with Washington's efforts to har-ness Gulf oil for Western Europe's and Japan's recovery and to promote Saudi leadership in the Arab world. In this respect, Aramco functioned almost as an unofficial arm of the US government.

If the Soviet threat to the Persian Gulf was largely conjectural, Britain and the United States faced an unmistakable challenge from Iranian nationalism. In 1951 the Iranian parliament nationalized the Anglo-Iranian Oil Company (AIOC) and awarded the premiership to Mohammed Mossadeq, who began a power strug-gle with the country's pro-Western shah. Seeing the nationalization as a direct challenge to its economic well-being and strategic position in the Gulf region,

Britain imposed economic sanctions against Iran and tried to enlist Washington in a military intervention in the country. The administration of Harry S. Truman (1945–53) cautioned that such a move would drive Iran into the Soviets' embrace and urged Britain to compromise with Mossadeq. But in 1953 a new American president, Dwight D. Eisenhower (1953–61), concluded that Mossadeq was already paving the way for a Soviet takeover. US and British intelligence agencies orchestrated an Iranian military coup that unseated the prime minister and granted the shah unquestioned authority. The nationalization of Iranian oil facilities remained formally in effect, but a consortium of foreign oil companies was allowed to control and market Iran's oil. The AIOC surrendered a large share of its operations to US oil companies, a telling indication of Britain's and America's diverging trajectories in the area.[10]

Over the next few years, the United States and Britain worked on integrating the Gulf region into a formal alliance structure. But disagreements between the two governments, combined with opposition from the Arab world, hampered these efforts. In 1953 John Foster Dulles, Eisenhower's secretary of state, proposed that Turkey, Iran, and Pakistan—the three nations constituting the Middle East's "northern tier"—form an anti-Soviet defense organization aligned with the West. Once the alliance had been successfully launched, Dulles hoped, its membership could be expanded to include Iraq and possibly Syria. In 1955 Britain implemented a variation of this plan. After Turkey and Iraq signed a mutual defense treaty, Britain joined the alliance and encouraged Iran and Pakistan to do the same. The enlarged organization became known as the Baghdad Pact. By including Iraq from the start, Britain hoped to shore up its dwindling influence in that country and solidify its position in the Gulf area. The Eisenhower administration, by contrast, thought it unwise to open the alliance to Arab membership so soon; the organization would be overwhelmed by inter-Arab controversies before it had a chance to establish itself. The US government endorsed the Baghdad Pact but, much to the dismay of British officials, declined to join it.[11]

As the Americans had feared, the formation of the Baghdad Pact drew a harsh reaction in the Arab world. Egyptian leader Gamal Abdel Nasser, who was then emerging as a pan-Arab figure, saw the alliance as an instrument of Western imperialism. He launched a region-wide campaign of propaganda and subversion to vilify Iraq and dissuade other Arab states from following its example. The pact also antagonized Saudi Arabia, a bitter rival of the Hashemite dynasty that then ruled Iraq and Jordan. The Saudis were already feuding with Britain over the Buraimi Oasis, a patch of territory in southeastern Arabia claimed by both Saudi Arabia and the Sultanate of Muscat and Oman, a British protectorate. The forging of an alliance between Britain and Iraq intensified Saudi Arabia's hostility to both countries; in 1955 and 1956 the kingdom threw its considerable financial weight behind Nasser's anti–Baghdad Pact campaign. Britain's insistence that the United States restrain its Saudi ally, and the Americans' reluctance to do so, caused considerable Anglo-US tension.[12]

The United States and Britain soon found themselves more sharply at odds in a crisis that bore profound implications for the politics and security of the Gulf region. In the fall of 1956, following Egypt's nationalization of the Suez Canal Company, Britain joined France and Israel in a military assault on Egypt to seize control of the canal and, apparently, topple Nasser from power. Though hardly sympathetic to Nasser, President Eisenhower saw the attack as a politically disastrous throwback to the age of European imperialism. Alongside the Soviet government, his administration publicly condemned the move. Eisenhower then placed extraordinary diplomatic and economic pressure on the three aggressors, forcing them to abandon their venture.[13] In the Middle East and beyond, both the United States and the Soviet Union gained considerable prestige for upholding Egyptian sovereignty. Nasser won even greater acclaim, having defiantly withstood an attack by great powers. Britain, by contrast, in failing so spectacularly to get its way, showed it could no longer be considered the primary Western power in the Middle East.[14]

To be sure, the damage to Britain's position was less visible in the Persian Gulf region than elsewhere in the Middle East. Unlike in Egypt, where the British had to relinquish control over the Suez Canal, or in Jordan, where they hastily negotiated an end to their treaty relationship, security arrangements in the Gulf were outwardly unaltered. But the Suez debacle had gravely weakened London's authority in the Gulf and rendered its allies there deeply vulnerable. Iraq was in an especially precarious position. Not only was it the sole Arab member of the Baghdad Pact but its role in a failed British-backed plot to overthrow the Syrian government had been exposed during the Suez War. A wave of domestic riots threatened the stability of the Iraqi regime.[15]

Eisenhower, having disassociated his government from imperialist aggression, now faced a new worry: the discrediting of Britain and its local allies had cleared the way for Soviet encroachment on the Middle East. The president needed some mechanism by which the United States could replace British power where it was receding and preserve it where it remained. In early 1957, in a policy known as the Eisenhower Doctrine, the United States offered increased economic and military aid and pledges of military protection to Middle Eastern countries willing to declare their opposition to "international communism." Though billed as a purely anti-Soviet initiative, the Eisenhower Doctrine was most immediately aimed at containing the influence of Nasser, whom US officials considered a dangerous, if perhaps unwitting, agent of Moscow.[16]

The Eisenhower Doctrine fared poorly in the Middle East, especially in the Gulf region. The policy's underlying strategy was to create a coalition of pro-Western Arab states to rival Nasser' influence. Two key members of the hoped-for coalition were the Gulf nations of Saudi Arabia and Iraq. Yet the strength of pro-Nasser sentiment in the Arab world, and of Saudi-Iraqi mutual mistrust, made it difficult for the two monarchies to play their assigned roles. Fearful and uncertain, they vacillated between confronting and appeasing Nasser, whose regional stature continued to rise. In July 1958 a group of army officers who appeared to be acolytes of Nasser's violently overthrew the Iraqi regime, extinguishing the Hashemite dynasty in Iraq. British prime minister Harold Macmillan proposed a joint Anglo-US military intervention to restore the Baghdad regime, but Eisenhower rejected the plan as too ambitious and risky. Instead, the United States and Britain landed troops in Lebanon and Jordan, respectively, each of whose governments was menaced by pro-Nasser rebels and had requested Western protection. In a simultaneous show of US force, one MIDEASTFOR vessel hugged the coast at Dhahran while another moved closer to Kuwait; a marine battalion from the US Pacific Fleet sailed toward the Persian Gulf. That these military moves were necessary at all showed that Washington's political strategy for containing Nasserism had failed. Later that year Eisenhower quietly abandoned his doctrine in favor of a less confrontational approach to that movement.[17]

Such a shift became more palatable in early 1959, when tensions unexpectedly arose between Cairo and Moscow. The dispute resulted from the Soviets' support for the new Iraqi government, which had sided with Iraqi communists in a power struggle against local Nasserists. Nasser's denunciation of Soviet interference in Arab affairs showed that the Egyptian leader was more independent than many American officials had assumed. The bad news, of course, was that the Soviets now had an oil-rich client at the head of the Persian Gulf. Still, the damage was limited. Although the Iraqi regime received substantial military aid from the Soviets, it recognized that Western Europe remained the primary market for Iraqi oil and honored its contracts with Western firms. Eisenhower found he could live with both the Egyptian and the Iraqi regimes.[18]

Into the 1960s the United States remained committed to preserving Britain's position as the primary Western power in the Gulf region. At the same time, the administration of John F. Kennedy (1961–63) sought to accommodate anti-imperialist and "progressive" elements in and around the Gulf and thus prevent them from turning irrevocably against the West. Ironically, the failure of such balancing measures prompted the United States to expand its own security profile in the Gulf region, lending credence to nationalist critiques of "American imperialism." In 1962 pro-Nasser rebels overthrew Yemen's monarchy and proclaimed the Yemen Arab Republic (YAR). Royalist forces, with Saudi support, took up arms against the new regime. When Egypt dispatched troops to shore up the YAR, the conflict became a proxy war between Cairo and Riyadh. Hoping to appeal to Arab nationalism without jeopardizing its relationship with Saudi Arabia, the Kennedy administration recognized the YAR while assuring the Saudis of continued support. This stance pleased neither the Egyptians nor the Saudis, whose mutual animosity escalated. Egyptian warplanes began bombing the Saudi border towns from which the loyalists launched their attacks. Saudi Arabia sought a more tangible demonstration of US backing, and Washington responded by sending a squadron of aircraft to patrol the kingdom's skies. US and United Nations (UN) mediation efforts failed to end the fighting, which continued off and on until 1970.[19]

In Iran the Kennedy administration balanced support for the shah with pressure on him to institute domestic reforms that might placate the country's increasingly vocal noncommunist left. After some resistance, the shah enacted a set of (largely self-serving) measures that not only failed to appease his domestic critics but also stirred up further opposition, from religious conservatives and from secular leftists alike. In June 1963 massive protests spread throughout the country, only to be crushed by Iranian security forces. Believing the reform agenda had reached its limits, and seeing no alternative to upholding the shah, the Kennedy administration increased its military aid to the Iranian regime.[20]

Thus, by the time of Kennedy's assassination in November 1963, his efforts to recast Gulf policy in a progressive-friendly mold had faltered. His successor, Lyndon B. Johnson (1963–69), did not even make the attempt. In the mid- to late 1960s, as US relations with Egypt sharply deteriorated, Johnson openly embraced America's traditional allies in the Gulf. The United States sold Iran and Saudi Arabia (especially the former) hundreds of millions of dollars' worth of military equipment. An extensive US military mission provided advice and training to the Iranian military and gendarmerie. The US Army Corps of Engineers constructed bases and power grids for Saudi defense forces. Still, the United States deployed very few operational troops in the Gulf, and MIDEASTFOR remained confined to only a handful of ships. Preoccupied with the escalating Vietnam War, the Johnson administration wanted Britain to keep bearing the main defense burden in and around the Gulf.[21]

Britain, however, found this increasingly difficult. In southwestern Arabia, Egyptian-armed insurgents fought to dislodge the British from their colony in Aden. In Oman's western province of Dhofar, leftist rebels tied down British and Omani troops. The British government was already facing severe financial difficulties and growing domestic pressure to scale back its overseas commitments. In two successive declarations in the mid-1960s, it pledged to grant Aden independence and withdraw all of its troops from the colony by 1968. It actually took these steps in late 1967, permitting the emergence of the Marxist-led People's Republic of South Yemen (called the People's Democratic Republic of Yemen after 1970). Possessing a military base at Aden had been essential to Britain's ability to project military power into the Persian Gulf; abandoning that position all but guaranteed a further retreat. In January 1968 Britain announced it would remove all of its military forces from the Gulf region by the end of 1971. The withdrawal was completed on schedule.[22]

Regional Proxies and Balancers, 1972–90

So began a new phase in which the United States relied on regional actors to secure the Persian Gulf against domination by hostile powers, from without or within. In the early 1970s, the United States anointed Pahlavist Iran as the pro-Western guardian of the Gulf and encouraged Saudi Arabia to assist in the effort. The collapse of the Iranian regime in early 1979, followed by the Soviet invasion of Afghanistan late that same year, prompted a scramble for new security arrangements. During the Iran-Iraq War of 1980–88, the United States lent de facto support to Iraq despite Baghdad's client relations with Moscow and despite Washington's proclaimed readiness to use its own forces to defend the Gulf. In fact, concerns about the war's potential to disrupt oil exports did produce a considerable US military buildup in the Gulf, and by 1987 US forces were directly tangling with their Iranian counterparts. These skirmishes merely hinted, however, at the massive US engagements to follow.

Britain's withdrawal decision of early 1968 had come as a rude jolt to Johnson administration officials, who knew that the United States would be hard-pressed to replace the departing British forces. Bogged down in Vietnam, the US military had few resources to commit to another theater. Moreover, growing domestic opposition to the war suggested there would be little public appetite for any new military ventures. Indeed, Britain's announcement of its planned withdrawal from the Gulf occurred in the same month as the start of the Tet Offensive, which swiftly undermined domestic support for the war.[23]

Yet inaction was scarcely an option, either, for US officials could not ignore the Persian Gulf's growing importance to the global economy. In the early postwar years, the world had experienced an oil glut. By the 1960s, however, rapid industrial development had brought a sharp increase in global demand for petroleum, much of it met by stepped-up production in the Gulf. (As in previous decades, domestic American consumption of Persian Gulf oil was negligible, but the US military depended heavily on Gulf oil for its operations in Vietnam.) During the Arab-Israeli War of 1967, Iraq, Kuwait, and Saudi Arabia had declared an embargo on oil shipments to the United States, Britain, and West Germany, accusing those countries of colluding with Israel. The embargo quickly fizzled, but the episode dramatized the industrialized world's growing dependence on Persian Gulf petroleum. In 1967 the United States had sufficient oil stockpiles to reallocate supplies to boycotted nations, but informed observers understood that these conditions could soon change.[24]

And now, with Britain planning to quit the Gulf, US officials worried that the Soviets would exploit the situation. The commencement in early 1968 of Soviet naval patrols in the Indian Ocean was, already, a troubling sign. In the Gulf itself, there were few indications of stepped-up Soviet activity. But it seemed likely that Moscow would seek to fill any strategic vacuum emerging in that area, if not by deploying its own forces, then perhaps by forging closer ties to Iraq, South Yemen, the Dhofar rebels, or other local radicals.[25]

Preferably, such a vacuum would be prevented from developing in the first place. But who, if not the Americans, could step into the breach? Britain proposed that Iran and Saudi Arabia cooperate with each other, and with the independent Arab states and federations that would succeed Britain's protectorates, to secure the Gulf region. The shah of Iran had other ideas. He had long aspired to be the hegemon of the Gulf region, serving as the guardian of its pro-Western geopolitical orientation and as the guarantor of its oil exports. Following Britain's withdrawal decision, he lobbied Washington for the wherewithal to assume this role. Though sympathetic to the shah, the Johnson administration endorsed Britain's more balanced policy, and the administration of Richard M. Nixon (1969–74) initially did so as well. But by 1972, largely at the president's personal behest, the administration had thrown its full weight behind Iran.[26]

This decision was in keeping with a broader reorientation of US foreign policy. By the late 1960s a relative decline in US global power, combined with the debacle of Vietnam, had suggested the wisdom of placing stricter limits on America's overseas commitments. In a July 1969 speech, Nixon declared that while the United States remained committed to its allies, the latter must play a larger role in their own defense.[27] The Nixon Doctrine, as this statement was called, provided the strategic justification for a reduction of US forces overseas and for a greater reliance on regional proxies—that is, powerful states that could protect Western interests in trouble spots around the globe. Thus, Nixon enthusiastically endorsed Iran's bid for hegemony in the Gulf, assuring the shah that he could purchase the most sophisticated conventional weapons in the US arsenal.[28]

Saudi Arabia was another beneficiary of the Nixon Doctrine. Although the Nixon administration saw Iran as the main guardian of the Gulf, it hoped the Saudis could assist in a secondary capacity. In the early 1970s, as rising global demand for oil and the geopolitical assertiveness of producing nations drove petroleum prices upward, Saudi Arabia found itself with rapidly expanding revenues. US defense companies stepped up their arms sales to the kingdom, especially in airpower. US military advisers and contractors modernized the Saudi Arabian National Guard and oversaw the expansion of the Saudi Royal Navy. The Nixon administration warmly encouraged these arrangements, partly to improve America's balance of payments, partly to retain Saudi friendship, and partly to empower Saudi Arabia to help Iran combat Soviet and radical influences in the Gulf region.[29]

As the US-anointed stewards of Western interests in the Gulf, Iran and Saudi Arabia accrued mixed records. In the early and mid-1970s, Iran did vigorously combat radical and Soviet-backed rivals in the Gulf area, with the Saudis playing a useful supporting role. On oil-related matters, however, each country pursued policies that at different times and in different ways damaged the Western and indeed the global economy. Worse still from Washington's standpoint, the shah's despotic and corrupt rule created the conditions for a revolutionary upheaval that propelled Iran out of the Western orbit and dramatically upset power relationships in the Gulf area and beyond.

The clearest examples of the Nixon Doctrine in action were the shah's skirmishes with left-leaning adversaries in the Gulf region. As in other times, Iran's principal rival was Iraq, which had improved relations with the Soviet Union after a period of strained ties in the late 1960s. Starting in the early 1970s, amid an ongoing dispute with Iraq over control of the Shatt al-'Arab waterway (a tidal river that borders Iran and Iraq and flows into the Gulf), the shah provided arms and encouragement to a Kurdish rebellion inside Iraq. The United States covertly supported this effort to weaken and harass Moscow's main client in the Gulf area. The campaign succeeded: In 1975 Iraq and Iran settled the Shatt al-'Arab dispute on terms favorable to Iran. Tehran and Washington then withdrew their support from the Kurdish revolt, which Baghdad crushed. Over the same period, Oman's Dhofar rebels, with support from the Soviet Union, the People's Republic of China, and South Yemen, intensified their struggle against the Omani government. In late 1973 Iran sent a brigade to Oman to help its government put down the uprising. Saudi Arabia and several other countries assisted the counterinsurgency, which succeeded a few years later.[30]

On other matters, however, Iranian and Saudi actions often clashed with Western interests. During the Arab-Israeli War of October 1973, several oil-producing

Arab states, including Saudi Arabia, retaliated against US military support for Israel by cutting off petroleum shipments to the United States and some Western European nations. The embargo, which lasted until March 1974, caused panic buying, hoarding, and real and imagined gas shortages throughout the West; these developments, in turn, severely dislocated the global economy. The Arab oil producers were operating in much tighter market conditions than in 1967, and the United States no longer possessed the same stockpile capacity it had enjoyed six years earlier. Thus the Arab producers now had far greater leverage. Non-Arab Iran eschewed the embargo and in fact supplied petroleum to US naval vessels operating in the Indian Ocean. (After the war, moreover, Iran aided US peacemaking efforts by selling oil to Israel, making it easier for the latter to return oil-rich portions of the Sinai Peninsula to Egypt.) But in December 1973, with the Arab embargo still in effect, the shah used his influence in the Organization of the Petroleum Exporting Countries (OPEC) to impose a drastic increase in OPEC's posted price—from $5.11 per barrel to $11.65. The shah had embarked on a massive arms-buying spree (mostly from US suppliers), and the embargo presented him with an irresistible opportunity to maximize Iran's revenues.[31]

With the resumption of Arab oil shipments in the spring of 1974, a struggle ensued within OPEC over the appropriate trajectory of oil pricing. While the Iranians pushed for additional price increases, the Saudis tried to bring prices down somewhat. Heedless price gouging, they warned, would further damage the global economy, harming Middle Easterners along with everyone else. The Saudis also worried about alienating the United States, the ultimate guarantor of the kingdom's security. From 1974 to 1978, oil prices were relatively stable, undergoing a modest nominal increase and even a slight decline when adjusted for inflation. Because the December 1973 price hike had been so wrenching to begin with, however, simply maintaining the new prices ensured a continuation of economic difficulties in the West and in much of the rest of the world.[32]

On the merits, US officials favored the Saudi position, and they did petition the shah to bring prices down. But these exhortations were often tepid and pro forma. Henry Kissinger, the US secretary of state from 1973 to 1977 and for most of that time the dominant figure in US foreign policy, championed the shah's role as guardian of the Gulf. Kissinger worked to keep contentious issues from intruding on US-Iranian relations, sidelined colleagues less partial to the shah, and recommended a continuation of lavish arms sales to Iran.[33]

The cumulative impact of Tehran's and Washington's policies was disastrous. By 1976–77, high oil prices had suppressed global demand for Persian Gulf oil, causing a drop in Iranian revenues. Yet the Iranian government continued to spend massively on arms and public works and ran up substantial deficits. Meanwhile, the exaggerated ebbs and flows of oil revenue had encouraged rampant corruption throughout Iran's government and society. This phenomenon, combined with glaring economic and social inequality, increasing official repression, and a rapid influx of weapons (including easily disseminated small arms), destabilized Iranian society. Starting in early 1978, antigovernment demonstrations and strikes spread throughout the country. The regime's efforts to put down the disturbances, though in some cases remarkably violent, failed to quell the unrest, and by fall the entire country was in revolutionary upheaval. Initially, the revolution drew in leaders and activists from across the political spectrum, but soon conservative Shia elements gained ascendancy within the movement—much to the surprise of Iranian and US officials, who had been preoccupied with the regime's enemies on the secular left. In early 1979 the shah fled the country, and his government collapsed. Ayatollah Ruhollah Khomeini, a Shia cleric who had lived in exile since the mid-1960s, returned home to preside over a new, theocratic government.[34]

The fall of the shah was a severe setback for the United States. Still, the administration of Jimmy Carter (1977–81) thought it could establish tolerable relations with the new Iranian regime, which was staunchly anticommunist and contained some moderate figures. This hope was dashed in November 1979 when Iranian students stormed the US embassy in Tehran and took scores of American diplomats hostage. The Iranian government blessed the action and continued to detain the Americans, who would be held for longer than a year. Weeks later came another shock. In late December 1979, eighty thousand Soviet troops entered Afghanistan to shore up that country's Marxist government, which was losing ground to an Islamist rebellion that drew inspiration from events in neighboring Iran.[35]

The Soviet move alarmed Washington. Events in Iran had already caused major dislocations in the global oil market. The revolution had temporarily halted all Iranian petroleum production, leading, as in 1973–74, to a spike in oil prices (up to $30 per barrel in 1980) and gas shortages throughout the West. With Soviet forces now rolling into Afghanistan, US officials worried that Moscow was embarking on a campaign to dominate the oil fields and sea-lanes of the Persian Gulf. The Carter administration imposed economic sanctions against the Soviet Union, persuaded Congress to increase military spending, and used Pakistan as a conduit for supplying military aid to anti-Soviet Afghan rebels. In a January 1980 statement that became known as the Carter Doctrine, the president warned: "An attempt by any outside force to gain control of the Persian Gulf . . . will be repelled by any means necessary, including military force."[36]

Even before the invasion of Afghanistan, Washington had begun acquiring the "means necessary" to project US military power directly into the Gulf. Since 1973 the United States had supplemented the essentially symbolic MIDEASTFOR with a modest naval buildup in the Indian Ocean and the Arabian Sea. These efforts took a quantum leap after the fall of the shah in early 1979. In the ensuing months, the Carter administration began planning for a Rapid Deployment Force, a mobile force drawn from all of the military branches that could be sent into areas where the United States lacked forward bases or facilities provided by friendly countries. Meanwhile, the administration concluded agreements with Oman, Somalia, and Kenya that granted the United States limited basing rights in those countries. In December 1979 (just before the invasion of Afghanistan), President Carter announced plans for the construction of "a new fleet of Maritime Pre-positioning Ships" that could carry massive amounts of military equipment into conflict zones to support mobile forces deployed there. By these mechanisms, writes the military historian Jeffrey R. Macris, the United States had developed a formula for future intervention in the Gulf: "fast-reaction troops from outside of theater swooping in when needed and meeting up with pre-positioned gear."[37]

Macris makes two broader observations about the emergence of the Carter Doctrine: First, "America's abandonment of the Nixon Doctrine, and its replacement by the willingness of the superpower to rapidly deploy its own forces, . . . grew out of the collapse of Iran, not as a reaction to Moscow"; second, it nonetheless "would take Soviet misbehavior . . . to elicit from Washington a formal declaration that the Persian Gulf had become a vital national interest, and that the US stood ready with armed might to defend it."[38] If the Iranian Revolution suggested the necessity of devising a new security doctrine for the Persian Gulf, then the invasion of Afghanistan proclaimed the urgency of doing so.

Strictly speaking, the Carter Doctrine had little bearing on subsequent US policy toward the Persian Gulf. Carter had warned against the encroachment of "any outside force" on the area, obviously referring to the Soviet Union. Over the next decade, however, Moscow caused the United States little trouble in the Gulf. Far from serving as a stepping-stone to that vital waterway, Afghanistan became a sinkhole for Soviet lives, treasure, and global prestige. The Afghan misadventure (which US support for Afghan resistance forces made more misadventurous) played a significant role in the later unraveling of the Soviet system itself. Instead, US Gulf policy in the 1980s focused increasingly on an indigenous foe, the Islamic Republic of Iran. And although the US military did directly confront Iranian forces in the late 1980s, for most of the decade Washington counted on regional powers to contain and weaken Iran. The main balancing power on which the United States relied—not quite a proxy but something approaching one—was Iraq under Saddam Hussein. Only after the collapse of the US-Iraqi understanding in 1990 did the United States start deploying military forces in the Persian Gulf on the ambitious scale Carter had envisioned, and even then America's adversaries remained entirely indigenous. If, however, the Carter Doctrine is more loosely interpreted as contemplating the use of American armed force to prevent any hostile power from dominating the Persian Gulf, or from challenging US domination of it, then we can say that the doctrine was partly implemented in the late 1980s and fully implemented from 1990 on.

Washington's alliance of convenience with Baghdad grew out of the Iran-Iraq War of the 1980s. Despite its official neutrality in the war, the administration of Ronald Reagan (1981–89) generally tilted toward Iraq. (The administration's arms-for-hostages dealings with Iran in the mid-1980s were a spectacular, though relatively minor, exception to this rule.) Although the Iraqi regime continued to receive Soviet assistance—and was a brutal dictatorship to boot—Washington found it less objectionable than the fanatical and disruptive Islamic Republic. One should not exaggerate the Reagan administration's partiality toward Iraq. When the administration took office in early 1981, its preference was for the two belligerents to neutralize each other in a stalemate. But in 1982–83, and again in the mid-1980s, Iran gained the upper hand and seemed headed for victory. To forestall this calamity, the administration furnished the Iraqi regime with satellite intelligence on Iranian troop dispositions. Meanwhile, without extending outright military aid, the United States provided the Iraqis with nonmilitary assistance that indirectly boosted their war effort, such as credits to purchase American agricultural products (thus freeing up Iraqi funds to acquire arms elsewhere) and licenses to buy US civilian equipment that could be put to, or upgraded for, military use. The Reagan administration also quietly encouraged France and Italy to sell arms to Iraq, and it asked Egypt to supply Iraq with spare parts for Soviet-made warplanes.[39]

Another way the United States helped the Iraqis was by tolerating their war crimes. In 1984 and 1988 Iraq used chemical weapons, the first time against Iranian troops and the second time against Iraqi Kurdish villages and towns in which Iranian-supported Kurdish resistance units were active. Thousands of civilians died in the 1988 operations. Although the Reagan administration criticized the Iraqis on both occasions, it did so in mild tones, and US support for Iraq continued.[40] "Praising with faint damnation" would be an apt characterization of Washington's attitude.

Meanwhile, the United States built up its own forces in the Gulf. Over the course of the war, MIDEASTFOR was expanded to ten vessels (up from the traditional three to five), and separate naval deployments brought the total number of US ships up to thirty.[41] A squadron of four US airborne warning and control systems (AWACS) aircraft based in Saudi Arabia (separate from the five AWACS planes sold to the kingdom in 1981) conducted radar surveillance of the Gulf. Kuwait furnished floating barges to house US Army helicopters and Navy SEAL and Marine Corps crews.[42]

In the later stages of the war, some of these US forces went into action against Iran. Throughout the conflict, but especially after 1984, Iran and Iraq attacked each other's merchant fleets, paying particular attention to oil shipments. Starting in late 1986, in response to Iraq's escalation of the shipping war, Iran targeted the maritime oil exports of Arab countries supporting Iraq, most notably Kuwait, and threatened to close the Strait of Hormuz. In 1987–88 the Reagan administration provided naval escorts to Kuwaiti oil tankers transiting the Gulf and permitted them to fly the American flag. As part of the escorts, the US Navy destroyed Iranian mine-laying boats and oil platforms that Iran used for intelligence gathering. When Iranian gunboats interfered with these operations, the US Navy sank them. The Strait stayed open throughout the war.[43] In the summer of 1988, Iran and Iraq concluded a truce on terms that essentially restored the prewar status quo. The United States drew down its forces.

Direct US Power, 1990 to the Present

The turn of the new decade brought about a third phase, which continues to the present day, in which the United States has projected massive military power directly into the Gulf region. Following Iraq's invasion of Kuwait in 1990, the United States led a multinational coalition to restore Kuwaiti sovereignty. In the aftermath of the first Gulf War, US forces remained heavily deployed in the area, arousing animosities that helped fuel the terrorist attacks of September 11, 2001. The US-led Iraq War, launched in 2003, scrambled the geopolitics of the Gulf region and created daunting new challenges for the United States. US forces pulled out of Iraq at the end of 2011, but the United States has remained heavily engaged in the Gulf region, a state of affairs likely to continue for the foreseeable future.

After the Iran-Iraq War ended in 1988, the United Sates tried to continue its cooperative relationship with Iraq, but Saddam Hussein's belligerent attitude toward his neighbors, including his erstwhile allies in the war, made this course difficult and ultimately impossible. In the summer of 1990, after an escalating dispute with Kuwait over debt payment, oil pricing, and other issues, Iraq invaded Kuwait, taking forceful possession of the country and ousting its ruling family. Hussein announced that Iraq had annexed its tiny neighbor. President

George H. W. Bush (1989–93) declared that the invasion would not stand. His administration secured resolutions in the UN Security Council demanding Iraq's unconditional withdrawal, imposing economic sanctions against the country, and authorizing collective security measures to restore Kuwait's sovereignty.[44] Meanwhile, the Bush administration gained Saudi Arabia's permission to station troops in the kingdom, and a massive US force, eventually numbering more than 500,000 personnel, materialized in the Saudi desert. The United States had withdrawn most of the naval forces that had been deployed in the Gulf during the Iran-Iraq War. Military planners quickly restored those forces and supplemented them with a growing air capability both at bases in Saudi Arabia and on aircraft carriers steaming into the Gulf. Thirty-three other nations, including several Arab ones, contributed forces to the anti-Iraq coalition, though the United States provided the bulk of the troops and dominated the decision making.[45]

In January 1991, after Iraq failed to meet a UN Security Council deadline to leave Kuwait, the US-led coalition launched extensive air attacks against Iraqi military positions in both Kuwait and Iraq and against industrial, communications, and transportation facilities inside Iraq. In February, with Iraq still refusing to withdraw, the coalition conducted a ground invasion of Kuwait and parts of Iraq, quickly defeating the Iraqi forces and ousting them from Kuwait. Saddam Hussein's regime was thrown into disarray, and two separate Iraqi rebellions, by the Kurds in the north and the Shia in the south, simultaneously erupted. In a decision that was widely criticized at the time (but seemed more prudent in retrospect), the Bush administration declined to aid either rebellion, fearful of being drawn into a quagmire. Instead, the US military established no-fly zones over northern and southern Iraq, preventing Baghdad from using military aircraft to attack Kurdish and Shia rebels or civilians. Though severely weakened by the defeat, Hussein clung to power and remained defiant of the United States and its allies.

At the end of the Persian Gulf War, the United States did not draw down its military forces in the Gulf to prewar levels as it had done after the Iran-Iraq War. Although most US troops left Saudi Arabia, several thousand remained, and the US Air Force continued to operate bases in the country. The US Navy maintained an extensive presence in the Gulf (and later renamed it the Fifth Fleet, as if to signify its permanence). In a broad sense, the United States stayed in the Gulf to deter any recurrence of Iraqi aggression. More particularly, US forces were needed to enforce the various restrictions placed on Iraq. As US warplanes took off from land bases and aircraft carriers to patrol Iraq's no-fly zones, American naval vessels policed Iraqi compliance with UN economic sanctions, which remained in effect despite the end of the war. For it turned out that Iraq had not only acquired (and used) chemical weapons but also made substantial progress toward developing biological and nuclear capabilities. The UN Security Council refused to lift the sanctions until Iraq had dismantled all of its WMD programs. To prevent Iraq from importing items banned by the sanctions, the US Navy aggressively patrolled Gulf waters, inspecting and sometimes interdicting maritime cargoes headed for Iraqi ports.[46] The Americans were in the Gulf to stay.

In the decade following Iraq's ouster from Kuwait, the United States faced few state-level challenges to its newly dominant position in the Gulf region. The year 1991 also marked the demise of the Soviet Union; henceforth, the United States was not even nominally concerned about threats to the Gulf from outside powers. Apart from Iraq, which was now ill equipped to menace its neighbors, virtually all of the Gulf Arab states welcomed the expanded US presence in the area. Some of them even permitted the United States to station troops or pre-positioned equipment and to conduct military exercises on their territory. The US relationship with Iran, though still hostile, grew somewhat more stable as the latter concentrated on recovering from its war with Iraq. Rather than confront the United States directly in the Gulf, Iran supported non-state actors, such as the Lebanese Shia militia Hezbollah, that battled America's allies elsewhere in the Middle East. In the late 1990s and early 2000s, a relatively moderate Iranian leadership sought improved relations with the West.[47]

Throughout his two presidential terms, Bill Clinton (1993–2001) worked to prevent Saddam Hussein's regime from circumventing the economic sanctions and to force it to cooperate with UN inspectors investigating the status of Iraq's WMD programs. On a handful of occasions, Clinton ordered military strikes to punish Iraq for specific transgressions or to degrade its military capabilities. In 1996 the Clinton administration secretly authorized a coup attempt in Baghdad, but when the regime thwarted the effort, Washington retreated. In public, Clinton grew increasingly willing to advocate "regime change" in Iraq, but apart from insisting that economic sanctions remain in force until Iraq had new leadership, he made no further attempt to realize this goal. Overall, the president treated Iraq as posing a relatively minor strategic threat. While some criticized this stance, it is now apparent that Iraq's military capabilities were far more modest than many international observers assumed at the time or than Hussein himself wanted his enemies to believe.[48]

Indeed, the United States had entered a new era in which its most effective adversaries were not hostile states but transnational opposition movements and ideologies, especially those rooted in political Islam. Throughout the Arab and Muslim worlds, the decline of secular nationalism had left a political vacuum that Islamists filled. Meanwhile, a communications revolution—video and computer technology, expanded television news coverage, cellular phones, the Internet—made it easier for political dissidents, among whom Islamists were ever more prominent, to forge discursive and operational linkages that transcended national borders. Struggles in Palestine, Lebanon, the Gulf region, Afghanistan, Kashmir, and elsewhere were increasingly enmeshed with one another, forming what the Middle East analyst Fred Halliday called a "new integrated West Asian crisis."[49]

In a complex dynamic, transnational Islamism both reflected and shaped events in the Persian Gulf. Throughout the 1990s, America's rising profile in the region, and the perceived injustice of its policies there, fueled a formidable Islamist opposition movement that mounted increasingly deadly attacks against the United States and its Middle Eastern allies. The intensification of those attacks early in the following decade provoked, in turn, a massive military response from the United States that upended the international politics of the Gulf.

As we have seen, following Iraq's invasion of Kuwait, the Saudi government agreed to host hundreds of thousands of US troops, a portion of whom remained in the kingdom after the Gulf War ended. The presence of non-Muslim soldiers on Saudi soil outraged conservative Islamists in the country, most notably Osama bin Laden, whose opposition to US and Saudi policies soon took a violent turn. Later in the decade, when bin Laden publicly launched his "Jihad against Jews and Crusaders," his bill of indictment included the economic sanctions against Iraq that had caused widespread suffering and death among Iraqi civilians. Whether bin Laden was genuinely moved by the plight of the Iraqi people or simply saw the sanctions as an exploitable grievance, the issue struck a chord with his Arab and Muslim audiences, enabling him to attract many additional followers and donations. Invoking these Gulf-based issues along with causes from elsewhere in the Muslim world (especially the struggle for Palestine), bin Laden and his network of operatives, now based in Afghanistan, followed the logic of their jihad to its ghastly culmination in the skies over New York City, Washington, DC, and Shanksville, Pennyslvania.[50]

The trauma of September 11, 2001, reverberated throughout American society and policymaking, significantly altering the ways in which the US government related to the outside world and to its own citizens. For the Persian Gulf, the tragedy's main consequence was to enlarge the influence of policymakers and commentators who insisted that Saddam Hussein's continuation in power was no longer tolerable. Although some of these figures actually claimed, baselessly, that Iraq was behind the terrorist attacks, the more common argument was that Iraq possessed, or would soon acquire, WMD capabilities that could be used against America's allies or transferred to terrorist groups that might use them against the United States. Some also predicted that the replacement of Hussein's dictatorship by a democratic government would unleash pro-democracy forces throughout the Middle East.[51]

The administration of George W. Bush (2001–9) was divided between advocates of regime change in Iraq and those seeking to focus the US military's response on bin Laden's network and on the fanatical Afghan government that harbored it. President Bush quickly gravitated to the regime-change faction. Although he did at first concentrate on Afghanistan—authorizing an invasion of that country that toppled its government and scattered bin Laden's forces—by early 2002 his administration had begun its relentless march toward war in Iraq. Over the ensuing year, Bush did seek international approval for his anti-Hussein campaign, persuading the UN Security Council to pass a resolution demanding that Iraq permit UN inspectors to resume their search for Iraqi WMD. But as of the spring of 2003, the inspections remained inconclusive, and the Bush administration, relying on questionable intelligence and tendentious analysis, had meanwhile convinced itself that Hussein must be hiding WMD somewhere. In March of that year, the United States invaded Iraq without UN authorization. Britain and a number of smaller countries took part in the operation, but as in the 1991 Gulf War the United States was the coalition's dominant member and driving force.

The US military had little difficulty defeating the Iraqi army and dislodging the Baghdad regime. Hussein went (quite literally) to ground and was later apprehended, tried for crimes against humanity, and executed. In other ways, however, the intervention was a grim fiasco. Despite scouring the country for more than a year, inspectors found no evidence that Iraq had possessed WMD stockpiles in March 2003. The war's central rationale was nullified. Meanwhile, a series of missteps by US authorities in Iraq—failing to provide adequate security, disbanding the Iraqi army, and outlawing Iraq's ruling Ba'ath Party—plunged the country into chaos, giving rise to a formidable anti-US insurgency and, later, a vicious civil war. Following the infusion of more than 20,000 additional US troops in 2007, and a transformation in the political attitudes of many Sunni Iraqis (resulting in closer cooperation between them and US forces), the level of violence abated, permitting a subsequent reduction in US forces and their full withdrawal from the country by December 2011. The war had removed a murderous dictatorship and permitted the establishment of more representative forms of government in Iraq. But it also had taken the lives of some 4,800 US soldiers and perhaps 160,000 Iraqi combatants and civilians.[52]

Moreover, by eliminating Iraq's fiercely anti-Iranian regime and facilitating the emergence of a Shia-dominated government friendly to Iran, the Iraq War enhanced Iran's regional position. To Washington, this was hardly a welcome development, for the war coincided with a sharp deterioration in US-Iranian relations. The main bone of contention was Iran's nuclear energy program. Iran claimed it was intended solely for civilian use but refused to disclose crucial information about it to the International Atomic Energy Agency, arousing suspicions that Tehran was seeking a nuclear weapons capability. The UN Security Council demanded that Iran stop enriching uranium and—under the prodding of President Bush and his successor, Barack Obama (2009–)—imposed increasingly stringent sanctions on the country. Iran insisted on its right to keep enriching uranium. Inflammatory statements about Israel and the Nazi Holocaust by Iranian president Mahmoud Ahmadinejad (2005–13) exacerbated Israeli and Western anxieties about a nuclear-armed Iran. Many of Iran's Gulf Arab neighbors, especially those with Sunni-dominated governments and populations, had fears of their own. Both the United States and Israel declared their determination to use all necessary means, including force, to prevent Iran from joining the nuclear club, with the Israelis expressing much greater urgency. Israel, of course, had acquired its own nuclear-weapons capability, prompting some commentators to argue that any long-term resolution of the Iranian issue must take cognizance of this fact.[53]

Whatever the merits of such linkage, international actors set their sights on a more focused diplomatic remedy. In July 2015 Iran and the "P5 + 1" nations— the United States, Britain, France, Russia, China, and Germany—concluded an agreement limiting Iran's ability to acquire and enrich nuclear fuels in exchange for the easing of sanctions against the country. Though hailed in many nations as an impressive and promising response to a dangerous international standoff, the agreement aroused considerable skepticism, even alarm, in Israel, within the US body politic, and in parts of the Sunni Arab world. Critics charged that the P5 + 1 nations had granted far too much sanctions relief for far too little assurance that Iran would, in the end, be blocked from crossing the nuclear threshold.[54]

US relations with Saudi Arabia also changed significantly after 2001. The fact that fifteen of the nineteen 9/11 hijackers came from Saudi Arabia—as did, of course, bin Laden himself—provoked an anti-Saudi backlash from the American public and Congress. US officials increasingly recognized that the American troop presence in the kingdom was more a liability than an asset. Saudi leaders themselves were eager for the Americans to leave, especially as it became clear that the United States would invade Iraq, a move deeply unpopular with the Saudi public. A few months into the Iraq War (in which the Saudi military played no part), the United States withdrew the five thousand US troops still deployed on Saudi soil and left behind only two hundred training personnel. The command center for US air operations in the area was transferred from Saudi Arabia to Qatar. US-Saudi relations were thereafter uneasy, marked by disagreement on some issues and cooperation on others. Saudi Arabia was among the skeptics regarding the US-backed diplomacy over Iran's nuclear capabilities. After the spring of 2015, however, the Obama administration provided logistical assistance for Saudi air strikes against the Houthi movement in Yemen's civil war.[55]

More generally in recent years, a note of chastened uncertainty has crept into official and public discourse on US involvement in and around the Persian Gulf. The costs and setbacks of the wars in Iraq and Afghanistan have shown the limitations of relying on massive force to achieve foreign policy goals. (This recognition clearly motivated President Obama's inclination to address the Iranian nuclear crisis diplomatically.) And yet the rise of the brutally resourceful Islamic State (IS) following the withdrawal of US troops from Iraq, to which the United States has responded with air strikes against IS positions and the reintroduction of military advisers into Iraq, demonstrates that US forces will have no easy exit from the Gulf region. Nor are unmanned drone attacks any panacea. The Obama administration's stepped-up use of them has provoked bitter resentment abroad and troubling legal and moral questions at home. Meanwhile, the upheavals of the Arab Spring have cast doubt on the stability of some US-allied regimes in the Gulf region and on Washington's power to shape political events there. Softening the sting of these insights—but also complicating the discussion—is the realization that US dependence on Persian Gulf petroleum has markedly declined due to a surge in domestic production. Some commentators have proposed, only half in jest, that the United States step aside and let China, which has become ever more dependent on oil from the Gulf, police the area instead.[56]

Of course, US interests in the Persian Gulf go well beyond the rate at which Americans consume its oil. The orderly export of the region's petroleum is still essential to the functioning of the global economy, and the United States will continue to see itself as the main guarantor of that process. Since the late 1970s, moreover, the Persian Gulf region has been a source of violent hostility to the United States and its allies and an incubator of extremist ideologies that foment such hostility. Xenophobic doctrines out of Arabia, "rogue" regimes in Iraq and Iran, chaotic upheavals in Iraq and nearby Syria and Yemen, nuclear capabilities in Iran (and, for that matter, not-too-distant Pakistan)—all have fastened Washington's attention on the Gulf region. Variations of these alarming patterns, we must assume, will command its attention for years to come. The Gulf remains too vital, and has become too dangerous, to be left alone.

Notes

1. Jeffrey R. Macris, *The Politics and Security of the Gulf: Anglo-American Hegemony and the Shaping of a Region* (London: Routledge, 2010), 11–25; Michael A. Palmer, *Guardians of the Gulf: A History of America's Expanding Role in the Persian Gulf, 1833–1992* (New

York: Macmillan, 1992), 1–19; and Rachel Bronson, *Thicker than Oil: America's Uneasy Partnership with Saudi Arabia* (New York: Oxford University Press, 2006), 15–19.

2. Britain blocked a possible German offensive from the west by winning the Second Battle of El Alamein in Egypt in the fall of 1942. In 1942–43 the Soviets halted the Germans at the Battle of Stalingrad near the Black Sea. Had Germany won that battle, it might have been able to advance southward through the Caucasus to the Persian Gulf. Macris, *Politics and Security*, 39–41.

3. Thomas A. Bryson, *Seeds of Mideast Crisis: The United States Diplomatic Role in the Middle East during World War II* (Jefferson NC: McFarland, 1981), 48–49; and Macris, *Politics and Security*, 43–44.

4. Bryson, *Seeds of Mideast Crisis*, 50–56; and Macris, *Politics and Security*, 44–46, 57–61.

5. Macris, *Politics and Security*, 69–79; and Bronson, *Thicker than Oil*, 36–42.

6. Macris, *Politics and Security*, 55–57, 61–62, 71.

7. W. Taylor Fain, *American Ascendance and British Retreat in the Persian Gulf Region* (New York: Macmillan, 2008), 25–26.

8. Macris, *Politics and Security*, 92–101; and Fain, *American Ascendance*, 25–35.

9. Daniel Yergin, *The Prize: The Epic Quest for Oil, Money, and Power* (New York: Simon & Schuster, 1991), 445–9; and Madawi Al-Rasheed, *A History of Saudi Arabia*, 2nd ed. (Cambridge: Cambridge University Press, 2002 [2010]), 92. In separate accounts, Robert Vitalis and Toby Craig Jones persuasively argue that Aramco significantly exaggerated its modernizing role in Saudi Arabia. Nonetheless, both authors document substantial company involvement in developing the country's infrastructure. Robert Vitalis, *America's Kingdom: Mythmaking on the Saudi Oil Frontier* (Stanford: Stanford University Press, 2007), 68–76, 106–10, 120–25, 131–33; and Toby Craig Jones, *Desert Kingdom: How Oil and Water Forged Modern Saudi Arabia* (Cambridge MA: Harvard University Press, 2010), 96–100, 103–4, 115–16, 119, 140.

10. For accounts of this episode, see Mary Ann Heiss, *Empire and Nationhood: The United States, Great Britain, and Iranian Oil, 1950–1954* (New York: Columbia University Press, 1997); William Roger Louis, "Britain and the Overthrow of the Mossadeq Government," in *Mohammad Mosaddeq and the 1953 Coup in Iran*, ed. Mark J. Gasiorowski and Malcolm Byrne (Syracuse NY: Syracuse University Press, 2004), 126–177; Malcolm Byrne, "The Road to Intervention: Factors Influencing US Policy toward Iran, 1945–1953," in ibid., 220–26; and Mark J. Gasiorowski, "The 1953 Coup d'État against Mosaddeq," in ibid., 227–60.

11. Steven Z. Freiberger, *Dawn over Suez: The Rise of American Power in the Middle East, 1953–1957* (Chicago: Ivan R. Dee, 1992), 50–54, 94–100, 105–6; and Nigel John Ashton, *Eisenhower, Macmillan and the Problem of Nasser: Anglo-American Relations and Arab Nationalism, 1955–59* (London: Macmillan, 1996), 43–51.

12. Anthony Nutting, *Nasser* (New York: Dutton, 1972), 77–78; Robert Stephens, *Nasser: A Political Biography* (New York: Simon & Schuster, 1972), 143–45; Macris, *Politics and Security*, 115–16; Fain, *American Ascendance*, 62–68; and Salim Yaqub, *Containing*

Arab Nationalism: The Eisenhower Doctrine and the Middle East (Chapel Hill: University of North Carolina Press, 2004), 44.

13. For accounts of the Suez crisis, see Keith Kyle, *Suez* (New York: St. Martin's Press, 1991); and W. Scott Lucas, *Divided We Stand: Britain, the United States, and the Suez Crisis* (London: Hodder & Stoughton, 1991).

14. Yaqub, *Containing Arab Nationalism*, 61–65.

15. Bonnie F. Saunders, *The United States and Arab Nationalism: The Syrian Case, 1953–1960* (Westport CT: Praeger, 1996), 48–51; and Kyle, *Suez*, 397–98.

16. For a study of the Eisenhower Doctrine, see Yaqub, *Containing Arab Nationalism*.

17. Ibid., 101–6, 121, 131–32, 142, 162–64, 167–69, 192–99, 219-35, 254–56; and Palmer, *Guardians of the Gulf*, 80.

18. Yaqub, *Containing Arab Nationalism*, 256–62; and Oles M. Smolansky, *The Soviet Union and the Arab East under Khrushchev* (Lewisburg PA: Bucknell University Press, 1974), 125–36.

19. Jesse Ferris, *Nasser's Gamble: How Intervention in Yemen Caused the Six-Day War and the Decline of Egyptian Power* (Princeton NJ: Princeton University Press, 2012); Macris, *Politics and Security*, 130–31; and Fain, *American Ascendance*, 125–34.

20. James A. Bill, *The Eagle and the Lion: The Tragedy of American-Iranian Relations* (New Haven: Yale University Press, 1988), 131–53; and April Summitt, "For a White Revolution: John F. Kennedy and the Shah of Iran," *Middle East Journal* 58, no. 4 (Autumn 2004): 560–75.

21. Bill, *Eagle and the Lion*, 154–80; and Macris, *Politics and Security*, 145–51.

22. Macris, *Politics and Security*, 133–39, 155–56, 188; and Fain, *American Ascendance*, 141, 150–58, 161–70.

23. Macris, *Politics and Security*, 171–74, 177, 190; and Fain, *American Ascendance*, 141–42.

24. Yergin, *The Prize*, 567–68; and Fain, *American Ascendance*, 147–48, 163–64.

25. Selig S. Harrison and K. Subrahmanyam, *Superpower Rivalry in the Indian Ocean: Indian and American Perspectives* (New York: Oxford University Press, 1989), 19.

26. Macris, *Politics and Security*, 159–82; Fain, *American Ascendance*, 175–91; and Roham Alvandi, "Nixon, Kissinger, and the Shah: The Origins of Iranian Primacy in the Persian Gulf," *Diplomatic History* 36, no. 2 (April 2012): 338–49, 353–57.

27. Nixon is quoted in Walter LaFeber, *The American Age: United States Foreign Policy at Home and Abroad: 1750 to the Present*, 2nd ed. (New York: W. W. Norton, 1989 [1994]), 638.

28. Ibid., 640; Bill, *Eagle and the Lion*, 183–202; and Alvandi, "Nixon, Kissinger," 369–71.

29. Bronson, *Thicker than Oil*, 109–13; and David E. Long, *The United States and Saudi Arabia: Ambivalent Allies* (Boulder CO: Westview Press, 1985), 47–48.

30. Bill, *Eagle and the Lion*, 204–8; Marianna Charountaki, *The Kurds and US Foreign Policy: International Relations in the Middle East since 1945* (Oxford: Routledge, 2011), 137–39; Andrew Scott Cooper, *The Oil Kings: How the U.S., Iran, and Saudi Arabia*

Changed the Balance of Power in the Middle East (New York: Simon & Schuster, 2011), 240–46; and Tore T. Petersen, *Richard Nixon, Great Britain and the Anglo-American Alignment in the Persian Gulf and Arabian Peninsula: Making Allies Out of Clients* (Eastbourne: Sussex Academic Press, 2009), 121–27.

31. Yergin, *The Prize*, 602–9, 613–32; and Cooper, *Oil Kings*, 143–47.

32. Yergin, *The Prize*, 633–42; and Cooper, *Oil Kings*, 161–62, 178–79, 220, 229, 252–55, 276–78, 311.

33. Yergin, *The Prize*, 642–45; Bill, *Eagle and the Lion*, 216–17; and Cooper, *Oil Kings*, 159–62, 200–203, 223–26, 250–55, 276–78, 336.

34. Bill, *Eagle and the Lion*, 233–60; Mansoor Moaddel, *Class, Politics, and Ideology in the Iranian Revolution* (New York: Columbia University Press, 1993), 93; and Cooper, *Oil Kings*, 263–65, 295, 297–98, 304–7.

35. Bill, *Eagle and the Lion*, 276–95.

36. Yergin, *The Prize*, 684–98; Steven M. Gorelick, *Oil Panic and the Global Crisis: Predictions and Myths* (Oxford: Wiley-Blackwell, 2010), 64; and Gaddis Smith, *Morality, Reason, and Power: American Diplomacy in the Carter Years* (New York: Hill and Wang, 1986), 224–30.

37. Macris, *Politics and Security*, 202–4, 208–10.

38. Ibid., 210.

39. Steven Hurst, *The United States and Iraq since 1979: Hegemony, Oil and War* (Edinburgh: Edinburgh University Press, 2009), 40–47, 52–60.

40. Ibid., 47, 66–70.

41. To compare these forces with the 1990–91 buildup, see Caitlin Talmadge's chapter 9 in this volume.

42. Macris, *Politics and Security*, 215, 221.

43. Hurst, *United States and Iraq*, 63–64; and Macris, *Politics and Security*, 213–17.

44. The fact that the Cold War was ending greatly facilitated these diplomatic efforts. The Soviet Union, which in an earlier era probably would have vetoed the anti-Iraq resolutions, was desperately seeking Western economic assistance and could ill afford to obstruct US Iraq policies. Moscow supported or acquiesced in the diplomatic measures against Iraq.

45. For accounts of the Persian Gulf crisis and war, see Steve A. Yetiv, *The Persian Gulf Crisis* (Westport CT: Greenwood Press, 1997); and Michael R. Gordon and Bernard E. Trainor, *The Generals' War: The Inside Story of the Conflict in the Gulf* (Boston: Little, Brown, 1995).

46. Macris, *Politics and Security*, 225–32, 234; and Hurst, *United States and Iraq*, 122–24.

47. Macris, *Politics and Security*, 229–30, 232–36; and Ray Takeyh, *Guardians of the Revolution: Iran and the World in the Age of the Ayatollahs* (New York: Oxford University Press, 2009), 111, 161–78, 196–204.

48. Hurst, *United States and Iraq*, 122–35, 139–43; and Robert J. Pauly, *US Foreign*

Policy and the Persian Gulf: Safeguarding American Interests through Selective Multilateralism (Burlington VT: Ashgate, 2005), 72–73.

49. Fred Halliday, "September 11, 2001 and Greater West Asian Crisis," in *Two Hours That Shook the World: September 11, 2001: Causes and Consequences* (London: Saqi Books, 2002), 38–40.

50. Peter L. Bergen, *Holy War, Inc.: Inside the Secret World of Osama bin Laden* (New York: Simon & Schuster, 2001 [2002]).

51. For treatments of the Iraq War's prelude, execution, and aftermath, see Terry Anderson, *Bush's Wars* (New York: Oxford University Press, 2011); Michael Isikoff and David Corn, *Hubris: The Inside Story of Spin, Scandal, and the Selling of the Iraq War* (New York: Crown, 2006); Thomas E. Ricks, *Fiasco: The American Military Adventure in Iraq* (London: Penguin, 2006); and John S. Duffield and Peter J. Dombrowski, eds., *Balance Sheet: The Iraq War and US National Security* (Stanford: Stanford University Press, 2010).

52. "Iraqi Deaths from Violence, 2003–2011," *Iraq Body Count*, January 2, 2012, https://www.iraqbodycount.org/analysis/numbers/2011/.

53. Takeyh, *Guardians of the Revolution*, 205–19, 242–50, 255–58; Trita Parsi, *A Single Roll of the Dice: Obama's Diplomacy with Iran* (New Haven: Yale University Press, 2012); and Shibley Telhami and Steven Kull, "Preventing a Nuclear Iran, Peacefully," *New York Times*, January 16, 2012, A23.

54. Michael R. Gordon and David E. Sanger, "Accord Is Based on Verification, Not Trust, Obama Says," *New York Times*, July 15, 2015, A1.

55. Tim Niblock, *Saudi Arabia: Power, Legitimacy and Survival* (Oxford: Routledge, 2006), 127–30; and Matt Schiavenza, "Saudi Airstrikes Intensify Yemen's Humanitarian Crisis," *The Atlantic*, April 22, 2015, http://www.theatlantic.com/international/archive/2015/04/saudi-airstrikes-intensify-yemens-humanitarian-crisis/391203/.

56. Marc Lynch, *The Arab Uprising: The Unfinished Revolutions of the New Middle East* (New York: PublicAffairs, 2012), 83–84, 105–7, 109–14, 135–41, 155–58, 193–235; Tom Gjelten, "US Rethinks Security as Mideast Oil Imports Drop," National Public Radio, November 14, 2012, http://www.npr.org/2012/11/14/165052133/u-s-rethinks-security-as-mideast-oil-imports-drop?start=10; and Keith Johnson, "China Is the New Power Broker in the Persian Gulf," *Foreign Policy*, March 26, 2015, http://foreignpolicy.com/2015/03/26/chinas-thirst-oil-foreign-policy-middle-east-persian-gulf/.

CHAPTER 2

Assessing Current US Policies and Goals in the Persian Gulf

Daniel Byman

The United States has long had a military presence in the Persian Gulf region and considered its security essential for US interests. Yet the perceived threat to the region—and views about the best US response to any dangers—has varied dramatically. Some of the supposed dangers are external, with Iran looming particularly large today. Others involve domestic threats such as terrorism or the risk of internal instability. This chapter argues that some of these concerns are overstated and thus require little or no US action. Other risks, however, are quite real. The United States can respond to some but not all of these dangers effectively and even shape the likelihood of their occurring, particularly with regard to proliferation and terrorism. However, the US role often involves heavy costs and trade-offs and can even make some of the region's problems worse. In some cases, such as supporting democracy, the United States has relatively little ability to shape events and forces in the Gulf region.

This chapter assumes the United States will retain a forward-deployed military posture in the Gulf region. However, it seeks to address the nature of the threats to the Gulf states, the ways in which the United States can (and cannot) mitigate these dangers, and the conflict and tension among various US interests in the region.

The first part of this chapter explores four posited US interests—preserving oil security, stopping proliferation, fighting terrorism, and supporting democracy—and the nature of the threats to each in the Gulf region. The second part briefly reviews past US security arrangements in the region and then details the nature of security relationships today. In part 3 the chapter reviews the advantages and disadvantages of using US military forces for protecting these interests. It concludes by discussing several alternative approaches for the United States in the Gulf region.

Posited US Interests in the Gulf and Associated Threats

US leaders have declared a range of vital (and not-so-vital) American interests in the Persian Gulf region. These interests have varied by administration and historical era, but they have long included ensuring the free flow of oil. The United States has also expressed a strong desire to prevent further nuclear proliferation in the Gulf and, since 9/11, placed particular emphasis on counterterrorism. In addition, Washington has demonstrated an episodic commitment to the spread of democracy in the region.[1] This section describes these interests, examines questions concerning their validity, and surveys potential threats posed to them.

Oil

Ensuring the free flow of oil represents perhaps the most constant, and many would say the most important, US interest in the Middle East. This interest is indeed critical, but for now the threat of a significant oil disruption is low and the US ability to protect against it with only modest resources quite high.

The states of the Persian Gulf are key oil producers, exporting far more than they consume. In 2013 the Persian Gulf states produced roughly 30 percent of the world's total oil output, with the United States receiving roughly 20 percent of its imports from the region in 2014. Europe, China, and Japan all also depend on oil imports for their energy needs. Saudi Arabia possesses much of the world's spare oil capacity (though the figure varies from year to year, and there is disagreement on specifics), enabling it to play a critical role in support of US policies. The kingdom's spare capacity allows it to mitigate disruption of the market in case of a price shock, such as the collapse of Libya's supplies during the Libyan Revolution and subsequent civil war, or an unexpected surge in demand.[2] Oil is in a global market; who supplies whom at any given moment matters far less than the overall supply and demand, which is what sets the overall price.[3]

One commonly noted danger is sudden price shocks. Scholars Eugene Gholz and Daryl Press, who are in general skeptical about the cost of potential supply disruptions, contend that the Gulf region may be an exception to their relaxed view of oil security. They argue the Strait of Hormuz is perhaps "the world's only true chokepoint," and they posit that preventing the conquest, and thus the consolidation, of major Persian Gulf suppliers represents an important US interest, albeit one that they do not see as facing serious threat today.[4]

Notionally the external threat to oil arises in two forms. A hostile state could invade and occupy an oil producer, attack Gulf shipping, and hit Gulf oil facilities, or it could cut off a key choke point such as the Strait of Hormuz. The hostile producer, of course, would almost certainly want to sell the oil; thus in the long term, supply would likely remain constant. However, the short-term disruption caused by invasion (and perhaps an insurgency or civil war in response) could prove highly disruptive. In addition, the invading power, if it gained control of a significant percentage of the world's reserves, would possibly acquire the ability to manipulate the market, deliberately creating price spikes and otherwise artificially inflating the price.

Since the end of the Cold War, only Iran and Iraq have posed a threat to oil from the Gulf region—Iraq from conquest, as it attempted in Kuwait in 1990, and Iran through subversion. With Saddam Hussein gone and Iraq in turmoil, in the near to medium term Iran represents the country of greatest concern with regard to invasion; however, even a cursory look at Iran's capabilities suggests how difficult it would be.[5] Tehran's military lacks the ability to project power outside its borders in a sustained way. Thus, attacks on oil facilities in Saudi Arabia would be highly difficult for Iran as it could not sustain operations should its forces somehow manage to cross the Gulf. Iran could use its missile force to try to disrupt the facilities, and the terrorizing impact of this threat would make operations harder, but for now Iran's missile forces lack a sophisticated precision guidance capacity. Tehran could also use terrorism to strike oil facilities, but the scale of damage would have to be massive and difficult to repair, while most terrorist attacks tend to be limited in scope and scale. In addition, the long-standing threat of Iranian terrorism, and the threat of al-Qaeda terrorism since 2003, has led the Kingdom of Saudi Arabia to increase its protections against possible terrorist attacks.[6]

Iraq's military is weak and unable to "balance" Iran, but Iran's seizure of oil-rich parts of Iraq would be difficult to achieve and would probably lead to a protracted insurgency on the part of local Iraqis. Striking across the Gulf at Kuwait and Saudi Arabia would be exponentially harder; it would require sea and air capabilities the Islamic Republic currently lacks and would expose attacking forces to strikes from the forces of the Gulf states, which are prepared for this eventuality. Politically Tehran does not claim the territory of any of its neighbors (a few minor islands aside), and the Islamic Republic still bears the scars from the country's long struggle with Iraq. Tehran has no appetite for another large-scale war.

One much-touted concern is that Iran might try to block the Strait of Hormuz, perhaps the world's most important choke point for oil supplies. Stopping traffic through the Strait would cut off more than 80 percent of the region's oil exports, drive up shipping costs, and cause a major spike in the price of oil—one that could not be quickly made up from other sources.[7] Scholar Caitlin Talmadge finds that Iran, using a combination of mines, antiship cruise missiles, and land-based air defense, has significant capabilities to close the Strait for perhaps a month.[8]

One reassuring counterargument is that it would be self-defeating for Iran to close the Strait as Iran itself depends on the Strait to export its oil and most of its trade. However, it is plausible (though not likely) that Iran might still try to close the passageway. Scenarios leading to such a shutdown might include a full boycott of Iranian oil because of a renewal of Iran's nuclear program, leaving Iran with no significant exports to lose, or the rise of a more ideological or desperate regime in Tehran. Iran might also miscalculate, believing that the threat of a closure and limited attempts to do so might lead its adversaries to cave to its demands but then, when a crisis develops, find itself politically cornered. A closure, however, would create a counterbalancing coalition, including Europe and China, that would lead to the further economic and diplomatic isolation of Iran and to support for an aggressive US military action.

Another risk comes from Iranian-supported subversion and perhaps even limited military strikes on Gulf oil facilities. Tehran in the past sponsored a coup in Bahrain and various terrorist attacks in Kuwait and Saudi Arabia. A renewed campaign of subversion at present is unlikely as Iran has learned that the Gulf Shia are not ripe for revolution, and Tehran is leery about a further escalation of conflict with its neighbors. However, the circumstances for this are far from impossible given tension over the Iranian nuclear program; the sense that the civil wars in Syria, Iraq, and Yemen are becoming a proxy war between Arab Gulf states and Iran; the growing polarization of Sunni and Shia in the Muslim world; and other issues. In 2011 US law enforcement officials disrupted an Iranian plot to kill the Saudi ambassador in Washington—a strike against two enemies that, if successful, would have been highly provocative and risked tremendous escalation, suggesting Iran can be less cautious in its use of terrorism than is often assumed.[9] Here the direct threat to supply would be smaller, but the increased risk premium would lead to price increases for oil and perhaps even a short-term spike until the situation stabilized one way or another.

Regional allies are also at risk of internal strife unrelated to foreign subversion. In Iraq during the height of the civil war in 2006, in Libya during the 2011 revolt against Muammar Qaddafi and during the subsequent civil war, and in Iran during the early days of the revolution, internal unrest led to significant decreases in oil production.[10] Depending on the extent and duration of the violence, this decline can last for years or more. Eventually the oil market adjusts, but should a disruption occur when there is little excess capacity and high demand, significant price increases are likely.

The Arab Spring and the unrest that followed embody the latest reminder that many regimes in the Middle East rest on fragile foundations. While oil-rich Gulf states have largely escaped massive unrest, they have witnessed some demonstrations. Bahrain in particular suffered unrest, which was put down forcibly and with Saudi Arabia's intervention on behalf of the ruling family. Instability there has continued, along with sporadic unrest in neighboring states. Most are outside the Gulf region, but in 2014 full-scale civil war returned to Iraq and began consuming Yemen. Because of its large share of global production and world spare capacity, Saudi Arabia represents a particular concern in terms of internal instability.[11]

Nuclear Proliferation

Halting the spread of nuclear weapons represents a central and often-cited US interest in the Middle East. In part this policy stems from the broader goal of preventing any hostile state from gaining enough power to threaten US interests regarding oil security. But this issue also involves concerns relating to the security of Israel and a more general viewpoint that proliferation is dangerous, particularly with regard to "rogue" or hostile regimes such as Iran.

The arguments against proliferation (or, more rarely, in favor of it) are well known and thus only briefly summarized here. While some contend that nuclear weapons make leaders more cautious, others argue that their spread risks the use of nuclear weapons in war or by accident, either way a catastrophic event. A particular fear is the so-called stability-instability paradox. According to this logic, even if states become more cautious in their willingness to go to war, they will be more willing to engage in limited aggression—including supporting terrorists and insurgents—in the belief that their nuclear capability insulates them from conventional attack.[12] As scholar Robert Jervis has argued, "To the extent that the military balance is stable at the level of all-out nuclear war, it will become less stable at lower levels of violence."[13] This more pessimistic view is the common wisdom in policy circles.

Today the biggest risk of proliferation comes from Iran. Tehran has developed an extensive nuclear program and has enriched uranium to 20 percent. Tehran is hostile to the United States and Israel, and its command-and-control and accident-prevention procedures are uncertain. However, should Tehran acquire a nuclear weapon, it is highly unlikely that it will use it as a "bolt from the blue" or will pass it to terrorist groups, though the possibility of an accident remains quite real.[14]

In 2015 the United States and several key allies negotiated the Joint Comprehensive Plan of Action (JCPOA) with Iran to end its nuclear weapons program though its ultimate effectiveness is hotly debated. Israel, Saudi Arabia, and other close allies in the region are at odds with Washington over the JCPOA. These allies do not believe that Iran negotiated in good faith, and the Gulf allies worry that the United States might seek a rapprochement with Iran that allows Tehran to exercise a dominant role in the Gulf region. They fear Iran will use the JCPOA to gain a nuclear capability either by cheating in the near term or by waiting until the pressure on it ends and being able to go forward without encumbrances.

An Iranian nuclear weapon would pose a potential threat to the flow of oil from the Persian Gulf region. Because a nuclear weapon would give Iran at least some degree of immunity from a US military response—or because Tehran's leaders may perceive it as such—Iran might be more willing to close the Strait of Hormuz, sabotage oil fields, or otherwise become more aggressive. It is also possible, though extremely unlikely, that Iran would use a nuclear weapon to attack Saudi Arabia's oil infrastructure or otherwise disrupt supply.

Tehran sponsors a range of terrorist and insurgent groups, and analysts fear that with a nuclear capability acting as a deterrent to conventional military attacks, it would become more belligerent. Especially given Iran's more aggressive use of terrorists and insurgents in recent years, a nuclear Iran could mean a heightened risk of greater terrorism, subversion, and support for insurgency. Given that the Gulf states—with US military backing—have the conventional advantage over Iran, there is little danger of Iranian-backed violence escalating immediately to the nuclear level. However, the likelihood of a significant conventional military response increases if Iranian actions become more aggressive. In some ways the situation is akin to that of India and Pakistan, where scholar Paul Kapur finds that "instability in the nuclear realm encourages instability at lower levels of conflict."[15] Even in the event of a deal, Iran might step up its support to militants around the region as a sop to hard-liners who lost out on the nuclear negotiations.

Another concern is so-called reactive proliferation: When one country's acquisition of a nuclear weapon triggers a response by that country's neighbors, greatly increasing the number of nuclear powers, the risk of accident and war also goes up. Saudi Arabia, Turkey, Egypt, and other regional countries are all named as potential reactive proliferators should Iran's program lead to a nuclear weapon. However, the analyst Philipp Bleek's research indicates that reactive proliferation is far from automatic, but it is more likely when a state exhibits an intense rivalry with another, possesses its own indigenous research and industrial base to build a bomb, and lacks a security guarantee from a nuclear-armed ally.[16] Iran's rivalry with its neighbors is significant but not necessarily intense when compared with the standards of, say, India versus Pakistan. Even more reassuringly, Saudi Arabia lacks the necessary resource base, though in contrast to most potential proliferators, it might have the ability to purchase a weapon outright from an ally like Pakistan. Turkey, however, possesses the necessary resource base, but it too does not have an intense rivalry that would drive the development of a weapon. Most important, many of the potential proliferators are US allies and thus can "balance" against the greater Iranian threat.

Terrorism

Since the attacks of September 11, 2001, in particular, the United States has prioritized counterterrorism in its policy toward the Middle East, with the Persian Gulf playing an important role. The United States can significantly advance its counterterrorism goals against al-Qaeda, the Islamic State, associated movements, and, to a lesser degree, Iran through partnerships with Gulf states. However, these partnerships at times hinder other US goals.

Al-Qaeda, associated movements, and other jihadist groups such as the Islamic State pose three categories of threats. First, they directly plot attacks on US and allied targets, both in the Middle East and in the West. The al-Qaeda core itself has attempted several attacks in Europe and the United States since 9/11, and al-Qaeda in the Arabian Peninsula nearly succeeded in its attempts to down a US passenger plane in 2009 and a US cargo aircraft in 2010.[17] Less directly, but more significantly for the region, al-Qaeda actively backs insurgencies and other parties in civil wars. Yemen is threatened by sizable insurgencies linked to al-Qaeda, and the organization attempted to foment an insurgency in Saudi Arabia in 2003. The Islamic State is a particular danger in this regard; a formidable force in Iraq and Syria in particular, it uses insurgent tactics as well as conventional warfare to spread its territorial control. It also resorts to terrorism to attack the governments it opposes, to expand its influence to neighboring areas, and to generate a sectarian backlash. The Islamic State also attacked Paris, France, in 2015 and inspired an attack in San Bernardino, California, that same year. Third, both al-Qaeda and the Islamic State back or work with rebels and terrorist groups outside the Arab world, such as in Nigeria, Somalia, Syria, Chechnya, and Pakistan.[18] These insurgencies and civil wars have claimed tens of thousands of lives and risk fundamentally destabilizing the countries in question.

Counterterrorism cooperation helps all concerned. Through cooperative efforts, the United States gains access to vital intelligence, and local services use their agents and capabilities to target and disrupt terrorists at home.[19] In 2010 the Saudis reportedly played a critical role in foiling an al-Qaeda in the Arabian Peninsula plot to bomb a US airliner and similar plans.[20] In Saudi Arabia and other wealthy Gulf states, both the George W. Bush and Barack Obama administrations pushed hard for a crackdown on terrorist financing and support for jihadist movements in general. The intelligence services of several regional allies have all reportedly penetrated al-Qaeda with human assets.[21]

A key argument against counterterrorism is that it often works against democracy promotion. By working with allies to fight terrorism, in reality, the United States is working to bolster their intelligence services, which are often the least democratic part of an undemocratic regime.

Perhaps the most common argument against prioritizing counterterrorism is that the threat today is low.[22] Since 9/11 the US homeland has suffered few terrorist attacks emanating from abroad, despite several near misses. Yet the United States has suffered more than six thousand deaths in Iraq and Afghanistan so far, or more than twice the fatalities on 9/11. Several reports suggest al-Qaeda's core has been hit hard and is far weaker than it was in 2005, when it carried out major attacks in London. The death of Osama bin Laden, the setbacks in Iraq, the Arab Spring, and an ideological critique within the Salafist community—all are cited as sources of the organization's decline.[23] In 2011 Defense Secretary Leon Panetta declared, "We're within reach of strategically defeating al-Qaeda."[24]

This argument, even if true, depends on whether al-Qaeda's weakness can be credited to a constant US counterterrorism campaign or whether it is largely independent of US actions. It also depends on whether al-Qaeda affiliate groups are considered as part of the core movement—and a threat to the United States—or as simply local groups that pose at best an indirect threat to US interests. The truth seems somewhat in between: The core is hit hard, but local groups are stronger. Some, like al-Qaeda in Iraq and al-Qaeda in the Arabian Peninsula, are far stronger than they were in 2008. These groups pose less of a direct threat to the US homeland, but they threaten American personnel abroad and the stability of US allies.[25]

A particularly important question concerns the status of the Islamic State. The group is the most dynamic terrorist organization in the world, and it attracts far more young jihadists than does al-Qaeda. In 2014 it declared a caliphate and proclaimed itself in charge of the Muslim world. Its actions have further destabilized Syria, helped bring about a return of all-out civil war to Iraq, and threatened the peace in Lebanon and other regional states, including Saudi Arabia. In 2015 it played a significant role in the violence in Libya, and it has declared "provinces" elsewhere in the Muslim world. The group's brutality and reactionary ideology make it a further threat to the civilians under its rule. From the US government's point of view, however, the Islamic State is primarily a threat to US interests in the Middle East. For now it does not prioritize attacks on the US homeland, but it has tremendous latent potential to do so, and its attacks in late 2015 suggest it is becoming more global in its focus.[26]

Counterterrorism against Iran, and its close partners such as the Lebanese Hezbollah, involves actions similar to deterring Iran's nuclear program. Tehran shares many ideological goals with terrorist organizations, thus leading it to establish close relationships with several after the 1979 Islamic Revolution. As time went on, however, strategic concerns rose to the fore. Tehran has used terrorists to assassinate dissidents, put pressure on Israel, undermine Gulf states, and threaten the United States.[27] In 2012, for instance, Iran was believed to be behind a bus bombing in Bulgaria that killed seven people, including six Israelis.

Because the support is linked to state policy, effective counterterrorism requires influencing the decision calculus of the Iranian regime. This is often difficult, as the low death toll from terrorism and the deniable nature of many attacks complicate victims' efforts to gain the political and diplomatic support they need to respond. In addition, Tehran also faces sustained pressure due to its nuclear program, and short of war or military strikes, it would be hard to significantly ratchet up this pressure over terrorism.

Democratization

The United States professes an interest in the spread of democracy throughout the world. However, though the Arab Spring has made this interest more immediate, the ability of the United States to promote democracy in the Gulf is quite limited at best and, at times, hinders other US objectives.

For many years various US administrations embraced a "Middle East exceptionalism," wherein the United States acted as if democracy in the region represented both an unlikely and undesirable development. This policy changed significantly in the George W. Bush administration, but the disastrous occupation of Iraq and the success of Hezbollah and Hamas in elections in Lebanon and Gaza, respectively, made the embrace of democratization appear naive and counterproductive.[28]

The unexpected occurrence of the Arab Spring, however, briefly returned democracy promotion to center stage. In different ways, the question of whether to support democracy has come up in Egypt, Libya, Syria, Tunisia, and Yemen, with US policy taking each revolution as it comes without developing an overall doctrine. In the Gulf, Bahrain reacted to democratic demonstrations with a brutal regime crackdown and elicited only weak and limited US protests.

Several arguments emerged for democracy promotion. Hosni Mubarak's Egypt, Qaddafi's Libya, Ali Abdullah Salih's Yemen, and other authoritarian regimes produced terrorists who often targeted the United States as well as local authorities. Dictatorship, it seemed, provided al-Qaeda with both a grievance to exploit and a large pool of recruits. In addition, American support for dictatorships tarnished the image of the United States in the eyes of many Arabs. Thus, democracy promoters anticipated that a change in policy would lead to a change in hearts, as democracy is genuinely popular in the region.[29]

Supporting democracy also aligns with US values, while strategically the most enduring and close US alliances are with strong democracies. Consequently, if democracy were successfully fostered, Israel would not be the only regional country with shared political values. Perhaps most powerful of all, some officials, including at times the American president himself, believed that the revolutionary wave represented an inevitability, and the United States needed to get behind it or risk being swept away.

Critics, however, point to several weaknesses in these arguments. First, a US endorsement of democracy under President George W. Bush, and then belatedly under Obama, has won little support for the United States in the Arab world. In Jordan after the Arab Spring, approval of the United States was barely greater than 10 percent. In Egypt, among Palestinians, and in other countries of the region, rates also remain low and largely unchanged since before the Arab Spring.[30]

Second, many of the dictators were staunch US allies, and those in Jordan and Egypt maintained peace with Israel—something far harder for popularly elected governments to accomplish given the widespread public hostility toward Israel. So in supporting democratic movements, the United States was in essence abandoning friends while their replacements remained unknown. Indeed, democratic regimes are not likely to be more pro-American than their authoritarian predecessors, and they have good reason to adopt a more hostile position. Broad anti-American sentiment in the Arab world suggests that regimes responsive to the mood of their people are likely to oppose close relations with the United States. In addition, Islamists did well in many of the initial elections, and many hold views on personal freedoms and the role of religious minorities, among other issues, that diverge sharply from those held by the United States, rendering the "shared values" objective a much less likely outcome.

Third, fighting terrorism requires strong governments, and for the short term in particular, democratization actually weakens governments while the risk of civil strife creates opportunities for al-Qaeda, the Islamic State, and like-minded groups.[31] So while the grievances that foster support for terrorists may decline, the abilities of governments to fight them will falter too. In addition, if governments are more hostile, then their intelligence services are less likely to cooperate with the United States.

Fourth, skeptics point out that the most important dynamics are domestic. Active US backing of democracy, if anything, backfired under President George W. Bush, and the Arab Spring had little to do with US policy. The United

States, the skeptics would contend, should simply pursue its interests unconcerned with the nature of regimes that govern the Arab world, as it cannot effect this type of change through its own efforts.

Regimes are entrenched and resist reform. New actors that come to power after the collapse of dictators may not accept the premise of democracy or may implement it fitfully. Most regional economies are in poor shape, and the rule of law is often weak. On the margins, Washington might influence these dynamics, but US intervention, even in small ways, could easily backfire, discrediting those we seek to help. Now that the initial energy of the Arab Spring is spent and chaos and counterrevolution have engulfed many states, the likelihood of change seems low.

Yet the threat posed to democracy is not completely internal. In Syria, Iran backed the Bashar al-Assad regime in its efforts to resist what began as a popular revolution. The governments of Saudi Arabia and United Arab Emirates (UAE) have given more than $10 billion to the military government in Egypt after it ousted the democratically elected Muslim Brotherhood regime in July 2013. Most dramatically the Kingdom of Saudi Arabia backed the Bahraini government's 2011 crackdown on dissent, deploying its troops to shore up government control. Middle East expert Bruce Riedel argues that Saudi Arabia is implementing a version of the Brezhnev Doctrine, using force and money to ensure that revolutions do not occur in its backyard.[32] Some of the previously mentioned regimes are US allies while others are enemies, but the standard mix of government-to-government threats and inducements may be more effective in preventing hostile intervention than would be efforts to shape domestic politics.

Fifth, and perhaps most relevant to the Gulf states, democratization seems unlikely in any of the Arabian Peninsula monarchies and Iran. Of course, the same could have been said for Tunisia or Egypt in 2010, but the poor track record of the Arab Spring has soured many in the region on the promise of democracy. Moreover, there is reason to believe the Gulf monarchies are more stable. Saudi Arabia has emerged as a leading counterrevolutionary state in its own neighborhood, willing to devote tens of billions of dollars—and, in the case of Bahrain, its military forces—to shore up monarchical rule. In addition, organized opposition is weak in all of these states, with the possible exception of Bahrain. In Iran the defeat of the so-called Green Revolution in 2009 led to the conservative consolidation of power, and democratic forces appear to have little chance of near-term success. Finally, much of the success of the Arab Spring depended on surprise, and the Gulf monarchies and Iran are ready and willing to put down any unrest that risks getting out of control.

US Security Arrangements in the Persian Gulf Region: A Brief Review

The United States has long had a strong security interest in the states of the Persian Gulf. The concerns, and associated policies, have varied considerably since the end of World War II, with dramatic changes occurring in the early 1970s, in 1979, in 1991, and in 2003. With the withdrawal of US forces from Iraq, and with US and allied differences over Iran's nuclear program, the United States may again be at a turning point.

Past Security Relationships

The United States has long had security relationships with states of the Persian Gulf owing to the region's energy supplies. After World War II the United States relied heavily on the United Kingdom as the primary security guarantor of the region, though British influence declined when the monarchy in Iraq collapsed in 1958. In addition, Washington had strong relationships with Mohammad Reza Shah Pahlavi's Iran and the Kingdom of Saudi Arabia—relationships that became more important after the United Kingdom withdrew east of the Suez in the late 1960s and early 1970s. To protect its regional allies, the United States provided military and financial aid, encouraged investment, and—in the case of Iran—backed the overthrow of an elected government in 1953.[33]

In 1979 the Soviet invasion of Afghanistan and the Islamic Revolution in Iran that overthrew the shah jolted this system. Washington feared that Moscow would continue marching south and threaten the oil-rich Gulf region while the United States lost the support of its most militarily powerful ally in the region. To reassure Arab allies in the Arabian Peninsula and to deter Moscow, the United States established the Rapid Deployment Joint Task Force—the nucleus of what became US Central Command—and increased its security arrangements with the Gulf states. During crises, such as Iranian attacks on Gulf state shipping during the Iran-Iraq War, the United States deployed its forces and attacked Iran's navy and infrastructure. For the most part, however, the US presence remained "over the horizon," a posture designed for rapid deployment during a crisis but not for a large boots-on-the-ground presence.

Much changed again with the 1990 Iraqi invasion of Kuwait and the subsequent US-led war in 1991 that pushed Iraq back. Saddam Hussein's regime, of course, did not fall, and US planners worried that Iraq would again attack the Gulf states if given a chance to do so. As a result US forces massively expanded their presence, with tens of thousands of troops stationed in Kuwait and Saudi Arabia in particular.[34] These forces enforced no-fly and no-drive zones in Iraq and at times conducted coercive strikes designed to pressure Hussein.

The 9/11 terrorist attacks on the United States strained US relations with the Gulf, with two concerns being paramount. First, the Gulf states, and Saudi Arabia in particular, were seen as having tolerated support for al-Qaeda; some citizens were major funders. Second, al-Qaeda claimed, and many observers accepted, that the US military presence in the Persian Gulf was an affront to the dignity of area Muslims and that it justified their terrorist attacks. This view significantly influenced the US decision to withdraw most of its forces from Saudi Arabia.

In 2003 another dramatic shift occurred when a US-led coalition toppled Saddam Hussein. Iraq soon plunged into chaos. Today it remains weak, removing, at least in the medium term, the most imminent military threat to US allies in the Arabian Peninsula. After the invasion of Iraq, the toppling of the regime there, and the occupation that became a quagmire, the United States withdrew much of its military presence from the Gulf states, particularly Saudi Arabia, and relocated many assets.

Security Relationships Today

The United States maintains a range of security relationships in the Middle East: defense cooperation agreements, basing and access rights, the prepositioning of equipment, and other "hard" forms of cooperation. In addition, the United States has made rhetorical commitments to several of its allies (as well as explicit and implicit threats to its enemies) and fulfills the role of major arms supplier to the region.

The US basing network in the Middle East is quite extensive, as illustrated in map 2.1. Even taking the US presence in Afghanistan out of the picture, the United States positions numerous bases and forces along the Gulf littoral, as well as in the eastern Mediterranean region and along the Horn of Africa. Taken together, these arrangements provide the United States the ability to deploy forces at or near a wide range of potential crisis points.

This basing network is reinforced by several thousand troops deployed in various states throughout the Persian Gulf: 15,000 in Kuwait, 7,500 in Qatar, 6,000 in Bahrain, and 3,000 in the United Arab Emirates. The United States also retains several dozen personnel in Oman and an advisory presence, reported at 270 personnel, in Saudi Arabia. In addition, the United States maintains several thousand troops afloat in the region at any given time.[35]

Washington also holds numerous long-standing security agreements with the smaller states of the Arabian Peninsula that give the United States access to facil-

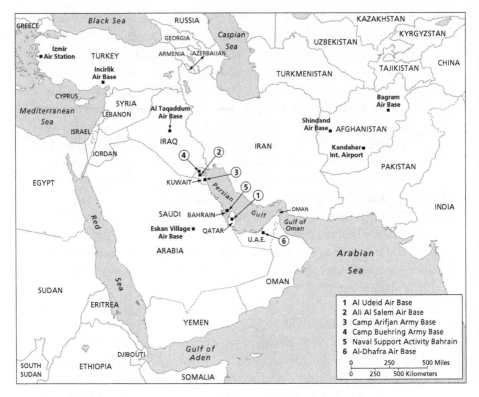

Map 2.1. Major US military bases in the Middle East, January 2015

Sources: Militarybases.com; militaryinstallations.dod.mil/MOS/f?p=MI:ENTRY:0; Heritage Foundation, specifically the "2015 Index of U.S. Military Strength"; *Washington Post*; *New York Times*; and additional edits by the author.

Note for the map key: Al-Dhafra Air Base was disclosed in Rajiv Chandrasekaran, "In the UAE, Washington Has a Quiet, Potent Ally Nicknamed 'Little Sparta,'" *Washington Post*, November 9, 2014 (accessed online September 30, 2015); and for Al-Taqaddum Air Base, see Michael R. Gordon and Julie Hirschfeld Davis, "In Shift, US Will Send 450 Advisers to Help Iraq Fight ISIS," *New York Times*, June 10, 2015.

Note: Many bases are temporary and/or foreign owned, and in general the specific bases for planned and actual operations often vary considerably by year. It is likely that secret basing arrangements also exist. In addition, per an agreement with Oman, the United States can use three Omani military airfields given sufficient advance notice and a specified purpose (see Kenneth Katzman, "Oman" [Washington DC: Congressional Research Service, December 23, 2013]).

ities and bases in the region and the right to preposition equipment. The agreements include the following arrangements:

- Bahrain houses the American Fifth Fleet and, per the US State Department, was designated a "Major Non-NATO [North American Treaty Organization] Ally" in 2002, thus enabling it to buy advanced American weapons systems. The United States has supplied Bahrain with surplus military equipment and helped Bahrain expand its air and coastal defenses.[36] During the wars in Iraq and Afghanistan, Bahrain provided basing and other support for US operations.
- Kuwait is also a major non-NATO ally and has served as a base for more than 20,000 US troops during the Iraq War. Despite the withdrawal of US forces from Iraq, Kuwait has remained an important regional hub, with the US bases there coordinating logistical and training support. The United States also deploys missile defense systems to the country and helps train the Kuwaiti military.[37]
- The United States has long used airfields in Oman and stored prepositioning equipment there. Oman, like Bahrain, provided support for US operations in Afghanistan. Although the size of the US presence fell in 2010, US forces maintain access to bases in Oman for contingencies and engage in a range of training programs and joint exercises with the Omani armed forces.[38]
- The United Arab Emirates hosts large numbers of US Navy and Air Force personnel and assets, with Jebel Ali serving as the most visited foreign port in the world for the American Navy. The United States positions several air defense systems in the country, which also functions as the base for the Integrated Air and Missile Defense Center, a training site for area militaries on air defense and on improvements to their interoperability and communication. The United States trains large numbers of Emiratis and other Gulf students in the UAE, and the United States also supports efforts to develop and support the country's air forces.[39]
- Qatar emerged as an important US base in the 1990s as the United States moved away from Saudi Arabia. Qatar became the forward-deployed base of Central Command and houses the Combined Air and Space Operations Center. Qatar acts as an important hub for US forces in Afghanistan (and did so for the Iraq War). In 2011 Qatar signed a bilateral security agreement with the United States regarding information sharing, aviation and cyber security, and other homeland defense–related issues. Qatar also hosts a missile defense radar station.[40]

The United States has long cooperated militarily with Saudi Arabia and has worked extensively—though without much success—to train the Saudi military. In 2015 the United States also provided logistical and intelligence support to the Saudi military intervention in Yemen against the Houthi rebels there. The United States is widely perceived as firmly committed to Saudi Arabia's security, but no formal defense agreement exists between the two countries. In the 1990s the United States deployed tens of thousands of troops to Saudi Arabia, primarily to defend the region against Iraq, but began to draw down forces after they peaked in the 1990s and almost completely withdrew forces following the 2003 fall of Saddam Hussein. Several hundred troops remain in the country to administer training programs. Washington has also undertaken a range of counterterrorism cooperation efforts with the Saudi regime, including measures to work together to combat terrorism financing, as wealthy Saudis represent an important source of funding for al-Qaeda and like-minded groups.[41]

In addition to formal defense cooperation agreements with traditional allies on the Arabian Peninsula, and the implicit guarantee of Saudi security, the United States signed a "strategic framework agreement" with Iraq in 2011. Although it promises cooperation in various areas, it comes after unsuccessful attempts to conclude a more formal defense arrangement, which foundered on Iraq's unwillingness to grant US forces a separate legal status. Washington also helps arm and train the Iraqi army.[42] When the Islamic State's forces swept much of western Iraq in 2014 and captured major cities such as Mosul, the United States began air operations against the group, increased training for local Iraqi forces, deployed more military advisers, and stepped up military support for the Iraqi government. However, given the American public's broad fatigue with Iraq—and the Iraqi public's fatigue with the US presence—the depth and longevity of any defense relationship remain open questions.

To back up these various formal agreements, the United States engages in repeated public declarations of support for the security of its allies in the region. President Obama and other senior US officials have repeatedly declared their commitment to individual states and to the security of the region as a whole.[43] The sense of the region's importance is widely shared among the political leadership of both major American parties.

States in the Middle East also serve as major purchasers of US military equipment. In December 2011 Saudi Arabia agreed to purchase more than eighty F-15SA fighter aircraft and upgrade its existing fleet of seventy F-15s, along with air-to-air and air-to-ground packages. The $29 billion sale was the largest of its kind to a single recipient. In recent years the UAE, though far smaller than Saudi Arabia, agreed to purchase more than $10 billion of US equipment, including eighty F-16s.[44] Additional sales to these and other regional states have included not only high-end aircraft, tanks, and other military systems but also packages for system support, logistics, and upgrades.

The United States also enjoys substantial trade relationships with several Middle Eastern states, though these connections are usually dwarfed by US trade with more advanced industrialized economies in Europe and Asia. In 2013 the United States exported almost $25 billion worth of goods to the UAE and almost $19 billion to Saudi Arabia, with aircraft, vehicles, and electronics being top categories. The United States imported more than $50 billion in goods, primarily petroleum, from Saudi Arabia and billions more from other Gulf states.[45] (Korea, in contrast, exported more than $68 billion in goods to the United States in 2013 and imported almost $60 billion.[46])

Advantages and Disadvantages of Military Forces

The current US forward-deployed military presence in the Gulf offers several advantages for protecting the previously discussed interests of the United States. At the same time, this presence also carries with it risks and potential dangers.

The US military presence in the Gulf region, along with alliances between the United States and countries in the region, is both a symbol of US commitment and a powerful show of force. This presence potentially advances US counter-proliferation objectives and deters an increase in Iranian-backed terrorism. Many US allies, particularly the smaller states of the Persian Gulf but also Saudi Arabia, have weak conventional military forces.[47] An alliance with the United States both enables them to resist pressure from hostile neighbors and simultaneously provides them protection from outright invasion. Indeed, it is possible that Iraq would have collapsed almost completely if the United States had not deployed its airpower and stopped the Islamic State's advance in 2014. So if Iran threatens the Gulf states with military force or increased subversion, then the presence of American troops is a visible symbol that the United States will aid its allies in resisting Tehran. This assurance makes the Gulf States less likely to engage in reactive proliferation as they can ensure their security via an alliance with the United States. Regarding Iran, since the 1988 clash between US and Iranian forces in Operation Praying Mantis, in which US naval forces sunk or damaged several Iranian vessels after Iranian mines hit a US warship, Tehran has repeatedly demonstrated a healthy respect for the strength of US military forces and avoided any confrontation.

The US presence in the Gulf also greatly improves the US ability to strike Iran should the United States seek to destroy Iran's nuclear program or to punish Iran for terrorism or other hostile actions. To ensure a military strike destroyed as many and as much of Iran's nuclear infrastructure as possible, the United States would have to conduct multiple sorties against numerous parts of Iran, such as the enrichment facilities at Natanz and Fordo, the heavy water production plant near Arak, and the uranium conversion facility at Isfahan, among others. One unclassified study identifies five main nuclear facilities and more than twenty ballistic missile bases and production facilities in Iran. Having bases close to Iran to minimize flight time and to allow aircraft to rapidly return, refuel, and rearm would be essential, particularly as many platforms could carry only one or two bunker-busting Massive Ordnance Penetrator munitions. Some of the aircraft would come from Diego Garcia or other bases outside the Gulf region, but fixed-wing aircraft from facilities in the Gulf and from the Gulf-based Fifth Fleet would be invaluable. Although Iran does not have an advanced or well-integrated air defense system or the most advanced aircraft, the United States would also want first to destroy Iran's most lethal air defense systems to ensure that US strike aircraft would face little risk and operate with maximum effectiveness.[48] This operation would require additional sorties and time, again making bases nearby particularly valuable.

Should such a strike happen, the United States would also seek to prevent any Iranian retaliation against the flow of oil. This effort might involve expanding and manning ballistic missile defense (BMD) facilities in the Gulf, providing technical assistance to stop infiltration, and bringing in forces prepared to strike infrastructure or other targets in Iran as part of a deterrent campaign to stop any Iranian escalation. Iran's oil infrastructure, power grid, and many military facilities would be among the vulnerable targets for retaliation. The United States has already provided BMD systems to Kuwait, the UAE, Qatar, and Oman, and it has deployed BMD-capable Aegis warships in the Persian Gulf.[49]

To react immediately to most threats, the United States would need a presence in the Persian Gulf comparable to what it has today. To be able to deploy relatively quickly in a crisis, the United States would at least need basing and access privileges and prepositioning. An Iranian nuclear weapon would greatly complicate US thinking on a military response and multiply the risk of even a limited military action. Even if the United States remained undaunted, then Iran might be more likely to risk closing the Strait, believing that it would deter any US response.

The US military presence also offers security benefits for outside the region. Gulf facilities have proven valuable for sustaining some of the US military and intelligence efforts in Pakistan and Afghanistan against al-Qaeda–linked targets there. A regional military presence is also potentially useful for strikes against the Islamic State or other foes in Iraq and Syria.

The US military presence also reduces the risk of rivalries within the Gulf. The US military presence is a visible sign of the US commitment, potentially calming the leaders of Saudi Arabia, the UAE, and other countries who are alarmed about the growing Iranian influence in the Middle East. The smaller Gulf states at times also fear Saudi hegemony, although Riyadh has not shown any interest in military domination of the region. In addition, minor border disputes—such as the Bahrain-Qatar disagreement over the Hawar Islands—might potentially escalate, and the US presence in and cooperation with both countries has a restraining effect. Particularly important here is US influence over (and often de facto control of) the logistics and communications networks of Gulf forces. It is hard for them to engage in sustained operations in opposition to US goals.

Finally the region, as is the overall neighborhood, is historically an unstable one. If the past is a guide, the ability to predict future contingencies in the region is limited. Forces there may be useful for unexpected crises involving, say, a resurgence of Iraqi militarism or growing dangers from outside the region, such as in Yemen or the Horn of Africa. In addition, the extensive facilities in the Gulf states might be used for contingencies in Pakistan, Syria, or Central Asia.

Costs and Risks

The United States at times has paid a heavy price for its willingness to use its military to deter and repel regional aggressors in the Middle East. Even putting aside the 2003 war in Iraq as a policy approach that is unlikely to be repeated, the human cost can be considerable. Future limited US uses of force and deterrence attempts may involve casualties comparable to the deterrence and coercion campaign of 1990 and 1991, after Iraq invaded Kuwait. More than a hundred Americans died in combat in the 1991 Gulf War, and almost five hundred were wounded.[50]

The financial costs are difficult to determine precisely. The Gulf states subsidize much of the cost of the US military presence. Moreover, given that the size of the US military is determined by multiple contingencies as well as domestic concerns, part of the air, naval, and ground presence in the region would have been developed and maintained for other reasons. However, as Eugene Gholz explores in chapter 6 in detail, if the United States decided to shift its planning from fighting two major regional contingencies to one, which would be consistent with the central role that the Persian Gulf has played in setting US requirements, then the United States would be able to save roughly $75 billion annually.

Furthermore, the US role in the region increases the risk of local "free riding" on the American security guarantee. The wealth of the Gulf states, and even their purchase of massive stocks of the most advanced aircraft, has not directly translated into military power. This weakness stems in part from the assumption that they can rely on the United States as a security guarantor and thus do not need to take the politically painful steps to dismiss incompetent generals, implement conscription or otherwise expand their militaries, and reduce coup-proofing measures to increase effectiveness.[51]

The US military's role on behalf of Gulf allies also contributes to anti-Americanism. US ties to authoritarian regimes have led political opponents of all stripes to see the United States as a force for repression.[52] The 2003 US war in Iraq was deeply unpopular among Arabs and Muslims in general, prompting conspiratorial charges that the United States sought to dominate the Arab world militarily, to subjugate Muslims, and to control the region's oil.

This anti-Americanism can weaken the stability of US allies in the region and further anger terrorist groups. A source of controversy in Saudi religious circles in the 1990s, the peacetime US military presence remains unpopular. The US military's regional role is still a concern though it represents a far less emotive issue today as sectarianism and the perceived Iranian threat have grown in importance. Even so, however, radical groups, including those linked to jihadists and those with Iranian support, are quick to deride any form of cooperation with the United States as a sign of the associated regime's fundamental illegitimacy. In their eyes, hosting US troops often represents the highest form of betrayal. And, indeed, the US presence signals that US allies are not able to ensure their own security, thus representing a potential humiliation. However, as the Syrian conflict has heated up and this and associated sectarian violence is dominant in the discourse, anti-Americanism is often less of a concern of many groups.

The US military presence plays little role in fostering democratization, and this anti-Americanism might make a democratic regime more hostile to the United States should it nonetheless take power. However, the presence of significant numbers of US military forces in a country and that country's anti-Americanism do not seem to be strongly correlated. Hostility toward the United States is high in Algeria, Jordan, and the Palestinian territories, none of which have a significant US military presence.

A bigger risk with democratization is that US military assistance to what was an authoritarian regime could bolster the military power of an emerging hostile democracy or revolutionary regime. This danger, however, is limited. First, US control of logistics, in particular, restricts the ability of any new regime to use equipment effectively without US support. Second, when they were in power, Islamist regimes in Egypt and Tunisia continued to cooperate with the United States.

Finally, even putting regime change aside, the United States cannot always use the military forces it has deployed to the Gulf region. During the 1990s, Saudi

Arabia and Kuwait, for example, restricted the US military's use of Gulf bases for its actions against Iraq. All of the Gulf states feel vulnerable to Iranian retaliation and might place similar restrictions for coercive measures against Iran, barring a direct and imminent threat to the security of the Gulf states themselves.

Options and Policy Implications

Based on the preceding analysis, three variants of the current approach deserve a brief discussion (a fourth, returning to an over-the-horizon posture, is discussed in Caitlin Talmadge's chapter 9). They include a deeper military commitment, a greater emphasis on political reform, and a lighter but still visible military presence.

A Deeper Commitment

The United States could push its Gulf allies to accept an expanded US presence. This larger footprint would involve, notionally, deploying several tactical air wings to various Gulf states and include reestablishing a more considerable US military presence in Saudi Arabia. It might also entail negotiating a basing agreement with Iraq and establishing a greater naval presence in the Persian Gulf and eastern Mediterranean. Politically, this commitment would be backed by more explicit guarantees—perhaps formalized in a treaty but also possibly only rhetorical—that the United States will take strong actions to defend the Gulf states against any perceived threat from Iran, whether it is nuclear or not.

The greater US presence would notionally make it easier for the United States to strike and destroy Iran's nuclear program and make it more likely that allies would stand up to Iran. The basing of US aircraft would help both suppress Iranian air defenses and escort bombers that might be based outside the region. However, the existing naval presence in the Gulf and other assets in the region can already perform many of these functions. Moreover, many of the hardest problems—gaining the political support to justify a preemptive strike, gathering enough actionable intelligence so that the strike destroys most of Iran's facilities, and managing the Iranian response to the attack—are no easier with a larger presence.

Politically a greater presence could inflame anti-US and anti-regime sentiment in the Gulf. The United States remains deeply unpopular, particularly regarding its uses of force in the region. To the extent that terrorism is motivated by the US presence, a greater footprint risks compounding the threat. More problematic, the greater presence also detracts from the legitimacy of US allies, making them more vulnerable to opposition at home. Currently this issue is not an important part of the discourse in most Gulf states, but a sudden a visible buildup could return it to the fore.

An Emphasis on Political Reform

In theory, the United States could encourage states in the region to open up their political systems and move forward on the path to democracy. Beyond its human rights value, such a move might have several benefits. First, if the furies unleashed by the Arab Spring suggest that change is inevitable, then it is better for regimes allied with the United States to get ahead of events and manage the transition rather than be toppled amid the chaos. Second, many American officials believe that the authoritarian nature of regional allies fuels terrorism. Finally, even if US efforts fail, being seen on the side of reform could improve the image of the United States in the region.

There are reasons to be skeptical of all three of these arguments. First, in helping push out Mubarak, the United States won few points with Egyptians, and there is little reason to expect other Arab publics would react differently. Second, the tide of democratization is not inexorable: The survivors of the unrest that broke out in 2011 seem strong and prepared to take on new demonstrations, and while only Tunisia remains democratic today, even its transition is facing many problems. Assuming other authoritarian regimes will fall would be a mistake. The tide seems particularly weak in the Gulf, where a combination of wealth, greater regime legitimacy (compared to the so-called Arab republics), and the Saudis' willingness to back up area regimes with force have inhibited dissent. Third, the link between authoritarianism and support for *anti-US* terrorism is quite weak. There are many authoritarian regimes but relatively few anti-US terrorists.

However, the costs of encouraging reform will be quite real and immediate. The US government's abandonment of Mubarak angered Saudi Arabia. Turning against other allies, particularly in Riyadh's immediate neighborhood, may lead to a reduction in counterterrorism cooperation; an increased risk of terrorism, at least in the short term; and a decline in Saudi cooperation to ensure oil price stability. Third, as the revolts in Libya, Syria, and Yemen indicate, a weak government or even chaos might replace a dictator. A reform process that results in a weak government may also exacerbate the terrorism problem and create new, and at times worse, human rights issues.

A Light but Visible Presence

The United States might further reduce its presence in the Gulf region by withdrawing completely from some of its bases, by cutting its forces still further in existing bases, or by pursuing both options. Such a measure may send a conciliatory gesture to Tehran that the United States does not plan a military action, and in theory, it could reduce any local hostility linked to the presence of US forces.

Going light has several advantages for other US foreign policy objectives. First, it potentially frees up forces for other parts of the world. So if the United States plans a security pivot to Asia, then having fewer forces in the Middle East better enables such a shift. Second, forces deployed abroad can be costly, and bringing them back home—or perhaps cutting them altogether—will save money.

The local advantages, however, are less likely to accrue. Halving the size of US forces, for example, is unlikely to satisfy critics of the US military's presence. The critics' objection is more philosophical, and the forces already are largely out of the public view in many countries. Tehran, for its part, is likely to see such a move as a retreat rather than a peacemaking gesture unless it was accompanied by a dramatic lessening of pressure on Iran. Similarly, the United States needs regional forces to combat the Islamic State in Iraq and Syria.

Policy Implications

If the United States is going to continue a forward-deployed strategy, it should recognize its limits and the trade-offs involved in any changes. Withdrawing from any particular country would be a mistake, assuming no dramatic change in the current political situation. Given internal instability and the vagaries of local politics, diverse basing is vital, for it allows the United States to pick and choose as necessary from backup capabilities should a regime turn against the United States or if the politics of the day make it difficult for that government to cooperate with the United States in a particular crisis. This issue of basing and access is also important for contingencies outside the region.

It is important, however, not to overstate either the role that the presence of US forces in the Gulf plays in leading to internal instability and terrorism problems or the ability of the United States to shape domestic politics in the Gulf. Elite Gulf politics are secretive, and the United States has few levers with which to move decision making. Mass-level politics are largely unformed, and the publics' low opinion of the United States makes many US efforts likely to be counterproductive. So the political effects of a further US withdrawal are likely to be limited.

In short, the United States may have found a reasonable balance with its current posture. The US presence is able to shore up deterrence and gain compelling options against Iran, but at the same time it is neither so costly nor so politically detrimental as to jeopardize other US objectives.

Notes

The author would like to thank the participants of a December 2012 workshop at George Washington University and Charles Glaser, Rose Kelanic, Michael O'Hanlon, and Caitlin Talmadge in particular for their additional comments. Tess deBlanc-Knowles provided excellent research support. This draft also draws on, and overlaps with, concurrent research I am coauthoring with Sara Bjerg Moller that is sponsored by the Tobin Project on the costs and advantages of the US military presence in the Middle East in general.

1. US support for the security of Israel is also a long-standing US objective, though this is not Gulf specific. The United States and Israel have long opposed common foes in the Middle East, ranging from pro-Soviet (or at least not pro-American) regimes such as Gamal Abdel Nasser's Egypt and Saddam Hussein's Iraq to the clerical regime in Tehran and, more recently, a range of terrorist groups, most notably al-Qaeda. Champions of the US-Israel alliance also stress that Israel represents an island of democracy in the authoritarian sea of the Middle East. In helping defend Israel, the United States is thus defending its own values. In addition, Israeli public opinion of the United States—in contrast to Arab state public opinions—is favorable, and the alliance is based on people-to-people as well as government-to-government relationships. However, this support is not at the core of US policy in the Gulf region although, as noted, some objectives such as opposing Iran's nuclear program are supported in part because of the risk these weapons would pose to US allies, including Israel.

2. BP, *BP Statistical Review of World Energy, June 2014*, http://www.bp.com/content /dam/bp-country/de-de/PDFs/brochures/BP-statistical-review-of-world-energy-2014 -full-report.pdf; US Energy Information Administration, "Frequently Asked Questions," last updated September 14, 2005, http://www.eia.gov/tools/faqs/faq.cfm?id=727&t=6; and Marianne Lavelle, "Iran's Undisputed Weapon: Power to Block the Strait of Hormuz," *National Geographic News*, February 6, 2012.

3. As discussed in this volume's introduction, improvements have enabled production from so-called tight oil, increasing overall world supply as well as the relative share of US and Canadian production. However, increases in global demand are likely to match supply increases—particularly if China and India continue high growth rates—though both the total likely additional demand and supply remain speculative at this point. Frank A. Verrastro, "The Role of Unconventional Oil and Gas: A New Paradigm for Energy," in *2012 Global Forecast: Risk, Opportunity, and the Next Administration*, ed. Craig Cohen and Josiane Gabel (Washington DC: Center for Strategic and International Studies, April 17, 2012); and Daniel Yergin, "America's New Energy Reality," *New York Times*, June 9, 2012. For an argument that tight oil will add dramatically to global oil supply, see Leonardo Maugeri, "Oil: The Next Revolution," Discussion Paper 2012–10 (Cambridge MA: Belfer Center for Science and International Affairs, Harvard Kennedy School, June 2012); and for a more skeptical view, see Claudia Cattaneo, "Will Tight Oil Change the World?," *Financial Post*, July 21, 2012.

4. Eugene Gholz and Daryl Press, "Protecting 'The Prize': Oil and the U.S. National Interest," *Security Studies* 19, no. 3 (2010): 463, 474.

5. For an in-depth discussion of the low probability of conquest by regional powers, see Joshua Rovner's chapter 5 in this volume.

6. Thomas Hegghammer, "The Failure of Jihad in Saudi Arabia," Occasional Paper

(West Point: Combating Terrorism Center, February 25, 2010), https://www.ctc.usma
.edu/posts/the-failure-of-jihad-in-saudi-arabia.

7. Daniel Yergin, "Ensuring Energy Security," *Foreign Affairs* 85, no. 2 (March–April
2006): 78.

8. Caitlin Talmadge, "Closing Time: Assessing the Iranian Threat to the Strait of Hormuz," *International Security* 33, no. 1 (Summer 2008): 82–117.

9. Benjamin Weiser, "Man Pleads Guilty in Plot to Murder Saudi Envoy," *New York
Times*, October 17, 2012, http://www.nytimes.com/2012/10/18/nyregion/mansour
-arbabsiar-expected-to-plead-guilty-in-bomb-plot.html?-r=0; and Daniel Byman, "Plausible Culpability," *Foreign Policy*, October 28, 2011, http://www.brookings.edu/research
/opinions/2011/10/28-iran-byman.

10. Jim Krane, "Iraq Oil Output Lowest since Invasion," *Washington Post*, April 28,
2006, http://www.washingtonpost.com/wp-dyn/content/article/2006/04/28/AR
2006042801082.html; and Clifford Krauss, "After the Revolution, Hurdles in Reviving
the Oil Sector," *New York Times*, August 23, 2011, http://www.nytimes.com/2011/08/24
/business/global/libya-faces-hurdles-in-reviving-its-oil-sector.html.

11. For more on subversive threats to Saudi Arabian oil specifically, see Thomas W.
Lippman's chapter 4 in this volume.

12. Kenneth Waltz, "The Spread of Nuclear Weapons: More May Be Better," *Adelphi
Papers* 21, no. 171 (London: International Institute for Strategic Studies, 1981); Scott
Sagan, *The Limits of Safety: Organizations, Accidents, and Nuclear Weapons* (Princeton:
Princeton University Press, 1993); and Peter Lavoy, "The Strategic Consequences of
Nuclear Proliferation: A Review," *Security Studies* 4, no. 4 (1995).

13. Robert Jervis, *The Illogic of American Nuclear Strategy* (Ithaca: Cornell University
Press, 1984), 31.

14. Daniel Byman, "Iran, Terrorism, and Weapons of Mass Destruction," *Studies in
Conflict and Terrorism* 31, no. 3 (2008): 169–81. For more on this general point, see Brian
Jenkins, *Will Terrorists Go Nuclear?* (Amherst NY: Prometheus Books, 2008); and Keir A.
Lieber and Daryl G. Press, "Why States Won't Give Nuclear Weapons to Terrorists," *Inter-
national Security* 38, no. 1 (Summer 2013): 80–104.

15. Paul Kapur, "India and Pakistan's Unstable Peace: Why Nuclear South Asia Is Not
Like Cold War Europe," *International Security* 30, no. 2 (2005): 129.

16. Philipp Bleek, *The Nuclear Domino Myth: Why Proliferation Rarely Begets Proliferation* (PhD diss., Georgetown University, 2010).

17. For a review, see Gregory D. Johnsen, *The Last Refuge: Yemen, Al-Qaeda, and America's War in Arabia* (New York: Norton, 2012).

18. Daniel Byman, "Breaking the Bonds between Al-Qaeda and Its Affiliate Organizations," Saban Analysis Paper 27 (Washington DC: Brookings, 2012), http://www.brookings
.edu/research/papers/2012/07/alqaida-terrorism-byman.

19. Daniel Byman, "The Intelligence War on Terrorism," *Intelligence and National Security* 29, no. 6 (December 2013): 837–63.

20. Yochi J. Dreazen, "Foiled Bomb Plot Highlights Growing CIA–Saudi Arabian Ties," *National Journal*, May 9, 2012; and "News Report: Would-be Bomber Was a Double-Agent," CNN, May 8, 2012.

21. Martin Rudner, "Hunters and Gatherers: The Intelligence Coalition against Islamic Terrorism," *International Journal of Intelligence and CounterIntelligence* 17, no. 2 (Summer 2004): 217.

22. John Mueller and Mark Stewart, "The Terrorism Delusion: America's Overwrought Response to September 11," *International Security* 37, no. 1 (Summer 2012).

23. Peter Bergen and Paul Cruickshank, "The Unraveling," *New Republic*, June 11, 2008; and Daniel Byman, "Al Qaeda's Terrible Spring: Why the Organization Might Not Survive," *Foreign Affairs*, May 2011.

24. Greg Miller, "Al-Qaeda Could Collapse, U.S. Officials Say," *Washington Post*, July 26, 2011, https://www.washingtonpost.com/world/national-security/al-qaeda -could-collapse-us-officials-say/2011/07/21/gIQAFu2pbI_story.html.

25. See Byman, "Breaking the Bonds," for a discussion.

26. For works comparing the threat that al-Qaeda and the Islamic State pose and the terrorism risk from the Islamic State to the Middle East and the West, see Daniel Byman, "The Homecomings: What Happens When Arab Foreign Fighters in Iraq and Syria Return?," *Studies in Conflict and Terrorism* 38, no. 8 (May 1, 2015); Daniel Byman and Jennifer R. Williams, "ISIS vs. Al Qaeda: Jihadism's Global Civil War," *The National Interest*, February 24, 2015, 10–18, http://nationalinterest.org/feature/isis-vs-al-qaeda -jihadism's-global-civil-war-12304; and Daniel Byman and Jeremy Shapiro, "Homeward Bound? Don't Hype the Threat of Returning Fighters," *Foreign Affairs* 93, no. 6 (October–November 2014), https://www.foreignaffairs.com/articles/iraq/2014-10-01 /homeward-bound.

27. Daniel Byman, *Deadly Connections: States that Sponsor Terrorism* (New York: Cambridge University Press, 2005).

28. For a review of this debate, see Tamara Wittes, *Freedom's Unsteady March: America's Role in Building Arab Democracy* (Washington DC: Brookings, 2008).

29. Pew Research Center, "Most Muslims Want Democracy, Personal Freedoms, and Islam in Political Life," *Global Attitudes and Trends*, July 10, 2012.

30. Pew Research Center, "Arab Spring Fails to Improve US Image," *Global Attitudes and Trends*, May 17, 2011, http://www.pewglobal.org/2011/05/17/arab-spring-fails-to -improve-us-image/.

31. F. Gregory Gause III, "Can Democracy Stop Terrorism?," *Foreign Affairs* 84, no. 5 (September–October 2005): 62–76.

32. Bruce Riedel, "Brezhnev in the Hejaz," *The National Interest*, September–October 2011.

33. For an extensive review of this history, see Salim Yaqub's chapter 1 in this volume.

34. Valuable works on this period include Thomas McNaugher, *Arms and Oil: US Military Strategy and the Persian Gulf* (Washington DC: Brookings, 1985); Thomas Lippman, *Inside the Mirage: America's Fragile Partnership with Saudi Arabia* (Boulder CO:

Westview, 2004); Parker T. Hart, *Saudi Arabia and the United States: Birth of a Security Partnership* (Bloomington: Indiana University Press, 1998); Rachel Bronson, *Thicker than Oil: America's Uneasy Partnership with Saudi Arabia* (New York: Oxford University Press, 2006); Maxwell Orme Johnson, *The Military as an Instrument of US Policy in Southwest Asia: The Rapid Deployment Joint Task Force, 1979–1982* (Boulder CO: Westview, 1983); and Nadav Safran, *Saudi Arabia: The Ceaseless Quest for Security* (Ithaca: Cornell University Press, 1988).

35. These figures are from a June 2012 Senate Foreign Relations Committee report, but the figures for Oman, Saudi Arabia, and troops afloat come from U.S. Senate, Committee on Foreign Relations, "The Gulf Security Architecture: Partnership with the Gulf Cooperation Council," Majority Staff Report, June 19, 2012; Department of Defense, "Active Duty Military Personnel Strengths by Regional Area and by Country," December 31, 2011; and Thom Shanker, Eric Schmitt, and David E. Sanger, "US Adds Forces in Persian Gulf, a Signal to Iran," *New York Times,* July 3, 2012. The United States in July 2012 deployed another aircraft carrier to the Gulf, further increasing the troop numbers. See Adam Entous and Julian E. Barnes, "Pentagon Bulks Up Defenses in the Gulf," *Wall Street Journal,* July 17, 2012.

36. Kenneth Katzman, "Bahrain: Reform, Security, and US Policy" (Washington, DC: Congressional Research Service, August 13, 2012); and US Department of State, Bureau of Near Eastern Affairs, "US Relations with Bahrain," Fact Sheet, July 31, 2012, http://www.state.gov/r/pa/ei/bgn/26414.htm.

37. Anthony Cordesman and Alexander Wilner, "Iran and the Gulf Military Balance: Conventional and Asymmetric Dimensions" (Washington DC: Center for Strategic and International Studies, June 28, 2012); and Kenneth Katzman, "Kuwait: Security, Reform, and US Policy" (Washington DC: Congressional Research Service, June 20, 2012).

38. Kenneth Katzman, "Oman: Reform, Security and US Policy" (Washington DC: Congressional Research Service, June 4, 2012); and Cordesman and Wilner, "Iran and the Gulf."

39. Kenneth Katzman, "The United Arab Emirates (UAE): Issues for US Policy" (Washington DC: Congressional Research Service, July 17, 2012); and Cordesman and Wilner, "Iran and the Gulf."

40. Agence France-Presse, "Qatar, US Sign Security Pact," *NOW,* January 2, 2011; Christopher M. Blanchard, "Qatar: Background and US Relations" (Washington DC: Congressional Research Service, June 6, 2012); and Entous and Barnes, "Pentagon Bulks Up."

41. Christopher M. Blanchard, "Saudi Arabia: Background and US Relations" (Washington DC: Congressional Research Service, April 30, 2009); and Cordesman and Wilner, "Iran and the Gulf."

42. See Kenneth Katzman, *Iraq: Politics, Governance, and Human Rights* (Washington DC: Congressional Research Service, August 21, 2012), http://www.fpc.state.gov/documents/organization/198107.pdf.

43. Among many, see, for example, Associated Press, "Obama: Kuwait Has Been 'Outstanding' Host," *CBS News,* August 3, 2009; Habib Toumi, "Clinton Reiterates US Com-

mitment to Security in the Gulf," Gulfnews.com, December 4, 2010; and Leon E. Panetta, "Remarks at the US Forces-Iraq End of Mission Ceremony," Baghdad, Iraq, December 15, 2011.

44. Defense Security Cooperation Agency, "Kingdom of Saudi Arabia–Intelligence, Surveillance, and Reconnaissance (ISR) Suites and Support," News Release, August 15, 2012; and Katzman, "United Arab Emirates."

45. Office of the United States Trade Representative (USTR), "U.S.–Saudi Arabia Trade Facts," May 6, 2014, https://ustr.gov/countries-regions/europe-middle-east /middle-east/north-africa/saudi-arabia; Office of the USTR, "United Arab Emirates: U.S.–United Arab Emirates Trade Facts," May 8, 2014, https://ustr.gov/countries -regions/europe-middle-east/middle-east/north-africa/united-arab-emirates; and Christopher M. Blanchard, "Saudi Arabia: Background and US Relations" (Washington DC: Congressional Research Service, June 19, 2012).

46. Office of the USTR, "United Arab Emirates"; Office of the USTR, "Korea," April 29, 2014, https://ustr.gov/countries-regions/japan-korea-apec/korea; and Blanchard, "Saudi Arabia" (June 19, 2012).

47. The problem for many of these states is not only their small size but also the overall skill levels of their militaries. In many cases they possess state-of-the-art arsenals, and regional predators' forces are weak, but US allies are unable to leverage the systems they own. See Kenneth Pollack, *Arabs at War: Military Effectiveness, 1948–1991* (Lincoln: University of Nebraska Press, 2002).

48. Jonathan Marcus, "Analysis: How Israel Might Strike at Iran," *BBC News*, February 27, 2012; and Anthony H. Cordesman and Abdullah Toukan, "Analyzing the Impact of Preventive Strikes against Iran's Nuclear Facilities" (Washington DC: Center for Strategic and International Studies, September 10, 2012), with briefing slides at http://www .csis.org/files/publication/120906_Iran_US_Preventive_Strikes.pdf.

49. Cordesman and Toukan, "Analyzing the Impact."

50. This figure excludes casualties from accidents. Dennis Cauchon, "Why U.S. Casualties Were Low," *USA Today*, April 20, 2003, http://usatoday30.usatoday.com/news /world/iraq/2003-04-20-cover-usat_x.htm.

51. James Quinlivan, "Coup-Proofing: Its Practice and Consequences in the Middle East," *International Security* 24, no. 2 (Fall 1999): 131–65.

52. For a discussion of this association regarding Saudi Arabia, see Bronson, *Thicker than Oil.*

PART II

Key Questions

CHAPTER 3

The Economic Costs of Persian Gulf Oil Supply Disruptions

Kenneth R. Vincent

Oil is unique among traded commodities. Production centers are not colocated with demand centers, and governments control a substantial portion of oil production. Further, the short-term supply of and demand for oil are inelastic, meaning that consumers cannot immediately shift their consumption patterns when the oil-based products they purchase increase in price and that most producers cannot rapidly expand output in response to shortages. Historically, most notably in the 1970s, oil supply shocks have harmed the US economy. These factors, along with the importance of oil in military operations, have combined to elevate oil supply stability to a US national security issue. The American military presence in the Middle East and the US maritime commitment to protecting the free flow of oil are driven, at least in part, by the assumption that oil supply security is critical to US prosperity. The empirical record appears to support this assumption: Oil price shocks have preceded ten out of eleven post–World War II recessions in the United States.[1]

Historical patterns notwithstanding, the US energy landscape is dramatically changing. Expanded tight oil production and moderating oil consumption are reducing the amount of oil that the United States must import. The US Energy Information Administration (EIA) projects that the share of imported oil in American liquid fuel consumption will bottom out at 14 percent in 2020, or down from 60 percent in 2005.[2] Some fear that these trends will reduce US engagement in the Middle East over the long term.[3] Despite these significant changes, the stability of the global oil market will matter greatly to the United States for the foreseeable future. Even the *World Energy Outlook* by the International Energy Agency (IEA), which projects that the United States will approach energy self-sufficiency by 2030, notes that "reducing its oil imports will not insulate the United States from developments in international markets."[4] Critically because the global price of oil is determined at the margin, the United States will remain vulnerable to oil price increases that harm the economy.

This chapter characterizes and assesses the potential economic costs of oil supply disruptions in the Persian Gulf in the context of changing market conditions. Any research endeavor that addresses the role of oil in US foreign policy and grand strategy must speak to the economic importance of oil and America's evolving vulnerability to oil supply disruptions. Some studies do not go much further than acknowledging this relationship.[5] Other analyses make more of a concerted effort to address the nature and complexity of the economic importance of oil.[6] However, these studies neglect to engage fully with the economic literature on oil supply shocks. To address this gap, I review the accumulated findings of economic research in this area, with specific reference to the potential economic consequences of a major Persian Gulf supply disruption. I identify which economic vulnerabilities will likely persist and which vulnerabilities will subside as US oil imports continue to fall.

A vigorous academic dialogue on the nature of the oil-macroeconomy relationship has been taking place for more than three decades. Among economists, a consensus on the existence, nature, and scale of the relationship between oil price shocks and macroeconomic aggregates remains elusive. The debate about this relationship has produced insights about the difference between oil demand and oil supply shocks, the specific mechanisms through which oil shocks affect the economy, the relative importance of how monetary policy reacts to oil supply shocks, and the variation in the significance of oil supply shocks across time and space. Economists have also developed multiple modeling approaches to address this issue and have arrived at varied empirical conclusions about the scale of the economic damage that oil shocks cause. Their different findings reflect the fact that any assessment of the impact of a major supply disruption is extraordinarily complex and necessarily laden with assumptions.

Although numerous scholars have surveyed the economic literature in great detail, few have attempted to "translate" this literature for decision makers and scholars who approach oil supply security from other disciplinary vantage points.[7] This analysis communicates the major findings of relevant economic research in terms that are accessible to readers who are not trained economists and presents the contours of this academic debate with specific reference to a Persian Gulf disruption. Nothing has the potential to roil energy markets like a major disruption in the Gulf. Even scholars whose position on oil supply security is relatively sanguine concede that certain adverse events in the Persian Gulf could exact an extraordinary toll on the world oil market.[8] In terms of the literature on this topic, many of the arguments that point to the reduced importance of oil supply disruptions fall flat in the context of a major Gulf supply outage. This remains the case even when reduced US imports are taken into consideration. Further, many of the concepts highlighted in the oil-macroeconomy literature, such as the way in which uncertainty stemming from oil shocks affects investment patterns and how the impact of oil shocks changes over time, hold particular salience in the context of assessing the impact of a Gulf outage.

As a key contribution, this chapter presents a range of the potential costs of oil supply shocks of varying magnitude and duration based on the findings of the economic literature. These estimates derive from the empirical findings of the literature reviewed in this chapter. Given that many debates in the oil-macroeconomy literature stand unresolved, it is no surprise that the range of potential damage from an oil price shock presented here is quite large. The range of potential losses in gross domestic product (GDP) can be thought of as a "confidence interval" designed to encompass the uncertainty highlighted in the following debates. Estimates of how severely the US economy would be harmed, therefore, represent guideposts for understanding the scale of the relationship as opposed to firm inputs to a straightforward cost-benefit analysis.

It is also important to note what this chapter does not do. First and foremost, it does not advocate any particular policy to address potential economic vulnerabilities. The chapter represents an unbiased, technical input to the volume's larger assessment. Second, the chapter does not take a position in the oil-macroeconomy debate and does not attempt to advance this literature. It communicates the findings of this body of scholarship and contextualizes them to inform a larger dialogue. Last, it does not evaluate the likelihood of particular supply disruption scenarios, for Thomas Lippman and Joshua Rovner address them in chapters 4 and 5, respectively. The analysis presented here outlines the potential price impacts of a major shock and a corresponding range of economic losses, but it does not present concrete outage/price/GDP loss scenarios.

The chapter begins with a discussion of some general preliminaries concerning oil markets. It explains why oil is important for the US economy, why oil shocks can occur, and why the Persian Gulf is critical in the world market. This section also explains the chapter's focus on oil prices as opposed to physical supply and how the world oil price translates into continued vulnerability of the US economy in the face of new US oil output. Next, the chapter reviews the literature on the relationship between oil shocks and the macroeconomy, focusing on the major questions addressed by this research, the relevance of these topics to Persian Gulf disruptions, and what the conclusions of this literature imply for assessing the impact of reduced US oil imports. The penultimate section presents estimates of the potential costs of major Gulf oil supply disruptions in terms of their price impacts and the associated GDP losses and wealth transfers to producing nations. To qualify these estimates, the section also discusses the uncertainty surrounding the price reaction to a Gulf supply shock and highlights the variety of estimated responses in the literature. The chapter concludes with a brief discussion of the major takeaways from this literature.

Oil, the US Economy, and the Persian Gulf

Any assessment of the role of oil in US foreign policy decision making must be made in the context of a dramatically changing North American petroleum market. Between 2008 and 2014, annual US crude oil production grew by close to 75 percent.[9] Further, the United States transitioned from being a net importer of refined products to a net exporter, and the share of American petroleum oil imports coming from Canada rose from around 20 percent to more than 50 percent. This transformation clearly changes the US energy security picture. However, four fundamental principles remain relevant:

1. Oil plays a central role in the US energy sector and economy.
2. Oil's supply and demand characteristics cause it to be unusually prone to price shocks.
3. The Persian Gulf plays a central role in the world oil market.
4. The United States is inextricably linked to the world oil market through the price mechanism.

The following section discusses these foundational elements of the US relationship with oil and explores how the energy revolution has (and has not) impacted them.

Continuity and Change in Petroleum Market Fundamentals

Oil plays a predominant role in the US energy sector. In 2014 petroleum accounted for 35 percent of American energy consumption, more than any other fuel.[10] Figure 3.1 breaks down US oil consumption. Recent increases in US natural gas production are changing the country's energy landscape, but the resulting reductions in oil consumption will not be transformational. Industrial oil consumption will shrink in coming years as cheap natural gas becomes the feedstock of choice in the petrochemical sector, but this sector accounts for only 24 percent of US oil consumption. Petroleum represents only 5 percent of residential energy consumption; however, reductions in this sector, driven by increased use of natural gas for home heating, will only slightly alter US demand patterns.

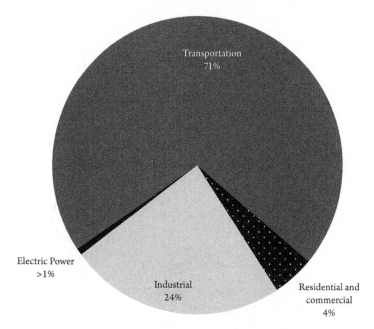

Figure 3.1. US oil consumption by sector, 2014

Data source: EIA, *Monthly Energy Review,* http://www.eia.gov/totalenergy/data/monthly/.

The easiest sector for fuel switching is power generation, but high oil prices have already pushed most of the oil out of America's power sector (see figure 3.2). This clearly illustrates that renewable energy resources such as wind and solar, which are power-generation technologies, cannot displace oil.

Moving away from petroleum has proven most difficult in the transportation sector, which accounts for the majority of US oil consumption and is projected to do so for the foreseeable future. Both market forces and regulations have vastly improved the efficiency of the US automobile fleet since 1970, but it is still *petroleum based.* Despite years of government efforts to increase the share of ethanol and biodiesel in the US fuel mix, these fuels are expected to account for a small fraction of transportation liquids by 2040. Many have pushed for a wholesale transition of the US automobile fleet to natural gas–powered, electric, fuel cell, and hybrid vehicles, but alternative vehicles combined are projected to account for only 16 percent of the US vehicle fleet in 2040. These technologies, along with mandated efficiency improvements, are projected to offset increased vehicle miles traveled and cause total US petroleum consumption to remain flat through 2040.[11] Expanded US oil production will not alter the fundamental characteristics of the US oil demand profile, nor will it shift oil's central role in the American fuel mix.

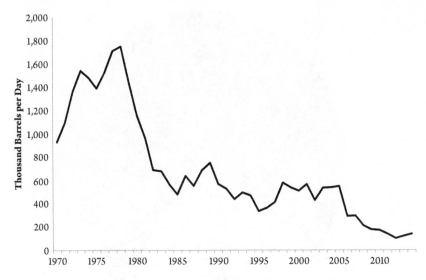

Figure 3.2. US power sector's petroleum consumption, 1970–2014
Data source: EIA, *Monthly Energy Review.*

In addition to playing a predominant role in the US economy, oil is unusually prone to price volatility because oil supply and demand are relatively price inelastic in the short term. Unlike many goods, oil production and consumption cannot respond quickly to price signals. On the demand side, most consumers cannot suspend their oil use when prices rise. While drivers might pass on a car trip, most cannot stop driving to work. Changes in behavior that materially reduce petroleum demand—for instance, purchasing a more fuel-efficient car or moving closer to one's place of work—do not occur quickly. Industrial entities usually cannot completely shift their activities to reduce oil consumption in response to price increases, either. On the supply side, bringing new conventional oil production on stream is remarkably expensive and time consuming. Further, outside of the nations of the Organization of the Petroleum Exporting Countries (OPEC), virtually all of the oil that can be economically produced is being produced. These short-run rigidities combine to make the price responses to oil supply disruptions very severe. Oil's basic market fundamentals, as opposed to speculation in the futures market, drive most of the volatility in the world market.[12] In short, oil is uniquely prone to price "shocks."

US tight oil production is set to moderate some of the supply-side rigidity. Because tight oil production functions more like a manufacturing process than like conventional oil production, shale producers can respond much more quickly to price signals than conventional producers can. This ability to ramp up production has caused some analysts to refer to the United States as the new "swing producer" in the world market.[13] This is only partially true. US tight oil production will increase the price elasticity of oil supply over time, but it will not equip the market with the capability to digest major supply shocks. In some circumstances, large-scale outages still could overwhelm shale producers' capability to rapidly ramp up production. Further, shale output does nothing to alter inflexibilities on the demand side of the oil market. While the US energy revolution is rationalizing the relationship between price and production in the oil sector to an important extent, it does not completely remove the threat of catastrophic oil price shocks (which are the core focus of this chapter).

The Continuing Importance of the Middle East

While expanding US oil output has dominated recent energy headlines, the role of the Persian Gulf in the world oil market cannot be discounted. The region holds a predominant position in terms of oil production, proved reserves, and spare production capacity. Close to 30 percent of the world's current oil supply comes from the Gulf region; this share is expected to increase through 2040.[14] Table 3.1 highlights the major producers in the Gulf region and their production volumes in global context. At the margin, the full or partial compromising of any one of these supply streams could wreak havoc on global oil markets. As US production peaks in the 2020s and other non-OPEC production declines, the Persian Gulf could actually increase in significance.[15] While expansions in other regions, notably the Western Hemisphere, are having a large impact on the world petroleum landscape, the Gulf region will remain pivotal.[16]

The share of proven oil reserves located in the region also contributes to this prominence (see figure 3.3). Close to half of the world's proven reserves lie in the Middle East. The share takes on a larger significance when one accounts for the production cost, which is on average far lower than in other regions. Some observers argue that the world has reached "peak oil" and that even supplies in the Middle East are not sustainable.[17] These concerns belie the history of the petroleum industry. Since the nineteenth century, concerns about impending shortages of oil have continually been shown to be wrong by ever-expanding proven global reserves. While in physical terms, petroleum could clearly be exhausted at some point, technology improvements and price trends have regularly made more oil available.[18] Recent expansions of oil production in Iraq and the United States have served to further discredit the peak oil theory. The Persian Gulf region will undoubtedly remain a critical component of this resource base.

Perhaps more important, all of the world's current spare oil production capac-

Table 3.1. Persian Gulf oil output volumes, 2014

	Oil production/transit (million barrels per day)	Share of world production (percent)
Iraq	3.3	3.5
Kuwait	2.8	3.0
United Arab Emirates	3.5	3.8
Iran	3.4	3.7
Saudi Arabia	11.6	12.5
Strait of Hormuz	17.0	18.3
Persian Gulf total	26.7	28.7

Data sources: EIA, *International Energy Statistics* (Washington DC: Department of Energy, 2015); and EIA, *World Oil Transit Chokepoints,* https://www.eia.gov/beta/international/regions-topics.cfm?Region TopicID=WOTC.

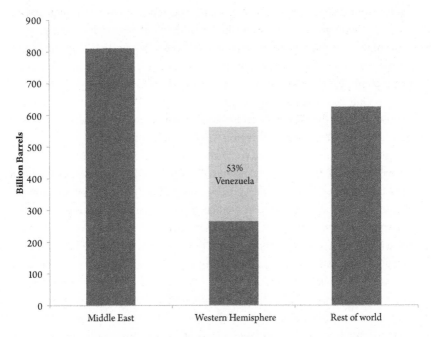

Figure 3.3. Proved world oil reserves by region, 2014
Source: British Petroleum, *BP Statistical Review of World Energy, 2014,* http://www.bp.com/content/dam /bp-country/de-de/PDFs/brochures/BP-statistical-review-of-world-energy-2014-full-report.pdf.

ity is located in the Persian Gulf region.[19] *Spare capacity* is defined as "production that can be brought on within 30 days and sustained for at least 90 days."[20] When the ratio of global spare capacity to global consumption is relatively low, the world oil market is considered "tight"; that is, it is relatively vulnerably to a supply shortage. The only players that can "turn on the spigot" in the event of a global supply shortage are select OPEC nations in the Middle East, and the vast majority of this spare capacity is located in Saudi Arabia.[21] Some observers argue that reliance on the kingdom constitutes a perilous energy strategy for the United States.[22] Others doubt Saudi Arabia's capabilities, arguing that the country is already producing at maximum levels.[23] The failure of Saudi Arabia to fully make up for lost Libyan production in 2012 lends some support to this claim. Any major disruption to Persian Gulf oil output would also likely affect the availability of this critical release valve.

No matter what happens with tight oil output, the United States will not be able to supplant Saudi Arabia in this regard. One of the chief reasons that the shale revolution has been so successful in the United States is that American landowners control mineral rights. Thus, outside of federal lands, oil production is a commercial decision as opposed to a policy decision. While tight oil producers can respond relatively quickly to price signals, they have no commercial incentive to hold back spare production capacity in the same fashion as Saudi Arabia and other Gulf OPEC members. In a crisis, American producers would not likely be able to surge their production in the same way that Gulf producers can. While recent OPEC (Saudi) policy decisions suggest a reluctance to throttle production to support high prices, Persian Gulf producers will likely remain the oil-producing countries that can help stabilize an oil supply crisis for the foreseeable future.

Why Focus on Prices?

The discussion in this chapter, and the literature on oil shocks more generally, focuses on price fluctuations rather than physical supply shortages. Given the prominent role that the concept of energy independence occupies in the public discourse on energy and national security, a brief note on the relative importance of supply and price is in order. It is especially relevant given declining US petroleum imports. Simply put, the physical supply of Persian Gulf crude oil to the United States is relatively unimportant. Only around a quarter of US crude oil imports come from the Persian Gulf.[24] Persian Gulf oil is critical to the United States not because of direct US consumption but because Gulf supplies are critical to the *world* market. Although US crude oil imports are projected to decline in the coming years, American energy autarky is not a plausible outcome. Oil is a globally traded, fungible commodity. While the sulfur content and specific gravities of different crude oils vary, the prices of different crude grades move together. Foreign oil is not the problem; rather, foreign disruptions that impact the global market are the problem.

Economic literature has addressed this issue at length. Morris Adelman's classic 1984 article "International Oil Agreements" provides a timeless metaphor for understanding global oil supply. He conceptualized the international oil market as a giant bathtub, with multiple spigots and multiple drains. In this context, worrying about which spigot's oil makes its way to your national drain is folly. The critical issue is keeping the bathtub full. Empirical economists followed this conceptual work with myriad studies, testing whether the prices of various crude oils moved together.[25] To date, the literature points to the co-integration of world crude oil prices on the spot market.

Even if regional logistical issues and refinery particularities cause some price heterogeneity among crude streams, the bathtub analogy still holds. Consequently, catastrophic supply shocks in the Persian Gulf would certainly have a major impact on the price of oil in the United States. A large supply disruption in the world market would take oil out of the world bathtub, driving up the price of the remaining oil. This global price escalation would likely have to be severe to adequately curtail world demand in response to a major cutoff, given the small price elasticity of demand discussed previously. The resulting reduction in US oil consumption would not be based on how much Gulf oil the country consumes but on its share of global oil consumption and the price elasticity of its oil consumption. The economic impacts of this phenomenon stem more from increased prices than from the physical availability of crude oil.[26]

The Literature on Oil Price Shocks and the Economy

After economic decline followed the oil shocks of the 1970s, the relationship between oil prices and economic activity became a topic of considerable interest to both economists and policymakers. Escalations of the world oil price tend to be followed by recessions (see figure 3.4). Exploring this phenomenon generated a large body of literature. After three decades of research, consensus on the exact nature of this relationship still eludes economists. That said, researchers in this area have built a considerable edifice of knowledge about how oil prices and economic aggregates interact. I explain next how several core questions addressed by existing research can illuminate the effects of potential Persian Gulf supply shocks on the American economy in light of a changing US petroleum landscape.

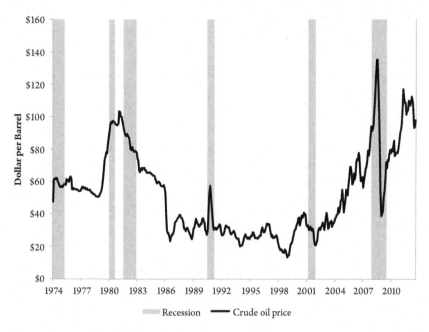

Figure 3.4. Real oil prices and US recessions, 1974–2012

Data sources: EIA, *Historical Real Oil Prices,* http://www.eia.gov/forecasts/steo/realprices/; and National Bureau of Economic Research, *US Business Cycle Expansions and Contractions* (Cambridge MA: NBER, 2012).

What Constitutes an Oil Shock?

In one sense, *oil shocks* are easy to define: episodes in which a substantial portion of global oil supply is removed from the market, causing an unusually large increase in the world oil price. More recently, oil shocks have also come in the form of price increases stemming from unexpected spikes in world oil demand. Table 3.2 summarizes the most notable supply shocks of the OPEC era. The supply outages are calculated based on the average monthly decrease in oil production as a share of global production in the month preceding the disruption. This table accounts for increases in production that occurred elsewhere in response to the supply shock. The price increases are based on the difference between the refiner acquisition cost of crude before the spike and the peak change in price during the episode. In each case, net outages of less than 5 percent of total global output led to major changes in world prices. All of these shocks originated in the Middle East.

Early studies on oil disruptions and economic output defined shocks in terms of simple price increases. As the following debates unfolded, the operational

Table 3.2. Major historical oil supply disruptions

Disruption event	Duration	Supply reduction (percent)	Price increase (percent)
October Arab-Israeli War and subsequent OPEC embargo	October 1973–March 1974	4.0	41
Iranian Revolution	November 1978–July 1979	1.3	39
Outbreak of Iran-Iraq War	October 1980–March 1981	1.2	26
Iraq-Kuwait War	August 1990–October 1990	2.9	72

Data source: James D. Hamilton, "Causes and the Consequences of the Oil Shock of 2007–2008," NBER Working Paper no. 15002 (Washington DC: Brookings, 2009).

definition of oil shocks evolved with the econometric specifications used to unpack their impact on the economy. A revised measure accounts for the difference between oil price increases stemming from exogenous events and oil price increases that follow cyclical price troughs.[27] Economists continue to use this measure, known as the net oil price increase. Subsequent scholars have further modified the definition. Some define oil shocks as a period during which the oil price exceeds the mean for the entire sample under consideration.[28] Others look at cumulative changes in the price of oil of more than 50 percent that have been sustained for more than four quarters.[29] Shifts in this definition can influence the econometric results of a model.

Other studies employ even more creative methods to meaningfully define oil shocks. One such study examines the major oil shocks beginning with the 1973 oil embargo and creates counterfactual scenarios for what countries *would have* produced in the absence of disruption events using extrapolations from similar producing countries.[30] The difference between what these countries would have produced and what they actually produced, expressed as a percentage of world production, represents the exogenous loss in global output. This measure allows for the examination of the impact of shocks over time. In a recent contribution, International Monetary Fund scholars developed a measure of shocks based on the impact of daily events chronicled in the trade press on daily oil price forecasts.[31] This methodology isolates the importance of surprise in driving oil price fluctuations. Both of these novel approaches to measurement advance the discourse on oil shocks by better isolating the specific impact of shock events.

In some ways, the back-and-forth about how to define oil shocks is unimportant for the nontechnical observer. Most of the preceding definition shifts matter only in terms of their impact on methodology. However, two points are particularly relevant to the topic of this chapter. First, under any definition, a large disruption of oil supplies from the Gulf region would constitute a supply shock. Second, past oil supply shocks point to a sobering fact about potential Persian Gulf disruptions: these outages were relatively small compared to total world output. None of the major oil shocks took more than 5 percent of globally traded oil off of the market, but they still coincided with major price increases. Bearing in mind the volumes listed in table 3.2, certain low-probability events in the Gulf region could clearly be larger than any oil market disruption on record.

Do Oil Shocks Really Harm the Economy?

Much like the democratic peace debate in political science, the oil-macroeconomy literature began with an empirical regularity that begged explanation. The correlation between oil price spikes and economic downturns is striking, but it does not equate to causation. James Hamilton wrote the seminal paper in this area of inquiry in 1983 and found that oil price spikes predicted decreases in gross national product to a statistically significant degree.[32] His article stakes one of the first formal claims regarding the relevance of oil shocks to the economy and remains the most widely cited study on this topic. Economists no longer regard Hamilton's original model as the ideal specification of this relationship, but it serves as a starting point for much of the following discussion.

Oil markets remained calm for the next few years after Hamilton published his initial study, and it altered the patterns in the time-series data upon which his model was based. Subsequent scholars published studies showing that Hamilton's argument was no longer sound.[33] Hamilton later revised his argument by updating his definition of an oil shock and demonstrating the relationship was nonlinear but strongly statistically significant.[34] Early literature reviews on the topic point toward the existence of a significant relationship between oil price shocks and economic output.[35] Still the evidence cannot be regarded as conclusive.

The most forceful challenge to Hamilton's foundational result comes from Lutz Kilian, who has authored and coauthored numerous articles questioning the importance of oil shocks to the macroeconomy. Robert Barsky and Kilian argue that major events in the Middle East cannot fully explain oil price spikes and deem the evidence of their impact on the macroeconomy inconclusive.[36] The larger contribution of their article, which serves as a precursor to some of the following major debates, is that it highlights the importance of demand in explaining the severity of oil shocks. Because economic output is a major driver of world oil demand and hence oil prices, shocks in the world oil price cannot be considered completely exogenous. Kilian's subsequent articles demonstrate both a moderate impact of Middle East supply interruptions on oil prices and small GDP consequences of these fluctuations, but Hamilton disputes these findings.[37]

This scholarly debate matters for the present assessment in two ways. First, the literature on this topic motivated investigations of specific aspects of the oil-macroeconomy relationship that have yielded a sophisticated understanding of how oil shocks unfold and have provided analysts with tools to assess how an oil shock might impact the economy under current conditions. Second and critically, the contentious discourse on this topic highlights the uncertainty surrounding the relationship between oil shocks and macroeconomic aggregates. While a major Persian Gulf supply disruption would definitely cause the US economy harm, estimates of the size or nature of this damage must be approached with this uncertainty in mind. The wide range of potential damage presented in the fourth section of this chapter bears this out.

How Do Demand and Supply Shocks Differ?

The most alarming oil price spike in recent years occurred in the summer of 2008. On July 3, 2008, the spot price of West Texas Intermediate—a light, sweet crude oil used as an indicator of market trends—reached a record price of $145.31.[38] Unlike previous significant oil price increases, no identifiable outage drove the fluctuation. Many public commentators at the time rushed to blame the price increases on speculators, but trading entities alone cannot account for the spike. As with the supply shocks of previous decades, this price increase was most likely driven by market fundamentals. Substantial increases in world demand caused the price spike of 2008. Supply at the time was stagnant but steady. The oil-intensive economic growth in countries that do not belong to the Organization for Economic Cooperation and Development (OECD) such as India and China pushed up global demand. Intuitively, it would seem that shocks caused by increasing demand stemming from a booming world economy would cause less economic harm.

Many empirical studies have confirmed this result: Oil shocks caused by increasing demand are less likely to depress economic growth than oil shocks caused by a supply outage. Kilian developed a variable that measures global real economic activity demand based on international freight rates.[39] He showed that aggregate oil demand shocks—that is, those driven by economic growth—do not harm the economy during the initial period of price escalation, although they do slow down growth in subsequent years. The initial correlation with economic expansion likely occurs because the aggregate impact of a thriving global economy dominates the growth-slowing impacts of high oil prices. Numerous other studies have confirmed that oil price shocks driven by broad demand expansions are less likely to harm the economy than supply shocks do.[40] This result holds across model types, countries, and time periods, including the 2007–8 fluctuations.

The most important lesson from this strand of the literature is that oil demand shocks represent less of an economic threat than oil supply shocks do. Kilian's full methodology, which drives his result challenging the relationship between oil shocks and the macroeconomy more generally, splits oil price shocks into those caused by supply shocks, demand shocks driven by broadly based growth (discussed earlier), and "precautionary" demand shocks. The logic behind this third type of shock is that adverse political events in oil-producing areas drive uncertainty in the market and lead actors to horde oil, driving up demand in a way that is unrelated to market fundamentals. Whether supply shocks or precautionary demand shocks drive price movement, one type of shock or the other would occur in the event of a major disruption to Gulf supply, ultimately harming the US economy.

How Do Oil Shocks Affect the Economy?

Research on oil shocks and the macroeconomy has identified four major mechanisms through which high oil prices result in decreased output. A brief review of these mechanisms highlights which types of harm would be particularly acute in the event of a Persian Gulf disruption. First, one basic explanation for how oil price spikes affect the economy is known as a classic supply-side shock. As energy, a critical input to national production, becomes more scarce and expensive, output and productivity suffer. Firms produce less with the same amount of capital and labor, causing them to eventually shed workers. This downsizing increases unemployment and causes aggregate economic output to decline. Simultaneously, escalation in the oil price leads to reduced real wages and rising inflation. This mechanism comports with the story of the "stagflation" that occurred in the 1970s.[41]

Oil price shocks also reduce output through demand-side channels. Empirical investigations at the consumer level illustrate the demand-side impacts of oil shocks well. Oil price increases reduce consumer expenditures by shrinking disposable income, stemming precautionary savings, and reducing purchases of oil-guzzling durable consumer goods.[42] For example, reduced purchases of American-made sport utility vehicles in favor of more fuel-efficient foreign imports in response to the 2007–8 escalation in oil prices had a significant impact on US output.[43] This period also witnessed a major decrease in consumer confidence, although this decline is difficult to separate from the larger economic problems occurring in the housing market. This finding highlights the importance of indirect demand-side impacts resulting from increased uncertainty and its influence, which can potentially be severe, on investment decisions.[44] As growth slows and disposable income fluctuates, consumers feel less comfortable spending money, perpetuating a cycle of economic decline.

Third, oil shocks can harm the economy through economic frictions known as adjustment or allocation costs. When oil prices increase suddenly, the capital stock and labor force of an economy do not immediately adjust to the new reality. The durability of energy-intensive capital goods, combined with the rigidity of labor markets, precludes the swift realignment of production inputs from more petroleum-intensive sectors to less petroleum-intensive activities. In other words, replacing oil-intensive equipment is expensive, and workers in oil-intensive industries cannot seamlessly migrate to other sectors. As a result, the economy performs below its optimal output level for a time.[45] Empirical work in this area suggests that allocation costs represent an important component of how oil shocks harm the economy. For example, oil price shocks lead to reduced employment, much of which is driven by reallocation across sectors.[46] Along with the severity of a given oil shock, the flexibility of the economy determines the extent of these costs.

Finally, oil shocks have the potential to curtail economic output by reducing investment. Oil price spikes increase firms' input costs and reduce demand for the goods that they produce, in turn decreasing the amount that they can invest. Further, the uncertainty generated by volatility in the oil market could also lead to an investment pause.[47] An empirical study demonstrating the differential effects of oil shocks across industries shows that uncertainty about the trajectory of future oil prices clouds the investment picture for petroleum-intensive industries, which have to make assumptions about oil prices in their financial planning.[48] Through this mechanism, oil shocks potentially play a major role in reducing investment at the firm level. Later empirical work calls the impact of oil price shocks on non-residential investment into question.[49] It still seems plausible that uncertainty generated by an oil price shock could lead investors to delay capital purchases, depending on the severity of the event.

In addition to the mechanisms that involve reduced economic output, oil shocks also hurt the economy by increasing the transfer of wealth from consumers in oil-importing countries to oil exporters. This shift constitutes an additional economic welfare loss, over and above the contraction in GDP.[50] Expenditures on foreign oil can be thought of as a "tax" on US consumers levied by foreign producers.[51] A large increase in the price of imported oil abruptly increases the revenue that is transferred to foreign producers. While some of these revenues are reinvested in the US economy or spent on US exports, the ratio is not 1:1. In effect, increased wealth transfers reduce the purchasing power of US consumers.[52] It is worth noting that these losses vary directly with the level of oil imports.[53]

Some observers rightly note that increased oil prices are not uniformly bad for all actors in the economy. The petroleum industry does profit handsomely during periods of high oil prices; however, the impact of these niche beneficiaries of oil shocks on the larger economy should not be overstated. Oil and gas accounts for only 1.6 percent of the US economy. To assess how vulnerability shifts as the importance of the petroleum sector changes in the economy, a recent study compared the economic sensitivity of all fifty states to oil price shocks and estimates that oil price escalations caused employment to suffer in forty-one states. The study concludes that the expanding role of the domestic oil sector will have only a minor impact on the overall vulnerability of the US economy to oil price shocks.[54]

As US oil production increases and imports decrease, the wealth transfer caused by a supply shock will decrease. However, increased US oil production will not substantially mitigate the economic output losses related to supply-side losses, reduced domestic consumption, allocation costs, and decreased investment. The impacts of oil supply disruptions and price increases cannot be escaped. A major Gulf outage constitutes the "scariest" possible event that could occur in the world oil market and would likely translate into considerable reductions in consumer confidence and extreme caution on the part of many investors. Despite reduced US dependence on foreign crude oil sources in the coming decades, the vulnerability of the American economy to a global oil shock will persist.

What Is the Relative Importance of Monetary Policy?

Petroleum price shocks simultaneously affect economic growth and inflation. Economic contraction occurs through the channels discussed earlier. Inflation escalates because of increasing consumer fuel costs and because higher fuel input costs drive up the prices of goods. This places monetary authorities in a difficult position. They can increase interest rates to address inflation worries and consequently exacerbate the slowdown in growth, or they can leave interest rates lower to offset the output losses and thus leave inflation unfettered. This trade-off presents central banks with a particularly unappealing set of choices that increases the likelihood of errors in monetary policy.[55] A significant strand of the oil-macroeconomy literature attempts to discern the relative importance of monetary policy and oil prices in driving the recessions that tend to follow oil price shocks.

Some scholars argue that monetary policy is the true cause of most of the post–oil shock recessions addressed in this literature. The most notable study staking this claim comes from Benjamin Bernanke, Mark Gertler, and Mark Watson.[56] They conducted a counterfactual simulation in which monetary policy does not respond to the oil price shocks that predated the recessions of 1973, 1979–80, and 1990. The authors found that in the absence of a major monetary policy reaction to an oil price shock, the economy contracts little. However, this result is partially statistical artifact, for while the model separates the monetary policy from oil price shocks, it fails to capture the strategic nature of investment decisions. In the event that the US Federal Reserve (the Fed) had done nothing to address the inflation impacts of a major oil price shock, the actors' expectations would have been different. This calls the economists' results into question, because their model was built on market data from a specific regime that led to a specific set of actor expectations.[57]

Despite this problem, Bernanke, Gertler, and Watson motivated further research that challenges their results on their own terms. Most notably, critics of their position point out that the scale of interest rate reductions that would have been necessary to offset the GDP losses that occurred were not plausible (e.g., a 900 percent reduction in the Fed funds' rate in 1974) and that the temporal structure of their model stacked the deck against the significance of oil price shocks.[58] Bernanke, Gertler, and Watson assume that the impact of oil shocks is only observable for the seven months following the shock. Once the impacts over a longer period are considered, oil price increases regain their significance.

It is unlikely that the monetary policy response that followed a major Persian Gulf oil supply disruption would matter more to US economic output than the disruption itself would. Economies are better able to weather oil price increases when interest rates and inflation are low, but these advantages might not prove decisive in the event of a major price shock.[59] For purposes of estimating how much a Persian Gulf supply disruption would harm the US economy, the main takeaway is that this third variable—monetary policy—would not be nearly as central to economic outcomes as the disruption itself would be.

How Has This Relationship Changed over Time?

During the post–World War II period, myriad changes have taken place in the world economy and in oil markets. Analyses of changes in the oil-macroeconomy relationship over time enable researchers to place current trends in context. Studying the history of this relationship helps answer some of the questions that have arisen about macroeconomic energy security in the wake of the US tight oil revolution. Issues such as the relative significance of decreasing imports and decreasing consumption, the impact of market volatility, and the potential boost the economy might see from lower oil prices—all are addressed in time-series studies within the oil-macroeconomy literature. Recent trends generally point to the reduced vulnerability of the US economy to oil shocks, although the exact source and scale of this reduction is not entirely clear.

A 2014 paper published by the Council of Economic Advisers makes a clear case for decreasing impacts of oil shocks on US GDP over time.[60] The authors point to reduced US oil imports as a key driver of this trend, but they note that the multiplicity of channels through which oil prices impact the economy preclude a single explanation of decreased vulnerability. Consumption patterns also play a significant role. Other studies point to changes in the US economy such as the increased credibility of monetary authorities, more flexible labor markets, and less regulation that reduce allocation and adjustment costs.[61] The reduced importance of the automobile industry in US aggregate output and changes in the structure of the auto industry itself likely also moderate the impact of oil shocks.[62] Automobile production now represents a smaller share of GDP, and US automakers have shifted production toward more efficient vehicles. Energy use patterns matter as well. A comparison of multiple countries show that reduced energy intensity of economic output—or the amount of energy required to produce a dollar of GDP—also lessens the impact of oil shocks over time.[63] The American economy has witnessed large decreases in energy and petroleum intensity since the first oil shocks and is therefore currently better equipped to deal with a supply outage than it was in the 1970s.

Analysis of the oil-macroeconomy relationship over time has also shed light on how conditions in oil markets influence the severity of economic problems caused by oil shocks. This understanding is especially important, given the severity of recent volatility in the world oil market. Oil shocks when the oil market is volatile appear to inflict less harm on the economy relative to those shocks that follow periods of stability.[64] The unanticipated component of an oil price shock is what jolts the market.[65] This finding might actually point to a smaller impact from a Persian Gulf supply outage than observers might expect, because much of the oil market volatility experienced in recent years has been driven by events in the Persian Gulf. For years analysts have argued that a "fear premium" is built into the world oil price.[66] If markets are already moving based on fears of a Gulf disruption, the price shock and resulting economic losses could be less severe than they would be in reaction to a totally unanticipated event.

Recent price changes have also raised questions about the extent to which the oil-macroeconomy relationship flows both ways. After the dramatic drop in the world oil price that took place in 2014 and early 2015, the dramatic boost to the US economy that some observers expected did not materialize.[67] In fact, some of the first attempts to examine the changes in this relationship over time were published after the oil price crash of the 1980s. Early studies of this period show that decreases in the oil price do not stimulate the economy to the same extent that increases in the oil price harm the economy.[68] Notably, when oil price increases are separated from oil price decreases, the impact of price increases on GDP becomes much larger. Empirical investigations suggest that the adjustment costs are the most likely driver of this asymmetry.[69] Asymmetry matters in assessing the cost of shocks, because even if oil prices return to pre-shock levels, much of the shock's damage likely will not be undone. That the oil price crash of 2014–15 has given the economy only a modest boost supports this conclusion.

In general, trends in the oil-macroeconomy relationship over time point to the reduced vulnerability of the United States. The national economy is better equipped to deal with changes in energy input prices than it was during the 1970s because of the reduced importance of petroleum in national output, increased flexibility of the economy, reduced levels of imports and consumption, and numerous other factors. Volatility in the world oil market also could actually mean that a major supply disruption would take a *less* severe toll on the economy. The only result that tempers this optimism is the asymmetric relationship between oil price changes and economic output. If major disruption causes considerable harm, subsequent oil price decreases will not sufficiently stimulate the economy to recoup the lost output.

How Do These Impacts Vary across Countries?

If a major oil supply disruption in the Persian Gulf roils the world oil market, virtually every nation in the world will experience the effects. The bulk of cross-national research on the oil-macroeconomy relationship focuses on advanced economies. The impact of oil shocks on both inflation and output varies across the Group of 7 (G7) economies, but the source of this variation is not clear.[70] Prior to the integration of European monetary policy, the G7 countries provided an excellent experimental space to test the importance of monetary policy responses to oil price shocks. Policy differences account for some of the variation across G7 countries in lost output caused by the 1990 oil price shock.[71] Other drivers of these differences across developed countries include the countries' net energy import status and the energy intensity of their economic output.[72] If the energy-intensity reduction across the OECD continues, the impacts in developed countries will probably continue to abate.

Research on how oil shocks affect industrialized countries that are self-sufficient in oil offers limited guidance in assessing whether increased US oil production might mitigate the impact of price shocks on the US economy. Price shocks have a less detrimental impact on economic output in producer countries such as Norway, the United Kingdom, and Canada. However, this finding might or might not hold for the United States because, unlike the producer countries, the United States will likely not become a net oil exporter. Kilian's analysis actually shows that the impacts in G7 countries that produce oil are more severe than in those countries that do not. He argues that "policy responses and institutional characteristics may matter in dealing with exogenous oil supply shocks."[73] Detailed analysis of exactly how oil price changes affected the OECD oil exporters would be needed to draw firm conclusions about how escalating US production translates into reduced vulnerability.

Comparatively less attention has been paid to the potential impact of oil shocks on non-OECD countries. This is partly because of the timing of most historical oil supply disruptions. During most of the post–World War II oil shocks, large developing countries were not yet major oil consumers. Two studies have examined China's response to oil price shocks. One shows that oil shocks did not harm China's stock markets from 1996 to 2007; the other finds that oil shocks from 1995 to 2008 did not harm China's GDP growth.[74] Given that most observers agree that during this period China was the primary driver of the global growth that led to price spikes, these results do not provide conclusive evidence on how China and other large developing nations would respond to an exogenous oil supply shock.

Two aspects of non-OECD countries might explain why they might suffer less from a shock to the price of oil. First, these countries' labor markets are far more flexible than those in the West. Thus, many of the allocation costs associated with oil price shocks might prove less severe, given the relative ease with which resources can be moved within the economy.[75] Second, the subsidies that non-OECD countries provide for petroleum products drive demand patterns. Consumers do not feel the brunt of oil price fluctuations because of fuel subsidies, which cost governments nearly a quarter of a trillion dollars in 2010.[76] Throughout the developing world, governments set price ceilings for fuels and pay the difference between the market cost of the fuels and the consumer price. This practice, which is beginning to be reformed in a lower oil price environment, leads to distorted consumption patterns and fiscal problems. However, given the capital surpluses enjoyed by countries such as China, these price supports might be able to insulate non-OECD economies from the worst impacts of a price shock.

A major disruption to oil supplies from the Persian Gulf would likely harm the economies of most oil-importing nations. OECD countries with relatively low oil intensity of economic output would be affected by a shock but not to the same degree as the United States. Emerging economies represent more of a wild card. Recent growth in non-OECD countries has greatly expanded these nations' oil consumption. While these countries have policies in place to withstand the worst impacts of an oil price shock, their economic output patterns are extremely energy intensive. If a major supply disruption took place, the subsidy systems and energy consumption patterns that underlie non-OECD growth could be thrown into disarray. Further, the impacts of economic slowdowns elsewhere could be more harmful to the United States than in the past, given the increased significance of international trade and investment in the US economy. While the United States will likely purchase a smaller portion of globally traded crude oil in the coming years, the country's increased economic linkages with other vulnerable oil importers could add to the impact of a price shock.

Estimating the Economic Impact of a Persian Gulf Oil Supply Disruption

A Persian Gulf supply disruption would hurt the US economy through changes in the world price of oil. A major world oil price escalation would result in a large wealth transfer to oil-exporting countries and significantly damage US GDP. The two determinants of the extent of economic losses are the size of the oil price change and the sensitivity of the US GDP to such a change. This section briefly discusses the economic literature on oil price movements and reviews empirical estimates of the magnitude of oil price shocks' impact on economic output. It then presents estimates of the potential impacts of a Persian Gulf supply disruption based on a range of price shock scenarios and GDP sensitivities.

The first determinant of the severity of economic losses that a Persian Gulf supply disruption would cause is the size of the oil price shock. The main strand of economic research on oil price fluctuations focuses on *elasticities*, which measure how much oil supply and demand respond to changes in price and income. Elasticities refer to the expected percent change in the quantity of oil demanded or supplied in response to a given percentage change in price.[77] Numerous studies have examined the magnitude of these elasticities.[78] Empirical studies confirm that both oil demand and supply are relatively unresponsive to price changes in the short term; consequently, shortages can cause severe price escalations. A recent study estimates an overall short-run disruption elasticity of −0.118, which suggests that oil prices will rise by 8.47 percent for every 1 percent of lost global petroleum production.[79] Thus, for every million barrels of oil taken off the market, the world oil price will rise by about $5 per barrel, given a baseline oil price of around $60 per barrel.[80] This suggests that a major outage in a relatively minor Gulf producer could cause a price escalation of up to 25 percent, that a large-scale disruption in Saudi Arabia could cause an upswing of 50 percent or more, and that a catastrophic regional disruption could result in the doubling of oil prices. These estimates are based on the scale of production activity in the region (see table 3.1) and oil market conditions at the time of this writing.

The problem with using estimates from the econometric literature to estimate the price impacts of particular supply disruptions is that this practice implicitly assumes that the future will be similar to the past. Most of the price movements that inform empirical estimates of elasticities take place in what might be considered normal conditions. In the event of a major Persian Gulf supply disruption, this history becomes less relevant. Further, it is not clear that the price response would be linear. At extremely high prices, the price change in response to a major outage could level off. Different sizes of exogenous oil supply shocks have different price impacts in percentage terms.[81] Consequently, we should understand econometric estimates of oil's price responsiveness to a supply shock as providing guideposts for analysis and not as exact predictions.

Nonacademic observers echo this uncertainty. A survey of market participants produces an extremely wide range of the price impacts of Gulf disruptions under different policy scenarios; market participants gave responses from as little as a few dollars to an increase of more than $100 when asked about the price impact of the closure of the Strait of Hormuz.[82] The US Energy Information Administration uses "rules of thumb" to estimate the impacts of a supply shock that account for market psychology. For instance, it projects that the price impact of a shock caused by a violent event such as a war will be more severe than a price escalation of the same scale caused by a nonviolent event.[83] No matter what analytical framework an observer uses to address the impact of a Persian Gulf supply shock, the true price outcomes of a major Gulf outage are fundamentally uncertain.

Part of this uncertainty derives from the potential policy responses that governments could undertake to address a supply shock. The main instrument that the United States has to address oil supply outages is the Strategic Petroleum Reserve, which consists of 696 million barrels of crude oil that can be released at a rate of 4.4 million barrels per day.[84] Other nations that belong to the International Energy Agency hold strategic stocks as well. Combined IEA oil stocks stood at more than 4 billion barrels in 2013.[85] In the event of a major Persian Gulf disruption, these resources could be deployed to address the shortfall in world markets. Numerous studies speak to the potential value of strategic stocks to offset the impact of major supply disruptions.[86] Still uncertainty surrounds exactly what a release of strategic stocks in response to a major supply disruption would look like.[87] While an oil stock response would undoubtedly moderate a price shock, the extent of its impact would depend on its timing and the amount of oil released. Stockpile actions are simply another element that drives the scale of price impacts.

The second key factor in determining the economic damage from a Persian Gulf supply disruption is the scale of the economy's response to the resulting price change. The empirical literature discussed in the preceding section has generated some quantitative estimates of these impacts, or oil price elasticities of GDP. These measures differ from demand and supply elasticities for products; they represent the impact of oil price shocks on GDP over time. Elasticities generated in the econometric literature are produced using time-series statistical models known as vector autoregressions. These models provide a dynamic framework in which the impact of a variable change at one juncture can be measured across time. An oil shock is introduced to the model at a given time, and the impact plays out over the remainder of the time series. The impact of oil shocks on output is measured by summing these "impulse responses" over time.[88] Estimates of the scale of these impacts in the literature vary, but they tend to cluster around −0.05.[89] Thus, a 100 percent increase in the world oil price would reduce GDP by about 5 percent.

Macroeconomic simulation models constitute the other major source of estimates concerning the impacts of oil price shocks on GDP. These models capture a variety of relationships across the economy using statistical techniques, but they often represent the economy using a one-sector production function. Consequently these models are unable to capture many of the economic frictions caused by oil supply disruptions, leading them to potentially underestimate the impact of oil shocks.[90] However, given that some evidence points to reduced allocation costs in the US economy, this study includes the average response to supply disruptions generated by these models (around −0.01) as a lower bound for the potential impacts of an oil shock.[91]

The range of potential economic impacts from a major Persian Gulf supply disruption is presented in table 3.3 and constitutes a "back of the envelope" calculation.[92] Oil price shocks of 25 percent, 50 percent, and 100 percent are examined with GDP elasticities of −0.01, −0.03, and −0.05. This approach captures the uncertainty surrounding both the potential price impacts of a Gulf supply disruption and the severity of potential economic impacts. The GDP impacts would unfold over a period of years, but they are presented in terms of current output levels for readability. Table 3.3 also includes the increased wealth transfer to exporting nations based on current import levels and prices. While these transfers are not included in GDP calculations, this measure should be included in our assessment as it speaks to the reduced purchasing power and returns to capital resulting from the shock. The wealth transfers are

Table 3.3. Estimates of the economic losses from a major oil supply disruption (billion US$)

			Oil price/GDP elasticity		
			−0.01	−0.03	−0.05
Price shock	25%	GDP loss[a]	$41	$122	$204
		Wealth transfer[b]	$9	$9	$9
		Total real income loss	$50	$131	$213
	50%	GDP loss	$81	$244	$407
		Wealth transfer	$18	$18	$18
		Total real income loss	$100	$263	$425
	100%	GDP loss	$163	$489	$814
		Wealth transfer	$36	$36	$36
		Total real income loss	$199	$525	$851

a. GDP loss estimated by multiplying the percentage loss derived from the elasticity by the 2012Q3 GDP estimate provided by the Bureau of Economic Analysis.
b. Wealth transfer calculated by multiplying import levels (2014) by the percent increase in the oil price (refiner acquisition cost of imported crude oil from May 2015) by ninety-one days. Data comes from EIA.

calculated solely for the quarter during which the shock occurs, constituting a conservative estimate.

These calculations do not capture the duration of a disruption. The methodology used in vector autoregression start with an oil price shock at a single juncture (e.g., one quarter), then measures the observed GDP responses over varying periods. In most cases, this approach implicitly assumes that a shock lasts for one month or one quarter, which is still instructive, given that most of the major outages in the post–World War II era have been relatively short lived. Longer disruptions would have two countervailing impacts. First, any strategic oil stock response would eventually be exhausted if a disruption lasted long enough. Although this outcome is unlikely, prices could ratchet up after stocks were exhausted. Second, longer-term price impacts would elicit a demand response from consumers and a supply response from tight oil producers. In other words, sustained major increases in oil prices would engender stronger reactions in consumer behavior that could reduce the price response. Further, the consumer reaction to a sustained escalation in oil prices could potentially be different than the reaction to a temporary price spike. It is therefore difficult to compare disruptions of varying duration with much accuracy.

Table 3.3 illustrates the wide range of potential impacts of an oil shock. Depending on which modeling approach and price impact an analyst deems appropriate, the conclusions can differ by more than a factor of ten. A smaller disruption could potentially cause less than $100 billion worth of damage, if GDP is relatively less responsive to price. Larger disruptions could cause close to $1 trillion worth of economic damage if the larger elasticities are correct. In all likelihood, the true response of the economy to a major oil shock lies between these two extremes, making the economic losses associated with an elasticity of −0.03 most relevant for the present analysis. It should be noted that under all of the scenarios, the majority of the economic losses associated with an oil shock stem from GDP reductions rather than wealth transfers. This is important because only the level of wealth transfers to oil-exporting countries will be affected by decreased oil imports. In other words, the vast majority of the costs of a global supply outage to the United States would not be attenuated by increased domestic oil production. The country remains economically vulnerable.

These calculations should be viewed as describing the potential boundaries of the impacts of oil supply disruptions on GDP based on the current state of knowledge in this area. Observers can then determine which point on this continuum is most likely based on their assumptions about how badly a Gulf shock would affect the world oil market and how resilient they deem the US economy to be. If a Gulf disruption is met with a robust IEA response, if consumers maintain confidence, and if the costs of reallocating resources in the economy prove minimal, then the smaller estimates likely capture the costs of a supply shock. In a scenario in which the amount of oil removed from the market even after a stockpile release is large, uncertainty paralyzes consumers and investors, and the economy experiences severe reallocation pains, then the larger impacts could unfold. Under almost all of the scenarios, the costs are substantial.

Conclusion

Despite economists' best efforts, the academic literature on how oil price shocks harm the economy has not yet produced a crisp consensus. Disputes on the existence and nature of this relationship still abound. Nevertheless, some conclusions can be drawn. A major oil supply disruption in the Persian Gulf could possibly constitute the largest oil shock that the world has ever seen. The economic impacts would be significant. A severe oil price escalation would decrease both consumer activity and business investment. It is unlikely that judicious monetary policy could preclude the problems that such a shock would cause. The potential for a major Persian Gulf supply shock to harm the US economy is clear.

That said, it appears that the oil-macroeconomy relationship is evolving. The oil shocks of the 2000s caused the US economy less harm than major shocks in previous decades did. This is partly because demand drove them rather than supply and partly because compared to previous decades the US economy is better able to adjust to a major oil price increase. As the US economy becomes less energy intensive and imports and consumption decline, its vulnerability to oil supply shocks could further decrease in the coming years. In addition, given that oil markets have been volatile in recent years, a Persian Gulf outage might cause less of a price spike than one might expect based on market fundamentals simply because the potential for such a shock is already built into global oil price movements. Although a shock would harm the economy, the most dire scenarios might not come to pass.

The biggest lesson from this literature is that the exact character of the oil-macroeconomy relationship is quite uncertain. The economic impact of an oil supply disruption in the Persian Gulf could be severe, but estimating the scale of the damage is difficult. As this chapter illustrates, the range of possible economic impacts is expansive. Depending on the assumptions an observer makes about the size of a price shock and the magnitude of a shock's impact on the US economy, the potential economic damage could range from tens of billions of dollars to close to $1 trillion. No matter what, a major Persian Gulf oil supply shock would almost invariably be followed by some degree of economic decline. The key for analysts will be to evaluate where in this continuum a shock is likely to fall.

In terms of the price impact of a shock, many factors point to the potential for a Persian Gulf outage to have a particularly severe impact on the world market. Despite growing production in the Western Hemisphere, the Gulf region will remain at the center of world oil markets for the foreseeable future. Robust demand and high prices mean that, outside of OPEC, oil producers will produce as much as they physically can and leave minimal spare capacity. As the budget challenges and domestic consumption grow in the Gulf, it is not clear how long the Gulf States, most importantly Saudi Arabia, will be able to maintain any spare capacity.[93] More important, the concentration of spare capacity in the Gulf means that in many supply shock scenarios, this release valve would be shut. If Persian Gulf supplies were disrupted, oil prices could hit unprecedented levels.

Some might point to increased domestic oil production and reduced imports in the United States as insulating the nation from this vulnerability.[94] It is true that as net oil imports decline, the wealth transfer to oil exporters during a shock will be reduced. Further, as US oil production expands, the economic boost that domestic drillers reap from high prices will increase. Two points should temper excitement caused by these trends. First, it is unlikely that any of the expanded activity in the American petroleum sector will lead the United States to hold large-scale spare production capacity. Although tight oil production can ramp up more quickly than conventional oil production, it is unlikely that this capability alone could address a catastrophic supply shock. Second, as long as the United States continues to engage in oil trade with other nations, Americans will have to pay the world market price for crude oil, because prices are determined at the margin. While the recent expansions in US oil production are impressive, the country will remain a net importer for the foreseeable future. Therefore, a shock to the world oil market will be a shock to the US market under almost any circumstance. Meaningful reductions in vulnerability would require substantially decreased oil demand or dramatically lower oil prices. US oil demand is not projected to grow in the coming years, but it will remain significant as long as mobility is based on petroleum-consuming automobiles. Barring unforeseen changes in the US landscape, some degree of vulnerability to a major oil shock will persist for decades.

Notes

The author is writing in a private capacity as a PhD candidate at George Washington University. All views expressed in the chapter are his own. This chapter does not advocate that the US government undertake any particular policy.

1. James D. Hamilton, "Causes and Consequences of the Oil Shock of 2007–2008," NBER Working Paper no. 15002 (Washington DC: Brookings, Spring 2009), 215–59.

2. US Energy Information Administration (EIA), *Annual Energy Outlook, 2015* (Washington DC: Department of Energy, 2015). This chapter uses EIA projections and data throughout. EIA is the authoritative source for data on US energy markets, and its projections have the advantage of policy neutrality. This is not intended to diminish projections from sources such as BP or the International Energy Agency (IEA); these sources are referenced where it is appropriate.

3. Brian Scheid, "US Oil Boom Fuels Security Fears in the Middle East," *Platts Oilgram News,* January 14, 2013.

4. IEA, *World Energy Outlook, 2012* (Paris: IEA, 2012), 2.

5. John Deutch and James R. Schlesinger, *National Security Consequences of U.S. Oil Dependency* (New York: Council on Foreign Relations, 2006); Pietro S. Nivola and Erin E. R. Carter, "Making Sense of 'Energy Independence,'" in *Energy Security: Economics, Politics, Strategies, and Implications,* ed. Carlos Pascual and Jonathan Elkind (Washington DC: Brookings, 2010), 105–18; and Michael Greenstone et al., *Energy Policy Opportunities and Continuing Challenges in the Presence of Increased Supplies of Natural Gas and Petroleum* (Washington DC: The Hamilton Project, Brookings, 2012).

6. John S. Duffield, *Over a Barrel: The Costs of U.S. Foreign Oil Dependence* (Stanford: Stanford University Press, 2008); and Keith Crane et al., *Imported Oil and U.S. National Security* (Santa Monica: RAND, 2009).

7. Regarding the literature, see Stephen P. A. Brown and Mine K. Yücel, "Energy Prices and Aggregate Economic Activity: An Interpretive Survey," *The Quarterly Review of Eco-*

nomics and Statistics 42 (2002): 193–208; Donald W. Jones, Paul N. Leiby, and Inja K. Paik, "Oil Price Shocks and the Macroeconomy: What Has Been Learned since 1996," *The Energy Journal* 25 (2004): 1–32; and Lutz Kilian, "The Economic Effects of Economic Price Shocks, " *Journal of Economic Literature* 46 (2008): 871–909. Notable "translations" of the literature include Marc Labonte, *The Effect of Oil Shocks on the Economy: A Review of the Empirical Evidence* (Washington DC: Congressional Research Service, 2007); and Blake Clayton, "The Link between Oil Prices and the U.S. Macroeconomy," *Georgetown Journal of International Affairs* 14 (2013): 175–84.

8. Such as Eugene Gholz and Daryl G. Press, "Protecting 'The Prize': Oil and the U.S. National Interest," *Security Studies* 19, no. 3 (2010): 453–85.

9. EIA, *Petroleum and Other Liquids: U.S. Net Imports by Country* (Washington DC: Department of Energy, 2014).

10. EIA, *Monthly Energy Review* (Washington DC: Department of Energy, 2014).

11. EIA, *Annual Energy Outlook, 2015.*

12. Robert J. Weiner, "Speculation in International Crises: Report from the Gulf," *Journal of International Business Studies* 36 (2005): 576–87; and James L. Smith, "World Oil: Market or Mayhem," *Journal of Economic Perspectives* 23 (2009): 145–64.

13. "The Oil Industry: After OPEC," *The Economist*, May 16, 2015.

14. EIA, *International Energy Statistics* (Washington DC: Department of Energy, 2012); and EIA, *International Energy Outlook, 2014* (Washington DC: Department of Energy, 2014).

15. IEA, *World Energy Outlook, 2014* (Paris: IEA, 2014).

16. Jason Bordoff and Michael Levi, "Power Shift," *Americas Quarterly*, Summer 2013.

17. Matthew Simmons, *Twilight in the Desert: The Coming Saudi Oil Shock and the World Economy* (New York: Wiley, 2005).

18. Daniel Yergin, *The Quest: Energy, Security, and the Remaking of the Modern World* (New York: Penguin Press, 2011).

19. EIA, *Short-Term Energy Outlook* (Washington DC: Department of Energy, December 2015).

20. EIA, *What Drives Crude Oil Prices* (Washington DC: Department of Energy, December 2015). In a June 2015 interview, Saudi oil minister Ali al-Naimi suggested that bringing this output online could take as many as ninety days. See Rania El Gamal, "Will Saudi Boost Oil Capacity? Naimi's Retort: Show Me 10 Pct Return," *Reuters*, June 4, 2015.

21. Robert McNally, *Energy Brief: Managing Oil Market Disruption in a Confrontation with Iran* (Washington DC: Council on Foreign Relations, 2012).

22. Amy M. Jaffe, "America's Real Strategic Petroleum Reserve," *Foreign Policy*, August 24, 2012.

23. Mamdouh Salameh, "The Shifting Sands under Saudi Oil Prowess," Paper prepared at the Annual Meeting of the United States Association of Energy Economics, Austin TX, 2012.

24. EIA, *Crude Oil: U.S. Net Imports by Country* (Washington DC: Department of Energy, April 2014).

25. For example, see Robert J. Weiner, "Is the World Oil Market 'One Great Pool'?," *The Energy Journal* 12 (1991): 95–107; Lance J. Bachmeier and James M. Griffin, "Testing for Market Integration: Crude Oil, Coal, and Natural Gas," *The Energy Journal* 27 (2006): 55–72; and William Nordhaus, "The Economics of an Integrated World Oil Market," Keynote for the International Energy Workshop, Venice, Italy, June 17–19, 2009.

26. This discussion assumes that in the event of a supply disruption, global markets will clear smoothly. Given the history of government intervention in the oil market, this assumption is heroic. Especially in crises, market institutions can break down. It might be the case in the context of a major oil crisis, although an analysis of the durability of oil market institutions is beyond the scope of this chapter. Such a breakdown would likely exacerbate, rather than ameliorate, the adverse impacts of a price shock.

27. James D. Hamilton, "This Is What Happened to the Oil Price–Macroeconomy Relationship," *Journal of Monetary Economics* 38 (1996): 215–20.

28. Rebecca Jiménez-Rodríguez and Marcelo Sánchez, "Oil Shocks and the Macroeconomy: A Comparison across High Oil Price Periods," *Applied Economics Letters* 16 (2009): 1633–38.

29. Olivier J. Blanchard and Jordi Galí, "The Macroeconomic Effects of Oil Price Shocks: Why Are the 2000s so Different from the 1970s?," in *International Dimensions of Monetary Policy*, ed. Jordi Galí and Mark J. Gertler (Chicago: University of Chicago Press, 2010), 373–421.

30. Lutz Kilian, "Exogenous Oil Supply Shocks: How Big Are They and How Much Do They Matter for the U.S. Economy?," *The Review of Economics and Statistics* 90 (2008): 216–40.

31. Tao Wu and Michelle Cavallo, *Measuring Oil-Price Shocks Using Market-Based Information*, IMF (International Monetary Fund) Working Paper (Washington DC: IMF, 2011).

32. James D. Hamilton, "Oil and the Macroeconomy since World War II," *Journal of Political Economy* 91 (1983): 228–48.

33. Douglas R. Bohi, "On the Macroeconomic Effects of Energy Price Shocks," *Resources and Energy* 13 (1991): 145–62; Douglas R. Bohi and Michael A. Toman, *The Economics of Energy Security* (Boston: Kluwer Academic, 1996); and Mark A. Hooker, "What Happened to the Oil Price–Macroeconomy Relationship?," *Journal of Monetary Economics* 38 (1996): 195–213.

34. Hamilton, "This Is What Happened," 215–20; and James D. Hamilton, "What Is an Oil Shock?," *Journal of Econometrics* 113 (2003): 363–98.

35. For example, see Nathan S. Balke, Stephen P. A. Brown, and Mine K. Yücel, "Oil Price Shocks and the U.S. Economy: Where Does the Asymmetry Originate?," *The Energy Journal* 23 (2002): 27–52; Jones, Leiby, and Paik, "Oil Price Shocks"; and Frank J. Atkins and S. M. Tayyebi Jazayeri, *A Literature Review of Demand Studies in World Oil Markets*, Discussion Paper 2004-07 (Calgary: University of Calgary, Department of Economics, 2004).

36. Robert B. Barsky and Lutz Kilian, "Oil and the Macroeconomy since the 1970s," *Journal of Economic Perspectives* 18 (2004): 115–34.

37. Lutz Kilian, "A Comparison of the Effects of Exogenous Oil Supply Shocks on Output and Inflation in the G7 Countries," *Journal of the European Economic Association* 6 (2008): 78–121; Kilian, "Economic Effects"; Kilian, "Exogenous Oil Supply"; Lutz Kilian, "Not All Oil Price Shocks Are Alike: Disentangling Demand and Supply Shocks in the Crude Oil Market," *American Economic Review* 99 (2009): 1053–69; Hamilton, "Causes and Consequences"; and James D. Hamilton, "Nonlinearities and the Macroeconomic Effects of Oil Prices," *Macroeconomic Dynamics* 15 (2011): 364–78.

38. EIA, *Petroleum and Other Liquids: Spot Prices* (Washington DC: Department of Energy, 2012).

39. Kilian, "Not All Oil Price Shocks."

40. Balke, Brown, and Yücel, *Oil Price Shocks*; Gert Peersman and Ine Van Robays, "Cross-country Differences in the Effects of Oil Shocks," *Energy Economics* 34 (2012): 1532–47; and Elizaveta Archanskaïa, Jerôme Creel, and Paul Hubert, "The Nature of Oil Shocks and the Global Economy," *Energy Policy* 42 (2012): 509–20.

41. An early survey of this literature found this account to be the most convincing. See Brown and Yücel, "Energy Prices."

42. Paul Edelstein and Lutz Kilian, "How Sensitive Are Consumer Expenditures to Retail Energy Prices?," *Journal of Monetary Economics* 56 (2009): 766–79.

43. Hamilton, "Causes and Consequences."

44. Kilian, "Economic Effects."

45. Paul N. Leiby et al., *Oil Imports: An Assessment of the Benefits and Costs*, Oak Ridge National Laboratory (ORNL)-6851 (Oak Ridge TN: ORNL, 1997).

46. Steven J. Davis and John Haltiwanger, "Sectoral Job Creation and Destruction Responses to Oil Price Changes," *Journal of Monetary Economics* 48, no. 3 (2001): 465–512.

47. Jones, Leiby, and Paik, "Oil Price Shocks."

48. Kiseok Lee and Shawn Ni, "On the Dynamic Effects of Oil Price Shocks: A Study Using Industry Level Data," *Journal of Monetary Economics* 49 (2002): 823–52.

49. Paul Edelstein and Lutz Kilian, "The Response of Business Fixed Investment to Changes in Energy Prices: A Test of Some Hypotheses about the Transmission of Energy Price Shocks," *The B.E. Journal of Macroeconomics* 7 (2007).

50. Paul. N. Leiby, "Estimating the Energy Security Benefits of Reduced U.S. Oil Imports," ORNL/TM-2007/028 (Oak Ridge TN: ORNL, February 28, 2007).

51. Alessandro Cologni and Matteo Manera, "Oil Prices, Inflation and Interest Rates in a Structural Cointegrated VAR Model for the G-7 Countries," *Energy Economics* 30 (2008): 856–88.

52. Labonte, *Effect of Oil Shocks.*

53. Stephen P. A. Brown and Hillard G. Huntington, *Backgrounder: Estimating U.S. Oil Security Premiums* (Washington DC: Resources for the Future, 2010).

54. Stephen P. A. Brown and Mine Yücel, *Energy Brief: The Shale Gas and Tight Oil Boom: U.S. States' Economic Gains and Vulnerabilities* (Washington DC: Council on Foreign Relations, 2013).

55. Brown and Yücel, "Energy Prices."

56. Benjamin S. Bernanke, Mark Gertler, and Mark Watson, "Systematic Monetary Policy and the Effects of Oil Price Shocks," *Brookings Papers on Economic Activity* 1997, no. 1 (1997): 91–157.

57. Jones, Leiby, and Paik, "Oil Price Shocks."

58. James D. Hamilton and Anna Maria Herrera, "Comment: Oil Shocks and Aggregate Macroeconomic Behavior: The Role of Monetary Policy," *Journal of Money, Credit and Banking* 36 (2004): 265–86.

59. Hillard G. Huntington, "The Economic Consequences of Higher Crude Oil Prices," Energy Modeling Forum, Stanford University, October 3, 2005.

60. Council of Economic Advisers, "New Report: The All-of-the-Above Energy Strategy as a Path to Sustainable Economic Growth," White House, Washington DC, May 29, 2014.

61. Congressional Budget Office (CBO), *The Economic Effects of Recent Increases in Energy Prices* (Washington DC: CBO, 2007); and Blanchard and Galí, "Macroeconomic Effects," in Galí and Gertler, *International Dimensions.*

62. Kilian, "Economic Effects."

63. Peersman and Robays, "Cross-country Differences."

64. Kiseok Lee, Shawn Ni, and Ronald A. Ratti, "Oil Shocks and the Macroeconomy: The Role of Price Variability," *The Energy Journal* 16 (1995): 39–56; and Jiménez-Rodríguez and Sánchez, "Oil Shocks."

65. Wu and Cavallo, *Measuring Oil-Price Shocks.*

66. John S. Duffield, *Over a Barrel: The Costs of U.S. Foreign Oil Dependence* (Stanford: Stanford University Press, 2008).

67. Justin Lahart, "Oil's Spoils Slow to Flow," *Wall Street Journal,* May, 11, 2015.

68. Knut Anton Mork, "Oil and the Macroeconomy When Prices Go Up and Down: An Extension of Hamilton's Results," *Journal of Political Economy* 97 (1989): 740–44.

69. Balke, Brown, and Yücel, "Oil Price Shocks"; and Brown and Yücel, "Energy Prices."

70. Kilian, "Comparison of the Effects."

71. Cologni and Manera, "Oil Prices."

72. Peersman and Robays, "Cross-country Differences."

73. Kilian, "Comparison of the Effects."

74. Rong-Gang Cong et al., "Relationships between Oil Price Shocks and Stock Market: An Empirical Analysis from China," *Energy Policy* 36 (2008): 3544–53; and Limin Du, Yanan He, and Chu Wei, "The Relationship between Oil Price Shocks and China's Macro-economy: An Empirical Analysis," *Energy Policy* 38 (2010): 4142–51.

75. Robert Weiner first raised this point in his initial formal review of this chapter in December 14, 2012. It might not be the case for all non-OECD economies.

76. David Coady et al., *Petroleum Product Subsidies: Costly, Inequitable, and Rising* (Washington DC: International Monetary Fund, 2010).

77. To calculate the price impact of a supply disruption based on elasticities, the

inverse of the sum of the elasticities of supply and demand is taken to calculate the price changes that are required to return the market to equilibrium. For a good discussion of this mechanism, see Smith, "World Oil."

78. Dermot Gately and Hillard G. Huntington, "The Asymmetric Effects of Changes in Price and Income on Energy and Oil Demand," *The Energy Journal* 23 (2002): 19–55; John C. B. Cooper, "Price Elasticity of Demand for Crude Oil: Estimates for 23 Countries," *OPEC Bulletin* 27 (2003): 1–8; Atkins and Tayyebi Jazayeri, *Literature Review*; and Smith, "World Oil."

79. Stephen P. A. Brown and Hillard G. Huntington, "Assessing the U.S. Oil Security Premium," *Energy Economics* 38 (2013): 118–27. This number is based on midpoint estimates from multiple surveys of multiple econometric studies of the price elasticity of oil supply and demand. It is worth noting that there is a wide range of estimates of these elasticities. Further, some recent studies suggest that the oil demand is becoming less price responsive. See Joyce M. Dargay and Dermot Gately, "World Oil Demand's Shift toward Faster Growing and Less Price-Responsive Products and Regions," *Energy Policy* 38 (2010): 6261–77. The notional oil price shocks outlined here should therefore be considered conservative estimates.

80. This number is based on a refiner acquisition cost of crude oil of $58.68 per barrel in May 2015 and a 2014 world oil output total of 93.018 million barrels per day. See EIA, "Petroleum and Other Liquids," http://www.eia.gov/dnav/pet/pet_pri_rac2_dcu _nus_m.htm; and EIA, "International Energy Statistics," http://www.eia.gov/cfapps /ipdbproject/IEDIndex3.cfm?tid=5&pid=53&aid=1.

81. Barsky and Kilian, "Oil and the Macroeconomy."

82. McNally, *Energy Brief*.

83. U.S. Government Accountability Office (GAO), *Strategic Petroleum Reserve: Available Oil Can Provide Significant Benefits, but Many Factors Should Influence Future Decisions about Fill, Use, and Expansion*, GAO-06-872 (Washington DC: GAO, 2006).

84. U.S. Department of Energy (DOE), *Strategic Petroleum Reserve: Quick Facts and Frequently Asked Questions* (Washington DC: Department of Energy, 2014).

85. IEA, *IEA Response System for Oil Supply Emergencies* (Paris: International Energy Agency, 2014).

86. David L. Greene, Donald W. Jones, and Paul N. Leiby, "The Outlook for US Oil Dependence," *Energy Policy* 26 (1998): 55–69; GAO, *Strategic Petroleum Reserve*; Duffield, *Over a Barrel*; McNally, *Energy Brief*; and Carmine Difiglio, "Oil, Economic Growth, and Strategic Petroleum Stocks," *Energy Strategy Reviews* 5 (2014): 48–58.

87. Jaffe, "Strategic Petroleum Reserve."

88. Jones, Leiby, and Paik, "Oil Price Shocks."

89. Brown and Yücel, "Energy Prices"; Atkins and Tayyebi Jazayeri, *Literature Review*; Jones, Leiby, and Paik, "Oil Price Shocks"; Rebecca Jiménez-Rodríguez and Marcelo Sánchez, "Oil Price Shocks and Real GDP Growth: Empirical Evidence for Some OECD Countries," *Applied Economics* 37 (2005): 201–28; and Brown and Huntington, *Estimating U.S. Oil*.

90. Jones, Leiby, and Paik, "Oil Price Shocks"; and Huntington, "Economic Consequences."

91. EIA's estimates, using a large macroeconomic model provided by Global Insight, are discussed in GAO, *Strategic Petroleum Reserve*. A broader discussion of these models shows that some of them suggest a stronger GDP response. See Clayton, "Link between Oil Prices."

92. This framework was adapted from Huntington, "Economic Consequences."

93. Salameh, "Shifting Sands."

94. For good discussion, see Michael Levi, *The Power Surge: Energy, Opportunity, and the Battle for America's Future* (New York: Oxford University Press, 2013).

CHAPTER 4

Saudi Arabian Oil and US Interests

Thomas W. Lippman

For more than half a century, the international relationships and strategic plans of the United States have assumed that the flow of oil from the Persian Gulf region, and from Saudi Arabia in particular, is essential to global commerce and that the United States is obliged to protect it. In the last quarter of the twentieth century, the United States also developed a broad array of other interests in the region, including the containment of revolutionary Iran, the security of Israel, the suppression of Islamic extremism, and the promotion of Arab-Israeli peace, but oil has remained the principal rationale for the US military presence there.

Although, in contrast to the past, the United States imports relatively little Saudi crude today, the US economy is still sensitive to the flow of Saudi oil. As discussed in previous chapters, oil sells on a global market; therefore, its price in the United States is essentially determined by the global price. Although the economic impact of a Saudi cutoff is uncertain, it would surely be immense. As Kenneth R. Vincent shows in chapter 3, there is no analytical consensus on the impact a cutoff would have on the global economy, but undoubtedly it would be large. To cite a 2012 report, analysts at the Heritage Foundation used computer models and calculated that in the event of a "total cessation" of Saudi production for one year, in the United States gasoline prices would rise to more than $6.50 per gallon, at least 1.5 million jobs would be lost, and annual economic output would decline by nearly $450 billion.[1] This estimate of the impact on US gross domestic product falls within the range of estimates presented in chapter 3. In addition, beyond the sheer amount of oil it produces, the Kingdom of Saudi Arabia is important due to its spare production capacity, which Riyadh has long used to temper the effects of supply disruptions elsewhere.

While the US interest in Saudi oil is not determined by the amount it imports, basic information about US imports provides valuable context. According to the US Energy Information Administration, of the 329 million barrels of crude oil and refined products imported to the United States in March 2012, a representative month, only 42.6 million came from Saudi Arabia.[2] This relatively low level of imports does vary, with the United States occasionally importing more Saudi crude. For example, a modest uptick in US oil imports from Saudi Arabia occurred in the summer of 2012, but it was mostly the result of temporary conditions in the market, such as a reduction in Gulf of Mexico production caused by the oil spill of 2010 and an imbalance in refinery capacity that limits the ability of US processors to use Canadian crude. Overall, despite this variation in the quantity the United States imports, the broad trajectory of US imports from Saudi Arabia and other Gulf producers is downward largely because of the substantial increase in domestic production derived from shale.[3]

The International Energy Agency (IEA) predicts that the central importance of Saudi oil to the rest of the world will continue. As the middle of this century approaches, the IEA estimates that "to compensate for declining output in some countries, those with the ability to expand will need to invest in expensive new technologies to meet global demand. The largest increase in oil production comes from Iraq, followed by Saudi Arabia, Brazil, Kazakhstan and Canada."[4] According to the IEA, though output in the United States will increase over the next decade, "quenching the world's thirst for oil," this trend is expected to be temporary. Middle Eastern oil is projected to provide the majority of global supply increases by the mid-2020s, while production from suppliers not participating in the Organization of the Petroleum Exporting Countries (OPEC) is expected to fall.[5]

President Barack Obama and his military and national security advisers have declared repeatedly that they will adhere to the same long-term US commitment to Saudi security as all of his predecessors back to Harry S. Truman have. After a meeting with leaders of Saudi Arabia and other principalities of the Gulf Cooperation Council (GCC) in May 2015, the president described that commitment as "ironclad."[6] The rise of the Islamic State and the corresponding deterioration of Iraq and Syria have led the United States to escalate rather than diminish its involvement in the region. But in the not-too-distant future, as the United States shifts its strategic assets to Asia and as Saudi Arabia increasingly finds new economic partners, the time may come to reevaluate this partnership, especially if the United States is able to resume a constructive relationship with Iran. It is also conceivable that defense spending constraints will challenge the long-standing bipartisan American consensus on securing the kingdom, pressuring leaders to reassess regional strategies and, in turn, to reprioritize global military commitments.

What would happen to Saudi oil exports if the United States pulled back from the Gulf, for whatever reason? To understand whether and how the withdrawal of the US security commitment might affect the reliability of Saudi supplies, it is essential to evaluate the nature and source of possible threats to the kingdom's petroleum industry. Conceivably, by itself, withdrawing that commitment might not threaten or undermine Saudi Arabia's oil industry, but it might alter the ambitions, tactics, and planning assumptions of a broad array of interested actors—from oil traders to al-Qaeda to the Iranian Revolutionary Guard Corps—in ways that are difficult to predict. More difficult still is anticipating how the actions of these groups will affect the global oil supply.

What event or development could put an end to Saudi Arabia's oil exports? The country is not prone to hurricanes, floods, earthquakes, or volcanoes, so a natural disaster of such magnitude would not likely take oil production completely offline. The kingdom faces very little threat of invasion or attack by another country; whether that threat would increase if the United States withdrew from the region is analyzed in other chapters. That leaves five possible reasons why an export shutdown could occur in Saudi Arabia: a rising domestic demand and dwindling resources that take Saudi Arabia out of the export market; a hostile seizure and closure of the oil industry by an anti-Western group such as the Islamic State; a civil war, possibly as a precursor to or a consequence of the hostile group's takeover; an act of sabotage by terrorists or insurgents on the oil installations; and a massive cyber attack that shuts down the industry's computer networks. These circumstances are assessed here in descending order of probability.

Rising Domestic Demand and Dwindling Resources

Saudi Arabia consumes a large and increasing percentage of the oil it produces. Over the next ten to twenty years, growing consumption will cut significantly into Saudi exports. In fact, if current trends continue unabated, Saudi Arabia will completely stop exporting oil in a few decades. Changes in Saudi policy are likely to slow its consumption growth and avert this extreme outcome, but Saudi exports are nevertheless expected to fall. The kingdom will face complex domestic challenges in righting the balance between exports and domestic consumption, adding increased uncertainty about the effectiveness of its future policies.

Already Saudi Arabia consumes nearly 30 percent of its oil output domestically to fuel its vehicles and aircraft and to generate electricity. The multinational oil company BP distributed an analysis in 2008 projecting that anticipated increases in domestic demand coupled with likely decreases in production could

Table 4.1. Oil and budget projections, 2005–30

Year	2005	2010	2015	2020	2025	2030
Oil production (mb/d)	9.4	8.2	9.3	10.0	10.7	11.5
Oil exports	7.5	5.8	6.3	6.0	5.6	4.9
Domestic consumption	1.9	2.4	3.1	3.9	5.1	6.5
Budget balance (billion Saudi riyal)	218	109	−50	−186	−512	−1,334
Break-even price ($ per barrel)	30.3	71.6	90.7	118.5	175.1	321.7

Data source: Jadwa Investments, Riyadh.

put an end to Saudi exports as early as 2025.[7] In 2011 the research staff at Jadwa Investment group in Riyadh offered this ominous projection: "Domestic consumption of oil, now sold locally for an average of around $10 per barrel, will reach 6.5 million barrels per day [mb/d] in 2030, exceeding oil export volumes."[8] According to Jadwa's analysis, the break-even price—that is, the export price Saudi Arabia would need in order to balance its budget—would rise to $321.70 per barrel, or nearly five times what it was in 2010.

An assessment of Saudi Arabia's oil and gas future by the US Energy Information Administration noted that while Saudi Arabia has one-fifth of the world's oil reserves, it is also

the largest oil-consuming nation in the Middle East. Saudi Arabia consumed approximately 2.9 million barrels per day (bbl/d) of oil in 2013, almost double the consumption in 2000, because of strong industrial growth and subsidized prices. Contributing to this growth is rising direct burn of crude oil for power generation, which has reached an average of 0.7 million bbl/d from 2008 to 2013 during the months of June to September, according to the Joint Oil Data Initiative (JODI), and the use of natural gas liquids (NGLs) for petrochemical production.

Khalid al-Falih, CEO of Saudi Aramco at the time, warned that "domestic liquids demand was on a pace to reach more than 8 million bbl/d of oil equivalent by 2030 if there were no improvements in energy efficiency" and current trends continued.[9] At the beginning of 2016, the government announced a reduction in gasoline subsidies, raising prices at the pump by a small amount.

These projections assumed that current fuel-use patterns will remain in place even as demand rises inexorably with a growing population. In fact, the government has recognized the ominous trend implied by the numbers and has committed itself to reducing domestic oil demand by changing the fuel mix in its power plants to conserve oil, by continuing to develop new wells, by developing new natural gas fields (so far with limited success), by devising advanced solar-generating techniques, and by creating civilian nuclear power plants. In February 2013 the government issued a notice to potential contractors that it would seek bids on the construction of 54 gigawatts of generating capacity from renewable sources—including geothermal and wind energy—by 2032.[10] A different government in Riyadh might pursue more vigorous conservation policies, though whether even these policies would be sufficient to preserve Saudi Arabia's place among the world's leading oil exporters is uncertain.

The Saudi government faces countervailing pressures to maintain high exports and to sustain the growth in domestic consumption. On the one hand, exports are essential to the economic health of the kingdom. More than 80 percent of government spending is dependent on oil revenue.[11] Consequently, allowing exports to decline to meet growing domestic demand would cause a severe revenue shortfall. On the other hand, some of the most obvious approaches for reducing consumption face serious barriers. For example, cutting subsides further would greatly increase the price of oil to Saudi consumers and would face substantial opposition. Both options—reducing exports and increasing domestic prices—risk both upending the social contract that has historically underpinned the kingdom's stable state-societal relations and fueling domestic instability.[12]

While there is no simple solution, the Saudi government clearly understands that efficiency gains must be part of the mix. The Saudis could also turn to their spare capacity to keep domestic prices low while maintaining exports. Unfortunately, this short-term solution would generate its own risks, including increasing the volatility of world oil markets, by eliminating much of the limited slack that the global market currently enjoys.[13]

Since the 1970s Americans have recognized that although access to affordable oil spurs economic growth, that growth is also tethered to the occasionally volatile global oil market. This trade-off was relatively easy to accept when oil prices were low. In fact, it was among the Saudis' goals when the government adopted a standing policy of maintaining low enough prices to keep consumers buying their product. However, if Saudi exports decrease, whether due to dwindling domestic supply or to growing domestic demand, then they will contribute to upward pressures on the global price of oil and lead to a more volatile market. Higher oil prices, in turn, will encourage further reductions in American consumption, reducing both its sensitivity to the global market and the importance it places on Saudi oil.

Finally, although the United States will not welcome reduced Saudi exports (assuming they do occur), there is virtually no role for US military forces in remedying this problem. The US military commitment is designed to maintain regional stability and, by extension, helps to moderate the global price of oil. Its commitment is not intended to influence Saudi domestic oil policy.

A Successful Cyber Attack

In the Stuxnet era, the most immediate disruptive threat to oil exports may come not from guns or explosives but from a cyber attack. Anyone who has visited the master control room at Saudi Aramco's headquarters in Dhahran can appreciate the extent to which the wells, pipelines, processing plants, and export terminals are linked in an electronic network. More generally, as Blake Clayton and Adam Segal write, one study found that "the energy sector, including oil and gas producers and infrastructure operators, was hit by more targeted malware attacks over a six-month period in 2012 than any other industry."[14] Though attacks have been frequent, they have not yet been able to disrupt physical infrastructure.[15]

In August 2012 an unknown group calling itself Cutting Sword of Justice claimed to have penetrated the Aramco network and unleashed a "malicious virus to destroy thirty thousand computers networked in this company." The object, the group said in its manifesto, was to send a message to what it called the corrupt, oppressive Al-Saud regime: "We invite all anti-tyranny hacker groups all over the world to join this movement. We want them to support this movement by designing and performing such operations, if they are against tyranny and oppression."[16] According to the *New York Times*, "The virus erased data on three-quarters of Aramco's corporate PCs—documents, spreadsheets, e-mails, files—replacing all of it with an image of a burning American flag."[17] Saudi Aramco confirmed that its main computer network had been put out of action on the day the hacker group claimed to have struck, but the company said oil operations continued because they are on a separate network.[18] The virus "originated from external sources," the company said at the time.[19]

Four months later, the oil company and the Ministry of Interior released a few details of their investigation. The ministry's spokesman Maj. Gen. Mansour al-Turki said it had been determined that "the planning and execution of the attack was carried out by an organized group from outside the Kingdom, operating from a number of countries." Reports in the Western media had suggested Iran was primarily responsible, but al-Turki did not name any country.[20] The *New York Times* had reported that the virus was implanted by a person with "privileged access" to the oil company's network, but al-Turki said that "none of the company's employees or contractors was involved."

According to the *Financial Times*, "The same cyber virus that targeted Saudi

Aramco, known as Shamoon, was also used—perhaps unintentionally—to attack systems at Qatar's RasGas, one of the largest producers of liquefied natural gas."[21] Given that Qatar has offered to help Iran develop its part of the giant offshore gas field they share, it is unclear why RasGas might have been the target of an Iranian cyber attack.[22] But as in other cases of industrial computer sabotage, identifying the nature of the malware used has been easier than pinpointing its origin.

The US Department of Defense has recognized cyber attack as a major threat to industrial and military operations around the globe, not just in the Middle East, and has created a new command in the armed forces to confront it—the US Cyber Command. In the fall of 2011, according to a Defense Department statement, Gen. Keith B. Alexander, the now-retired head of Cyber Command, told a conference on this subject that "when you look at the vulnerabilities that we face in this area, it's extraordinary. . . . What we see is a disturbing trend, from exploitation to disruption to destruction." At the same event, Regina E. Dugan, former director of the Defense Advanced Research Projects Agency, spoke in stark terms of the potential for devastation in this new theater of war. "Malicious cyber attacks are not merely an existential threat to our bits and bytes," Dugan said. "They are a real threat to an increasingly large number of systems that we interact with daily, from the power grid to our financial systems to our automobiles and our military systems."[23] The well-publicized hacker penetration of Sony Pictures Entertainment in 2014 amply dramatized Dugan's warning.

In a 2012 study of this threat, the security analyst Andrew Krepinevich noted that industrial computer networks worldwide are vulnerable because of a computer "monoculture" in which almost everyone, friend or foe, uses the same tools—namely, Microsoft programs and Intel chips. He wrote:

> As the cyber competition appears to favor the offense, and potentially by a considerable margin, even a cyber defense with access to an unlimited budget could not eliminate the possibility of intrusions, as new vulnerabilities are constantly being identified. General Alexander summed up the competition well when he stated, "In cyberspace the only 'perfect' defense is the static one: to disconnect [from networks] and thereby forfeit the cyber realm and its economic and social benefits to one's adversaries." Mounting a serious defense against a major cyber attack would likely require, at a minimum, intrusion detection and intrusion prevention on a nationwide scale. This seems unfeasible, however, as the networks that comprise the Internet are typically not segmented along national boundaries. Put another way, there are no national borders when it comes to the cyber world.[24]

That being the case, it appears unlikely that the Saudis, even with American assistance, could fully insulate their oil industry from electronic disruption. Balancing this concern is the likelihood that any cyber-based disruption of the oil industry would be brief and would not result in a long-term export cutoff.

Because the United States itself confronts cyber threats, US efforts to help Saudi Arabia and other friendly countries in the region protect themselves against this new danger would be likely to continue despite a US military withdrawal from the Gulf. Unlike a civil conflict in which US military intervention would probably cause civilian deaths and provoke potentially dangerous responses from insurgents, from non-state groups, and from other countries, cyber warfare represents an arena in which the US military could intervene with no casualties, relatively little political fallout, and perhaps even without public knowledge. But unlike a shooting war, these battles in the cloud would not end with a victory, a surrender, the arrest of participants, or the disarmament of rebels. The attackers could regroup, reprogram their computers, and strike again, perhaps while holding down respectable day jobs that would give them cover.

An Act of Sabotage

Judging from the experience of Nigeria, where rebels frequently blow up pipelines and processing facilities, periodic acts of sabotage represent an expensive nuisance and sometimes pose a danger to nearby residents, but they do not come close to shutting off a country's entire production. Oil and gasoline pipelines across open and remote terrain are easy to blow up, but the effects of such acts are usually minimal and short lived. Large-scale oil-processing and shipping facilities are better guarded, but they are also highly visible and usually clustered near population centers, rendering them vulnerable to infiltration and sabotage on a scale that could at the very least prompt a spike in prices.

Concern about this possibility is not a recent development. As long ago as May 1977, world oil markets, already skittish, were thrown into chaos for a few days when a fire and explosion at Aramco's giant Abqaiq refinery complex shut down more than half of Saudi Arabia's exports. John J. Kelberer, then chairman of Aramco, flew visiting journalists to the site in a corporate plane in an effort to calm the markets and showed that the explosion was accidental, not the result of sabotage.[25]

Damaging oil installations to inflict economic pain on the United States and the West has long been enshrined in al-Qaeda doctrine. Students of jihadist ideology often quote a treatise titled "The Religious Rule on Targeting Oil Interests" by a radical theorist named Abdel Aziz al-Anzi, who wrote that "targeting oil interests is lawful economic jihad. Economic jihad in this era is the best method to hurt the infidels."[26] The idea that foreign companies have "stolen" Arab oil was a central tenet of Osama bin Laden's worldview and is reflected in the writings and statements of his followers.

In 2004 when he was the head of al-Qaeda in the Arabian Peninsula—before Saudi security forces gunned him down—Abdul Aziz al-Muqrin issued "targeting guidance" that called for "hitting oil wells and pipelines [to] scare foreign companies from working there and stealing Muslim treasures."[27] Two years later the group attempted to put this instruction into practice by attacking the same Abqaiq complex that had been damaged in the 1977 accident. On the afternoon of February 24, 2006, heavily armed men wearing Aramco uniforms drove two cars packed with explosives into the mile-square Abqaiq compound and opened fire. They penetrated the outermost of three security fences before Aramco guards intercepted them. The attackers died when their vehicles exploded, and the resulting damage was slight because they had not been able to approach key facilities. Nevertheless, Abqaiq is such a hugely important—and highly symbolic—component of the industry in Saudi Arabia that this episode caused alarm in Riyadh and Washington, which recognized a need to harden security around the kingdom's essential installations.[28]

Aramco has had a security force since its early years, when guards were hired to prevent pilferage from storage sheds. But except during a bout of labor unrest in the 1950s and occasional protests by the area's Shiite population, the oil region of the Eastern Province was largely untroubled by politics until the rise of al-Qaeda in the 1990s. The 2006 Abqaiq attack made clear, if there was any doubt, that al-Qaeda intended to heed Al-Muqrin's and other jihadist manifestos' "targeting guidance."

The Abqaiq raid was a "psychological shock" to the Saudis, as a US diplomat put it in a classified cable to Washington. It prompted them to seek an even deeper security relationship with the United States. Americans had been training and equipping the Saudi Arabia National Guard since the 1970s. After September 11, 2001, Washington coaxed and bullied the Saudis into working closely with American intelligence and security operatives to identify and track down al-Qaeda members and collaborators and to cut off their funding. In the wake of Abqaiq, the Saudis recognized their vulnerability and turned again to their American partners.

In November 2006 Vice Adm. Patrick Walsh, then commander of the US Navy's Bahrain-based Fifth Fleet, met with Rear Adm. Fahad al-Kayyal and a delegation of Saudi military and security officials at the King Abdulaziz Naval Base in Jubail, which is on the Gulf coast and in the heart of the oil region. Reporting on this meeting in a classified cable to Washington, US ambassador James Oberwetter used this subject heading: "Unprecedented meeting between USG [US government] and SAG [Saudi Arabian government] on petroleum infrastructure protection." According to Oberwetter's account, al-Kayyal "stressed the difficulties confronting the RSNF [Saudi navy] in policing an Arabian Gulf populated with many thousands of small fishing boats" and determining which vessels might have hostile intent. The Americans had no difficulty grasping this concept. They well remembered the attack on the destroyer USS *Cole* in 2000, when a small fishing boat pulled alongside while the ship was refueling in the harbor of Aden, Yemen, and exploded, blowing a huge hole in the hull. That attack, for which al-Qaeda claimed responsibility, killed seventeen American sailors and injured thirty-nine.

Admiral Al-Kayyal emphasized the "vulnerabilities" of the critical export terminal at Ras Tanura and said intelligence reports indicated that al-Qaeda was using satellite imagery to identify potential targets. Another Saudi officer said that most onshore facilities were sufficiently protected, but he warned that giant tankers, which often moor some distance offshore, "were significantly more at threat." An attack on one of those tankers would not shut down or even necessarily reduce Saudi production, but as Al-Kayyal told Walsh, "Terrorist groups only needed to cause minor damage to a crude oil facility to shake up international oil markets through media publicity." In response, as Oberwetter reported, Walsh "stressed the US Navy's willingness to be of assistance in protecting critical Saudi petroleum maritime infrastructure."[29]

In another bilateral meeting six months later, recounted in a separate cable, Maj. Gen. Saad al-Jabri of the Interior Ministry expressed "deep concern with the threat posed by Iran to Saudi Arabia's petroleum infrastructure" and requested a briefing from US intelligence agencies on Iran's capability to strike. He also warned of "the threat posed by internal sabotage from Saudi Aramco employees," some of whom the Interior Ministry knew "to be members of extremist groups."

One outcome of these and other meetings was that a technical team from the US Department of Energy's Sandia National Laboratory designed what US chargé d'affaires Michael Gfoeller described as "a highly rigorous, mathematical and engineering based model" to evaluate the threats. It ranked the facilities as Tier I, II, or III, "according to their criticality to the kingdom and the world," and began training the Saudis in how to evaluate "threat-related information."

During President George W. Bush's visit to Riyadh in May 2008, the two countries then set up a Joint Commission on Infrastructure and Border Protection to secure the oil installations and other critical facilities against attack or subversion, whether by Iran or by domestic militants. The most significant known outcome of this agreement has been the creation of an entirely new quasi-military force assigned specifically to protect oil installations and water desalination plants. This 35,000-man force is trained and equipped by American civilian advisers under military command, in an arrangement similar to that through which Americans have been training the Saudi National Guard for more than thirty-five years. Minister of Interior Prince Muhammad bin Nayef, a nephew of the king and now crown prince, controls this new force as well as the national police and the border security forces. These roles make him one of the most powerful people in Saudi Arabia after the king himself. Prince Muhammad has a long record of working closely with US security advisers and intelligence officials, and from Washington's perspective, he can be assumed to be politically reliable.

Because their dependence on the United States for security is a political liability for the Saudi rulers, neither Saudi Arabia nor the United States has divulged much information about the security force. In a speech in November 2011, former ambassador to the United States Prince Turki al-Faisal said in Washington,

> I am glad to report that Saudi Arabia's oil producing infrastructure has proven, and will continue to prove, safe from attack. This is not only due to the money spent on security and surveillance, but also due to the creation of a 35,000-strong Facilities Security Force. These troops come from across the Kingdom and receive extensive training through a US technical training program. This specialized force, which did not exist before 2005, has the exclusive responsibility of guarding all energy installations against both internal and external threats.[30]

He gave no further details.

In April 2012 a Saudi newspaper, reporting on a graduation ceremony for the first contingent of trainees, quoted the chief of the force, Maj. Gen. Saad al-Majed: "The newly set up Facilities Security Force has taken all necessary measures to protect oil and power installations and water desalination plants throughout the Kingdom in cooperation with the Ministry of Interior, the National Guard, and the Ministry of Defense and Aviation." He was quoted as saying that in three years the force had recruited 8,191 of its planned 35,000 members and that 4,588 were "ready to serve."[31]

The 2006 attempt on Abqaiq "exposed some weaknesses in command and control, and in coordination—and the fact that the [previous] Aramco protective force were not allowed to carry any weapons," a senior official of the Ministry of Petroleum acknowledged in June 2012. "That's all changed now with American help. A very well-trained force is being deployed. But where the Americans really helped was with satellite and cellphone intercept information."[32]

Beyond the forces dedicated to protecting key installations, the Saudis have developed measures to ensure that any disruption would be short lived. Redundancies exist, and potential targets are widely dispersed, making attacks designed to shut down Saudi production and exports extremely difficult for terrorist groups.[33] For instance, Aramco has prepositioned replacement parts across the country, enabling the company to repair damaged pipelines within thirty-six hours.[34] While it is unclear how long repairing a complete shutdown of the Abqaiq facility would take, one study estimates that by dipping into government-controlled oil reserves worldwide, fifteen months could elapse before the loss affected global oil consumption.[35] Finally, even if a terrorist group were able to elude Saudi security personnel and penetrate Abqaiq, at least ten stabilization towers would need to be destroyed to lower Abqaiq's capacity below 2009 processing levels.[36]

Overall, the threat of terrorist attacks is real, but existing infrastructure presents these groups with a range of targets that are difficult to destroy or disrupt for a significant time. Indeed, even Saudi Arabia's neighbors would have trouble halting Saudi oil production and exports with conventional attacks.[37] That said, simply because waging an attack is difficult does not imply that the US commitment should be eliminated. Instead, it shows that the United States might be able to secure its interests at a much lower cost. For instance, withdrawal would not preclude the United States from continuing to share satellite and cellular phone intercept information with the Saudis and to provide assistance in training their Facilities Security Force.

A Radical, Hostile Group Seizes Power

Whether the United States is present in the region or not, a radical takeover of Saudi Arabia that, in turn, shuts down the oil industry to damage Western economic interests is very unlikely, at least in the short to medium term. Even if it did occur, the likelihood that the new regime would shut down oil exports for reasons of politics or ideology can be excluded from strategic planning.

Saudi Arabia, for all its wealth, faces many difficult and well-known problems: a fast-growing population that is outstripping its resources; a geriatric leadership, which is now somewhat energized by the elevation of younger princes under King Salman; a set of weak and often corrupt government agencies; an increasing poverty and urban crime rate; an outdated education system; an often cruel and arbitrary legal system; a volatile controversy over the status of women; a nationwide shortage of housing; and an inability or unwillingness to resolve the grievances of its Shia-minority population. Many citizens in Saudi Arabia are dissatisfied and increasingly vocal. Nevertheless, the Al-Saud family's hold on power faces no immediate or substantial threat. The regime put down an armed insurgency by al-Qaeda in the Arabian Peninsula that began in 2003, largely because the population refused to support the rebels, and it was mostly undisturbed by the 2011 uprisings known as the Arab Spring that brought down other governments in the region.

In a perceptive analysis of those events, Professor Jack Goldstone of George Mason University noted that most popular revolutions fail. The few that succeed, as in Egypt, do so only when a number of conditions come together: "The government must appear so irremediably unjust or inept that it is widely viewed as a threat to the country's future; elites (especially in the military) must be alienated from the state and no longer willing to defend it; a broad-based section of the population, spanning ethnic and religious groups and socioeconomic classes, must mobilize; and international powers must either refuse to step in to defend the government or constrain it from using maximum force to defend itself."[38]

None of those conditions prevails in Saudi Arabia. Goldstone's last criterion, losing the support of foreign powers, might occur without an American security commitment. That is unlikely to be fatal to the regime, however, because for many other reasons, the kingdom is not seriously threatened.

The most important one is that even most of their domestic critics widely perceive the royal family of Al-Saud to be the legitimate rulers of the country. The members of the Al-Saud are not usurpers, they did not invade, they did not seize power in a coup, and no outside power—the Central Intelligence Agency or the British—installed them on the throne. On the contrary, the Al-Saud and their religious partners, rising from the Nejdi heartland, have ruled much of the Arabian Peninsula since the eighteenth century with only brief interruptions. They did not take over Saudi Arabia; indeed, they created it, forging a country out of a tribal wilderness that had not been unified since the era of the four "rightly guided" caliphs who ruled after the death of the prophet Muhammad in 632.

In the past twenty years, academics and other intellectuals, sometimes with the support of the country's powerful business tycoons, have circulated several petitions for reform and modernization of the government. However, they have called for making improvements to the present system, such as greater transparency in decision making, rather than replacing the system.

The Saudi people are generally averse to violence and disorder, an attitude that reflects what they are taught in schools and mosques from their youngest years. Looking at the countries around them and even at the United States, they have not identified a system of government or social organization that would be preferable to their own. Westerners raised in a tradition of democratic secularism tend to assume that citizens of countries outside that tradition must aspire to join it, but such is not the case in Saudi Arabia, where values of religion and family outweigh conventional politics.

During the Arab Spring uprising, Saudi Arabia's well-trained, well-armed security forces — hardened by their street battles with al-Qaeda from 2003 to 2007 — made clear that they would not tolerate mass demonstrations or violence, and people believed them. The rulers had powerful allies in the country's religious leaders, who proclaimed that public protest against the regime would be contrary to Islam. This message resonated powerfully among the people, who are committed to the belief that Islam is the most important function of human society and that it requires their allegiance to any ruler who adheres to the principles of the faith. These lessons are instilled in every Saudi child from the first day of school, and the result is a population that is steeped in the faith and in the belief that the Saudi way of practicing it is the right way.

In the 1950s and 1960s, the era of Gamal Abdel Nasser and Arab nationalism, Saudi Arabia had a small, homegrown leftist movement that advocated parliamentary democracy. Virtually no such movement exists today. Indeed, the most serious challenges to the rule of the Al-Saud—the 1979 armed takeover of the Grand Mosque in Mecca and the 2003–7 al-Qaeda insurgency—came from Islamic absolutists who accused the regime of being insufficiently religious, not excessively so.

Since the unification of the modern country in 1926, the Al-Saud leaders have labored assiduously, and spent billions, to instill in the population the belief that their regime is the personification of the Islamic ideal. Apart from the brief mosque takeover and al-Qaeda's attacks, they have had considerable success. As Andrew Hammond, a British journalist, writes in his recent book on the unique role of religion in Saudi Arabia, the members of Al-Saud have invested heavily in depicting themselves as not simply another royal family but also the authentic embodiment of the Islamic "utopia" in accordance with the principles of shariah and the Sunnah: "Saudi Arabia sees itself as the true heir of the Islamic Utopia of Medina under the leadership of the Prophet and the four 'Rightly-Guided' caliphs who succeeded him."[39] The educational and legal systems of the country have been dedicated for generations to perpetuating that idea among the people. Thus, what passes for political debate in Saudi Arabia is more likely to be about what attire is proper for Muslims than about the form of government.

Unlike the Shiite imams of Iran who were economically independent of the shah, the theologians and jurists of the Saudi religious establishment are well-paid employees of the state and have little incentive to risk their jobs by antagonizing the king who appointed them. They do the regime's bidding.

Nor is rebellion in the air over economic grievances. Saudi Arabia's economic situation cannot be compared to the stagnation that prevailed in Tunisia and Egypt in 2010. The Saudi impoverished underclass is far outnumbered by those citizens who have benefited from the existing system — through government jobs, state-funded benefits, and business partnerships with the ruling family — and who therefore have no incentive to jettison the regime. The expanding Saudi economy does provide some opportunities for educated young people and even women. While these opportunities are not enough, by far, for the growing population, they well exceed what existed in Egypt and Tunisia, where the masses understood that only the corrupt elite had prosperous futures.[40]

For half a century after the big oil money began to flow in, the rulers of Saudi Arabia could placate the disenfranchised populace by constructing everything their underdeveloped country needed. All around them people could see schools, roads, hospitals, electric power plants, and airports where there had been none; the oil riches were indeed benefiting them. Now that the country is almost fully developed, materially if not politically, that message of progress through construction is harder to maintain. Some of the most ambitious projects currently sponsored by the government are widely perceived as white elephants that will benefit mostly those who are already rich. And the population is growing faster than the government's ability to provide jobs and housing for the younger generation. The volume of popular grumbling and complaint is much higher than in the past. Nevertheless, even the most liberal of Saudi political thinkers concede that the people are not in an insurrectionary mood. If King Salman and the revamped government he installed early in 2015 prove to be flexible and creative, the citizens can be placated.

Moreover, there is no sign of dissent in Saudi Arabia's military or security forces, whose well-paid, well-equipped members are resolutely apolitical. Leaders of the security forces, other than the princes at the top, stay out of the public arena. There is no Saudi equivalent of Douglas MacArthur or David Petraeus, men whose military stature might inspire aspirations to rule.

One of the risks of Saudi Arabia's 2015 intervention in the civil war in Yemen is that a mortifying failure could stir resentment in the armed forces. So far there is no sign of such a development, but a cardinal rule of intelligence is that one doesn't know what one doesn't know. Few analysts foresaw the Egyptian Revolution of 1952 or the Iranian Revolution that erupted in 1978. For planning purposes, it is theoretically possible to envision a sequence of events in Saudi Arabia that would bring catastrophe to global oil markets and put the United States in an untenable position: Perhaps triggered by an Israeli attack on Iran or by Saudi-inflicted civilian casualties in Yemen, propelled by long-standing resentment of the US presence in the Gulf and Iraq, and stoked by religious extremists, a burst of popular outrage metastasizes into an armed conflict similar to the one in Syria. Unable to sustain its detachment as the global economy craters, Washington has little choice but to side with the regime, further provoking the opposition. Dissidents in the security forces side with the insurgents. An airline pilot sympathetic to al-Qaeda's ideology and to the rebels flies his plane into the Abqaiq oil-processing facility or the shipping terminal at Ras Tanura.[41] Infighting paralyzes the ruling family. Tankers flee the Gulf. After prolonged strife, the king and senior princes leave the country, and the regime collapses.

Such a sequence is beyond unlikely, but assuming it were to occur, what is the probability that the successor regime would shut down oil exports rather than repairing facilities damaged in the conflict and resuming full production? History demonstrates that such an outcome lies somewhere between extremely improbable and out of the question. Since the beginning of the petroleum age in the nineteenth century, no nation that has been a major producer of oil has voluntarily shut down its oil industry. Regardless of the type of regime running the country (royal, military, authoritarian, or democratic) and of how that regime came to power (inheritance, coup, revolution, or election), the flow of oil has continued more or less without interruption. Thus, a rebellion that overthrew the Al-Saud regime might well damage the oil industry as it unfolded, but its shutting down oil commerce is so unlikely that it can be disregarded in strategic planning. The most recent evidence is provided by the Islamic State, which did not shut down the oil facilities it captured in Iraq; instead, it began marketing their output because it needs the money.

In a few instances, natural disaster or acts of war, most notably in Kuwait during Operation Desert Storm in 1990–91, have shut down the oil fields of a particular country, but these disruptions have never come at the volition of the ruling authority. Restoring full production may take several years, depending on the severity of the damage and the amount of investment capital available to finance reconstruction, but it is eventually accomplished. In the case of Kuwait, though repairs necessitated by the Gulf War took two years, some exports resumed within nine months and reached more than 80 percent of prewar levels by 1992.[42]

Political upheavals and civil wars have resulted in temporary disruptions, as in Libya and Iraq in recent years, but whatever regime has emerged victorious has always made restoring oil exports one of its highest priorities. During the Middle East War of 1973–74, some Arab members of OPEC, including Saudi

Arabia, cut off sales to the United States and the Netherlands, but the flow of oil to other purchasers continued. In other cases where oil commerce between the United States and a particular nation has been interrupted—as with Libya for many years or with Iran—the United States initiated the cutoff, not the producer.

The reason for this immutable fact of history is that regardless of politics, ideology, or religion, the producer states need the money that oil brings. The greater the percentage of state revenue derived from oil sales, the less flexibility the ruling regime has to tamper with the flow of exports. In Saudi Arabia, oil exports generated 90 percent of state revenue in 2012—higher than in the preceding years—and the need for cash is insatiable.[43] This dependence on oil is unlikely to diminish much in the near future.

Saudi Arabia is a vast landmass where a growing population expects free education and health care, massive capital projects are essential to continued development, almost all drinking water comes from desalination plants that are expensive to build and operate, and troublesome neighbors require prolific defense spending. The kingdom is mostly a developed, modern country in which citizens expect to live more like Europeans than like Third World peasants. That lifestyle costs money.

Even Osama bin Laden, at the height of his remote-controlled jihad against the Saudi state, said that al-Qaeda's purpose in attempting to attack oil facilities was to punish the West by driving up the price, not to shut off the flow. "We are not going to drink it," he said.[44]

That being the case, there is little reason to fear that the ouster of the Saudi monarchy in some political upheaval would result in the Saudis' withdrawal from the global oil market. If a radical revolutionary regime gained control of all the kingdom's more than $540 billion in gold and foreign currency reserves—it probably could not, because most of those holdings are in Western banks—the regime could survive for quite some time without oil income, but it would have a ruinous impact on the country.[45] A successor regime that was hostile to the United States or to Western interests might try to find alternate customers for the country's exports, but the total amount of oil flowing to global markets would not change much. Besides, the biggest purchaser of Saudi oil is China, which presumably would not be a political target of the revolutionaries.

A radical regime might reduce oil production to drive up prices, pursuing a revenue-neutral policy that would inflict economic pain on consumer nations, as bin Laden and other theorists of jihad have advocated. In the short term, such a policy could be effective, and consumer nations would find it difficult to justify foreign intervention to oblige the new Saudi government to discard the policy. The men who run the kingdom's oil industry well understand, however, that price increases will backfire at some point, one at which their consumers will rebel and their market will dwindle. The quest for long-term market share trumps the quest for immediate cash, not just in Saudi Arabia but also in OPEC.[46]

Saudi Arabia weathered the upheavals of the Arab Spring with some economic strain but little political turmoil; the Al-Saud neutralized any serious threat to the regime with a $130 billion outlay on, among other things, social welfare improvements.[47] Given the age of its leadership, however, the pressure for reform from a new generation of better-informed citizens—and a growing population that threatens to overwhelm food and water supplies—means that the potential for trouble cannot be discounted entirely. If a change of regime were to happen, oil exports would be disrupted only to the extent that facilities were closed or damaged in the struggle. Once firmly in power, new leaders would have to restore full exports as soon as possible, as happened in Libya after the conflict that brought down Muammar Qaddafi.

A Civil War

For the same reasons that a radical takeover of Riyadh is unlikely, the prospect of civil war during the next two decades is remote. Who would be the combatants? Unlike the former Yugoslavia or Iraq, for example, Saudi Arabia is basically homogeneous. Its people have tribal resentments but no ethnic rivalries, and the only religious conflict is between the ruling Sunni majority and the long-oppressed Shia minority. Shia leaders interviewed by Arab and Western media almost always assert that they desire only to be full citizens of Saudi Arabia. They seek neither to break up the country nor to make common cause with Shiite Iran.

Short of an armed rebellion, a major work stoppage by dissatisfied employees of the state oil company could possibly disrupt production, especially if the workers disabled Saudi Aramco's computer network. When the oil company was still American owned, security forces responded quickly and forcefully to labor actions in the 1940s and 1950s; the impacts were short lived. The security forces today are far better trained and equipped than they were in that earlier era; thus, presumably any effort to organize a strike and lead workers off the job would be dealt with in short order.

For the sake of argument, however, let us posit a scenario that leads to civil war. The Shiite majority of nearby Bahrain finally overthrows the minority monarchy and comes to power. Their fellow Shiite Arabs of Saudi Arabia's Eastern Province, despairing of winning concessions from the Riyadh regime and following the suggestions of a few Shiite radicals, decide to secede from the kingdom and join Bahrain. Iran, perceiving an opportunity, provides arms and assistance to the new Shiite country. Because the oil fields of Saudi Arabia are in the Shiite communities of the Eastern Province, the royal government in Riyadh sends armed forces to foil the secession. Thus, a civil war breaks out. (This scenario may appear far-fetched, but such a conflict did develop in Nigeria, a major OPEC country, with the Biafra secession of 1967–70.) Unless Iran intervened directly, such a conflict in Saudi Arabia would probably be brief as the Shiites lack the population and weapons to resist the government's military power. Because of the geography, however, some damage to oil facilities might be inevitable, and the secessionists might block export terminals along the Gulf to shut off the government's revenue stream.

Even so, depending on the intensity and scope of the conflict, significant oil exports could continue. For example, during the Biafra war, Nigeria's oil output dropped by more than half but was not cut off entirely. More recently, a Nigerian rebel group attacked an oil facility four days prior to the 2006 attack on Abqaiq. According to Khalid R. Al-Rodhan, "This caused Shell to shut its operations and production of a fifth of Nigerian oil output, approximately 0.45 million barrels a day."[48] Algeria contended with similar issues during that country's civil war of the 1990s. Oil production and exports from Algeria continued with little disruption, however, because the oil fields were far from the coastal towns where most of the violence occurred. By contrast, when Russia's Bolsheviks took over Azerbaijan in 1920, the oil industry around Baku was virtually shut down until the Soviet government could rebuild it. Vladimir Lenin recognized the need for export revenue. As Daniel Yergin recounts in his history of oil, "The Soviet oil industry, virtually dormant from 1920 to 1923, thereafter revived quickly, helped by imports of large amounts of Western technology, and the USSR soon reentered the world market as an exporter."[49] Regarding the Strait of Hormuz, the narrow shipping channel at the exit of the Persian Gulf, in the unlikely event of an extended closure, some exports from Saudi Arabia and the United Arab Emirates could continue via constructed pipelines that bypass that maritime choke point.

In a Saudi conflict, the extent and duration of oil disruption might depend on the weapons used, the extent to which outside powers intervened, and the desire of both sides to preserve facilities intact in order to resume full production after the fighting ceased. An armed conflict in the oil fields could panic world markets, disrupt supplies temporarily, and damage facilities that would be expensive to repair, but whoever won would work quickly to restore full production.

The Role of the United States

This era is one of uncertainty and upheaval throughout the Middle East. The list of countries in which it cannot be said with certainty which individual or group will be in charge ten to twenty years from now includes Libya, Egypt, Syria, Iran, Yemen, and Iraq. The possibility of war hangs over the Gulf. Turkey is asserting itself as a regional power for first time since World War I. Jordan appears increasingly fragile. The Islamic State has seized large swaths of Iraq and Syria and has affiliates in other countries that are wedded to the same extreme and violent ideology. In that environment, Saudi Arabia, for all its flaws, represents stability, continuity, and a welcome commitment to work closely with Washington on security matters. The "succession crisis" that many Western analysts feared might develop upon the death of King Abdullah did not occur; indeed, his successor, King Salman, quickly established his authority and engineered an orderly transition to the next generation of princes.

For half a century the United States, which has positioned troops, ships, and aircraft from Incirlik in Turkey to Diego Garcia in the Indian Ocean, has borne responsibility—for better or for worse—for maintaining stability and ensuring the free flow of oil and other goods across the region. In two wars with Iraq and the Tanker War of the 1980s, the United States has demonstrated its willingness to use military force. For substantial elements of the mostly Muslim populations of the region, the mere presence of those American units is at least an irritant, if not an incitement to violence. Raising the US military profile in any part of the region carries the risk of popular backlash; lowering it might have the opposite effect. That is one reason the Obama administration has limited the US role to air power, rather than deploying troops, in the fight against the Islamic State.

In the case of Saudi Arabia especially, the circumstances in which US military involvement would be constructive are very limited. Oil is important, but the impact of a price spike or temporary shortage might be easier to accept than the unforeseeable consequences—for the United States and for its friends—of military intervention. In the absence of a regional war or outright invasion, there is no inherent reason why Saudi Arabia could not or would not maintain its oil export capacity, so long as resources last, without a US security commitment or a US military presence in the Gulf.

If Saudi exports shut down, however, the economic shock to the United States and other industrialized nations would compel them to respond in some way but not necessarily with military force. Some elements of an international response to a shutdown of Saudi exports are in place, beginning with the release of crude stocks from the strategic reserves of the United States and other countries. Beyond that measure, the nature of the response and degree of US responsibility for it—as well as its success—would depend on the cause of the shutdown.

Even in the absence of a standing US military presence in the Gulf, another country is unlikely to invade or attack Saudi Arabia directly. The Saudis regard the

Houthis, the rebels who seized control of most of Yemen in 2015, as hostile proxies of Iran, but they pose little threat to the kingdom itself. No other hostile states border the kingdom. Its armed forces are more powerful than those of its neighbors, with the possible exception of Jordan. If Iran were to attempt to attack from the sea, it might well inflict serious damage on Saudi oil installations along the Gulf coast. Without a standing military presence in the Gulf, the United States would need some time to respond militarily to an Iranian attack, but eventually, in its own interest, it would almost certainly do so. The region's Sunni Arab populations might welcome a US intervention in this one scenario.

On the one hand, if termination of the US security commitment entailed not only the withdrawal of its armed forces but also the end of its training and equipment assistance to Saudi security forces, then the kingdom's vulnerability to insurgency and sabotage would increase, but to what degree is not quantifiable. On the other hand, the US security presence in Saudi Arabia and neighboring states is a source of political and religious grievance to large segments of the Saudi population that might be assuaged if the "crusaders" departed. As Rachel Bronson wrote in her definitive history of the US-Saudi strategic partnership, "The blowback from King Fahd's decision to welcome half a million American troops to the kingdom [to confront Iraq in 1991] continues to reverberate through Saudi society. The Saudi leadership has learned firsthand the perils of an overt American presence."[50]

A dozen years after that massive deployment of foreign troops into the kingdom alienated large segments of the Saudi population and inspired Osama bin Laden's campaign against the United States, the removal of Saddam Hussein and his Ba'athist regime in the war of 2003 eliminated the need for international enforcement of flight restrictions over Iraq. Thus, the United States had a convenient reason to withdraw its air combat units from Saudi Arabia without appearing to do so at bin Laden's behest. Since that time, US security planning in the region has assumed, correctly, that American military deployment inside the kingdom for any reason other than defense against invasion would cause more trouble than it would cure. The US Air Force and Navy units available for protecting Saudi Arabia are deployed in other countries of the region, but their presence nearby remains an inflammatory talking point for al-Qaeda and like-minded groups.

In reality there is little reason to fear a civil conflict in Saudi Arabia would grow to such proportions that it would disrupt more than half of oil exports. If it did occur, however, it is difficult to imagine that the United States would stay completely disengaged from such a conflict, especially if Iran were aiding the rebels.

US government officials take it for granted that a Saudi oil cutoff would severely damage US economic interests and, therefore, would require intervention in some form but not necessarily direct military involvement. While a civil war in Libya or the Congo has few economic implications for the rest of the world, Saudi Arabia is in another category entirely. A clear statement of this position comes from a Heritage Foundation paper that sought to calculate the economic impact of a Saudi oil cutoff. It projected that such a crisis would require US military intervention aimed at "ensuring that a hostile, radical Islamist power does not seize control of key oil and gas infrastructure in Saudi Arabia and the Persian Gulf."[51]

For reasons already discussed, that mission would be risky and dangerous for the armed forces, and it would require Herculean feats of diplomacy to convince the Arab combatants that the American forces were there not to support either side but solely to protect the vital installations that all sides would wish to preserve anyway. If Riyadh's forces were unable to put down a rebellion quickly and the oil fields became a battleground, Washington would probably be forced to take a side—namely, the side of the Al-Saud government, however unpalatable its domestic political system might be to advocates of democracy. If the antigovernment side represented Islamic militancy or Iranian meddling, a US position allied with the regime would be politically sustainable, but what if—like the uprisings in Tunisia and Egypt—the rebellion presented itself as the face of reform, the will of the people, a struggle for justice? If the United States sided with an oppressive regime against a genuine popular uprising in order to protect US economic interests, surely an anti-American backlash would occur in Saudi Arabia if that regime were overthrown and elsewhere in the Muslim world even if it were not. As Shibley Telhami demonstrates in his recent book, the United States is deeply unpopular with the Arab masses. They would understand that any US action to keep the oil flowing would also keep the money flowing to the Saudi government's bank accounts in London and New York; by definition, that action would represent US support for the regime.[52]

Throughout the uprisings known as the Arab Spring, the United States had to weigh multiple, sometimes conflicting interests in deciding whether to intervene and, if so, in what way. The United States and its allies had obvious interest in promoting democracy and averting humanitarian disaster. But Washington also wished to deter Iranian meddling, protect Israel, preserve the Egyptian-Israeli peace treaty, stabilize Iraq, contain al-Qaeda and like-minded groups, keep sea-lanes open, avoid involvement in any combat that would cost lives and money, and uphold military alliances such as the one with Bahrain.

These interests are not always compatible, as evident in the case of Bahrain. That tiny island state provides a useful if imperfect window into the difficulties the United States might face in dealing with an uprising in Saudi Arabia. Bahrain's people are mostly Shia Muslims, but an autocratic monarchy has ruled with a firm hand ever since independence in 1971. The people took to the streets and protested in early 2011. Some of their grievances were legitimate, and if human rights were the only issue, the United States might have sided with the protestors. The United States and Bahrain, however, have been military and strategic allies for more than twenty years. The US Navy's Fifth Fleet is headquartered in Bahrain, and the country holds the official legal status of "Major Non-NATO [North American Treaty Organization] Ally" of the United States, a distinction it shares with countries such as Japan and Israel. Despite its long and close association with Washington, Saudi Arabia has not achieved that status, which allows those holding it greater access to American weapons and training.

The Obama administration was fortunate in that the Bahraini uprising has been about Bahraini politics and religion, not about the US military presence, and Bahrain produces little oil. The United States has therefore been spared the need to become involved or to take sides. Washington issued a few relatively mild statements chastising the regime for its harsh response to the demonstrators, but once it was clear that the conflict presented no threat to larger US strategic interests, Washington sat it out, leaving the Saudis to help the regime put the lid back on the cauldron. The Saudis did so by sending in troops. This position may have caused some embarrassment in the administration, but it did not become a major issue.

Bahrain is a negligible factor in the global economy. If a similar crisis occurred in Saudi Arabia, the stakes would be far higher. The United States would have compelling reasons to intervene, but any form of US military presence almost certainly would become an issue and stoke further conflict. Washington would have no easy choices and perhaps no good choices.

As for sabotage, there is no way to quantify the extent to which a withdrawal of US assistance and advice would exacerbate the Saudis' vulnerability to such a campaign. There would surely be some impact, but here again, separating the Al-Saud government from its longtime protectors might remove the most important provocation for a sabotage campaign in the first place. The Saudis could seek assistance from Britain, France, or perhaps Russia; from other Muslim countries such as Jordan or Pakistan; or from their largest customer, China. The Saudis' capabilities and their access to US intelligence assistance might diminish but so might their political vulnerability. Consequently, any level of American commitment must weigh the costs of sabotage against the potentially moderating effect withdrawal could have on the probability that sabotage will occur.

A regional war would disrupt oil commerce and probably require US military intervention in some form, even if the United States had already pulled back from the Gulf. In the kingdom, however, the United States has very little influence on Saudi political affairs—certainly less than it may have had in the era when Saudi Arabia was poor and dependent—and overt US intervention in Saudi domestic developments would only exacerbate whatever trouble it was intended to address.

On balance, then, oil alone is not a compelling reason for the United States to maintain its role as security guarantor of the Kingdom of Saudi Arabia indefinitely. Indeed, this chapter highlights the multiple potential ways oil will continue to flow absent an American commitment. A US military presence cannot remedy—and, in fact, might exacerbate—many of the most likely vulnerabilities facing the Saudi oil industry. In short, these vulnerabilities require political solutions guided by Saudi society and its government. Finally, a US-Iran rapprochement could eliminate most of the other reasons that the United States maintains a presence in the region as well. If such an agreement were to happen, Saudi Arabia might well be left to fend for itself; thus, so many Saudis fear that possibility.

At President Obama's Camp David meeting with leaders of the Gulf Arab principalities in May 2015, the GCC states—including Saudi Arabia—agreed to accept as potentially beneficial a pending agreement between Iran and the United States and its negotiating partners about the scope and size of Iran's nuclear program. They had little choice: The president made clear that he was determined to press ahead and would not be deterred by protests or petulance from the GCC. He clearly hoped that such an agreement would eventually lead to a more constructive relationship between the United States and Iran. There is no inherent reason why such a rapprochement would be detrimental to US-Saudi relations, but it could provide one more reason for the United States to reduce its security commitments in the Gulf.

Notes

1. Ariel Cohen et al., "Thinking the Unthinkable: Modeling a Collapse of Saudi Oil Production," Heritage Foundation Backgrounder no. 2671 (April 9, 2012), http://report .heritage.org/research/reports/2012/04/thinking-the-unthinkable-modeling-a-collapse -of-saudi-oil-production. For estimates of the costs of a full closure of the Strait of Hormuz, see William Komiss and LaVar Huntzinger, "The Economic Implications of Disruptions to Maritime Oil Chokepoints" (Arlington VA: CNA, March 2011), 25–44. They find the cost estimates to be lower.

2. US Energy Information Administration (EIA), "Petroleum and Other Liquids: U.S. Imports by Country of Origin," March 2012, http://www.eia.gov/dnav/pet/pet_move _impcus_a2_nus_ep00_im0_mbbl_m.htm. It is worth noting that even though the aggregate level of imports is relatively low (approximately 13 percent of the US total),

its effect on the US economy is inflated by the fact that Saudi Aramco, the giant state oil company, and its joint venture partner Royal Dutch/Shell operate three large refineries in the United States that specifically purchase Saudi crude.

3. Clifford Krauss, "US Reliance on Saudi Oil Goes Back Up," *New York Times*, August 17, 2012, 1.

4. International Energy Agency (IEA), "Executive Summary," *World Energy Outlook, 2011* (Paris: IEA, 2011), http://www.iea.org/publications/freepublications/publication/executive_summary.pdf.

5. IEA, "Executive Summary," *World Energy Outlook, 2013* (Paris: IEA, 2013), http://www.iea.org/publications/freepublications/publication/WEO2013_Executive_Summary_English.pdf.

6. Barack Obama, "Remarks in Press Conference after GCC Summit," Camp David, May 14, 2015, https://www.whitehouse.gov/the-press-office/2015/05/14/remarks-president-obama-press-conference-after-gcc-summit.

7. John Busby, "Oil and Gas Net Exports," *BP Statistical Review, 2008* (June 29, 2008), http://www.after-oil.co.uk/oil_and_gas_net_exports.htm.

8. See "Saudi Arabia's Coming Oil and Fiscal Challenge," Saudi-US Relations Information Service, July 30, 2011, http://susris.com/2011/07/30/saudi-arabias-coming-oil-and-fiscal-challenge.

9. EIA, "Country Analysis Brief: Saudi Arabia," September 10, 2014, 3, http://www.eia.gov/beta/international/analysis_includes/countries_long/Saudi_Arabia/saudi_arabia.pdf.

10. King Abdullah City for Atomic and Renewable Energy (K.A.CARE), "Proposed Competitive Procurement Process for the Renewable Energy Program," 2013, http://kacare.gov.sa/en/wp-content/uploads/K.A.CARE-Proposed-Competitive-Procurement-Process-for-the-Renewable-Energy-Program-2013.pdf.

11. See Glada Lahn and Paul Stevens, *Burning Oil to Keep Cool: The Hidden Energy Crisis in Saudi Arabia* (London: Chatham House, 2011), 1–2.

12. The Saudis could also increase domestic prices to compensate for revenue shortfalls. This, too, would strain state-society relations. The following material discusses this option.

13. See Lahn and Stevens, *Burning Oil*, 1.

14. Blake Clayton and Adam Segal, "Addressing Cyber Threats to Oil and Gas Suppliers," *Energy Brief* (Washington DC: Council on Foreign Relations, June 2013), 3.

15. Indeed, it is difficult but not impossible to target production and distribution infrastructure. As Clayton and Segal note, "The operational hurdles would typically require significant planning, financial resources, technical expertise, and inroads within the corporation or facility being targeted. Though high, these barriers would not be insurmountable to certain skilled operators, many of whom work for or under the auspices of foreign governments or are available to them for hire." Ibid. Also on the difficulty, see Christopher Bronk, "Hacks on Gas: Energy, Cybersecurity, and US Defense" (Houston: James A. Baker III Institute for Public Policy, Rice University, February 5, 2014), 14.

16. An English version of the Cutting Sword of Justice manifesto was published online at http://pastebin.com/HqAgaQRj.

17. Nicole Perlroth, "In Cyberattack on Saudi Firm, U.S. Sees Iran Firing Back," *New York Times*, October 23, 2012.

18. While seemingly true, it can be noted that Saudi Aramco reportedly took "almost two weeks to fully restore its network and recover from a disruption of its daily business operations caused by data loss and disabled work stations resulting from the incident." Christopher Bronk and Eneken Tikk-Ringas, "Hack or Attack? Shamoon and the Evolution of Cyber Conflict," Working Paper (Houston: James A. Baker III Institute for Public Policy, Rice University, February 1, 2013), 3.

19. "Saudi Oil Producer's Computers Restored after Virus Attack," *New York Times*, August 27, 2012, B4.

20. "Saudi Aramco, Ministry of Interior Discuss Cyber Attack," Aramco ExPats, December 12, 2012, http://www.aramcoexpats.com/articles/2012/12/saudi-aramco -ministry-of-interior-discuss-cyber-attack/.

21. The malware may have migrated unintentionally beyond its intended targets. See Clayton and Segal, "Addressing Cyber Threats," 3; and Camilla Hall and Javier Blas, "Aramco Cyber Attack Targeted Production," *Financial Times*, December 10, 2012.

22. See "Qatar Ready to Help Iran Develop Its Share of Common Gas Field," *Natural Gas Asia*, December 23, 2013, http://www.naturalgasasia.com/qatar-ready-to-help-iran -to-develop-its-share-of-common-gas-field-11343.

23. Gerry J. Gilmore, "DOD, Industry Address 'Intense Challenge' of Cyber Security," *Defense News*, November 7, 2011, http://www.archive.defense.gov/news/newsarticle .aspx?id=65988. For more information on the vulnerability of electrical grids and oil and gas infrastructure, see Bronk, "Hacks on Gas."

24. Andrew Krepinevich, "Cyber Warfare: A 'Nuclear Option'?" (Washington DC: Center for Strategic and Budgetary Assessments, August 24, 2012), 45.

25. The author of this chapter was one of the journalists on that flight.

26. See, for example, Alex P. Schmid, "Terrorism and Energy Security: Targeting Oil and Other Energy Sources and Infrastructures," in *Terrorism: What's Coming: The Mutating Threat*, ed. James O. Ellis III (Oklahoma City: Memorial Institute for the Prevention of Terrorism, 2007); and Michael Scheuer, Stephen Ulph, and John C. K. Daly, "Saudi Arabian Oil Facilities: The Achilles Heel of the Western Economy" (Washington DC: Jamestown Foundation, May 2006), 10n2, http://www.jamestown.org/uploads/media /Jamestown-SaudiOil.pdf. See also Peter Bergen, "Al Qaeda, the Organization: A Five-Year Forecast," *Annals of the American Academy of Political and Social Science*, vol. 618, *Terrorism: What the Next President Will Face* (July 2008): 14–30; and Bruce Riedel, "Al Qaeda Strikes Back," *Foreign Affairs* 86, no. 3 (May–June 2007): 24–40.

27. "Al-Qaeda Targeting Guidance—v1.0" (Alexandria VA: Intel Center/Tempest Publishing, April 1, 2004), 4, http://www.intelcenter.com/Qaeda-Targeting-Guidance -v1-0.pdf.

28. Mark Weston, *Prophets and Princes: Saudi Arabia from Muhammad to the Present*

(Hoboken NJ: Wiley, 2008), 470; and Anthony Cordesman, *Saudi Arabia: National Security in a Troubled Region* (Santa Barbara CA: Praeger Security International, 2009), 283.

29. Unless otherwise specified, all diplomatic cables quoted in this chapter are from the WikiLeaks compilation distributed by McClatchy Newspapers, June 13, 2011, http://www.mcclatchydc.com/news/special-reports/article24655390.html.

30. Prince Turki al-Faisal, Address to the World Affairs Council, National Press Club, Washington DC, November 5, 2011.

31. Mohammad Al-Umairi, "Force Ready to Defend Oil and Power Plants," *Saudi Gazette*, April 2, 2012, 1.

32. Private conversation with the author, June 2012.

33. See EIA, "Saudi Arabia," February 26, 2013; and Joshua Shifrinson and Miranda Priebe, "A Crude Threat: The Limits of an Iranian Missile Campaign against Saudi Arabian Oil," *International Security* 36 (2011): 167–201.

34. Shifrinson and Priebe, "Crude Threat," 177.

35. Note that this assumes 2008 consumption rates. Ibid., 194–95.

36. Ibid., 199.

37. Ibid.

38. Jack Goldstone, "Understanding the Revolutions of 2011: Weakness and Resilience in Middle Eastern Autocracies," *Foreign Affairs* 90, no. 3 (May–June 2011): 8

39. Andrew Hammond, *The Islamic Utopia: The Illusion of Reform in Saudi Arabia* (London: Pluto Press, 2012), 56.

40. On the potential of oil-rich exporting states to maintain domestic stability, see Benjamin Smith, "Oil Wealth and Regime Survival in the Developing World, 1960–1999," *American Journal of Political Science* 48, no. 2 (April 2004): 232–46; and Benjamin Smith, "The Wrong Kind of Crisis: Why Oil Booms and Busts Rarely Lead to Authoritarian Breakdown," *Studies in Comparative International Development* 40, no. 4 (Winter 2006): 55–76.

41. The damage caused by these attacks could be significant depending on where the plane hits and the aftermath of the initial impact. That said if the Abqaiq oil-processing facility were completely destroyed, Saudi Arabia would only be able to produce and stabilize approximately 5.6 mb/d of oil. Striking individual shipping terminals, however, would be relatively less damaging for Saudi exports. Exports would diminish, but the use of other smaller terminals and pipelines would allow Saudi Arabia to continue exporting 6 mb/d to 8mb/d. Estimates differ on these amounts for a variety of reasons. See EIA, "Saudi Arabia"; and Shifrinson and Priebe, "Crude Threat."

42. Shifrinson and Priebe, "Crude Threat," 194.

43. Figures provided by Finance Minister Ibrahim al-Assaf in announcing the 2013 government budget. See "Saudi Arabia Announces 2013 Budget," Saudi-US Relations Information Service, January 3, 2013, http://susris.com/2013/01/03/saudi-arabia-announces-2013-budget/.

44. Quoted in Scheuer, Ulph, and Daly, "Saudi Arabian Oil Facilities."

45. The reserve figures are in the statistical appendix to Saudi Arabian Monetary

Agency (SAMA), "Forty-Eighth Annual Report: The Latest Economic Developments" (Riyadh: SAMA, August 2012), http://www.sama.gov.sa/en-US/EconomicReports/AnnualReport/5600_R_Annual_En48_2013_02_19.pdf.

46. For an overall review of Saudi oil policy, see Thomas W. Lippman, *Saudi Arabia on the Edge: The Uncertain Future of an American Ally* (Washington: Potomac Books, 2012), chap. 2.

47. While $130 billion is a significant amount of money, the king's reserves in 2010 reached $214 billion. Neil MacFarquhar, "In Saudi Arabia, Royal Funds Buy Peace for Now," *New York Times*, June 8, 2011.

48. Khalid R. Al-Rodhan, "The Impact of the Abqaiq Attack on Saudi Energy Security" (Washington DC: Center for Strategic and International Studies, February 27, 2006), 4.

49. Daniel Yergin, *The Prize: The Epic Quest for Oil, Money and Power* (New York: Simon & Schuster, 1991), 240.

50. Rachel Bronson, *Thicker than Oil: America's Uneasy Partnership with Saudi Arabia* (New York: Oxford University Press, 2006), 252.

51. Cohen et al., "Thinking the Unthinkable," note 4.

52. Shibley Telhami, *The World through Arab Eyes: Arab Public Opinion and the Reshaping of the Middle East* (New York: Basic Books, 2013), chap. 7.

CHAPTER 5

After America: The Flow of Persian Gulf Oil in the Absence of US Military Force

Joshua Rovner

This chapter analyzes the possibility of interstate conflict and Persian Gulf oil disruptions if the United States severs its military commitments to the region. It addresses three common fears of life in the Gulf after America departs. The first fear is that in the absence of US forces, a new regional hegemon will take its place and gain control over so much oil that it can threaten to manipulate global oil prices. The second is that a major regional war that would threaten the flow of oil—by damaging infrastructure, destroying shipping, or deterring oil merchants from operating in dangerous waters—would be more likely without the stabilizing presence of the United States. The last fear is that Iran will be able to threaten shipping through the Strait of Hormuz, thus increasing uncertainty about international oil and putting the global economy at risk.[1]

The following analysis assumes that the United States completely exits the Gulf and does not make any attempt to operate there for at least twenty years, even if there is substantial domestic or international pressure to return. In other words, it imagines the political and military conditions in the Persian Gulf region without any US forces present and without any hope that they will arrive in a crisis. In the last part of the chapter, however, I evaluate what US forces might be necessary to safeguard the flow of oil. While the United States has conducted a large withdrawal from the region since 2011, it still maintains land, air, and naval bases throughout the Gulf. Some land forces have also returned in response to the emergence of the so-called Islamic State (IS). My analysis discusses which of these forces are necessary to fulfill the oil mission.

In my analysis I make three major arguments. First, no regional hegemon will arise over the twenty-year period regardless of US decisions over force posture. Only three countries could conceivably make a bid for dominance—Saudi Arabia, Iraq, and Iran—and none of them will have the wherewithal to do so even if they so desired. A combination of military and economic weakness, along with internal threats to the political order, will force them to focus on domestic matters and downplay whatever regional aspirations they possess. To the extent that they seek to expand their influence, they are almost likely to do so through proxies. While this approach can certainly cause problems, it cannot do much to interrupt the flow of oil to market. Second, a large regional conventional war is unlikely not only because the possible combatants all lack power projection capabilities, making a sustained cross-border campaign difficult to imagine, but also because they are focused on domestic threats and have more practical ways of injuring one another. Third, Iran can plausibly threaten the Strait of Hormuz even if it cannot close it completely. This task will be far easier without US forces around to keep it open. A modest residual US force, however, should be capable of deterring Iran from harassing shipping or mining the Strait. If Iran is not deterred, then the same small force will be able to quickly restore safe passage for oil tankers.

Why There Will Not Be a Regional Hegemon

In theory, a hostile power in the Persian Gulf region could jeopardize the international economy by threatening oil or by withholding it from international markets. More than 30 percent of all traded oil comes from the Gulf region, which also contains more than 40 percent of the world's proven reserves. The United States has long worried that if a single country controlled a very large fraction of Persian Gulf oil, then it would have the ability to manipulate the global oil market and could use this capability coercively to advance interests that conflicted with American interests. US concern about the dangers posed by a regional hegemon played an important role in its reaction to Iraq's 1990 invasion of Kuwait, for the United States feared it might be the first step toward invading Saudi Arabia.

A dominant regional power would enjoy the most coercive leverage if global oil demand was high and rising because supply disruptions could cause price spikes. For a number of reasons, however, demand is expected to fall in 2016.[2] Continued uncertainty about global growth, along with a large glut in supply, has held oil prices in check. But even if the market reverses course, there is little strategic reason for concern, because the chance that a regional hegemon will emerge in the Persian Gulf during the next twenty years is slim to none. This is true even if the United States decides to withdraw completely. Only three states are large and wealthy enough to harbor dreams of dominance: Iraq, Saudi Arabia, and Iran. Internal problems plague all three, forcing them to focus inward for the foreseeable future. None of them will be able to acquire or produce the kind of offensive military capabilities necessary for sustained power projection. Nor will they be able to build and maintain the logistics infrastructure needed to manage a hegemonic presence in the Gulf. In addition, existing capabilities in all three countries, along with a host of other factors, will favor the defense. Thus, while regional powers are likely to meddle in regional affairs, they are unlikely to do so in ways that will cause anything more than mischief. Nothing they can do in the next twenty years will promise the kind of physical or political control over neighboring states that a hegemon enjoys.

Iraq

The following discussion briefly traces the history of Iraq's armed forces and assesses its current capabilities. It covers more historical ground than other contributions to this volume do, but a look back is essential for understanding why the Iraqi armed forces are in such dire shape today. Iraq's military poverty did not happen by accident, and the causes of its downfall also explain why it will not be able to rebuild any meaningful power projection capabilities in the near or medium term. For this and other reasons described in this section, Iraq is unlikely to risk its meager conventional forces in a bid for regional hegemony. Subsequent sections also analyze Saudi Arabia and Iran, asking whether they have current or latent capabilities and the political will to move aggressively against their neighbors.

Iraq lacked meaningful power projection capabilities for decades after World War II. The postwar Hashemite regime had a tiny army, and beyond rhetorical support it could not offer much to the Arab-Israeli War in 1948. A military coup in 1958 ended Iraq's relationship with the West but opened the door to arms imports from the Soviet Union. Dependence on Moscow, however, put Iraq at a relative disadvantage to regional powers that had access to technology from multiple Western suppliers. In addition, Iraq was forced to maintain a large garrison at home to deal with the threat of a Kurdish rebellion, thus sharply constraining its ability to act outside its borders.[3]

Circumstances changed in the 1970s when the Ba'ath regime was able to use oil revenues to fund a vast military expansion. Total defense spending in current dollars rose from $252 million to $1.66 billion from 1969 to 1979, and total military manpower rose from 78,000 to 212,000 over the same period.[4] The fourfold rise in oil prices after 1973 also enabled a fourfold increase in arms imports.[5] Thus, Iraq was able to continue to buy weapons from the Soviet Union while reducing its dependence on Moscow. By the end of the decade, Iraq was openly buying arms from Western European countries, including advanced antitank weapons from France and ships from France and Italy.[6] The army doubled in size by adding four armored and two mechanized infantry divisions, which it equipped with the Soviet Union's most modern tanks, armored personnel carriers, and combat aircraft, as well as advanced French fighters.[7]

Events over the next two decades shattered this force. The Iran-Iraq War, enormously destructive, left Iraq in deep debt. Saddam Hussein invaded Kuwait in 1990 partly as a way out of the debt trap, but it only brought in the United States, which annihilated a huge amount of Iraqi hardware in Operation Desert Storm. The ensuing twelve years of international sanctions dashed any Iraqi hopes of rebuilding its conventional strength. Iraq had been heavily dependent on arms imports throughout the 1970s and '80s, but those sources were now unavailable. The Ba'ath regime did what it could to cannibalize parts from other systems to field some semblance of an army, but by the end of the 1990s its force relied on systems that were "decaying, obsolete, and obsolescent."[8] Worse, the sanctions shattered the Iraqi economy, leading to crippling inflation and driving a deeply indebted regime into further distress. And every year that its forces atrophied made it that much harder and more expensive to rebuild. Anthony Cordesman estimated that by 1999, Iraq would have needed to spend almost $48 billion in arms imports to return to its pre–Gulf War average and $12 billion *simply to sustain the post–Gulf War force.*[9] Such expenditures were impossible. The Ba'ath regime barely had the resources to sustain its fractured forces, and it had no way of growing new ones. Annual defense spending in the 1990s amounted to a paltry $1.4 billion, down from $19 billion on average in the 1980s.[10]

The US invasion in 2003 erased any doubt about the capabilities of the Iraqi military. While the country was awash in small arms—a major problem for US occupation forces—it had no ability to sustain conventional operations, to say nothing of its ability to project power in the region. Several years of civil war forced the fledgling Iraqi security services to concentrate on rebuilding the kind of force capable of dealing with internal unrest, not waging war against other powers in the region. As of 2011 Iraq employed a little more than 800,000 personnel in the Ministry of Defense, the Ministry of the Interior, and the prime minister's counterterrorism force. Only a third of the total force resided within the Ministry of Defense, and according to the International Institute of Strategic Studies, it was "primarily designed to impose order on Iraq's own population."[11] The total defense budget was $4.8 billion, most of which was devoted to personnel costs and weapons systems designed for internal stability missions. The army fields only one armored division along with fifteen light divisions and three brigades. By way of comparison, the army was able to put nine heavy divisions in Kuwait in fall 1990, the last time it attempted to project power in the region.[12] The air force is made up of a mix of light utility fixed- and rotary-wing aircraft along with some medium transport planes. The only important exceptions are eighteen

F-16 Block 50/52 fighters purchased from the United States that began arriving in late 2014. As of this writing Iraq possesses no substantial striking power or strategic airlift capabilities and certainly nothing that would give it the ability to sustain offensive operations.[13]

Iraq remains mired in the bloody process of state building, which will further reduce its willingness and ability to deploy substantial power projection capabilities. A decade of vicious, overlapping ethnic and sectarian conflicts has not permanently resolved basic questions about the internal political order. Such wars often elevate ruthless risk takers, whose actions exacerbate the underlying sources of violence. Before his ouster in 2014, Prime Minister Nouri al-Maliki aggrandized power at the expense of his rivals, leading to increasing Sunni support for (or at least tolerance of) radical militants. Among other things, Maliki was criticized for inserting *dimaj* officers—really apparatchiks—into the ranks. These officers owed their allegiance to sectarian parties, and their principal function is to ensure that still-serving Sunni officers from the Ba'athist period do not act on any desire to restore their old power.[14] The prime minister's counterterrorism force gained a reputation for repression and secret violence against regime opponents.[15] While these methods helped keep Maliki in power, they also created new enemies for Baghdad and forced the Iraqi government to focus on internal security at the expense of regional politics for the indefinite future.

The government's intense security regime proved unable to stop the advance of IS militants or to prevent them from holding more than a quarter of Iraq's total territory. Indeed, the Iraqi army fell apart almost immediately as IS occupied several major Sunni cities and the Kurds took control of Kirkuk. The subsequent call to arms from Grand Ayatollah Ali al-Sistani led to a rapid mobilization of Shia fighters, and that, in turn, has prompted concerns that sectarian militias are replacing the national army.[16] The status quo today is a rough balance of power between the Shia-dominated areas in Baghdad and the south, the Sunni-dominated west, and the Kurdish north. The Iraqi civil war, now in its second decade, is far from over. Even if Iraqi officials respond to US calls for more inclusiveness, Sunnis will almost certainly fear that they face permanent persecution at the hands of the majority Shia population.

Meanwhile, much to the chagrin of the government, Kurdish leaders made a deal with Turkey for an oil and gas pipeline that would bypass Baghdad. They also independently invited foreign oil companies to work on Kurdish soil, infuriating the Maliki government. Driven together by IS, the Kurdish Regional Government and Baghdad reached an agreement on oil revenue sharing in December 2014, but the deal was tenuous and for months seemed to be on the verge of collapse.[17] These events, along with the recent seizure of Kirkuk, have convinced some observers that the Kurdish Regional Government might declare full independence in the next few years. This and other internal problems will dominate Iraq's attention for at least the next decade and rule out any dreams of Iraqi regional hegemony.[18]

Iraqi leaders, many of whom experienced the Iran-Iraq War and the Gulf War personally, may also feel chastened by that experience. In 1980 Iraq was arguably at the peak of its powers in terms of raw military capabilities, the Ba'ath regime had consolidated power, and the last Kurdish rebellion had been demolished. At that moment it faced off against revolutionary Iran, which was suffering from an ongoing civil violence, a serious economic crisis, and a purge of the officer corps. Despite it all, Iraq could not translate early battlefield victories into lasting success, and it fell into a war of attrition that wrecked the economy and took nearly a quarter million lives. Saddam Hussein acted on his dreams of regional predominance at a moment that seemed perfect for conquest, but the result showed the limits of Iraqi power projection even against a vulnerable neighbor. Given this experience and the dreadful state of Iraq's current conventional capabilities, it is highly unlikely that current leaders have any intention of trying again. Moreover, the next generation of Iraqi leaders will have no choice but to grapple with civil war and internal dysfunction. Necessity will force them to look inward and discourage thoughts of expansion.

Saudi Arabia

Simply by virtue of its vast oil wealth, Saudi Arabia is the second candidate for regional hegemony. It produces about 12 million barrels of crude oil per day, and Saudi leaders have recently speculated that the country could increase that number to 15 million. It also sits on 265 billion barrels of proven oil reserves—about one-fifth of the global total—and it has traditionally used its spare capacity to add or remove production to stabilize international markets.[19] All of this oil has led to astonishing state revenues. Saudi Arabia was a sparsely populated and impoverished state when oil was first discovered there in the 1930s. By the 1950s the kingdom was able to invest in a large number of social welfare and development projects. It also benefited greatly from the transformation of the global oil market in the late 1960s and early 1970s, as demand soared, prices skyrocketed, and Middle East producers were suddenly flush with cash.

But unlike some other Gulf states, Saudi leaders did not launch a massive military buildup. Instead, they outsourced their regional security needs to the United States while focusing on technology and imports. As a result, Saudi Arabia has built a very robust national defense but is in no position to project conventional military power in the region. In all likelihood it will continue to focus its attention on domestic problems and spend its considerable resources on regime stability while seeking to influence regional politics through proxies.

The exception is the kingdom's ongoing air war against Houthi rebels in neighboring Yemen. The air strikes began in March 2015, with logistics and intelligence support from the United States, but the campaign seems to have had little effect against the Houthis, who possess very modest air defenses.[20] This relatively minor effort to project airpower outside Saudi borders reveals the kingdom's inability to wage expeditionary warfare against comparable enemies with competent conventional forces.

Saudi Arabia's import strategy has allowed it to build a durable technological base for national defense. While Saudi forces are numerically inferior to those of Iran and Iraq, Saudi Arabia outspends both countries on Western weapons by a large margin. Annual defense spending in the kingdom is nearing $50 billion, which is more than four times what Iran can muster. Moreover, Riyadh has purchased a range of systems that directly offset Iranian weapons that might put its key facilities at risk, including Patriot advanced capability–3 (PAC-3) missile defense systems to ward off putative Iranian attacks on Saudi oil nodes and advanced fighters to maintain air superiority and put Iranian facilities at risk. Beyond sustaining the technological lead, Saudi investment clearly aims to deter any Iranian thoughts of aggression. As one analyst concluded in the wake of a recent massive arms buy from the United States, "The Saudi aim is to send a message especially to the Iranians—that we have complete aerial superiority over them."[21]

Saudi forces are organized for deterrence and defense. While not large, they are the richest and most technologically advanced in the Gulf, and they benefit from close relations with the United States, Great Britain, and France. The Royal Saudi Land Forces, which number only seventy-five thousand, comprise three armored brigades and five mechanized brigades. The force fields about three hundred M1A2 Abrams main battle tanks, with two hundred more in storage, and maintains more than a thousand surface-to-air missiles. According to the International Institute of Strategic Studies, the army and the Saudi Arabia National Guard are devoted to internal security and border defense. Recent purchases of American helicopters bolster the internal mission, but because Saudi Arabia lacks any logistical capability that would be needed for sustained cross-border operations, it is doubtful they could be used for power projection. The air force recently purchased advanced American- and European-made fighters, along with supporting equipment, munitions, and upgrades to existing aircraft. Together these purchases give it the ability to sustain air superiority over Gulf rivals indefinitely and to make their moving over Saudi territory extremely difficult.[22] The navy is geared toward maritime patrol, fielding three destroyers, four frigates, and thirty coastal ships. It also maintains a small number of modern mine countermeasure (MCM) ships and four older minesweepers.

The Saudi order of battle emphasizes deterrence by denial: Foreign forces are deterred from acting against a technologically sophisticated opponent with clear superiority on local soil. Even if US forces left the Gulf immediately, the weapons that the United States has already sold to the kingdom are likely to enable Saudi Arabia to sustain this posture through at least 2035. Its oil revenues will also allow it to buy many more.

However, domestic turmoil is likely to force the kingdom to continue focusing its security services on internal threats rather than on foreign wars. Following a surge in terrorist violence, it conducted an intense campaign against al-Qaeda in the Arabian Peninsula (AQAP) from 2003 to 2006. The Interior Ministry, writes terrorism analyst Thomas Hegghammer, "constructed state-of-the-art training facilities and electronic surveillance systems. The training of Special Forces was intensified with considerable assistance from the United Kingdom. CIA [Central Intelligence Agency] analysts and technical experts came to Riyadh to work side by side with their Saudi counterparts. Advances in technical surveillance gave the authorities de facto hegemony over the Internet, the telephone network and the road network."[23] In addition to this dragnet, Saudi Arabia offered two rounds of amnesty for AQAP members in 2004 and 2006, and the kingdom launched a public hearts and minds campaign to dampen popular enthusiasm for violent Islamism. But while these efforts were largely successful, Saudi officials remain concerned that AQAP has simply relocated to Yemen and from its base across the border may yet pose a threat to the regime. The Islamic State's claim of responsibility for the May 2015 mosque bombing in the port city of Dammam are likely to reinvigorate Saudi domestic counterterrorism efforts.[24]

The regime has also intensified counterintelligence in the Eastern Province, home to the majority of the country's Shia population and where low-level protests have been continuing for the last few years. News reports suggest that Saudi leaders see Iranian machinations behind the protests as part of the escalating proxy conflict between the two countries, and in 2013 Saudi Arabia arrested sixteen Shia individuals on allegations of spying.[25] More broadly the intensifying Iraqi civil war has also led to some concern about a deepening regional Shia-Sunni conflict, which might spill over into Saudi Arabia. Although how this might occur is not clear, the mere prospect of a restive Shia population in the oil-rich area will almost certainly be enough to convince Saudi leaders to pay close attention. They may also increase countrywide efforts after reports that jihadists have been using the events in Iraq to recruit new supporters in their campaign against the Saudi ruling family.[26]

Finally, the regime reacted quickly to the Arab Spring protests to preempt any similar uprising in the kingdom. In February and March 2011, King Abdullah announced $100 billion in new spending, which included raises for state workers, many more new state jobs, and cancellations to planned cuts in state subsidies.[27] This episode is evidence not only that the Al-Saud family can still use extraordinary oil revenues to shore up its position but also that it remains extremely sensitive to domestic opposition. Until this priority changes, it is unlikely to think seriously about power projection beyond its already vast territory.

Iran

Internal problems and external pressures have repeatedly interrupted the historically slow growth of Iranian conventional power. Its current capabilities are far short of what would be required if it had any hopes of winning and consolidating power in a major regional war. Moreover, it continues to suffer from acute domestic political problems that will force it to look inward for the foreseeable future.

Despite ambitions to transform Iran into a formidable regional power, the shah of Iran was unable to develop any serious power projection capabilities for most of the 1950s and '60s. Part of the problem was a lack of revenue for procurement and operations until the oil boom of the early 1970s. Iran could muster only $1.5 billion for new weapons from 1950 to 1972.[28] It could barely maintain the small forces it cobbled together in the postwar period, a problem that internal political crises exacerbated. A major power struggle in the early 1950s led to massive defense budget cuts and a purge of the officer corps. The army recovered over the next decade, but it was unable to start thinking about power projection until after 1965. While the size of the regular army grew to about 200,000 by the end of the 1960s, Iran lacked a reliable mobilization system for reservists. Until the mid-1960s the small air force concentrated on air defense and close air support, and the navy, for its part, was "virtually ignored."[29]

The oil boom dramatically reversed the fortunes of the Iranian military. In 1970 the total defense budget was $900 million. In 1977 it had risen to $9.4 billion, and all the services benefited. Sudden wealth allowed the army to buy weapons, including US and Soviet armored personnel carriers, modern rifles, machine guns, and antitank guided missiles, at breakneck speed from the United States and other Western suppliers. Iranian armor, which previously relied on older US tanks, received more than two thousand new British Chieftain main battle tanks to counter the Soviet tanks operating in Iraq. A new army aviation command operated 220 helicopter gunships and nearly 400 other helicopters for a variety of missions, all of which led to significant improvements in air mobility. The

Iranian air force also expanded, purchasing modern aircraft and in-flight refueling capabilities. And the Iranian navy grew in parallel. According to Iranian military analyst Steven Ward, "Iran's naval forces were more than large enough to ensure Iran's dominance of the Persian Gulf littoral."[30]

During the 1970s Iran relied on imports while simultaneously pursuing an import substitution strategy in the hopes that it would be able to indigenously design and build modern weapons in time. The Iranian Islamic Revolution interrupted this process, and while Iran vastly expanded its defense industry as a result of its war with Iraq, what it produced tended to be of lower quality, especially in terms of the platforms required to project power.

Decades of international pressure since the fall of the shah have exacted a high toll on Iranian military power. The continuing embargo against Iran has exacerbated old problems, while the ongoing currency and inflation crisis hinders its ability to generate new capabilities. Moreover, the combined defense budgets of the Arab states vastly exceed Iran's, despite its much larger population. Iran's total defense budget of $10 billion–$11 billion is less than a quarter of what Saudi Arabia spends. Its procurement budget of a little more than $3 billion is about the same as procurement spending in the United Arab Emirates (UAE), which incidentally has launched a major program to acquire sea, air, and missile defense systems in order to counter Iran.

Like Iraq, Iran relies on an increasingly outdated arsenal, and its efforts to retain readiness have probably forced it to cannibalize parts from other systems. This problem is especially acute for the Iranian air force, which struggles to maintain its fleet of 1970s-era US and European aircraft. Iran announced that it had begun work on the indigenous Azarakhsh (Lightning) fighter in 1997, but the Iranian press only reported the first flight test in 2007. How many fighters have been produced is unclear.[31] Similarly, Iran's effort to produce an indigenous attack aircraft, the Shafagh (Twilight), is stagnant. And apart from its effort to develop tactical transport aircraft with Ukrainian assistance, Iran has very little lift capability. Beyond these technical limitations, Iran also suffers from severe shortages of skilled technicians and pilots.[32]

The Iranian army is also struggling. Of the 350,000 troops in the regular army, more than two-thirds are conscripts. About 125,000 soldiers make up the more professional land forces of the Iranian Revolutionary Guard Corps. On paper the army appears impressive, organized into four armored divisions, two mechanized divisions, and four infantry divisions, but like the air force, it relies on very old technology. Most Iranian armor consists of old Eastern Bloc T-72 and T-55 main battle tanks along with some US M60A1 Pattons. In 1994 Iran announced that it would begin producing the indigenous Zulfiqar main battle tank; however, not only did the design suspiciously resemble a modified T-72, but also its self-propelled howitzers were based on Soviet designs.[33]

None of this is to say that Iran will avoid meddling in neighboring countries; rather, it will likely rely on asymmetric means to do so. In 2015 the terrible state of its conventional military means that it cannot project military power, and the depths of its economic crisis will not enable it to rebuild power projection capabilities for at least twenty years. The Iranian government issued an ambitious twenty-year economic program in 2005, but the economy has been under increasing strain since that time, with unemployment and inflation adding fuel to protests against the regime. In addition to the increasingly onerous effects of the Western sanctions regime, Iran also suffers from numerous political and ideological roadblocks to recovery and will continue to struggle even if the West lifts sanctions as part of the deal to rein in Iran's nuclear program.[34] The deal reportedly lifts the freeze on about $100 billion in Iranian assets, but a large percentage of those assets is either committed to nondefense-related international projects or is in the form of nonperforming loans held by Iranian banks.[35] Thus, rather than trying to rebuild the industrial and logistical capacity to project conventional military power, Iran will try to influence politics by cultivating sympathetic officials and by supporting non-state proxy groups.

Similarly, it has invested primarily in assets designed to make life difficult for naval vessels and commercial ships operating in the Gulf rather than funding the capabilities necessary for large-scale amphibious or ground operations. During the 2000s, for instance, it focused on missiles and unmanned aerial vehicles, though some analysts suggested that the latter were technologically unsophisticated drones.[36] Iran now has a large arsenal of short-range ballistic missiles as well as a growing indigenous production capability. Though its missiles are reported to be quite inaccurate, Iranian leaders may hope that they can saturate a small area such as the Strait of Hormuz to disrupt and deter shipping.[37] Finally, Iran has invested heavily in a variety of mines, all of which might be used if it decides to make good on its periodic threat to close the Strait.

In short, Iran lacks the capabilities needed to make a bid for regional hegemony, and its procurement behavior suggests that Iranian leaders realize this situation. Instead of acquiring the hardware necessary to seize and hold large chunks of territory, it has procured what it believes is required to gain coercive power by threatening the flow of oil. Even if Iran changed direction immediately and decided to invest in the capabilities required to project power, it would take many years to translate that investment into a functional capability. In the meantime, such a conspicuous change in Iran's buying habits would lead Saudi Arabia to redouble its own defensive effort. And because the Saudis have much deeper pockets, the net result of Iran's military buildup would be a *decline* in relative power versus that of its rival.

The other main reason Iran is unlikely to expand in the Persian Gulf region is that it faces enduring domestic problems that will force the regime to focus a great deal of its attention inward. Persians, the majority ethnic group, only account for a little more than half of the country's population. The government has mostly tamped down sectarian and ethnic controversies by successfully combining Shia Islam with nationalism.[38] However, since 2003 a Sunni Balochi movement has been orchestrating violent attacks, including one in 2009 that killed six Iranian Revolutionary Guard Corps commanders.[39] Similarly, while the regime has successfully exiled most of the opposition groups that present a possible challenge to its rule, the Mujahedeen-e-Khalq continues to operate from Iraq and has attracted high-level supporters in the United States and Europe. In 2012 Secretary of State Hillary Clinton removed the group from the State Department's list of designated terrorist organizations, fueling suspicions in Tehran that the United States sought to use it against the Islamic Republic.[40]

The 2009 Green Revolution revealed potentially bigger problems. Mass protests against alleged vote rigging devolved into broader criticisms of the Islamic Republic. Most Iranians are too young to remember the Islamic Revolution and are not imbued with its revolutionary fervor. Indeed, the hallmark of the Green Revolution was the open disdain that youthful protestors showed toward the government, which they accused of corruption, nepotism, and gross mismanagement of the economy. Although the regime successfully cracked down against the opposition, the protests undoubtedly caused alarm among those regime officials who are on guard against dissent, especially in the current context of economic stagnation. Iran is likely to focus its security activities inward for all these reasons, whatever its pretentions about exporting its revolution.

Of course, policymakers have long been concerned that Iran might acquire a modest arsenal of nuclear weapons. They worry that Iran's possession of even a handful of these weapons might encourage Tehran to become more aggressive in the region, given that the United States would be more hesitant to interfere. What are the implications of a nuclear-armed Iran on the foregoing analysis?

First, a nuclear-armed Iran would still have an impoverished conventional military. Acquiring nuclear capabilities may give Iran false optimism and encourage aggressive behavior, but it will find expanding and holding ground difficult. Second, it is not clear that a nuclear-armed Iran would seek to use nuclear weapons as cover for conventional military offensives. It may be encouraged to continue supporting its proxies in the region without fearing retaliation from the United States or other powers. Third, Iranian leaders might simply acquire nuclear weapons to improve national security and to deter attacks and not have any intention of trying to translate nuclear possession into political power.

In addition, the United States has the ability to deter Iran from using nuclear weapons as cover for aggression by improving the local conventional balance of power. Bolstering local allies, who already enjoy a substantial technological advantage over Iran, is likely to send a clear signal about the futility of aggression. Iran's nuclear posturing has already led its neighbors to call for security guarantees from the United States, and Washington has been eager to comply through arms sales and promises of US support.[41]

In sum, whether or not the United States exits the scene, the chance that any regional power will try to establish hegemony in the Persian Gulf is vanishingly small. None of the three possible hegemons has the military capability to become a hegemonic contender, and all of them face serious internal security problems. Iraq, Saudi Arabia, and Iran—all are likely to continue competing in the region, but the nature of that competition will not include a large-scale land grab that would put oil security in doubt.

Why There Will Not Be a Major Regional War

The outbreak of a major regional war if the United States withdraws from the Gulf represents a second serious concern. Unlike a regional hegemon, which could manipulate the flow of oil to coerce or punish oil-importing states, a major regional war could inadvertently threaten global oil markets by severely damaging the region's oil infrastructure and by making the transportation of oil too dangerous. The implicit logic of an enduring presence is that visible US capabilities deter regional states from initiating hostilities against one or more of their rivals. Knowing that the United States has stated its commitment to "security and stability" in the Gulf for more than three decades, and fearful of challenging a vastly superior American conventional force, would-be aggressors have no choice but to put aside their regional ambitions. If US forces left, however, what would deter these states from giving war a chance?

In fact, there is very little chance of major war breaking out and largely for the same reason there is no regional hegemon: None of the possible aspirants has the ability to sustain large-scale offensive operations. Unless a power resolves its internal problems and successfully builds power projection capabilities, the chance of a major regional war will remain very low.

Major war is also unlikely because the regional powers, despite their obvious weaknesses, have the ability to deter each other. Saudi Arabia can rely on deterrence by denial because it is now so densely defended that any large-scale attempt to destroy its forces and occupy its territory would almost surely fail. Even if Iran made initial gains, holding on to new territory would be exceedingly difficult given both its own logistical shortcomings and the necessity of having to rule over a majority-Sunni and inherently hostile population. Iran, however, does have significant defensive advantages that protect it against a large land invasion. It has the largest land forces in the region and can count on favorable geography to discourage would-be attackers from launching major conventional operations. (The last to try was Saddam Hussein in 1980, after Iraq had engaged in a huge military buildup, and Iran was reeling from the Islamic Revolution. Today Saddam is dead, and the Iraqi military is decimated.) Iran can also fall back on deterrence by punishment, given its growing arsenal of ballistic missiles. While these weapons are not particularly accurate, Iran would not need to be precise if it only sought retaliation.

The most vulnerable state is Iraq. As described previously, Iraq's military is still rebuilding after a decade of civil war, and the central government has not been able to consolidate its rule over the Sunnis in the west or the Kurds in the north. Internal fractures may weaken Iraq, which does not enjoy the natural obstacles that protect Iran and Saudi Arabia. Thus, it may not be able to deter aggression either by denial or punishment. That said, Iraq's neighbors are very aware of the costs of occupying the country, having witnessed the painful US experience of the last decade. Given these costs and their lack of power projection capabilities to act anyway, they more likely will continue to use proxy groups in Iraq to wage a low-level proxy war against one another.

Another way of forecasting the likelihood of a conventional war is to measure the offense-defense balance among the possible combatants. Offense-defense theory predicts that war will be more likely when conquest is relatively easy.[42] But in each of the relevant dyads—Iran and Iraq, Iran and Saudi Arabia, and Iraq and Saudi Arabia—the defense is dominant and will remain so indefinitely. Deterrence is likely to hold under these conditions because defenders can deny easy conquest to challengers, and none of the key states in the region are likely to launch a major war when the costs of offensive action are extremely high relative to the costs of defense.

The *offense-defense balance* is "the ratio of the cost of the forces that the attacker requires to take territory to the cost of the defender's forces."[43] Measuring the ratio between any two states requires assessing a host of factors. Technology may enable mobility and thus rapid offensive maneuver. Firepower, however, tends to make exposed offensive forces especially vulnerable. Geography will usually favor the defense if natural barriers inhibit or channelize offensive forces while providing cover for defenders, especially if offensive forces need to travel long distances that stretch out supply lines and make coordinating operations more difficult. Favorable force-to-force and force-to-space ratios may enable offensive operations, but they will face serious difficulty if they come up against dense defenses. Nonmaterial factors also complicate offensive action. A strong sense of nationalism, for example, will cause defenders to make tremendous sacrifices in defense of their home territory even against long odds.[44]

Defense dominates the Iran-Iraq dyad for a number of reasons. Geographic features, including the Zagros Mountains and the Shatt al-'Arab, are natural barriers to sustained large-scale offensives, but admittedly Iraq is less well protected. Both countries enjoy substantial depth, and neither can expect to acquire the kind of capabilities needed for large-scale maneuver. Finally, nationalism is very strong in both countries and offsets the sectarian solidarity among the Shia in both countries. Despite the internal fissures in both countries, leaders in Baghdad and Tehran have been successful in rallying support by playing on nationalism. In Iran, for instance, the government has gained support from across the political spectrum for its nuclear program by appealing to the popular notion that it is a symbol of national technological prowess.[45] Sectarianism threatens nationalism in Iraq, though, interestingly, some sects have chosen to use Iraqi nationalist symbols to rally supporters. Indeed, even those Shia leaders who received great criticism for sectarianism have also proven hostile toward outside powers. Prime Minister Maliki was "no puppet of Iran," according to Kenneth Pollack. "In his own way, he [was] a staunch Iraqi nationalist and, like most Iraqi Shiites, appears to dislike the Iranians more than he likes them."[46] While external powers are able to exploit sectarian fissures through proxies, the enduring sense of nationalism in Iran and Iraq places limits on their ability to act overtly.

Mutual hostility and distrust characterize relations between Iran and Saudi Arabia, but geography and technology strongly favor the defense as large land buffers (Iraq and Kuwait) and a large sea buffer (the Gulf itself) separate the two countries. Any Iranian attempt to mobilize for war would require such preparations to overcome those barriers that they would be easy to spot. Moreover, technology favors the defense. Saudi investments in air defense, missile defense, early warning radar, and air power all counterbalance Iran's advantages in mass. Saudi Arabia has spent so lavishly on defense, in fact, that it now "ranks among the world's most densely armed nations, and it has ambitious plans to further upgrade its arsenal."[47] This balance is likely to hold indefinitely, especially given the sanctions regime and Iran's crippling currency problem. Even if Iran were able to legally import the kinds of technologies that could seriously threaten Saudi Arabia's defensive advantages, it might not be able to afford them.

The Iraq–Saudi Arabia dyad is somewhat different. With far fewer geographic barriers to offensive action, Iraq posed a threat to Saudi Arabia in 1990 after it quickly conquered Kuwait. Moreover, because abundant oil fields are located in southeastern Iraq, in theory Riyadh could profit greatly from limited offensives designed to seize and hold that territory rather than having to conquer vast stretches of land. But as Saudi Arabia is already concerned about instability in the restive majority-Shia Eastern Province, why would it believe that it could occupy the Rumaila oil fields around Shia-dominated Basra? Technological factors also make offensive actions costly and make defensive actions cheap. Contemporary offensive operations against a well-funded defender require armor, air forces to protect them, mechanized infantry to rapidly move troops, a command-and-control infrastructure, and intelligence, surveillance, and reconnaissance (ISR) to keep tabs on the enemy. Iraq has none of these things. As a result, it could only hope to achieve offensive successes against a very weak defender.

The southern Gulf states, which sit on large oil reserves, are inherently vulnerable due to their size and limited manpower. In this sense they do not enjoy the obvious defensive benefits of their larger neighbors. Nonetheless, it is unlikely that any of them are at risk of a major offensive à la Iraq's conquest of Kuwait in 1990. The destruction of Iraqi military power has removed the main conventional threat to their sovereignty, and Tehran has replaced Baghdad as the focus of their attention. While Iran enjoys a considerable advantage in personnel—it can boast more than 500,000 men in uniform compared to about 70,000 for the UAE and fewer than 20,000 for Kuwait—the Gulf states have attempted to make up for their quantitative weaknesses through cash and qualitative superiority. The UAE's defense budget is roughly equal to Iran's, and total defense spending in the Gulf Cooperation Council (GCC), even excluding Saudi Arabia, is much higher. Arms sales and military assistance from the United States have given the Gulf states access to technologies that are far superior to those of their Iranian counterparts. In addition, they have specifically invested in the kind of systems to offset areas of particular concern. For instance, both the UAE and Kuwait have acquired PAC-3 missile defense systems in response to Iranian investment in ballistic missiles, and Qatar and the UAE have also contracted to buy two terminal high-altitude area defense batteries.[48]

The major problem for the Gulf states is their reluctance to coordinate military actions. The GCC is notoriously riven, and mutual mistrust among the smaller states, as well as lingering fear of Saudi domination, inhibits full cooperation. Nonetheless, the shared fear of Iranian meddling has increased in the last few years, especially after the Shia uprising in Bahrain in 2011. The belief that Iran instigated the uprising triggered balancing among the Gulf states and declarations of resolve to strengthen cooperation.[49] The United States has encouraged this trend, and some American analysts have called for GCC reforms to make it a deeper and more durable security body.[50] The combination of wealth, technology, and balancing is likely to restore the Gulf states' defensive position, especially given Iraq's dysfunction and Iran's limitations.

While defensive advantages reduce the risk of major conventional war in the Persian Gulf, relations between these states are likely to remain fraught. Long-standing grievances, old disputes, sectarian and nationalist conflicts, and security competition characterize the politics of the Gulf. Thus, even though major war is unlikely, the pattern of proxy fights among non-state actors, covert operations, and harassment is likely to continue indefinitely.[51] US forces in the Gulf could do little to prevent these actions; indeed, the covert war between Iran and Saudi Arabia heated up after the United States occupied Iraq and stationed more than 200,000 troops in the region. That the proxy war escalated during the US forces' presence in the region suggests that the nature of the conflict would not dramatically change even if the United States withdrew completely.

Why the Risk to Oil Shipping Will Increase

Every day about 17 million barrels of oil, or about 20 percent of global demand, transit the Strait of Hormuz. Almost all of the oil from the Persian Gulf region reaches international markets on twenty enormous tankers that go through the Strait each day, passing in both directions through a shipping lane only four miles wide at its narrowest point. The Strait is widely recognized as a critical choke point for energy supplies, and there is great concern that attacks on shipping in the Strait could have serious consequences for the global economy. In addition to the sudden drop in the supply of oil, a successful attack would inhibit Saudi Arabia from using its spare capacity to soften the blow. Unless and until exporters build substantial overland alternatives for getting oil to market, the security of the Strait will remain an enduring concern.

But analysts remain divided over Iran's ability to inhibit the flow of oil by cutting off traffic at the Strait of Hormuz, either by attacking shipping directly or by making the area so dangerous that tankers are deterred from making the trip. Some argue that the threat is overblown, given the numerous practical problems involved in any attempt to inhibit shipping. In addition, because shipping companies have proven remarkably risk acceptant even in high-threat areas—and willing to pay higher shipping insurance rates, as they did during the Tanker War in the 1980s—Iran would have to physically disable tankers rather than simply deter them from making a run through the Strait.[52]

Iran has a number of options for attacking tanker traffic in the Gulf. Analysts worry most about the use of shore-based missiles, fast boat attacks, or mines; all might pose a serious threat to large and slow-moving targets transiting predictable routes in a narrow shipping channel. Eugene Gholz and members of his policy research project, however, argue that Iran will face enormous operational challenges if it attempts to attack Gulf shipping using any of these weapons. Target identification will be essential for missile or fast boat attacks, but Iranian spotters will find it difficult because of the sandstorms, the dust, and the blurred vision caused by the extreme heat in the Gulf. Assuming that tankers cut off all electronic emissions during high-threat periods, Iran will necessarily have to rely on visual identification, and distinguishing tankers from other vessels might be problematic. Target interception will be tough should Iran choose to attack via small suicide boats. To do so they will have to navigate the very large bow wave of huge tankers, and this problem has stymied pirates who have targeted large vessels. Gholz and his group also estimate that a concerted Iranian mining effort would disable no more than twenty tankers over the course of a whole campaign, and that number would not significantly affect the oil market. Most Iranian mines, they also note, are old and unreliable. Iran does possess more than a thousand newer models, but that number is actually quite small to seed the Strait, which includes a twenty-mile-wide path of navigable water at its narrowest point. And even if they are struck, modern tankers—double-hulled behemoths that are more than three hundred meters long—are very hard to sink. Apart from their sheer size, they come equipped with various safety measures to protect the ships against catastrophic fire even if struck by small boats, missiles, or mines.[53]

Pessimists note that given a substantial share of the world's oil transits the Gulf, even a temporary blockage could have very serious economic effects. The geography of the Gulf could allow Iran to effectively deny access to external powers that might otherwise intervene to protect shipping. The Gulf offers Iran the ability to operate on interior lines and with short lines of communication. These factors would not only permit small boats and fast-attack craft to engage and disengage quickly but also enable a variety of vessels to lay mines without being noticed. Very short times might also allow Iran's mobile missile batteries to "shoot and scoot," making them less vulnerable to counterbattery fire, and their extensive knowledge of the geography of the coast would enable opportunities to hide. Pessimists also note that Iran has invested heavily in mines, antiship cruise missiles, and naval facilities along the coast. All of these capabilities could be put to use in attempts to cut off oil exports. Iran's procurement pattern, along with fears that it will equip non-state proxies and coordinate their efforts, suggests that it can pose a serious threat to shipping via conventional strikes and suicide attacks.

At a minimum it can make navigating the Strait so risky that foreign navies and shipping companies will think twice about entering the Gulf.[54]

These fears are overstated. As Caitlin Talmadge points out, despite Iranian investments, the United States continues to enjoy a substantial technological advantage, especially in its ability to target Iranian missile sites ashore. The US Navy is also capable of mine clearance, and in 2007 Talmadge estimated that depending on the nature of the attack, a comprehensive mine-clearing operation in the wake of an Iranian effort to close the Strait would take twenty-eight to forty days. A parallel effort to counter Iranian antiship cruise missile capabilities would require nine to seventy-two days. The total time required would be approximately one to four months if counter-mine and counter-missile efforts were conducted in tandem.[55]

Talmadge's estimate, however, was based on the assumption that the United States still maintained a sizable military presence in the Gulf. This presence offers at least four major benefits in terms of keeping oil flowing. First, access to land bases in the Gulf region provides air bases for high-altitude, persistent ISR. Second, only land bases have runways long enough to service refueling tankers, which may be necessary for a sustained air campaign against Iran's shore. Third, access to naval bases provides a home for dedicated MCM ships. Keeping these slow-moving ships docked at Fifth Fleet Headquarters in Bahrain will make it easier to rapidly begin mine-clearing efforts in the event that Iran tries to close the Strait. Maintaining the MCMs' presence will be necessary at least until Saudi Arabia demonstrates that it can independently handle such operations. Fourth, access to bases provides the logistical skeleton to surge more forces in later if necessary.[56]

The United States would sacrifice this infrastructure if it completely severed its military commitment to the Gulf. This withdrawal, in turn, would make deterrence harder because Iran might not be convinced that any force could deny its ability to close the Strait. Unlike the other scenarios described in this chapter, the threat to oil shipping would increase significantly in the absence of US forces. Although Iran would still face serious operational hurdles if it launched an attack on oil, they would be much easier to overcome if Iranian planners did not have to anticipate a rapid US response. Iranian missile operators could be much more deliberate and precise if they did not have to fear counter-missile attacks. Iranian maritime forces could likewise lay down much larger minefields if they did not need to act quickly and covertly. Attacking oil shipping will remain a very difficult challenge, to be sure, and skeptics are right to point out that several mechanisms allow the oil market to bounce back quickly after shocks: rerouting shipping, increasing production elsewhere, and tapping into countries' strategic petroleum reserves to soften the blow in the event of any turmoil in the Gulf.[57] But the more that Iran is able to act with a free hand against shipping, the more stress will be put on those mechanisms. Rerouting tankers in dangerous waters is a great deal easier when they enjoy the protection of naval forces. And while we should expect to see increasing production and the use of oil reserves, these steps may not do much in the short term, especially if Saudi Arabia is physically unable to play its traditional role of stabilizer by increasing production and getting it to market.

For these reasons, a visible US force remains necessary both to deter Iran from acting on its threats against oil traffic and to mitigate the consequences if deterrence fails. This does not mean, however, that the United States must rebuild its presence in the Gulf to its 1990s-era force level. Quite the contrary, the requirements for ensuring the flow of oil are quite modest. Enormous advantages in US intelligence, communications, speed, and precision mean that it can safely station most of its surface fleet away from the Gulf and count on early warning to bring it back if Iran begins to move against the Strait.[58]

Conclusion

The United States has already removed the bulk of its forces from the Persian Gulf region. US end strength in the region peaked at more than 230,000 in December 2008. Four years later it was down to about 50,000.[59] But while the scale of the drawdown is noteworthy, the actual effects on the Gulf balance and the flow of oil are not particularly important. No regional power will have the wherewithal to launch a bid for regional hegemony, and in any case the only possible candidates for regional expansion are riven with domestic fissures that will force them to look inward. Deterrence against major conventional war is also likely to hold both because the likely combatants benefit from technology and geography that favor the defense and because neither has shown any indication that they seek to build meaningful power projection capabilities. Over the last several years the politics among the major Gulf powers have become increasingly ugly, and they have clashed via proxies in Iraq, Syria, and Yemen. But they have not chosen conventional war and have tried to keep their roles covert. This suggests they fully understand the regional balance of power and the limits of their military capabilities.

The rise of the Islamic State has deepened the humanitarian disaster in Syria and Iraq and complicated any effort at achieving a durable political settlement in either country. But it has had little effect on Gulf oil. IS captured territory in eastern Syria and northern and western Iraq, far from the huge proven oil reserves of the Gulf. The large and hostile Kurdish population in northern Iraq and the

Shia population in the south have inhibited its ability to press farther. Indeed, one of the chief problems facing IS is that it is surrounded by people who hate it. Whatever its grandiose ambitions, it remains trapped in a natural containment regime that includes Syria, Turkey, Iran, Iraq, and Saudi Arabia. All of these actors will inhibit IS's outward expansion and, in so doing, limit its ability to affect the movement of oil to market.

Iran presents a more plausible threat, and its ability to put oil at risk will increase if the United States removes its dedicated MCM ships and dismantles its ISR and logistics infrastructure in the Gulf. The good news is that the United States can forestall this possibility by sustaining a light footprint, much as the British did in the 1950s and '60s. During that time Great Britain played the role of stabilizer in the Gulf, deterring would-be regional hegemons and otherwise ensuring that oil continued to flow, but it did so on the cheap. The Royal Navy routinely deployed ships to the Gulf, and the air force operated from bases in Bahrain and Sharjah, but the total British land presence was only about six thousand men. The logic behind Great Britain's approach was that it could intervene in force as long as it could count on prepositioned equipment and reliable warning intelligence. As a result, it avoided the financial and political cost of maintaining a large and visible foreign force. Moreover, Great Britain was able to draw down its force because the security environment was relatively benign. With the possible exception of Iraq in the 1960s, no regional power had the ability to seriously threaten a large-scale land invasion.[60]

The situation today is similar. Although states such as Saudi Arabia have invested in huge arms buildups, the regional powers are all oriented around deterrence and defense. None poses a serious challenge to the other's oil facilities, nor can any power plausibly threaten to make a land grab that would leave it in control of so much oil that it could affect global markets by withholding supply. And like the British, the United States enjoys substantial advantages in ISR and speed. As long as it commits to maintaining a modest base structure in the Gulf, it can use these advantages to deter attempts to interrupt the flow of oil or, if deterrence fails, rapidly defeat them. In short, it can sustain an inconspicuous force posture that ensures access to Gulf oil indefinitely and at a relatively low cost.

Notes

1. The other most commonly cited threat to oil security is intrastate disruptions. Thomas Lippman covers that issue in chapter 4 of this volume. Here I focus on interstate concerns.

2. Holly Ellyatt, "Global Oil Demand to Slow in 2016: IEA," CNBC.com, July 10, 2015, http://www.cnbc.com/2015/07/10/global-oil-demand-to-slow-in-2016-iea.html.

3. On modern Iraq's early military stumbles, see Timothy D. Hoyt, "Iraq's Military Industry: A Critical Strategic Target," *National Security Studies Quarterly* 4, no. 2 (Spring 1998): 33–50; Chaim Herzog, *The Arab-Israeli Wars: War and Peace in the Middle East*, rev. ed. (New York: Vantage Books, 2005); Kenneth M. Pollack, *Arabs at War: Military Effectiveness, 1948–1991* (Lincoln: University of Nebraska Press, 2002); and Timothy D. Hoyt, *Military Industry and Regional Defense Policy: India, Iraq, and Israel* (London: Routledge, 2007).

4. International Institute for Strategic Studies (IISS), *The Military Balance, 1968–1969* (London: IISS, 1969), 43; and IISS, *The Military Balance, 1978–1979* (London: IISS, 1979), 37.

5. Anthony H. Cordesman and Abraham R. Wagner, *Lessons of Modern War*, vol. 2, *The Iran-Iraq War* (Boulder CO: Westview Press, 1990), 46.

6. Anthony H. Cordesman, *The Gulf and the Search for Strategic Stability: Saudi Arabia, the Military Balance in the Gulf, and Trends in the Arab-Israeli Military Balance* (Boulder CO: Westview Press, 1984), 398–99.

7. Pollack, *Arabs at War*, 182; and IISS, *Military Balance, 1978–1979*, 38.

8. See Anthony H. Cordesman's briefing book, *The Conventional Military Balance in the Gulf in 2000* (Washington DC: Center for Strategic and International Studies, 2000), 80, http://csis.org/files/media/csis/pubs/gulfbalance2000[1].pdf.

9. Ibid., 81.

10. George A. Lopez and David Cortright, "Containing Iraq: Sanctions Worked," *Foreign Affairs* 83, no. 4 (July–August 2004): 90–103.

11. IISS, *The Military Balance, 2011* (London: IISS, 2011), 309.

12. "Ground Forces—Order of Battle—1991 Desert Storm," Global Security.org, http://www.globalsecurity.org/military/world/iraq/orbat-ground-91.htm.

13. IISS, *Military Balance 2011*, 308–28. Iraq has reportedly made a second purchase in order to bring its inventory up to thirty-six jets. "Iraq Says Signed Contract for 18 F-16 Fighter Jets," Reuters, October 18, 2012, http://www.reuters.com/article/2012/10/18/us-iraq-military-jets-idUSBRE89H14B20121018#Wde3eEcAR4WzjTBR.97.

14. As the army increasingly focused on coup proofing, it became less competent as a fighting force, and this situation partly explains why it broke down so quickly in the face of the recent Sunni militant onslaught. Keren Fraiman, Austin Long, and Caitlin Talmadge, "Why the Iraqi Army Collapsed (and What Can Be Done about It)," *Washington Post* (online), June 13, 2014, https://www.washingtonpost.com/news/monkey-cage/wp/2014/06/13/why-the-iraqi-army-collapsed-and-what-can-be-done-about-it/.

15. On Maliki's methods, see Yochi J. Dreazen, "Strong Man," *National Journal*, October 13, 2011; and Kenneth M. Pollack, "Reading Machiavelli in Baghdad," *The National Interest*, November–December 2012, http://nationalinterest.org/article/reading-machiavelli-iraq-7611?page=show.

16. US secretary of defense Ashton Carter has criticized the Iraqi army for lacking the will to fight. Others believe the Iraqi army is a fiction. See Barry Posen, "The Iraqi Army No Longer Exists," *Defense One*, June 7, 2015, http://www.defenseone.com/ideas/2015/06/iraqi-army-no-longer-exists/114607/.

17. Matt Bradley, "Iraq, Kurdistan Oil Deal Close to Collapse," *Wall Street Journal,* July 3, 2015.

18. On Iraq's severe internal problems, see Henri J. Barkey, "Spinoff: The Syrian Crisis and the Future of Iraq," *The American Interest,* December 26, 2012, http://www.the-american-interest.com/2012/12/26/spinoff-the-syrian-crisis-and-the-future-of-iraq.

19. US Energy Information Administration, "Saudi Arabia Country Analysis Brief," February 26, 2013, http://www.eia.gov/beta/international/country.cfm?iso=SAU.

20. Saudi Arabia claimed to have destroyed Yemen's major defenses, which had been previously captured by the Houthis, in late March. Some antiaircraft artillery was visible around the capital in mid-April. See Alan Taylor, "The Saudi Arabia–Yemen War of 2015," *The Atlantic,* May 7, 2015, http://www.theatlantic.com/photo/2015/05/the-saudi-arabia-yemen-war-of-2015/392687/.

21. Roula Khalaf and James Drummond, "Gulf States in $123bn US Arms Spree," *Financial Times,* September 20, 2010.

22. IISS, *Military Balance, 2011,* 311–15.

23. Thomas Hegghammer, "The Failure of Jihad in Saudi Arabia," Occasional Paper (West Point: Combating Terrorism Center, February 2010), 18.

24. Lizzie Dearden, "Saudi Arabia Mosque Bombing: Isis Suicide Bomber 'Disguised as Woman' Targets Shias," *The Independent* (UK), May 29, 2015.

25. "Saudi Arabia Shi'a Leaders Criticise Arrests," BBC News, March 21, 2013, http://www.bbc.co.uk/news/world-middle-east-21876520.

26. Glen Carey and Deema Almashabi, "Jihadi Recruitment in Riyadh Revives Saudi Arabia's Greatest Concern," *Bloomberg* (online), June 16, 2014, http://www.bloomberg.com/news/2014-06-15/jihadis-recruitment-drive-in-riyadh-revives-biggest-saudi-threat.

27. F. Gregory Gause, III, "Why Middle East Studies Missed the Arab Spring," *Foreign Affairs* 90, no. 4 (July–August 2011): 81–90, 87.

28. Steven R. Ward, *Immortal: A Military History of Iran and Its Armed Forces* (Washington DC: Georgetown University Press, 2009), 193–94.

29. Ibid., 186–87. Iran's regular army achieved the shah's goal by the end of the 1970s, when it numbered 285,000 active-duty troops.

30. Ibid., 199.

31. "Iran: Weapons: Azarakhsh," Globalsecurity.org, http://www.globalsecurity.org/military/world/iran/azarakhsh.htm.

32. Anthony Cordesman and Martin Kleiber, *Iran's Military Forces and Warfighting Capabilities* (Washington DC: Center for Strategic and International Studies, 2007), 41.

33. Information Handling Service (IHS), "Iran," in *Jane's World Defence Industry,* 2014.

34. Jahangir Amuzegar, "Iran's 20-Year Economic Perspective: Promises and Pitfalls," *Middle East Policy* 16, no. 3 (2009), http://mepc.org/journal/middle-east-policy-archives/irans-20-year-economic-perspective-promises-and-pitfalls.

35. Eric Pianin, "Lew: Iran Not Getting the Full $100 Billion of Frozen Assets," *The Fiscal Times,* July 26, 2015, http://www.thefiscaltimes.com/2015/07/26/Lew-Iran-Not-Getting-Full-100-Billion-Frozen-Assets.

36. IHS, "Iran."

37. Mark Gunzinger and Chris Dougherty, *Outside-In: Operating from Range to Defeat Iran's Anti-Access and Area-Denial Threats* (Washington DC: Center for Strategic and Budgetary Assessments, 2011), 33–38.

38. Keith Crane, Rollie Lal, and Jeffrey Martini, *Iran's Political, Demographic, and Economic Vulnerabilities* (Santa Monica CA: RAND, 2008).

39. Roger Hardy, "Profile: Iran's Jundullah Militants," BBC News, June 20, 2010, http://news.bbc.co.uk/2/hi/middle_east/8314431.stm.

40. Scott Shane, "Iranian Dissidents Convince U.S. to Drop Terror Label," *New York Times*, September 21, 2012; and Associated Press, "Iran Condemns US for 'Double Standards' over MEK Terror De-listing," *The Guardian*, September 29, 2012.

41. While this chapter imagines a region completely devoid of US forces, a limited US capability in the region will further dissuade Iran from the notion that it can offset its weaknesses by pulling off a surprise attack. For a description of this capability, see Joshua Rovner and Caitlin Talmadge, "Hegemony, Force Posture, and the Provision of Public Goods: The Once and Future Role of Outside Powers in Securing Persian Gulf Oil," *Security Studies* 23, no. 3 (July–September 2014). For a discussion of behavior problems associated with deterring emerging nuclear powers, see Joshua Rovner, "After Proliferation: Deterrence Theory and Emerging Nuclear Powers," in *Strategy in the Second Nuclear Age: Power, Ambition, and the Ultimate Weapon*, ed. Toshi Yoshihara and James R. Holmes (Washington DC: Georgetown University Press, 2012). For more on the consequences of a nuclear-armed Iran, see Joshua Rovner, "After Proliferation: How to Deter Iran When It Goes Nuclear," *The National Interest* (online), November 21, 2011, http://nationalinterest.org/blog/the-skeptics/after-proliferation-how-deter-iran-when-it-goes-nuclear-6179.

42. This is the major argument in Stephen Van Evera, *Causes of War: Power and the Roots of Conflict* (Ithaca NY: Cornell University Press, 1999). The seminal statement of offense-defense theory remains Robert Jervis, "Cooperation under the Security Dilemma," *World Politics* 30, no. 2 (January 1978): 167–214. For an important elaboration, see Sean M. Lynn-Jones, "Offense-Defense Theory and Its Critics," *Security Studies* 4, no. 4 (Summer 1995): 660–91.

43. Charles L. Glaser and Chaim Kaufmann, "What Is the Offense-Defense Balance and Can We Measure It?" *International Security* 22, no. 4 (Spring 1998): 46.

44. Ibid., 61–67.

45. Bahman Baktiari, "Seeking International Legitimacy: Understanding the Dynamics of Nuclear Nationalism in Iran," in *Nuclear Politics in Iran*, ed. Judith S. Yaphe (Washington DC: Institute for National Strategy Studies, 2010), 19–34.

46. Pollack, "Reading Machiavelli in Iraq." See also Dina al-Shibeeb, "Iraqi Nationalism Then and Now: The War Anniversary's Bigger Picture," *Al Arabiya*, March 16, 2003.

47. Library of Congress, Federal Research Division, "Country Profile: Saudi Arabia" (Washington DC: Library of Congress, September 2006).

48. For a useful overview of comparative military programs in the Gulf, see

Anthony H. Cordesman and Alexander Wilner, "The Gulf Military Balance in 2012," Working Draft (Washington DC: Center for Strategic and International Studies, May 16, 2012), http://csis.org/files/publication/120518_Gulf_Military_Balance_2012.pdf. On rising Gulf Cooperation Council spending, see Marcus Weisberger, "Gulf Cooperation Council Defense Budgets Steadily Rising," *Defense News*, November 19, 2013. On missile defense, see "US Clears Sale of Lockheed Missile Defense System to UAE, Qatar," *Reuters*, November 6, 2012.

49. See, for example, Charles McDermid, "Standing Up to Iran: Gulf Alliance Flexes Its Muscles," *Time*, April 6, 2011.

50. Kenneth M. Pollack, "Security in the Persian Gulf: New Frameworks for the Twenty-First Century," *Middle East Memo* no. 24 (Washington DC: Saban Center, Brookings, June 2012), http://www.brookings.edu/~/media/research/files/papers/2012/6/middle%20east%20pollack/middle_east_pollack.pdf.

51. On the so-called Saudi-Iran Cold War, see Bill Spindle and Margaret Coker, "The New Cold War," *Wall Street Journal*, April 16, 2011.

52. Eugene Gholz and Daryl G. Press, "Footprints in the Sand," *The American Interest*, March–April 2010, 59–67.

53. Eugene Gholz et al., "Threats to Oil Flows through the Strait of Hormuz," unpublished ms., LBJ School of Public Affairs Hormuz Working Group, Austin, December 2009.

54. See especially Gunzinger and Dougherty, *Outside-In*, 21–43; and Daniel Dolan, "Rethinking the Strait of Hormuz," *Proceedings* 138, no. 5 (May 2012): 40–46.

55. Caitlin Talmadge, "Closing Time: Assessing the Iranian Threat to the Strait of Hormuz," *International Security* 33, no. 1 (Summer 2008): 82–117.

56. See Caitlin Talmadge's chapter 9 in this volume.

57. Steve A. Yetiv, *Crude Awakenings: Global Oil Security and American Foreign Policy* (Ithaca NY: Cornell University Press, 2004); and Eugene Gholz and Daryl Press, "Protecting 'The Prize': Oil and the US National Interest," *Security Studies* 19, no. 3 (Fall 2010): 453–85.

58. Put another way, the United States can provide public goods in the form of oil security without having to invest a large force in the region. See Rovner and Talmadge, "Hegemony, Force Posture."

59. See Secretary of Defense Leon Panetta, quoted in Rowan Scarborough, "U.S. Arms to Gulf Allies Hint of Strategy," *Washington Times*, December 16, 2012; and Amy Belasco, *Troop Levels in the Afghan and Iraq Wars, FY2001–FY2012: Cost and Other Potential Issues* (Washington DC: Congressional Research Service, July 2, 2009), 6.

60. Rovner and Talmadge, "Hegemony, Force Posture."

CHAPTER 6

US Spending on Its Military Commitments to the Persian Gulf

Eugene Gholz

A reasonable estimate of the defense budget cost of protecting the Persian Gulf (and especially of protecting the production and transit of oil) would make an important contribution to a rational assessment of the desirability of continuing to include this mission as part of US military strategy. Producing such an estimate is not an easy task. An ideal estimate would incorporate three sources of defense budget cost: the avoidable future investment to acquire the force structure to perform the mission, the cost of the force posture linked to the mission (the incremental cost of forward basing, specific training exercises that could be canceled, etc.), and the intermittent cost of military operations in the region (whether surges of forces to deter potential adversaries or actual wars). Each of these subestimates presents significant analytical challenges. Even the best estimate will necessarily be rough, but a credible budget cost figure would significantly help to determine whether this mission should remain in the US military strategy.

I estimate that as long as the United States retains its current two-war strategy, the avoidable cost of the US military's role in defending Persian Gulf oil is very small (compared to overall US defense spending), or about $5 billion per year from the baseline budget plus an unknown expected value of the cost of intermittent military operations. However, in public discussion and in the minds of politicians, the engagement of US military forces in the Persian Gulf has provided a key part of the justification for the current US strategy that prepares to fight two overlapping regional wars. If dropping the Persian Gulf oil missions led to a shift to a one-war or a one-and-a-half-war strategy, the United States could make greater cuts, holding constant the current levels of strategic risk in other regions, and perhaps save as much as $75 billion per year. These estimates compare to a fiscal year 2016 defense budget of $573 billion, including both the base budget and the funds for overseas contingency operations.[1]

This chapter by itself is not intended as an argument for a different strategy; instead, it is a rough-cut budget exercise. It also is a building block of a rational argument about national security and not a study of the actual ways that the sausage of US national security policy is made.[2] Consequently, the chapter proceeds as if US strategy determines the budget. It initially applies the current US strategy, which calls for a force that can win two nearly simultaneous regional wars, and assumes that the United States will want to maintain this two-war capability even if it decides that it will not fight an oil-related war in the Persian Gulf region. Later the chapter briefly considers the reasonable potential budget savings of a shift to a one-war or a one-and-a-half-war strategy.

I begin by explaining the key analytical challenges that make the budget estimates difficult and have undermined previous attempts to estimate the defense budget costs of defending Persian Gulf oil. In the following section, I describe the various US military missions linked to defending Persian Gulf oil—that is, the missions to which the challenging budget analysis applies in this case. The third substantive section explains the very low savings estimate under the two-war strategy, and the final section reviews estimates of the potential savings from a change in US strategy.

Analytical Challenges

The difficulty of constructing a budget cost estimate stems from three key sources. First, the United States buys general-purpose forces rather than forces dedicated to specific regions or missions, so determining which forces and costs could be eliminated from the defense budget if a specific region were dropped from US military plans is problematic.

Even during the Cold War, when the ultimate force-sizing construct was a truly global war in which the military might need to plan to fight simultaneously in all theaters, the United States bought general-purpose forces because depending on the scenario the enemy might devote different levels of effort to different theaters; thus, the same US forces were earmarked to fight in several different places. As a result, reducing the assessed likelihood of having to deploy to or fight in a particular theater might have had little effect on force structure, because the forces were also prepared to deploy and fight elsewhere. Only a few region-specific bases might have been cut.[3] This fact made credible the oft-cited Department of Defense (DOD) estimates of the early 1990s that threats to oil security in the Persian Gulf did not add much to the US defense budget.[4]

The planning problem changed with the end of the Cold War, which unfortunately exacerbated the difficulty of efforts to attribute a direct force structure cost to the mission to protect oil production and transit routes. Now US strategy considers a number of potential adversaries, each of which is only powerful enough to confront the United States in a single region. To describe this sort of war, the United States developed the well-known force-sizing construct of the major regional contingency (MRC), which at other times has been called a major theater war.[5] In practice, the United States worries about having to confront more than one adversary at nearly the same time. Official strategy documents since the 1991 Base Force Review, including the Bottom-Up Review of 1993 and a series of *Quadrennial Defense Review* and *National Security Strategy* statements, all argue based on strategic logic that the United States faces many threats and that it cannot know in advance which will materialize into actual military deployments. The result has been a series of capabilities-based strategies that directs the military to prepare to fight two regional wars nearly simultaneously without designating where those wars will take place.[6]

Specific regions do not play a headline role in US strategy, so dropping a region would not have a direct, necessary consequence for the defense budget. In fact, while the regional combatant commanders who actually command US military forces during field operations provide input to the budget process, they do not have their own budget lines and only indirectly face a budget constraint. The regional commanders have no natural way of knowing how much the forces that they rely on cost.

This argument is not purely an administrative point. In the early 1990s with the Gulf War very much on leaders' minds, a Persian Gulf contingency was routinely considered one of the canonical two wars. That said, many other potential scenarios were considered even then. At various times contingencies ranging from waging a war on the Korean Peninsula to defending against a resurgent Russia or a rising China to imposing stability on a chaotic, narco-trafficking Colombia to ending a vicious ethnic or sectarian conflict such as Rwanda or Syria were all considered plausible MRCs. Figuring out which forces would only defend Persian Gulf oil or which ones would be excess to fighting in remaining, perhaps-less-stringent contingencies is not an easy task.[7]

The second major challenge in calculating the defense budget implications of dropping the defense of Persian Gulf oil from US strategy is that the defense budget involves a bewildering variety of different types of costs. It combines the fixed cost to generate any military capability at all (recruitment, payroll administration, research and development [R&D] investment), the cost that varies with the size of the force structure (pay and benefits, base infrastructure, procurement, training, most strategic systems), and the cost that varies with the activities of the force (combat pay differentials, fuel consumed in operations, incremental maintenance as equipment is used, and tactical intelligence collection and analysis). Separating out the fixed-cost component of American defense spending is really important. Foundational choices about the kind of military that the United States maintains—a highly trained, well-educated, professional, technology-intensive, and generally deluxe military—make the US military's fixed cost higher as a proportion of total spending than the similar cost component for most other militaries. Independent of its recurring spending on force posture and current operations, the US military needs many specialty schools, training grounds, R&D programs, and advertising and recruiting initiatives, all of which are types of fixed costs. So in any accounting of the defense budget effects of reducing the missions assigned to the US military, analysts must be very careful to reduce only the right cost categories and decrement spending on specific operations and on specific elements of force posture connected to the mission that has been cut.

Unfortunately that task is made still more complex by the need to include a few fixed costs in the projected spending cuts—for example, the incremental cost of the forward military bases that could be closed if the United States determined that it would not protect a particular region in the future. The bottom line is that eliminating 30 percent of the US military's missions will only yield a significantly smaller than 30 percent reduction in the defense budget. Yet the simplest method used in previous estimates of the cost of defending Persian Gulf oil—what has been called the total cost approach—ignores this nonlinearity. The total cost approach allocates a share of the overall defense budget or of the overall budget for each military service to each combat unit. Each combat unit bears a proportional share of the fixed cost of the military establishment.[8] In one sense, this is a fair accounting as someone has to "pay" for the overhead, but this accounting also substantially exaggerates the potential savings of dropping the defense of Persian Gulf oil from US strategy. Even if ending the mission would allow force structure cuts, most of the overhead spending would continue almost unaffected to support the remaining missions.[9]

An alternative strategy to handle the fixed-cost problem is to estimate the savings from eliminating particular types of units from the force structure based on the record of past force structure cuts. The RAND Corporation produced a high-quality study in 2009 that estimated the annual cost of each unit type by comparing defense budget reductions through the 1990s to force structure reductions during that period.[10] This method presumes that an army unit or a fighter squadron today costs the same as it did in the 1990s. On the one hand, units are likely more expensive today than they were in the 1990s given that military pay has increased substantially, and each unit's equipment is now somewhat different and costs more.[11] On the other hand, the RAND calibration comes from a time when fixed costs were a smaller fraction of the total defense budget (because they were spread across more units) and when the Base Realignment and Closure (BRAC) Commission process, not yet politicized, had some success in shrinking the overhead part of the defense budget—that is, force structure cuts then were more likely to lead to proportional cuts in the overall defense budget than they are today.[12] The former factor implies that RAND underestimates the potential savings of eliminating force structure in the 2010s; the latter factor implies that RAND overestimates the potential savings. Perhaps the two issues counterbalance, at least at the level of accuracy that analysts can hope for in these rough budget analyses of force structure reductions, and make the RAND estimate a reasonable one—as long as we know which parts of the force structure could be cut if the Persian Gulf mission were dropped.

The third major challenge to estimating the potential defense budget savings is that defense spending rapidly becomes a sunk cost. Even if we can identify forces purchased in the past specifically for the mission of defending Persian Gulf oil, the United States cannot "save" money that has already been spent. What the United States can potentially save is the future cost of continuing that mission; that is, it could save the money that would have been spent in the future on operating, maintaining, and investing in replacements and improvements to the forces that would no longer be required absent the mission. This challenge focuses on the equipment part of the defense budget. Consider the following hypothetical situation: If in 2014 the United States bought a large increment of capability for a particular mission, and if that capital investment has a twenty- or even forty-year life cycle in the force, the present value of planned future investment spending that could be cut by eliminating the mission will be quite low. The expenditures that can be avoided in the future are for operations and maintenance, and operations and maintenance cuts are only possible if the equipment is not required for other missions that keep it in the force structure despite the elimination of the primary mission used to justify its acquisition in the past.[13]

This problem notably features in political scientist John Duffield's high-quality estimate of the costs of protecting Persian Gulf oil. Duffield systematically identifies equipment on which the US military depends for its Persian Gulf engagement and carefully counts both its acquisition cost and its annual operating cost. He estimates that buying and operating this equipment in the 1980s, along with other investments in new Persian Gulf–related capability, cost the United States some $28 billion to $36 billion each year (inflation adjusted to 2006 dollars).[14] Focusing on one particular area of spending, the acquisition of strategic lift, highlights the difficulty with this estimate. Duffield notes that the United States started a major round of investment in strategic lift in the 1980s after the creation of the Rapid Deployment Joint Task Force, which was intended to protect the Middle East.[15] But once this equipment was purchased, a future reduction of the US commitment to the Persian Gulf would not recoup the money invested. At best the US military could avoid the need to purchase new lift assets when those purchased in the 1980s wear out. As of 2015 US investment plans do not call for significant purchases of new air- or sealift assets until after fiscal year 2040.[16] Duffield's cost estimates are commendably focused, but they are retrospective. A contemporary equivalent of only some of the costs that Duffield identifies could be avoided if the United States changes its future role in protecting Persian Gulf oil supplies.

The Persian Gulf in US Strategy

US strategy calls for several types of operations in the Persian Gulf, and each requires an increment of force structure, mostly accounted for by general-purpose forces. But the potential Persian Gulf operations would also use a few dedicated assets. Understanding the range of missions underpins the analysis of potential defense budget savings associated with dropping the defense of Persian Gulf oil from US strategy. Proceeding methodically through the various Persian Gulf missions and the demand that each places on US general-purpose forces suggests that, given the current strategy, most missions are lesser included cases of the major regional contingency mission.

The most obvious mission that the United States prepares to execute as part of its commitment to defend Persian Gulf oil is a major regional contingency. The United States has twice deployed joint forces to the region to fight conventional combined-arms wars against a medium power, and both conflicts had intuitive connections to oil. In justifying Operations Desert Shield and Desert Storm in 1990–91, many US officials openly linked the need to defend Saudi Arabia to the need to prevent Saddam Hussein from consolidating control over oil supplies, and they likewise highlighted the maintenance of another independent oil producer as a key benefit of liberating Kuwait. In 2003 government officials did not list oil as one of the main factors in choosing to fight the Iraq War, but many people believe that oil played a role.[17] President Barack Obama's January 2012 *Strategic Guidance* discusses roles and missions in the Middle East but does not mention defending oil supplies, and it explicitly states that the United States will no longer plan and invest to prepare for long-term stability operations.[18] Nevertheless, in the common association, one of the two MRCs in the current US strategy prepares for a Persian Gulf scenario because of the oil resources there, and each MRC requires multiple divisions of ground troops, about 25 percent of the US fighter aircraft inventory, and a surge deployment of five carrier strike groups.[19]

However, the forces required to conduct a Persian Gulf MRC are not constant. They depend on technology, the quantity and quality of forces available to the potential opponent, and the expected end state after the MRC. In the 2001 *Quadrennial Defense Review,* the George W. Bush administration declared regime change the normal goal as part of its definition of "decisively defeating" an opponent, but it was not the goal in the 1991 Gulf War nor apparently the goal set in President Obama's 2012 *Strategic Guidance.* While the official public document does not comment on whether current US strategy includes regime change or offensive operations designed to conquer other countries as part of its force-sizing constructs for regional contingencies, the tone of the Obama administration, in contrast to that of the Bush administration, suggests that operations to protect Persian Gulf oil under current circumstances would be more defensively oriented. If so, the logical conclusion is that current plans to defend the Persian Gulf in an MRC require fewer forces than the four ground divisions that invaded Iraq in 2003 or the very large rotation base that required nearly all US ground forces, active and reserve, for the 2007 surge phase of the stability operation in Iraq.[20] Indeed, with modern precision-guided weapons and US military expertise in hitting enemy ground formations moving in open terrain, relatively small numbers of tactical aircraft might handle the bulk of the fighting.[21]

More important than changes in US goals, though, are changes in the regional military balance.[22] Prior to 2003 Iraq had a large military with relatively modern (if under-maintained) equipment; to some eyes, Iraq seemed a fairly formidable foe, though less so than it had been in 1991. Since the United States smashed the Iraqi military in the Iraq War, no regional military has appeared to have much conventional offensive capability. The Saudi military, while equipped with high-tech weapons, is quite small, and analysts persistently question its effectiveness. The Iranian military, while considerably larger, mostly lacks the modern weapons and transportation suitable for an MRC-style offensive to threaten oil fields; instead, it focuses on asymmetric warfare strategies, razzle-dazzle, and internal security. Thus, the US military already does not need to maintain the same force structure it once required for a Persian Gulf MRC (regardless of the level of US commitment to defend Persian Gulf oil). Intuition suggests that the adaptation to a force prepared for a post–Iraq War MRC has included a greater reduction to ground forces than to air and naval forces, yielding a reasonable MRC force size of two ground divisions, some three hundred US Air Force fighters and bombers, and a surge of four carrier strike groups.

But an MRC along the lines of the Gulf War or the Iraq War is not the only US military mission currently involved in protecting Persian Gulf oil. The United States has explicitly announced its intent to protect freedom of navigation through the Strait of Hormuz, especially because Iran regularly threatens to close it and stop the transit of some 17 million barrels of oil each day from producers to consumers.[23] While this scenario would not involve many US ground forces, it would involve an armada of US Navy and Air Force assets: attack aircraft to destroy Iranian bases, to suppress Iranian antiship missile launchers, and to wage a substantial air superiority campaign, along with surface combatants and helicopters to protect commercial shipping from small-boat attacks and to safeguard the slow, steady work of mine sweepers.[24] Much of the required force structure overlaps the requirements of the Persian Gulf MRC; defending the Strait requires a US Navy– and Air Force–intensive subset of the MRC force.

The other potential military mission in the Persian Gulf is much more controversial than the first two, and it has never been part of declaratory US strategy. After the 1973 oil shock, several analysts wondered why the United States did not consider a "normal" military response to the extortion of the Organization of the Petroleum Exporting Countries, one along the lines of past great power interventions against massive economic threats. Specifically, why not occupy Saudi oil fields to pump sufficient crude to supply global consumers at "reasonable" prices?[25] Analysts suggested that the United States could have accomplished the mission with about four divisions of ground troops (plus air and naval support), a force large enough to grab and hold the territory and to resist possible Soviet counter-intervention. Critics, however, pointed out the significant risks and reasons the mission might have required additional forces.[26]

The analogous mission today would be to occupy and protect the oil fields in a crisis such as a Saudi civil war, perhaps an unlikely scenario but one with a potentially huge impact on the global economy. Today the mission would not require the same combined-arms force to keep out other great powers. Instead, seizing or protecting oil infrastructure would be an extreme example of a stability operation, with the significant population and geographical extent of the area in question requiring a large occupation force backed up by a substantial rotation base of ground forces at bases in the United States. Moreover, American troops unfamiliar with the local language and culture deployed (perhaps on hostile terms) into the country that adopts the role of protector of the Muslim holy cities of Mecca and Medina might be especially ineffective in this mission and might encourage an especially strong, violent local nationalist response. If the United States secretly plans for this mission as part of its commitment to protect Persian Gulf oil (or if an "objective" analysis of a rational strategy suggests that the United States should plan for this mission), then US ground forces might need to grow somewhat from the size that enabled the surge deployment in Iraq.[27]

Finally current US strategy prepares to use the military in the Persian Gulf region for missions beyond those that protect oil. Counter-proliferation and counterterrorism missions both direct much of the military's attention to the Persian Gulf. The existence of these other missions led economist Paul Leiby to exclude any effort to account for the defense budget costs of defending the Persian Gulf from his well-known estimate of the "oil import premium" that American consumers pay when they buy gasoline and other petroleum products.[28]

In fact, the regional contingency most discussed in public does not directly relate to protecting oil; rather, it has been the prospect of launching a strike against Iran's nuclear program. The official US line has famously been that "all options are on the table" for dealing with potential Iranian nuclearization. Some advocates respond to the criticism that air strikes would likely only temporarily set back the Iranian program by suggesting that the United States should prepare to repeatedly strike until Iran tires of starting the program over again.[29] Even as long as the July 2015 deal to constrain Iran's nuclear program remains in effect, the military option will lurk in the background as the presumed way that the United States would try to prevent Iran from violating the deal and building a nuclear arsenal. The official US policy that calls for a continuing capability to threaten air strikes against Iran suggests at least a substantial air force role in the Persian Gulf beyond the mission to protect oil. The counter-proliferation mission might also support substantial ground and naval roles to protect against potential Iranian conventional retaliation in the wake of air strikes (e.g., Iranian retaliation against US allies such as Iraq and Kuwait).[30] And the United States apparently invests a good deal of resources in cyber activity directed toward the Iranian nuclear program, as revealed by the Stuxnet cyber attack on Iran's nuclear enrichment centrifuges, activity that involves very specific investment in understanding and exploiting Iranian process control computers.[31] Presumably some fraction of continuing US military cyber investment is connected to the Persian Gulf, largely through the counter-proliferation mission.[32]

Counterterrorism also focuses US military attention on the Persian Gulf. Special operations forces (relatively small in numbers and equipment costs), private contractors, and the intelligence community—forces that do not overlap much with those required for defending oil or counter-proliferation—handle most of this mission.[33] Today some of the US military presence at Persian Gulf bases supports intelligence, surveillance, and reconnaissance missions connected to counterterrorism, notably with unmanned aerial vehicles. The need to continue this attention on Yemen and other parts of the region might constrain changes to the US force posture regardless of what happens to the mission to defend oil.

Of course, it is possible that the Iranian nuclear issue will be settled (one way or another) within a few years, and counterterrorism concerns may move away from the Persian Gulf region, even if the activities of the so-called Islamic State and of al-Qaeda affiliates in Iraq and Syria make this prospect seem unlikely as of the fall of 2015. In this scenario, though, continuing concern over oil would perhaps justify a US role in the Persian Gulf as part of American national security strategy. Consequently, it is still useful to know the savings the United States might achieve by avoiding potential conflicts associated with defending Persian Gulf oil, because in a favorable future with respect to counter-proliferation and counterterrorism, the United States could potentially enjoy some defense budget savings if it chose to discontinue the defense of Persian Gulf oil.

Finally, current US strategy includes one more important Persian Gulf mission—namely, forward presence—that might constrain force structure choices and surely influences the cost of US force posture. As a reminder that the US military is ready for the other missions, as a way of building understanding of the local geography and political-military conditions, and as a way of bolstering allies' confidence and deterring potential adversaries, the US military forward deploys to the region in peacetime.[34] While few forces are permanently based in the Persian Gulf (e.g., a few minesweepers, patrol boats, and helicopters in Bahrain and some headquarters units in Bahrain and Qatar), units from all of the military services routinely rotate through the region. The incremental cost of forward deployment for ground forces and aircraft compared to keeping these forces trained and equipped at bases at home is marginal (up to a few billion dollars per year, depending on other choices), and the decision to rotate these forces does not significantly expand the overall force structure.[35]

But the forward presence mission substantially affects the US Navy. Because the United States is so far from the Persian Gulf, maintaining a ship on station there requires multiple ships in the overall fleet to account for the long steaming time to and from the Gulf and for other factors. The US Navy nominally requires a roughly 8:1 station-keeping multiplier for the Persian Gulf.[36] However, given the stated station-keeping multiplier and the total of eleven carriers in the US fleet in recent years, the United States has done the impossible and maintained a virtually continuous presence of two carrier strike groups in the area of responsibility for Central Command (CENTCOM). In practice, the ships' deployments are more flexible than the station-keeping multiplier implies; and while keeping two carriers on station near the Persian Gulf has strained the US Navy, it suggests a more practical multiplier of perhaps 5:1 for the theater. Moreover, in 2014 the US Navy shifted to a new deployment plan, the "Optimized Fleet Response Plan," which will enable an even lower station-keeping multiplier for the fleet.[37] Going forward, after the drawdown from the war in Afghanistan, the US Navy should be able to sustain a multiplier of 5:1 or even 4:1 for the current strategy's long-term peacetime force posture of keeping one carrier continuously on station in CENTCOM's area of responsibility without leaving gaps in coverage of other regions, which have lower station-keeping multipliers than the Gulf does. In total, the United States might need ten carrier strike groups to keep carriers on station in peacetime in the Persian Gulf (four), the Pacific (three, counting the carrier homeported in Japan), and the Atlantic near Europe and Africa (three).[38] In other words, covering the Persian Gulf as part of the peacetime presence mission requires the United States to keep four additional carrier strike groups in the fleet, the same number likely allocated to fight a defensively oriented Persian Gulf MRC, given today's strategic situation (or one fewer than the number used historically in offensively oriented Persian Gulf MRCs).

Overall, the potential MRC is the constraining factor likely to drive the Persian Gulf region's contribution to US force structure requirements, assuming that the United States is not secretly planning for the mission to occupy Saudi oil fields. A few specialized assets such as forward-deployed minesweepers are associated specifically with missions to defend oil, but the vast majority of the forces associated with potential Persian Gulf operations are general-purpose forces.

Potential Savings under a Two-MRC Strategy

Even without planning to defend Persian Gulf oil, US military strategists and inside-the-Beltway experts can easily envision two or more regional contingencies that might engage US troops. Consequently, eliminating the defense of Persian Gulf oil from US strategy does not necessarily imply a shift to a smaller force-sizing construct. If the United States were to keep the two-MRC strategy, a starting point for estimating the savings from dropping the Persian Gulf mission from the budget for general-purpose forces would be (1) to calculate roughly the force structure, force posture, and operational costs required for the two most demanding contingencies outside the Persian Gulf region and (2) to subtract that estimate from the overall spending planned for the next few years under the current strategy, which includes plans to defend the Persian Gulf. A full accounting would also need to incorporate the cost of forces specifically dedicated to Persian Gulf missions, adding to the savings in the general-purpose forces.

An even better evaluation would be slightly more complicated because the most demanding force-sizing constructs might be different for each service or major unit type. For example, the scenarios that limit the ability to cut US ground forces suitable for high-intensity warfare might not be the same as those that determine the minimum force structure for land-based strike aircraft or for air-superiority capability.

This proposed estimating method more or less follows the stated DOD practice in building each year's military budget proposal. In principle, the military plans its spending with an enormous staff effort that constructs notional force-sizing scenarios; rests on detailed intelligence estimates of potential adversaries' orders of battle, doctrine, and unit and equipment quality; and uses sophisticated campaign models to simulate force-on-force outcomes. The process enables planners to estimate the force structure that is sufficient to execute the missions called for by US strategy.[39] No academic analysis can replicate the supporting effort that goes into the normal defense planning, programming, and budgeting process, but fortunately such resources are not required to produce a valuable rough-cut budget approximation. Instead, we can think in broad terms about the relative forces required for scenarios that are generally accepted as part of US strategy to decide how US spending might change under a two-MRC strategy that does not include the Persian Gulf.

Force Structure

While the force structure required for a Persian Gulf MRC has dwindled in recent years, the requirements for other potential contingencies have increased. Analysts cannot infer from the stickiness of US force structure and budgets that the Persian Gulf mission is as important as it once was in the trajectory of current and future US military investment, especially in general-purpose forces. Most notably, Chinese military capability has significantly increased as the People's Liberation Army has professionalized, its budget has soared, and its format has shifted in the direction of a technology-intensive force. Even more important, military technology has shifted rapidly. Early in the post–Cold War era, the United States gained great benefit from its long-range precision strike capability, which has enabled small forces to project power relatively cheaply. Now that the precision and sensor revolution is spreading, especially to China, it has created what the US military refers to as the anti-access/area-denial (A2/AD) challenge, which requires the United States to build larger and more complex forces to prepare and execute its strategy in the Pacific.[40] Responding to the emerging A2/AD environment drives a great deal of defense R&D investment and even current procurement spending.

The connections between spending driven by simultaneous changes in different theaters are complex. In principle, force structure choices aimed at the Pacific should be independent of decisions about US engagement in the Persian

Gulf. If the cost of Pacific operations increases while the role of the Persian Gulf in US strategy remains constant, then presumably the strategy-driven budget's top line should increase. Any savings from eliminating Persian Gulf missions would accrue relative to an expected trajectory of Pacific-driven increases in the US defense budget (rather than counting the savings relative to the current top line). But to the extent that spending in the recent past has been driven by the Pacific MRCs while the overall defense budget has remained relatively flat or even dropped, analysts can infer that spending related to the Persian Gulf has already fallen; thus, the potential future savings from eliminating Persian Gulf missions are smaller than they would have been in the past.

For a future two-MRC strategy without the Persian Gulf, two widely discussed East Asian scenarios will demand large air and naval capabilities at least equivalent to the capabilities in the current force. The bulk of a fight to defend Taiwan (or another part of Northeast or Southeast Asia) from China would be an air and naval battle, struggling for air superiority over the Taiwan Strait, suppressing missile attacks on Taiwan, and hunting Chinese submarines and other naval assets threatening American allies.[41] Similarly, the US contribution to defending South Korea from North Korea would involve a major deployment of air and naval forces to suppress North Korean long-range artillery that could otherwise shell Seoul, to provide air superiority and close air support to contribute to the ground war, to provide counterforce attacks against North Korea's weapons of mass destruction (WMD) capabilities, and to strike leadership and other strategic targets to try to end the war quickly.[42] Potential US adversaries could decide to initiate these two scenarios independently, and US forces deployed to fight in one scenario would not simultaneously contribute to the defense in the other scenario; that is, these two scenarios would account for the full range of US air and naval forces required for a two-MRC strategy.

It is more difficult to think of two simultaneous MRCs that would require large deployments for the US Army. The US Army presumably would play a relatively minor role in a Taiwan scenario, and the risk of other regional contingencies involving large numbers of ground forces, such as defending Europe against a resurgent Russia or countering political instability in Colombia or elsewhere in Latin America, seems to have faded.[43] One contingency that obviously includes a significant ground forces requirement remains—deterring North Korea from attacking South Korea.[44] Even there, though, the US role is dwindling as South Korea provides more and more of the ground forces for its defense; indeed, overall command of the allied ground forces in wartime has shifted to the South Korean army.[45] Instead, a potential mission to help provide stability and control WMD if the North Korean regime were to collapse sustains the need to prepare for deploying large ground forces in the Koreas. The United States would probably not provide the majority of the troops or stay for an extended duration, but an initial surge of American participation, as in an MRC, is likely.[46]

Beyond the Korea scenarios, though, the only ground forces–intensive potential MRC that seems plausible is one that US strategy has never openly embraced—protecting Saudi oil infrastructure.[47] Assuming that the United States does not plan for that scenario, the two-MRC requirement for US ground forces is probably quite similar to the alternative strategy of one MRC plus a humanitarian mission. Under the current two-MRC strategy, US ground forces would likely fight in only one substantial MRC; thus, US ground forces are already headed to the force structure they would have under a less-than-two-MRC strategy. The expansion of the ground forces during the Iraq War (enacted to support a long-term stability operation) has already been reversed, and current plans to cut at least an additional 40,000 soldiers will bring the US Army to 450,000 soldiers or fewer.[48] The upshot is that even while maintaining a role for the Persian Gulf in American strategy, spending for ground forces is shrinking. Currently envisioned Persian Gulf missions probably do not play a big role in providing a floor under the ground forces' numbers, so eliminating the mission to defend Persian Gulf oil may not yield much further savings from the budget for ground forces.

In addition to the general-purpose forces, a few military assets are specifically allocated to CENTCOM in the Persian Gulf region. The most notable examples are the four *Avenger*-class minesweepers homeported in Bahrain that are mainly associated with the Hormuz scenario. Without the Persian Gulf oil mission, some planners would surely call for reallocating these ships to the Pacific, where they think the United States is accepting too much risk now as Chinese mine warfare capabilities increase. But analytically, to separate the cost of the Persian Gulf from other military costs, analysts should hold the level of risk in the Pacific constant.[49] Currently each *Avenger*-class minesweeper costs about $5 million per year in operations and maintenance spending, meaning about $20 million per year could be saved if the four ships in Bahrain were decommissioned.[50]

Because the *Avenger*-class ships were purchased in the 1980s, their acquisition cost is a sunk cost; however, eliminating the dedicated minesweeping mission could save from the acquisition budget as the United States is currently buying a new mine-hunting capability to replace the *Avengers*. The new class of ships, the littoral combat ship (LCS), will perform the mine-hunting and other roles. Overall plans call for fifty new LCSs, eight of which would be stationed in Bahrain.[51] If we assume that the United States could buy only forty-two LCSs without the Persian Gulf mission, then the acquisition budget could save the cost of those eight new ships, or about $2.5 billion in present value.[52]

In total, the force structure savings from dropping the defense of the Persian Gulf from US military plans would be quite small under a two-MRC strategy. While not true in the past, it is increasingly true as force requirements for the Pacific increase (due to China's growth and to the spread of A2/AD technology) and as force requirements for the Persian Gulf shrink (due to the weakness of the remaining adversaries there and to the administration's choice to swear off stability operations). Two plausible major contingencies in East Asia would require roughly the current air and naval forces in the US inventory; meanwhile, with or without the Persian Gulf commitment, the demand for US ground forces is dropping substantially. So given the general-purpose nature of US forces and the continuing relevance of the two-MRC force-sizing construct, the United States is probably in a situation similar to the official DOD estimate from 1990: The budget cost of Persian Gulf force structure is very small. The minor exception would be the few billion dollars of acquisition, operations, and maintenance costs for the dedicated Persian Gulf assets such as minesweepers.

Force Posture

Changing the US force posture by dropping the Persian Gulf oil mission from US strategy without changing the overall two-MRC force-sizing construct would add some savings. The Department of Defense pays for forward bases through many different accounts, complicating the effort to estimate the cost of forward presence. For example, DOD pays for base operating costs, such as building maintenance and heating and air-conditioning; overseas allowances to personnel stationed outside the United States; moving costs, which are higher for relocating personnel overseas than for changing their stations in the United States; and training costs at forward bases that differ from those at bases located in the United States. Note that these costs concentrate on the incremental changes stemming from the overseas presence. If a foreign base were closed but the force structure remained unchanged, the forces currently stationed overseas would have to move to another base, and the variable cost component of the foreign base's operating cost would simply shift to the variable cost component of another base (although the cost per person of military personnel stationed at the "old" base would not necessarily be the same as the cost per person at the "new" base).

The marginal cost of Persian Gulf deployments, exercises, and bases turns out to be relatively small, at most a few billion dollars a year. A 2012 RAND study of the cost of the US Air Force's forward presence estimated that shifting US posture to maintain a forward presence in Asia but not in the Middle East would allow the United States to close eight bases where 13,300 military personnel are currently stationed, saving $900 million in annual operating costs.[53] This estimate presumes that the United States would continue the mission to defend the Persian Gulf as part of its strategy but would do so from over the horizon. The RAND analysis actually would eliminate support bases in Spain, Portugal, Korea, Japan, and Australia while keeping open all current US bases in Bahrain, Kuwait, Oman, Qatar, and the United Arab Emirates but under "more austere" conditions.[54]

Eliminating Persian Gulf missions entirely would presumably allow the closure of additional base infrastructure in the region itself, saving additional money.[55] Data is scarce and difficult to assemble across all the accounts that contribute to the costs of forward bases. Unfortunately the authors of the best public study of global basing costs could only assemble enough data on US, European, and Asian bases as they built their cost model.[56] Assuming that the operating and sustainment installation-support costs are of the same order of magnitude for Persian Gulf, Pacific, and European bases, the Persian Gulf installations cost US taxpayers some $825 million per year.[57] As noted, the Persian Gulf commitment also increases the defense budget by an additional increment due to the increased personnel costs of locating forces there (dominated by overseas allowances and costs of moving), totaling perhaps $125 million, and by the cost of deploying rotational forces to the Gulf, or approximately $830 million per year after the end of the Iraq and Afghanistan Wars.[58] Overall, eliminating the region from the US force posture might save $1.8 billion.

Cost of Operations

Dropping the Persian Gulf region from US strategy would also enable the United States to avoid significant spending on military operations, including crisis deployments to try to deter potential adversaries and actual fighting from time to time in the region. Fighting wars is genuinely expensive. Militaries blow up or wear out plenty of costly equipment, operations consume a great deal of pricey fuel, and mobilization diverts labor and capital from its normal productive trajectory into the war effort. The first two categories of costs appear in the defense budget.

Previous analyses of the cost of Persian Gulf commitments have been especially weak on the cost of operations, not because the analysts were lacking, but because the topic is simply intractable. Forecasting the plausible cost of a war is even more difficult than analyzing the long-term budget implications of changing force structure and posture, because the cost of war depends on the particulars of the scenario, including the size of the fight, the type of forces involved, the length of the fight and of the prewar preparatory phase, and the terms of the postwar settlement. At the low end of the scale, in relatively recent history the United States deployed forces to the Persian Gulf to escort reflagged Kuwaiti oil tankers during the last year of the Iran-Iraq War (Operation Earnest Will cost a little less than $500 million when converted to 2013 dollars) and to deter Iraq from a second invasion of Kuwait in October 1994 (Operation Vigilant Warrior cost a little less than $400 million when converted to 2013 dollars).[59] But at the high end of the scale, the United States fought the Gulf War in 1991 (around $105 billion in 2013 dollars, some $92 billion of which was paid by coalition allies) and the much more expensive 2003 Iraq War and ensuing occupation (around $930 billion in 2013 dollars).[60] The costs of future operations in the region are likely to vary substantially, as they have in the past.

Furthermore, assessing the cost of a strategy of protecting the Persian Gulf through an expected value calculation also requires an estimate of the probability (or frequency) of each type of possible war in the region. That prediction may be even more difficult than the estimate of the costs of operations.[61] Several analysts have tried the assumption that the operations over a future decade might approximate the actual operations over some representative decade.[62] Unfortunately, no pattern of operations in a previous decade has matched the pattern in any other previous decade, making it impossible to reasonably designate any decade as representative. For example, the United States did not intervene at all in the 1970s (except the unsuccessful hostage rescue mission, often called Desert One, in Iran), only interceded through Operation Earnest Will in the 1980s, fought the Gulf War and engaged in a series of anti-Iraq operations in the 1990s (including monitoring the no-fly zone of Operation Southern Watch and strikes such as Operation Desert Fox and the previously noted Operation Vigilant Warrior), and waged the much bigger Iraq War in the 2000s. None of this history suggests a pattern of repeated activity that would inform an expected value calculation for the cost of future operations in the Persian Gulf.

Perhaps the natural solution to the problem of projecting the expected future rate of operations in the Persian Gulf is to conduct a region-specific analysis of the emerging strategic environment. Experts may be able to judge, based on the balance of forces and interests among Persian Gulf countries and other factors, whether the decade after the publication of this book looks more or less conflict-prone than the past and whether the United States, given its current strategy, would intervene in those conflicts. If the experts based their expectation that the United States would intervene on their judgment that the benefits of intervention would outweigh the costs, then they would only be offering an informal assessment of the conclusions that this book attempts to draw based on more careful study. The experts' assessments could not be reasonably used as a systematic input without making this study's logic circular. Of course, the experts could base their forecasts on their sense that the United States would intervene for reasons other than a rational attempt to implement US strategy. But if the United States decides to intervene without reference to its strategy, then dropping the mission to defend Persian Gulf oil from the strategy cannot be presumed to change future US defense budget spending.

Any future interventions in the Persian Gulf designed to protect oil under the current strategy will have real budgetary implications for the United States. These interventions are far from free, and the cost of past Persian Gulf interventions shows the wide range of possible costs for future operations. Unfortunately, we have no analytically rigorous way to estimate the expected budgetary cost or frequency of future operations.

Total Savings

Focusing on the force structure and posture contributions to the defense budget, the experience of the 2012 *Strategic Guidance* provides rough corroboration of the relatively small estimate of savings from shifting regional focus without changing the two-MRC strategy. The much-heralded pivot, or rebalancing, to Asia and the Middle East (and by implication away from Europe) led to minor budget savings that were consistent with the baseline numbers in the 2011 Budget Control Act without contributing to the required follow-on cuts forced by "sequestration."[63] The cuts announced with the *Strategic Guidance* depended not only on the rebalancing but also on a proposed shift away from the full-on two-MRC force and its replacement with a force that would decisively win in one contingency while simultaneously "spoiling" the aggressor's plans in the second MRC. In practice, DOD officials rapidly reaffirmed their commitment to winning quickly in both theaters (backing away from anything that resembled the "win-hold-win" strategy that was floated and rejected in the early 1990s). But to find the limited savings announced in January 2012, DOD had to plan both to shift its regional focus and to cut back its mission set. It is no wonder that a proposal only to shift focus away from the Persian Gulf yields even more limited savings. The total estimate for annual cost savings combines the force structure and force posture savings detailed earlier, yielding an aggregate figure of about $5 billion.

Savings from Cutting Back the Two-MRC Strategy

Cutting the defense of Persian Gulf oil from US strategy would achieve larger defense budget cuts if it would allow the strategy to change the current two-MRC requirement. The expectation that the United States should prepare to fight an MRC in the Persian Gulf has long been one of the key pillars supporting the two-MRC strategy. If the United States decided that it would no longer plan to fight there, then it might also shift to a strategy that planned only to fight one MRC at a time or to fight one MRC while simultaneously conducting missions such as humanitarian support operations that are generally presumed to require fewer forces (a "one-and-a-half-war" force structure). A reasonable first-cut estimate of the potential savings of this shift might be as large as 15–25 percent of the US defense budget, or some $100 billion to $170 billion. It would more or less leave the global components of the budget alone (DOD-wide spending and the US Navy budget, which could in principle protect "the commons") but cut the US Air Force and Army budgets nearly in half to reflect their diminished mission requirements.[64] More meticulous estimating methods suggest similar though somewhat smaller savings.

The choice of a two-MRC force since 1990 has been based on a risk analysis. Although an MRC is unlikely to start on any given day, American leaders worry that should a first MRC start, one of their aggressive or barely rational adversaries might launch an opportunistic attack and draw the United States into a second major conflict immediately after the first MRC commenced. Consequently, the United States has chosen to prepare to fight two MRCs nearly simultaneously.[65] However, if American leaders judge that Persian Gulf adversaries are no longer so aggressive or no longer have the capabilities to launch important offensives, or if American leaders judge that the offensives that Persian Gulf states could launch no longer matter enough to US interests to justify a prompt US military response, then the risk of a second simultaneous MRC might be low enough that the United States could rationally shift its overall strategy and only build a one- or one-and-a-half-MRC force.

This strategy shift might be especially likely because the essence of the two-war strategy requires that the United States be prepared to fight in two theaters "nearly simultaneously." Even from the beginning, the military acknowledged that it could not really defend in two theaters literally on the same day, but its discussion focused on defeating a second attack that started three weeks after the first enemy offensive. The idea was that defense could not wait in either theater until after the other MRC was won because the harm in both regions would be so immediate. This logic seemed right when the canonical scenarios required the United States to blunt a North Korean offensive that threatened millions of civilians in Seoul at the same time that a Persian Gulf adversary threatened to unhinge the world economy by stopping the flow of a huge fraction of the world's daily oil supplies.

Some other MRC scenarios, including, for example, a counter-WMD strike, might allow the United States to choose the timing of the start of the fight. Even in the case of a Persian Gulf war that threatened oil supplies, the US Strategic

Petroleum Reserve and additional reserves held by other countries and coordinated through the International Energy Agency could replace a significant amount of Persian Gulf oil on the global market for a significant period. Thus, the United States could defer fighting the Persian Gulf contingency and, in this case, make the MRCs sequential rather than simultaneous.[66] Nevertheless, American presidents have judged the risks sufficiently high since the end of the Cold War to maintain the two-MRC strategy.

US military leaders likely would always *prefer* to maintain forces fully capable of fighting two simultaneous MRCs. Given the expense of a large military and the public distaste for actually fighting many wars, however, a leadership decision not to prepare to fight for Persian Gulf oil might change the political calculus enough to shift US strategy to preparing for two *sequential* rather than *simultaneous* MRCs. This posture would allow a significant force structure cut and budget savings.

In a 2009 study that explicitly links a shift away from defending the Persian Gulf to a shift away from a two-MRC strategy, RAND analysts suggested that potential defense budget savings of up to $75 billion (2013 dollars) were possible from force structure cuts.[67] They took the forces that the United States used for Operation Iraqi Freedom as the baseline combat units required for an MRC: 2.67 US Army division equivalents, 1.33 Marine Corps division equivalents, 5 carrier strike groups, and 344 Air Force fighters and bombers. When the analysts cut these units from their notional force structure, they put back some units, notably including the entire 1.33 Marine Corps division equivalents and 3 of the carrier strike groups, that the United States would want to keep for other contingencies. To convert force structure into dollars, they estimated a per-unit annual cost of each unit type by comparing defense budget reductions through the 1990s to force structure reductions during that period.[68] Because the Iraqi Freedom force seems larger than any force likely to be allocated to a foreseeable future Persian Gulf contingency—and the United States has already made some of the force structure cuts envisioned in the RAND study even while maintaining its commitment to a two-MRC strategy—RAND's cost estimate should be treated as an upper bound for the potential savings of shifting US strategy; but the estimate is useful nonetheless.

The RAND analysis focuses on complete major regional contingencies—that is, a reduction from a two-MRC force to a one-MRC force. The two-MRC force historically has enabled the United States to contemplate intervening not only in two nearly simultaneous MRCs but also in a different scenario that would involve one MRC plus a humanitarian emergency. Because the humanitarian intervention was always presumed to involve fewer forces than the second MRC would require, and American leaders assumed that they could forego deployments for humanitarian reasons in the midst of the nightmare scenario of two nearly simultaneous MRCs, the United States did not separately budget for the humanitarian-oriented force structure in the past. Under a future less-than-two-MRC strategy, the United States might well choose to maintain some force structure to conduct humanitarian missions simultaneously with a single MRC, thus creating what is sometimes called a one-and-a-half-MRC force. In budget terms, the cut from the two-MRC force would then save less money than the $75 billion that RAND estimated. If the humanitarian intervention force were limited to two army brigade combat teams plus some of the Marine Corps forces that the RAND authors decided not to cut in their projected force structure, the shift to a one-and-a-half-MRC force would still enable the bulk of the $75 billion in budget cuts, or perhaps some $65 billion to $70 billion.[69]

Conclusion

The military is an extremely expensive tool of US grand strategy. Even if a military defense of Persian Gulf oil is highly valuable to US national interests, in principle the cost of providing that defense might be too high to make the effort worthwhile in a strict cost-benefit calculation. Because the United States has invested in forces, bases, and training to perform this mission since the 1980s, the real question is how much the United States might deduct from its defense spending by stopping this mission. Unless the shift in the military's focus from the Persian Gulf led to a broader adjustment to US military strategy, the potential savings are probably quite small, or roughly $5 billion per year (plus some increment of expected cost of operations); however, cutting from a two-MRC force structure to a one- or one-and-a-half-MRC force structure would increase the potential annual savings to as much as $75 billion. Even that higher number is only a fraction of the overall defense budget and thus highlights the tremendously high fixed costs of the American way of war. So while an understanding of the defense budget costs of current US military commitments is theoretically important for comprehensive strategic analysis, in practice the potential fiscal effects of changing the US approach to the Persian Gulf only make a minor contribution to the resulting assessment.

Notes

1. Leo Shane III, "2016 Defense Budget Deal Finally Nailed Down by Congress," *Military Times*, December 18, 2015.

2. In practice, US strategy may provide only vague guidance for policymakers, and the defense budget is almost certainly influenced by many bureaucratic interests and polit-

ical economy pressures. Harvey M. Sapolsky, Eugene Gholz, and Caitlin Talmadge, *US Defense Politics: The Origin of Security Policy*, 2nd ed. (London: Routledge, 2014), esp. chaps. 2 and 6.

3. Local allies bear a substantial fraction of the cost to build and maintain bases, complicating even the calculation of the budget savings from overseas base closures. For a clear framework and careful assessment of the limited evidence available, see Michael J. Lostumbo et al., *Overseas Basing of US Military Forces: An Assessment of Relative Costs and Strategic Benefits* (Santa Monica: RAND, 2013).

4. US Government Accounting Office (GAO), *Southwest Asia: Cost of Protecting US Interests*, GAO/NSIAD-915–250 (Washington DC: US Government Printing Office [GPO], August 1991).

5. For convenience and consistency, I will refer to MRCs throughout this chapter without intending to draw a substantive distinction from major theater wars or any other name for US power projection to fight a regional conflict with a medium-sized power that is using the full extent of its conventional military capabilities.

6. For a useful summary, see Daniel Gouré, "The Measure of a Superpower: A Two Major Regional Contingency Military for the 21st Century," Special Report no. 128 on National Security and Defense (Washington DC: Heritage Foundation, January 25, 2013).

7. For an attempt to tackle the "problem" of general-purpose forces head-on, see Roger J. Stern, "United States Cost of Military Force Projection in the Persian Gulf, 1976–2007," *Energy Policy* 38, no. 6 (June 2010): 2816–25. Stern noticed that the US Army and Air Force almost never fight without the presence of US Navy forces, so he used the latter's deployment patterns as a proxy measure to allocate shares of the defense budget to different regions. Unfortunately, although the US Navy participates in essentially all deployments of ground and air forces, ground and air forces do not participate in all navy deployments, nor are the proportions of ground, air, and naval units involved the same for each mission. The Persian Gulf requires a very large naval rotation base to accommodate both the transit time to the theater and the relatively long maintenance and refit time for ships. Army units deploying to use prepositioned equipment and air units flying to the theater do not require anywhere near the same rotation base that naval forces require for the Persian Gulf. Both of these factors lead Stern to overestimate the fraction of US spending on air and ground forces to allocate to the Persian Gulf. Finally, Stern's data based on observed deployments does not tell us the minimum requirement for activity in each theater or mission. Other theaters are counting on having access to certain forces currently deployed to the Persian Gulf if a simultaneous crisis were to break out elsewhere. Absent stresses in other theaters, the United States probably sent more air and naval forces to Central Command than the true minimum requirement called for. The upshot is that Stern's estimate that five-sixths of the defense budget can be attributed to defending the Persian Gulf substantially exaggerates the true cost.

8. Earl C. Ravenal, *Designing Defense for a New World Order: The Military Budget in 1992 and Beyond* (Washington DC: Cato Institute, 1991); and William W. Kaufmann and John D. Steinbruner, *Decisions for Defense: Prospects for a New Order* (Washington DC: Brookings, 1991).

9. In a more recent study, Mark A. Delucchi and James J. Murphy optimistically hope that a rational base realignment and closure (BRAC) process and other potential adaptations of supporting infrastructure for the US Department of Defense (DOD) would enable the fixed cost of defense to shrink proportionally to the variable cost. However, the BRAC process is severely limited by political barriers to closing bases, and overhead costs include many spending categories beyond base infrastructure that could not be cut even if a "rational strategic analysis" simply wishes away the reality of the American defense policy process. Even Delucchi and Murphy recognize that they need to allocate a portion of the defense budget's fixed cost to the combat units, but they do not explain their reasoning behind their choice of the amount to include. Mark A. Delucchi and James J. Murphy, "US Military Expenditures to Protect the Use of Persian Gulf Oil for Motor Vehicles," *Energy Policy* 36, no. 6 (June 2008): 2253–64.

10. Keith Crane et al., *Imported Oil and US National Security* (Santa Monica: RAND, 2009).

11. On the one hand, it seems reasonable to think that any cuts due to reducing US strategic commitments to the Persian Gulf would phase out the older equipment in the US inventory. We should expect that older equipment to account for a disproportionate share of today's maintenance spending and to have a higher maintenance cost today than it did in the 1990s. On the other hand, in the 1990s the United States followed a similar process of reallocating equipment during cutbacks, phasing out older, hard-to-maintain equipment; so perhaps the magnitude of the savings from those cuts are close to the magnitude of comparable savings from potential force structure cuts in the future.

12. The actual cost savings realized through the BRAC process are also controversial and difficult to measure. See, for example, Charles S. Clark, "BRAC Savings Estimates Were Flawed, Report Says," *Government Executive*, March 8, 2013.

13. This continued spending on operations and maintenance would be caused by analytical point 1 on general-purpose forces rather than by analytical point 3 on sunk costs.

14. John S. Duffield, *Over a Barrel: The Costs of U.S. Foreign Oil Dependence* (Stanford: Stanford University Press, 2008), esp. 162–64, 174. However, during the 1980s, the United States was still committed to defending Europe from a Soviet attack, and planners constantly cited strategic lift as a key constraint on the ability to fulfill that core mission of the North Atlantic Treaty Organization (NATO). The United States might well have purchased a significant increment of strategic lift that Duffield counts in the 1980s even absent the Persian Gulf commitment, including the KC-10s, the re-winging of the C-5s, the stretching of the C-141s, and the launching of the C-17 program. The subset of new ships and equipment specifically prepositioned near the Persian Gulf seems naturally associated with Persian Gulf defense rather than with pure general-purpose forces.

15. The Rapid Deployment Joint Task Force evolved into US Central Command in 1983.

16. Office of the Undersecretary of Defense (Comptroller/CFO), *Program Acquisition Cost by Weapon System: United States Department of Defense Fiscal Year 2016 Budget Request* (Washington DC: DOD, February 2015), http://comptroller.defense.gov

/Portals/45/Documents/defbudget/fy2016/FY2016_Weapons.pdf; and DOD, *Annual Aviation Inventory and Funding Plan, Fiscal Years (FY) 2016–45* (Washington DC: DOD, April 2015), http://news.usni.org/wp-content/uploads/2015/04/Annual-Aviation -Plan-2016-2020.pdf.

17. See Duffield, *Over a Barrel*, 179–81.

18. DOD, "Sustaining U.S. Global Leadership: Priorities for 21st Century Defense" (Washington DC: DOD, January 2012).

19. Crane et al., *Imported Oil*, 68–70.

20. If a future president decided that strategic conditions required a return to offensive-oriented MRCs as part of US strategy, then that president would presumably have to increase defense spending at that time to build up the offensive-oriented force structure. If a subsequent president decided to drop the defense of Persian Gulf oil from US strategy, then the budget savings would be greater at that point than they would be if President Obama had decided to drop Persian Gulf oil defense from US strategy in 2015.

21. For relevant background, see Daryl G. Press, "What If Saddam Hadn't Stopped?: The Myth of Coalition Vulnerability in the Early Days of Desert Shield," *Breakthroughs* 3, no. 1 (Spring 1994): 1–11.

22. Eugene Gholz and Daryl G. Press, "Protecting 'The Prize': Oil and the U.S. National Interest," *Security Studies* 19, no. 3 (Fall 2010): esp. 474–76. See also Joshua Rovner's chapter 5 in this volume.

23. Thom Shanker, Eric Schmitt, and David E. Sanger, "US Adds Forces in Persian Gulf, a Signal to Iran," *New York Times*, July 3, 2012.

24. Caitlin Talmadge, "Closing Time: Assessing the Iranian Threat to the Strait of Hormuz," *International Security* 33, no. 1 (Summer 2008): 82–117. Talmadge estimates the required US air assets (both US Navy and US Air Force) to be comparable to those required for the 1998–99 Kosovo War. The baseline requirement calls for one to two carrier strike groups (essentially the force that the US Navy has kept on station in the CENTCOM area of responsibility steadily for the past several years) augmented by extra Aegis air-defense ships plus two to three squadrons of US Air Force attack aircraft. Note that these force requirements are substantially smaller than those called for in the canonical MRC scenario, except the Hormuz scenario's higher use of so-called low-density, high-demand assets such as electronic warfare aircraft and aerial refueling tankers would require a significant portion of the US inventory.

25. Robert W. Tucker, "Oil: The Issue of American Intervention," *Commentary* 59, no. 1 (January 1975): 21–31; and Miles Ignotus, "Seizing Arab Oil," *Harper's*, March 1975, 45ff.

26. Thomas L. McNaugher, *Arms and Oil: US Military Strategy and the Persian Gulf* (Washington DC: Brookings, 1985), 183–97. Perhaps most tellingly, McNaugher points out that the key region of Saudi Arabia includes at least one major urban area, and handling that population in which potential insurgents or anti-American terrorists might hide would present significant challenges and probably require more troops. For a careful, critical analysis from the mid-1970s, see US Congressional Research Service (CRS), *Oil Fields as Military Objectives: A Feasibility Study* (Washington DC: GPO, 1975).

27. Gholz and Press, "Protecting 'The Prize,'" 481–82. Also, Eugene Gholz and Daryl G. Press, "Footprints in the Sand," *The American Interest*, March–April 2010, 59–67.

28. Leiby instead focuses on issues such as the OPEC cartel's ability to raise oil prices above their competitive price. Paul N. Leiby, "Estimating the Energy Security Benefits of Reduced US Oil Imports," Oak Ridge National Laboratory Paper (ORNL)/TM-2007/028 (Oak Ridge TN: ORNL, February 28, 2007), 15.

29. Alan J. Kuperman, "There's Only One Way to Stop Iran," *New York Times*, December 23, 2009.

30. Lostumbo et al., *Overseas Basing*, 301, judge that the recent increase in the rotational presence of US forces in the Persian Gulf region is mainly driven by the Iranian threat.

31. Jon Lindsay, "Stuxnet and the Limits of Cyberwar," *Security Studies* 22, no. 3 (September 2013): 365–404.

32. The cyber component of the US defense budget has surged in recent years, but the bulk of the effort almost certainly focuses on China. "APT1: Exposing One of China's Cyber Espionage Units," Mandiant Intelligence Center Report (Alexandria VA: Mandiant, February 18, 2013).

33. At the height of the Iraq occupation, US ground forces there were closely involved in tracking terrorists, many of whom were locals simply resisting the American occupation or engaging in sectarian violence. That role for ground forces ended with the occupation.

34. Richard L. Kugler, "Naval Overseas Presence in the New US Defense Strategy," in *Globalization and Maritime Power*, ed. Sam J. Tangredi (Washington DC: National Defense University, 2002).

35. Lostumbo et al., *Overseas Basing*, esp. 214–24 and appendix C. See also Lynn E. Davis et al., *US Overseas Military Presence: What Are the Strategic Choices?* (Santa Monica: RAND, 2012).

36. Stern, "United States Cost," 2820, reports the raw multipliers. The discussion that follows is based on email correspondence with Eric Labs at the Congressional Budget Office (CBO), June 10–11, 2013.

37. Lance M. Bacon, "Fleet's New Deployment Plan to Lock in 8-Month Cruises," *Defense News*, April 6, 2014. The US Navy initially proposed a plan called Enhanced Carrier Presence that would have improved the station-keeping multiplier still further, but that plan required increased operations and maintenance funding that has not been available under the strictures of the Budget Control Act. Enhanced Carrier Presence is presumably still an option that the US Navy could choose to pursue under different circumstances in the future, reducing the force structure burden of the forward presence mission. For extensive discussion of the interaction of the forward presence mission with naval force structure, see CBO, *Preserving the Navy's Forward Presence with a Smaller Fleet* (Washington DC: CBO, March 2015), especially 19n25.

38. For a reference to the traditional 3:1 peacetime station-keeping multiplier used for back-of-the-envelope analysis, with a note that the US Navy can actually sustain 2:1 for significant periods, see Crane et al., *Imported Oil*, 70.

39. In practice, this effort involves too many variables and too many unknowns to yield

any specific, technical answers that define the "right" force structure. Instead, the real process relies to a large extent on professional judgment, a general sense of balance among various capabilities that might respond to threats, and inertia informed by the results of the complex scenario analyses. For a classic article on the role of military judgment in force planning, see Stephen P. Rosen, "Systems Analysis and the Quest for Rational Defense," *Public Interest*, Summer 1984, 3–17.

40. Office of the Secretary of Defense, "Annual Report to Congress: Military and Security Developments Involving the People's Republic of China, 2013," http://www.defense.gov/Portals/1/Documents/pubs/2013_China_Report_FINAL.pdf; and David C. Gompert, *Sea Power and American Interests in the Western Pacific* (Santa Monica: RAND, 2013), esp. 119–54.

41. Roger Cliff et al., *Shaking the Heavens and Splitting the Earth: Chinese Air Force Employment Concepts in the 21st Century* (Santa Monica: RAND, 2011). For an analysis less favorable to Chinese capabilities (but that predates some of the Chinese investments and doctrinal shifts highlighted in the RAND study), see Michael O'Hanlon, "Why China Cannot Conquer Taiwan," *International Security* 25, no. 2 (Fall 2000): 51–86.

42. For a somewhat dated analysis that is still a good analytical listing of the types of operations required in a Korean War scenario, see Michael O'Hanlon, "Stopping a North Korean Invasion: Why Defending South Korea Is Easier than the Pentagon Thinks," *International Security* 22, no. 4 (Spring 1998): 135–70. For a more recent description of some characteristics of likely US air operations in Korea, see Kier A. Lieber and Daryl G. Press, "The Next Korean War," *Foreign Affairs*, April 1, 2013.

43. Even though Russia's role in the Ukraine conflict and Russia's potential threat to NATO allies in the Baltic have led to expanded prepositioning of ground equipment in Eastern Europe and rotations of ground forces for exercises intended to deter Russia, most of the discussion has considered the threat of "hybrid warfare" scenarios rather than a direct force-on-force conventional fight like an MRC. See "Russia a Threat to Baltic States after Ukraine Conflict, Warns Michael Fallon," *The Guardian*, February 18, 2015. However, some analysts still see a possibility of a full-on MRC in the Baltics that would perhaps provide the justification for maintaining the current scale of US ground forces under the two-war strategy. For example, Christopher S. Chivvis, "The Baltic Balance: How to Reduce the Chances of War in Europe," *Foreign Affairs*, July 1, 2015.

44. Thomas J. Bickford et al., *The Role of the US Army in Asia* (Arlington VA: Center for Naval Analyses, May 2015), 39, 47. The US Army would play a role in a counter-A2/AD campaign in a Taiwan scenario, and while the forces for that campaign would not all be a lesser case of the Korea contingency, the additional forces would be far smaller than a second MRC force would be. Ibid., 65–66.

45. "US Changing Its Mission in Korea," *Washington Times*, March 5, 2009.

46. Bruce W. Bennett and Jennifer Lind, "The Collapse of North Korea: Military Missions and Requirements," *International Security* 36, no. 2 (Fall 2011): 84–119.

47. If a potential Russia scenario (along with the canonical Korea scenario) justifies maintaining the current size of ground forces for two nearly simultaneous MRCs, then for the same reason that the Korea and Taiwan scenarios would justify maintaining the

current size of US naval and air forces for two overlapping MRCs, dropping the mission to protect Persian Gulf oil from the US national security strategy will have little effect on ground force structure and the defense budget.

48. Dan Lamothe, "Army Details How It Will Cut to Its Smallest Size since before World War II," *Washington Post*, July 9, 2015.

49. The United States currently divides its minesweeping fleet into three increments: four ships homeported in Bahrain, four ships homeported in Japan, and six ships homeported in San Diego. In 2012 the US Navy sent four extra minesweepers from San Diego to Bahrain, leaving behind only two ships for training use. Presumably in a Pacific regional contingency, the ships from San Diego could alternatively have augmented the four minesweepers that are homeported in Japan. Essentially, the San Diego ships are the general-purpose component of the minesweeping inventory, and the ones in Bahrain and Japan are theater-specific assets. Christopher P. Cavas, "US Doubling Minesweepers in Persian Gulf," *Navy Times*, March 15, 2012.

50. "Navy Minesweeper to Be Dismantled after Running Aground off Philippines," FoxNews, January 30, 2013.

51. Lostumbo et al., *Overseas Basing*, 13, 301; and "LCS: The USA's Littoral Combat Ships," *Defense Industry Daily*, May 28, 2013.

52. This estimate is very rough. The savings would come on ships 43–50, which are scheduled for construction roughly twenty years in the future; thus, the savings need to be discounted to net present value in 2013 (the estimate in the text assumes a 5 percent discount rate). Additionally, by the time ships 43–50 are built, the cost overruns caused by challenges in the ships' development will presumably have passed, and learning effects and economies of scale should have driven down the unit cost; that is, the savings would come from the relatively "cheap" end of the acquisition process. Present plans call for a cost as low as $348.5 million per ship but as high as $500 million per ship (across the long production run); for estimating purposes that maximize potential savings, figure a savings of $4 billion (future dollars) by cutting eight ships. Beyond the cost of the ships themselves, the LCS design relies on "swappable" mission modules; that is, each hull sometimes will specialize in mine warfare, sometimes will specialize in antisubmarine warfare, and sometimes will specialize in surface warfare. Presumably all three mission module types will be relevant to the Hormuz scenario. The current budget proposal allocates $2 billion for development and procurement of the first twenty-two mission modules between 2013 and 2017, suggesting a reasonable estimate of at least $100 million per module purchased in the future for the Bahrain-dedicated ships. Assuming that reducing the ships destined for Bahrain will cut six of twenty-four planned mine warfare modules, two of sixteen planned antisubmarine warfare modules, and four of twenty-four planned surface-warfare modules yields a savings of roughly $1.2 billion on mission modules. (Cost estimates derived from "LCS: The USA's Littoral Combat Ships," *Defense Industry Daily*, May 28, 2013; and Sydney J. Freedberg Jr., "LCS: Production Surges, Price Drops," *Breaking Defense*, July 16, 2015.) Note that operations and maintenance costs for the ships in Bahrain would add a few million additional dollars per year to the total bill.

53. If the forward-deployed weapon systems and personnel were dropped from the force structure, the total savings would be $2.3 billion, but that would double-count savings covered previously in the discussion of force structure changes due to dropping the Persian Gulf mission. Davis et al., *US Overseas Military*, 28, table 3.1.

54. Ibid., 14.

55. The following calculations apply the RAND model for estimating basing costs to the following US bases (drawn from Lostumbo et al., *Overseas Basing*, 24, table 1.3): Ali Al Salem Air Base, Kuwait; Al Dhafra Air Base, United Arab Emirates (UAE); Al Udeid Air Base, Qatar; Camp Arifjan, Kuwait; Camp As Sayliyah, Qatar; Camp Buehring, Kuwait; Fujairah, UAE; Jebel Ali Port, UAE; Kuwait Naval Base, Kuwait; and Naval Support Activity (NSA) Bahrain, Bahrain. I assume that US Air Force units currently on rotational deployments to Al Mussanah and Thumrait Air Bases in Oman and Ahmed Al Jaber Air Base in Kuwait are linked to the current conflict in Afghanistan rather than part of long-term US posture in the Persian Gulf region.

56. Lostumbo et al., *Overseas Basing*, 173.

57. Ibid., 195, table 8.9. This calculation does not include the estimated cost of recapitalizing the fixed plant at these bases because host nations provide the US bases in the Persian Gulf. For completeness, note that expanding the number of ships homeported in Bahrain from four *Avenger*-class to eight littoral combat ships will slightly increase basing costs there—by about $11 million per year—and if the United States dropped Persian Gulf missions, then that $11 million per year would be saved beyond the text's estimates, which refer to the current cost of the bases. Ibid., 370, table B.3.

58. The figures given in the text apply specific estimates for overseas personnel allowances (ibid., 181, table 8.3) and costs for permanent changes of station outside the continental United States (ibid., 183, table 8.4) to the roughly six thousand people permanently stationed at NSA Bahrain, and they use the rotational costs given in ibid., 362–66, table B.1 for other bases in the region.

59. US GAO, *Southwest Asia*, 2; and US GAO, *Contingency Operations: DoD's Reported Costs Contain Significant Inaccuracies*, GAO/NSIAD-96–115 (Washington DC: GAO, May 1996), 13.

60. Crane et al., *Imported Oil*, 73; and Amy Belasco, *The Cost of Iraq, Afghanistan, and Other Global War on Terror Operations since 9/11*, CRS RL33110 (Washington DC: CRS, GPO, March 29, 2011), CRS-3, table 1. This estimate of Iraq War costs is significantly lower than Joseph Stiglitz and Linda Bilmes's well-known $3 trillion estimate. Their estimate includes some cost categories that the CRS estimate does not. For example, Stiglitz and Bilmes attempt to include the present discounted value of the increase in future veterans' health care costs related to war injuries, a cost borne by the government budget, but they also take into account a pure guess at the "security premium" added to global oil prices because of Iraq War–related instability. This guess should not count as a defense budget cost even if it were accurate. See Joseph Stiglitz and Linda Bilmes, *The Three Trillion Dollar War: The True Cost of the Iraq Conflict* (New York: W. W. Norton, 2008).

61. A third factor, the appropriate choice of a discount rate, also complicates computing the present value of future costs.

62. For example, using a related method, Delucchi and Murphy focus on the major cost contributors, assume that the sequence of a war such as the Gulf War followed by a war like the Iraq War will happen once every fifty years, and compute an annualized cost of operations of $15 billion to $25 billion in current-year dollars into the future. Delucchi and Murphy, "US Military Expenditures," 2257.

63. DOD, "Defense Budget Priorities and Choices" (Washington DC: DOD, January 2012). Note that the pivot as described in the *Strategic Guidance* relies principally on general-purpose forces in "rebalancing" US attention toward the Pacific but not necessarily requiring the expansion of force structure or a major expenditure to change US force posture in East Asia.

64. For example, Barry R. Posen, "Pull Back: The Case for a Less Activist Foreign Policy," *Foreign Affairs* 92, no. 1 (January/February 2013). Based on actual FY2012 defense outlays of $677.9 billion. See "US Federal Budget Actual Spending Breakdown, 2007–2012: Budget," USgovernmentspending.com, http://www.usgovernmentspending.com /federal_budget_detail_2012bs12012n_30#usgs302.

65. The most recent formulation says that the United States "will be capable of defeating a regional adversary in a large-scale, multi-phased campaign while denying the objectives of—or imposing unacceptable costs on—another aggressor in a different region." Joint Chiefs of Staff, "The National Military Strategy of the United States of America 2015: The United States Military's Contribution to National Security" (Washington DC: DOD, June 2015), http://www.jcs.mil/Portals/36/Documents/Publications/National _Military_Strategy_2015.pdf.

66. For data and analysis on the effects of strategic reserves, see Eugene Gholz and Daryl G. Press, "All the Oil We Need," *New York Times*, August 20, 2008, A23.

67. Crane et al., *Imported Oil*, 68–71.

68. Over the next few years, analysts may be able to apply the RAND methodology to yield an updated estimate for budget savings from force structure cuts, especially for cuts to ground forces. The US Army is in the process of shrinking by more than ten brigade combat teams. Comparing changes in budget outlays to changes in force structure will allow an updated estimate of the cost per unit that could be applied to an assessment of potential savings by moving away from a two-MRC force. During the period of cuts, some forces will be reorganized, and the simultaneous reorganization will complicate future cost analysis.

69. That is the size of the humanitarian intervention force that Alan Kuperman proposed in his excellent analysis of a potential anti-genocide mission to Rwanda in 1994. See Alan Kuperman, *The Limits of Humanitarian Intervention: Genocide in Rwanda* (Washington DC: Brookings, 2001).

CHAPTER 7

Resilience by Other Means: The Potential Benefits of Alternative Government Investments in US Energy Security

John S. Duffield

US incentives to use military force to maintain the flow of oil in the Persian Gulf revolve largely around the economic costs of an oil supply disruption. To an important extent, these costs depend, in turn, on baseline levels of US petroleum supply and consumption and how quickly the United States could alter those levels in the event of a disruption. What measures could the United States take to reduce the economic consequences of an oil supply disruption both in the short term and in the longer run? This book proceeds from the assumption that American policy should depend on a comparison of the potential costs and benefits of such measures with those of a comparable investment in US military capabilities intended to reduce the likelihood, size, and/or duration of an oil supply disruption. Thus, if the United States could limit its vulnerability to a major oil supply disruption, then it might be able to cut commensurately its need for military forces.

This chapter explores ways that the US government could potentially decrease the economic costs of a future oil supply disruption, thereby reducing the incentives to be politically and militarily involved in the Persian Gulf in order either to prevent a future disruption or to restore the flow of oil as quickly as possible should a disruption nevertheless occur. After briefly reviewing the potential direct economic costs to the United States of an oil supply disruption, costs that are examined in detail in chapter 3, this chapter identifies and evaluates some of the principal policy alternatives on both the supply and demand sides and both at home and abroad. On the supply side, the chapter emphasizes potential measures to ramp up domestic oil production and the size of the Strategic Petroleum Reserve (SPR). On the demand side, it focuses on the transportation sector, which is responsible for some 70 percent of US oil consumption. Here leading options include raising taxes on petroleum products, increasing fuel economy standards for cars and trucks, promoting the production and substitution of alternative fuels, and supporting the electrification of the transportation sector. The chapter also examines how—and to what extent—the United States could promote similar policies in other oil-producing and -consuming countries. Because oil is a global commodity, and because US energy security is linked to the global price of oil, other countries' preparations for dealing with oil shocks also bear on US security.

Could the United States increase its energy security or achieve an equal level of energy security at less cost by investing at home and abroad in such measures? This chapter finds no panacea. The US economy will be affected by oil supply disruptions as long as the United States consumes a substantial amount of petroleum and oil can be freely traded across US borders. No single policy by itself promises to reduce significantly the cost of a future oil supply disruption. In combination, however, these options could make a substantial difference both by reducing the exposure of the US economy to a jump in world oil prices and by damping the impact of a supply disruption on those prices. Indeed, the United States could arguably reduce its vulnerability eventually to the point where the biggest impact of an oil supply disruption would be felt indirectly—that is, through its effects on the economies of other countries with which the United States is economically interdependent. In contrast, as the penultimate section of the chapter argues, the ability of the United States to help or ensure that other countries adopt similar measures seems highly limited.

Before proceeding, an important caveat is in order. This chapter does not evaluate the potential environmental consequences of various policy options. Of particular concern is the impact on levels of greenhouse gas emissions, which are implicated in climate change. Although a thorough cost-benefit analysis should consider such externalities, this chapter remains limited to examining the contributions to reducing US vulnerability to oil supply disruptions in the Persian Gulf.

Incentives for Involvement in the Persian Gulf: The Potential Economic Costs of Oil Supply Disruptions

To lay the foundation for an analysis of measures that can reduce the cost of oil supply disruptions, we need to identify the key ways in which a disruption could hurt the US economy. Concerns frequently focus on shortages of petroleum products such as those that seemed to occur because of the oil shocks of the 1970s, when long lines appeared at some US gasoline stations. In fact, however, most of those shortages resulted from domestic policies, such as price controls, that created bottlenecks in the supply chain. And the prospects for physical shortages have further diminished as the international oil market has become more liquid, with prospective purchasers generally being able to meet their needs at some price. In any case, by 2011 the United States received only 16.4 percent of its oil imports from the Middle East.[1]

The biggest impact of an oil supply disruption in the United States is likely to take the form of higher oil prices. Depending on the size and expected duration of a disruption, the world price of oil could rise substantially. Such an oil price shock would affect the US economy in three main ways.[2] First, it would result in increased outlays for oil imports, transferring wealth to oil-producing countries and thereby reducing aggregate demand at home. Next, it would reduce the country's economic output as businesses cut back on energy use in response to the higher prices, causing production and productivity to decline. Both of these effects, however, are not unique to sudden supply disruptions; even a gradual increase in oil prices produces similar results. Instead, the most distinctive cost of an oil price *shock* would be macroeconomic adjustment costs, which represent a temporary drop in output below the country's economic potential.

This summary of the potential economic costs of an oil supply disruption suggests four general strategies for reducing these costs. One is to lower the share of oil that is imported, thus limiting the wealth transfer cost. Another is to cut the baseline level of oil consumption, a move that would curb the costs of lost economic output and reduce adjustment costs. Both of these strategies could also help to lower the average cost of oil, although a reduction in price alone would not necessarily decrease the marginal cost of an oil price shock. Two other strategies would seek to reduce the economic costs by limiting the price increase caused by an oil supply disruption. The first is to increase temporarily the amount of oil on the market, and the other is to lessen quickly, if only temporarily, the demand for oil. Both tactics would also effectively compensate for some of the loss from the disruption. The range of possible strategies can also be organized in terms of whether they concern the supply or demand side and whether they are designed to have sustained or short-term effects on supply and demand (see table 7.1).

Possible Supply-Side Solutions

We turn first to possible supply-side solutions to the problem of oil supply disruptions. This area would seem to be the logical place to start as it addresses most directly the potential problem of reduced supply. Here we find two main options. One, increasing US oil production, could reduce US oil imports and bring down commensurately the amount of money sent abroad both during a supply disruption and in normal periods. The other option is to increase US oil reserves so that

Table 7.1. Summary of possible measures and potential benefits

	Sustained effects	Temporary effects
Supply side	*Measures:* Increase in baseline level of domestic oil production via subsidies, price supports, etc. *Benefits:* Reduction of oil imports and wealth transfer	*Measures:* Short-term increases in oil supply (i.e., releases of strategic stocks) *Benefits:* Moderation of price increase due to an oil shock
Demand side	*Measures:* Reduction of baseline level of oil consumption via taxes, higher energy efficiency, alternative fuels, etc. *Benefits:* Reduction of spending on oil	*Measures:* Short-term decreases in oil consumption (e.g., fuel switching, rationing, etc.) *Benefits:* Moderation of price increase due to an oil shock and reduction in spending on oil

they could be released more quickly or for a longer period in the event of a supply disruption and help moderate likely price increases.

Increase US Oil Production

After a long period of decline, production of hydrocarbon liquids in the United States has grown substantially in recent years. This positive trend has had three main causes. One is that offshore production of crude oil has been increasing since 2008.[3] Another is a rise since 2005 in the output of natural gas plant liquids as a by-product of greater natural gas production.[4] But the most important cause is the increased production of so-called tight oil from shale and other underground rock formations through the use of hydraulic fracturing (fracking) and horizontal drilling.

Considerable uncertainty attends estimates of future US oil production in part because of the drop in world oil prices in 2015. For example, the most recent US Energy Information Administration (EIA) projections show US crude oil production in 2040 ranging from 7.1 million barrels per day (mb/d) to 16.6 mb/d, depending on oil prices and the ultimate size of US oil resources.[5] Given these wide ranges, a promising place to begin an analysis is with the EIA's reference case, which assumes no change in current laws and regulations. The central trend in the EIA's reference case is generally positive, with total liquids production (crude oil plus natural gas plant liquids) rising more or less steadily from 10.05 mb/d in 2013 to 14.6 mb/d in 2020 and then declining slowly thereafter. Largely as a result of this increase, the EIA projects that net oil imports will drop from 6.2 mb/d in 2013 to 2.7 mb/d, or only 14 percent of liquid fuels consumption, in 2020 and then rise again slowly.[6] This trend marks a dramatic improvement over the high point of US import dependence in the middle of the 2000s, when oil from abroad accounted for more than 60 percent of petroleum consumption.[7]

What steps could the United States take to increase further domestic petroleum production? The federal government currently provides about $500 million a year in subsidies to the domestic petroleum industry. Presumably additional subsidies could incentivize even more production, but they would seem to be politically infeasible in view of the low price of oil and current fiscal constraints.[8] Instead, the most common recent policy proposals for increasing production have involved opening up the Arctic National Wildlife Refuge (ANWR) and hitherto restricted areas in the outer continental shelf to exploration and production. According to the most detailed government estimates, however, the potential for raising US oil output through these measures is relatively modest. In 2008 the EIA estimated that the coastal plain region of ANWR contained between 5.7 billion and 16.0 billion barrels of oil that could be produced using current technology, with a mean estimate of 10.4 billion barrels. Assuming that production would begin in 2018, ten years after approval to develop the area was given, output would peak in the mean case at 780,000 barrels per day in 2027 and decline slowly thereafter.[9] A 2009 EIA analysis noted that the undeveloped areas of the outer continental shelf contained approximately 18 billion barrels of technically recoverable oil, although that estimate was highly uncertain given the absence of previous exploration and development activity. Assuming that those areas were open for development, the EIA estimated that US crude oil production would be 270,000 barrels per day higher in 2020 and 540,000 barrels per day higher in 2030.[10] In the longer term, the US government might take other steps to promote higher levels of domestic oil production. Injecting carbon dioxide into depleted wells to boost their pressure and exploiting America's vast reserves of oil shale are thought to hold particular promise. But the widespread use of these techniques is currently constrained by a number of technical, economic, and environmental factors.[11]

Increased domestic production would cause net US imports to decline by a roughly equivalent amount. Thus, it would bring down the US import bill for oil by an amount equal to the number of barrels times the world price of oil, especially if US consumption stayed roughly constant, and that benefit would be magnified in the event of a sharp increase in world oil prices following an oil supply disruption in the Persian Gulf. Higher US output could also exert downward pressure on world oil prices. But exactly what impact it would have would depend critically on the responses of consumers and other producers.

Lower prices would promote both greater consumption and production cuts, causing prices to rise again. Thus, the 2008 EIA analysis estimated that opening ANWR would reduce oil prices by only 75 cents per barrel in 2025, or a little more than 1 percent, and by less in subsequent years in the mean resource case.[12] As perhaps the most thorough recent analysis of the subject concludes, "Letting US production rise would help keep a lid on prices, which might otherwise rise more. Anything much beyond that, though, seems unlikely, at least in the long run."[13]

Higher production levels alone, moreover, would not provide protection against the other economic costs of oil shocks. For that, the United States would need the ability to increase domestic production quickly in response to unanticipated supply disruptions elsewhere. This is precisely what occurred during the Suez crisis of 1956 and the unsuccessful Arab oil embargo of 1967. Since about 1970, however, US oil fields have been producing at 100 percent of their capacity, eliminating their ability to provide a supply cushion in the event of an emergency. In theory, the government could require producers to hold some of their production capacity in reserve, similar to the state-regulated prorationing system that prevailed from the 1930s through the 1960s, but such an arrangement would likely prove highly unpopular among both producers and consumers as it would involve keeping oil off the market.

Increase the Strategic Petroleum Reserve

The limitation on production has been addressed since the 1970s by maintaining strategic stocks of oil. In 1975, following the first oil shock, Congress mandated the creation of a Strategic Petroleum Reserve with a capacity equivalent to ninety days of crude oil imports, or about 500 million barrels at the time. Two years later, the Jimmy Carter administration increased the planned capacity to a billion barrels and ordered it to be done by 1985. For various reasons, the filling of the SPR proceeded more slowly than originally planned and stalled at a little less than 600 million barrels in the early 1990s. Following the attacks of September 11, 2001, however, President George W. Bush ordered that the SPR be filled to its then full capacity of some 727 million barrels, and that goal was achieved in 2009.[14]

In the event of an oil supply disruption, oil could be released from the SPR at a rate of as much as 4.4 mb/d for ninety days. Over the next ninety days, the withdrawal rate would decline steadily to approximately a third of the maximum amount.[15] A 2006 Government Accountability Office study found that using the SPR, especially in combination with other existing international reserves, could neutralize the economic impact of all but the largest supply disruptions. A larger combination of reserves, however, would be needed to compensate for a three-month-long closure of the Strait of Hormuz or a multiyear loss of Saudi Arabian oil production because of the volumes of oil required.[16]

The 2000s witnessed two unsuccessful efforts to increase the size of the SPR. The 2005 Energy Policy Act (EPACT), the first major US energy legislation since the early 1990s, directed the government to expand the SPR to its authorized capacity of a billion barrels. That effort would require enlarging the existing storage sites or adding at least one new facility. And in his 2007 State of the Union address, President Bush called for doubling the then size of the SPR to 1.5 billion barrels by 2027. This proposal, however, was not included in that year's energy bill, and in 2011, the process of adding new capacity was canceled.[17]

Nevertheless, expanding the SPR remains a policy option. What is unclear is its optimal size, which depends, in turn, on the likely amount and duration of a potential oil supply disruption. The optimal size is also contingent on the size of the strategic reserves maintained by other countries. The International Energy Agency (IEA) mandates that its members hold reserves equal to ninety days of imports, and several developing countries, notably China, have recently created their own reserves. A unilateral increase in the size of the SPR, however, might encourage other states as well as private actors to limit or even to reduce their own stockpiling efforts.[18] Thus, the success of such a move might require the participation of and cooperation by other countries and perhaps the increased regulation of private stockpile obligations. Whether and how the United States could encourage other governments to increase the size of their reserves is discussed later.

Another question regarding increasing the SPR is the cost involved. The Department of Energy recently put the capital cost of expanding the SPR's capacity by 273 million barrels at $3.7 billion and estimated the cost of operating and maintaining the expanded portion of the SPR at $35 million to $40 million per year.[19] Thus, the bulk of the cost of expanding the SPR would come from acquiring crude oil. Even with the price of oil running at roughly $60 per barrel in mid-2015, to add 300 million barrels to reach the total capacity of a billion barrels would carry a price tag of roughly $18 billion. Creating a reserve of 1.5 billion barrels would require purchasing approximately $48 billion worth of oil at $60 dollars a barrel plus capital costs of about $10 billion and an additional $100 million per year for operations and maintenance. This investment would be substantial, but when compared with the level of military spending intended to maintain the flow of oil, expanding the SPR might still be a cost-effective move in terms of avoiding potential economic damage in the event of a major oil supply disruption. For example, an SPR of 1.5 billion barrels, supplemented by existing international reserves and assuming a proportionate increase in the maximum drawdown rate, would compensate sufficiently for all but the most extreme scenario considered in the Government Accountability Office's analysis.

Possible Demand-Side Solutions

We now turn to possible demand-side solutions for reducing oil consumption. In 2014 the United States consumed an average of 18.0 mb/d of petroleum products, down from a peak of 20.8 mb/d in 2005.[20] The Energy Information Administration projects that, assuming no change in current laws and legislation, total petroleum consumption will remain at roughly the same level, rising to 18.6 mb/d in 2020 and then gradually declining to 18.1 mb/d in 2040.[21]

This section focuses on what could be done to further reduce petroleum consumption in the transportation sector. In 2013 that sector alone accounted for 70.5 percent of petroleum consumption, with most (24.7 percent) of the rest being used in industry, and the EIA projects that the share of liquid fuels consumed by transportation will decline only slowly, remaining at least 65 percent through 2040.[22] Another reason for this focus is that transportation is the sector most dependent on oil. Despite a noteworthy increase in the use of biofuels over the past decade, 92 percent of the energy used in transportation is still derived from petroleum.[23] Hence, the sector is especially vulnerable to the consequences of oil supply disruptions.

Two broad approaches can cut petroleum consumption in the transportation sector—reduce total fuel demand and displace petroleum with alternative fuels and energy sources, especially those whose prices are not determined by the price of oil. Over the years, the United States has tried both approaches, but it has not come close to exploiting fully the potential of either.

Reducing Transportation Fuel Demand

Transportation fuel demand can be reduced in two general ways. One is to change behavior. For example, people might be encouraged or required to drive less frequently and shorter distances, to use public transportation, or to operate their vehicles in a more energy-efficient manner. The other is to make vehicles more energy efficient. For example, a 2008 National Research Council report estimated that if future improvements to gasoline-powered engines were used exclusively for fuel economy gains, then oil consumption per mile traveled could be reduced by almost 30 percent by 2020, more than 40 percent by 2035, and about 50 percent by 2050. Likewise, evolutionary improvements in hybrid-electric vehicles could reduce fuel consumption for new vehicles by about 50 percent by

2020, more than 60 percent by 2035, and nearly 70 percent by 2050 when compared to current conventional gasoline engines.[24]

Governments have pursued two main strategies for reducing transportation fuel demand—regulations, primarily in the form of fuel economy standards, and various types of taxes intended to alter consumer incentives. US policy has emphasized the former, but the latter has even greater potential to bring about reductions in petroleum consumption.

INCREASED FUEL ECONOMY

In the United States, light-duty vehicles (LDV) in the form of passenger cars and light trucks account for 60 percent of total transportation energy use. Thus, it is not surprising that US efforts to improve energy efficiency have focused on this important segment of the transportation sector. In 1975 Congress established the Corporate Average Fuel Economy (CAFE) standards for LDVs, and they were phased in between the late 1970s and the mid-1980s. During the following two decades, the standards remained at approximately 27.5 miles per gallon (mpg) for passenger cars and 20.5 mpg for light trucks. Because of the increasing popularity of minivans and sport utility vehicles (SUVs), which qualified under the lower light truck standard, and because on-road fuel economy is about 20 percent lower than test results, the actual fuel economy of the entire light vehicle fleet stood at 20 mpg in 2005.[25]

Since the mid-2000s, US fuel economy standards have been rising. In 2003 the Bush administration issued a rule to boost the fuel economy of light trucks to 22.2 mpg by 2007.[26] Much more significant, the 2007 Energy Independence and Security Act (EISA) mandated an effective 40 percent increase in the tested fuel economy for all LDVs, from an average 25 mpg to 35 mpg, by 2020. It also established for the first time a fuel economy program for work trucks and commercial medium- and heavy-duty trucks.[27] After taking office in 2009, the Barack Obama administration accelerated the introduction of the new standards and raised them slightly, setting a new target of 35.5 mpg by 2016.[28] Because of the discrepancy between on-road and tested fuel economy, however, the EIA projected that actual average fuel economy of new light vehicles would reach only around 30 mpg. Add in the relatively slow replacement rate, and the actual fuel economy of the entire LDV stock was projected to rise much more slowly than the standards, reaching only 25.6 mpg in 2025 and 28.2 mpg in 2035.[29] Thus, according to various estimates, the higher standards introduced by EISA would reduce US oil consumption by 1.1 mb/d to 1.2 mb/d by 2020 and total liquid fuel use (including biofuels) by 2.1 mb/d by 2030 as the US LDV fleet gradually turned over.[30]

In 2012 after intensive negotiations with automakers, the Obama administration announced an even more dramatic increase in fuel economy to 54.5 mpg on an average fleet-wide basis by 2025. Because of various credits, the actual fuel economy of new vehicles was expected to be about 49 mpg on average, but this figure would still represent a rough doubling of recent levels.[31] To be sure, the overall fuel economy of the entire LDV fleet would not increase nearly as much given the large number of older vehicles still on the road. Nevertheless, the EIA projects that actual on-road fuel economy for all vehicles in use will increase from an average of 21.9 mpg in 2013 to 28.5 mpg in 2025 and then to 37.0 mpg in 2040, or 75 percent. In addition, thanks to these newest standards, the total consumption of liquids in the transportation sector would be an additional 0.6 mb/d lower in 2025 and 1.5 mb/d lower in 2040, and about 90 percent of the reduction would be in petroleum.[32]

One attraction of fuel economy standards is that the cost to the federal government is minimal. Instead, the direct costs of raising fuel efficiency are borne by auto manufacturers and especially by consumers, who must pay more for new vehicles; however, future savings on outlays for fuel may offset the additional cost to the average consumer. Nevertheless, fuel economy standards do not reduce the fuel consumption of existing vehicles. Moreover, by making driving less costly in new vehicles, they may actually encourage more driving in a phenomenon known as the "rebound" effect. In addition, projected efficiency gains have been not nearly as great for heavy trucks and commercial aircraft, which have lacked equally demanding fuel economy standards; yet these vehicles will account for an increasing share of transportation energy use—from 27.2 percent in 2013 to 36.0 percent in 2040—as the fuel economy of LDVs rises.[33] Thus, the rate at which overall petroleum use in the transportation sector can decline will be limited, especially until fuel economy standards are broadened to include other important categories of vehicles.

TAXES

The principal alternative way to reduce transportation fuel consumption is through the use of taxes. Indeed, economists argue that imposing taxes on oil and/or petroleum products is the most efficient way to do so. Rather than favoring particular technologies, such taxes allow manufacturers and consumers to decide how to reduce the use of petroleum in the most cost-effective manner. As a result, higher taxes would probably reduce consumption through a variety of mechanisms. In the short run, they would prompt consumers to drive fewer miles and in ways that were more fuel efficient. They would encourage drivers to live closer to their workplaces or use alternative forms of transportation. And taxes would provide incentives for consumers to demand—and for manufacturers to provide—vehicles that had better fuel economy or that used other forms of technology, such as all-electric or natural gas–powered vehicles, even in the absence of other government mandates or incentives.[34] According to various estimates, the overall economic cost of reducing gasoline consumption by raising fuel economy standards can be 2.4 to 13 times as expensive as using a gasoline tax, and a tax could produce greater immediate savings because it would affect all vehicles rather than only new ones.[35]

Most other advanced industrialized countries have used taxes on gasoline and diesel to reduce fuel consumption in the transportation sector. Indeed, in many countries, such as Britain, France, and Germany, taxes accounted for more than half of the cost of gasoline in 2011, even with oil at nearly $100 a barrel.[36] So far, however, the United States has not tried this approach. The federal government has imposed an excise tax on gasoline (and subsequently diesel) since 1932, but the purpose has never been to discourage consumption. Rather, the proceeds have been used both to fund the federal highway program and, since 1983, mass transit and to raise general revenues for the government. As a result, US fuel taxes have been among the lowest in the industrialized world. Indeed, the real value of the federal gasoline tax—fixed at 18.4 cents per gallon since 1997—has been generally at or below where it stood before the first oil shock in 1973.[37]

Nevertheless, increasing taxes on petroleum products could potentially yield large dividends in terms of realizing lower use. According to one common rule of thumb, a 10 percent increase in the price of gasoline could eventually reduce consumption by 6–9 percent.[38] Other estimates by economists are more conservative, but they still suggest that a 10 percent increase in the price of gasoline would reduce consumption by roughly 3–5 percent over a range of prices.[39] Thus, in 2004 both the Congressional Budget Office and the Department of Energy estimated that an increase on the order of 50 cents per gallon, when gasoline prices were fluctuating between $1.50 and $2.00 per gallon, would cut gasoline use by 10–15 percent.[40]

Consequently, the last decade has seen proposals for raising the federal tax on gasoline by $1.00 or $2.00 over five to ten years. The cost to the government would be limited to collecting the tax. Indeed, a tax could raise substantial revenue, especially given that US gasoline consumption exceeds 100 billion gallons per year. One problem is that such a tax would be regressive, hitting harder those poorer consumers who spend a higher proportion of their income on transportation fuel. Thus, most proposals involve returning the revenues to consumers through reductions in income and/or payroll taxes and through financing improvements in transportation infrastructure.[41]

Another type of tax, widely known as a "feebate," provides an ongoing incentive for consumers to place greater emphasis on fuel economy in their vehicle-purchasing decisions. Under such a system, the government would impose a tax or fee on vehicles that fall below a certain fuel economy benchmark and offer a rebate for vehicles above that point. The size of the feebate would be proportional to the difference between the expected fuel consumption and the benchmark. Currently the United States maintains a truncated feebate system in the form of the "gas guzzler" tax that starts at $1,000 and rises as high as $7,700 on vehicles rated at less than 22.5 mpg. But no rebate exists for more efficient vehicles, and the tax applies only to passenger cars and not the many other LDVs.[42]

One recent study proposes a feebate of $120 for each incremental change in fuel consumption of a gallon per thousand miles. The benchmark would initially be set at slightly lower than the current model year average mpg (e.g., 30 mpg is equivalent to 33 gallons per thousand miles), but it would steadily increase over time. Approximately 98 percent of all vehicles would fall somewhere between receiving a $2,000 rebate and paying a $2,000 fee, with the average consumer receiving a $240 rebate. Such a feebate system would cost the federal government several billion dollars per year, but it could drive improvements in fuel economy by 20–30 percent in the absence of other measures.[43]

In this regard, the feebate bears comparison with fuel economy standards. The latter provides the certainty of increases in fuel economy, but the former is generally regarded as more cost-effective. A feebate is viewed as especially effective when adopted in conjunction with a fuel tax, because consumers do not fully value the lifetime fuel expenses associated with a vehicle purchase.[44] But like fuel economy standards, the feebate does not reduce fuel consumption by the existing vehicle fleet.

All of these measures, including fuel taxes, have one further limitation: Although they would reduce the economic costs of a future oil supply disruption by lowering the baseline level of US oil demand and possibly the baseline price of oil, they would not increase the ability of the United States to mitigate the impact of a disruption by quickly reducing consumption an additional amount for the duration of the disruption. Indeed, higher taxes would reduce the impact of a rise in oil prices on behavior because the price of oil would represent a smaller share of a gallon of gasoline. For such short-term flexibility in consumption, we must look at the potential to substitute other energy sources for petroleum.

Displacing Petroleum with Alternative Fuels and Energy Sources

The other general approach for reducing US oil consumption in the transportation sector is to replace petroleum with alternative fuels and energy sources.

Here we find three main options: alternative liquid fuels, especially biofuels, that have many of the same properties as petroleum products; other on-board fuels, such as natural gas and hydrogen; and electricity from the electric power grid.[45] In evaluating each approach, we must consider three issues: the production of the alternative fuel or energy source in question, the means of distributing it, and the modifications that vehicles require in order to use it.[46]

Thus far, US policy has emphasized the first option and promoted the production of biofuels, which have been most readily substitutable for petroleum-based fuels. But recent years have seen increasing numbers of opportunities and proposals for making more radical changes in the way the US transportation fleet is powered.

BIOFUELS

Federal government support for biofuels dates back to the late 1970s, but biofuels only reached 1 percent of transportation energy use in 2004.[47] It was not until the US government established a renewable fuel standard (RFS) in the 2005 Energy Policy Act and then greatly expanded it in the 2007 Energy Independence and Security Act that the production and use of biofuels took off. The EPACT mandated that the amount of ethanol and biodiesel in the nation's fuel supply rise to 7.5 billion gallons per year by 2012, after which the share of renewables would be held constant. The EISA raised the standard to 36 billion gallons by 2022 while capping the amount of ethanol that could be derived from cornstarch at 15 billion gallons. This limit was meant to ensure that a growing share — and eventually the majority — would consist of advanced biofuels, especially ethanol derived from cellulose.[48] When fully implemented, the RFS would provide the equivalent of about 1.6 mb/d of gasoline, thereby reducing US petroleum demand by an equivalent amount. Recent studies have put the country's long-term sustainable ethanol production potential at as much as 90 billion gallons per year, or the equivalent of 4 mb/d of gasoline.[49]

Implementing the RFS proceeded quickly at first but then encountered obstacles. By 2011 production had plateaued at around 14 billion gallons, or less than 40 percent of the ultimate goal, because of difficulties with scaling up the production of advanced biofuels, especially cellulosic ethanol. Since 2010 the government has been forced to cut the target for cellulosic ethanol substantially. The extensive use of corn for ethanol production, which consumes as much as 40 percent of the US corn crop, has generated much criticism, especially during times of drought and high corn prices. Thus, the EIA projected in 2012 that biofuel consumption would reach only 22.1 billion gallons in 2022 and not meet the standard of 36 billion gallons until sometime in the early 2030s.[50] In 2013 and 2014, however, the EIA dramatically cut its projection of renewable biofuel consumption in 2035 to less than 16 billion gallons.[51]

In the longer term, moreover, fully implementing the RFS and increasing production of biofuels more generally may depend on investments in new vehicles and infrastructure. Although ethanol is very similar to gasoline, the widespread concern is that most gasoline-powered cars and trucks currently on the road cannot use concentrations of ethanol greater than 10 or 15 percent (E10 and E15)—the so-called blend wall—because of its corrosive properties. As a result, the EIA projects that the volume of blended ethanol will peak at 13 billion gallons per year in 2025 before rising again in the late 2030s.[52] Thus, especially as gasoline consumption declines because of fuel efficiency increases, full exploitation of the RFS will require greater use of much higher concentrations of ethanol, most commonly E85, in so-called flexible fuel or flex-fuel vehicles (FFVs) that can run on almost any combination of gasoline and alcohol.

Although FFVs made up 3 percent (7.1 million) of the light-duty vehicles on the road in 2010, only about 1 percent of ethanol production was used in E85 that year.[53] One reason is the lack of dedicated refueling infrastructure. Again, because it causes corrosion, ethanol cannot be readily transported through the existing extensive network of pipelines for petroleum products and may require its own distribution system as well as dedicated storage tanks and fuel pumps. Thus, in 2012 the publicly accessible E85 refueling sites in the United States numbered only 2,500—compared with about 160,000 conventional refueling stations—and were heavily concentrated in the upper Midwest.[54]

One possible solution to these bottlenecks is substituting so-called drop-in biofuels, which are largely compatible with existing fuel infrastructure, for ethanol. Of particular interest in this regard is butanol, which can be produced by virtually the same process used for ethanol but whose chemical properties are more similar to those of petroleum products. As a result, it can be blended with gasoline in higher concentrations and shipped via pipeline. In addition, butanol's energy content per gallon is almost the same as that of gasoline. Thus, several companies are currently exploring the conversion of ethanol plants to produce butanol.[55]

Greater penetration of biofuels would also be facilitated if the government were to require or strongly incentivize auto manufacturers to produce a much higher percentage of FFVs. According to a number of estimates, the added cost of building new gasoline-powered vehicles capable of using alcohol fuels is on the order of $100 to $200, and existing vehicles can be retrofitted as FFVs for less than $500. Legislation to establish an open fuel standard has been pending before Congress since 2005, but not one of the proposed measures has passed.

Alternatively, an annual government subsidy of $1 billion to $2 billion could finance the production of 10 million new FFVs per year, or the majority of the light-duty vehicles produced each year.[56] Each additional 10 million FFVs on the road, if consistently fueled with E85, could reduce gasoline consumption by an additional 2.7 billion gallons per year, or 0.2 mb/d.

If the number of FFVs increased substantially and larger amounts of cellulosic and other second-generation forms of ethanol became available, transport fuel distributors and retailers would have a greater financial incentive to invest in dedicated E85 refueling infrastructure, such as storage tanks and fuel pumps. Here, too, however, the federal government could accelerate the process by mandating the necessary investments or by offering subsidies. Indeed, the 2005 EPACT provided a 30 percent tax credit (up to $30,000) for investments in alternative fueling equipment.[57] At this rate, the cost to the government of subsidizing the installation of E85 equipment at 100,000 fueling stations, or roughly two-thirds the number of conventional refueling stations, would be about $3 billion.

Without any major change in US policy, however, the EIA projects that FFV sales will amount to only 11 percent of new vehicle sales in 2035.[58] This level of production would represent an improvement, but it would fall well short of the potential for increasing biofuel use in the United States. Thus, biofuels would contribute to reducing US petroleum consumption over the long term but quite possibly not to the same extent as planned increases in fuel economy standards will. Certainly the prospects for phasing in the RFS on schedule, not to mention raising the target for biofuels even further, are dim.

One potential advantage of biofuels over fuel economy standards and taxes is that they could give the United States some fuel-switching capability in the event of an oil supply disruption, thereby helping to moderate an oil price shock. As the price of gasoline rose, consumers could use gasoline blends with a higher proportion of ethanol. To make a significant difference, however, the United States would have to maintain either substantial stocks of ethanol or substantial excess capacity in ethanol production. For example, it would take increasing the supply of ethanol to about 60 million gallons per day—a rate equivalent to 22 billion gallons per year—to bring down oil consumption by 1 mb/d, and that calculation assumes that sufficient flex-fuel capacity existed in the transportation fleet to take advantage of the increase. In addition, the United States could not count on benefiting from a surge in biofuel imports from other countries because it is now, and is likely to remain for some time, the world's largest producer of biofuels.[59] Given that ethanol is likely to be much more expensive to stockpile than oil is and assuming the availability both of sufficient feedstocks to produce the additional ethanol and of FFVs to consume it, the most cost-effective approach will likely be for the government to pay for the creation of excess ethanol production capacity. Assuming that the cost of producing cellulosic ethanol can be brought in line with that of corn-based ethanol, the cost of building sufficient production capacity to replace 1 mb/d of oil would be roughly $20 billion, and the exploitation of that capacity would depend on the availability of sufficient feedstocks on short notice. One would also have to compare the cost-effectiveness of such a policy with that of increasing the withdrawal rate and overall capacity of the SPR by a comparable amount.

NATURAL GAS

Another potential substitute for petroleum in the US transportation sector is natural gas. Indeed, the attractiveness of natural gas as a transportation fuel has grown substantially in recent years, thanks to the widespread application of hydraulic fracturing and horizontal drilling technology and the resulting boom in US natural gas production. In addition, natural gas–powered vehicles already exist. Indeed, natural gas accounts for nearly 25 percent of the energy used by city transit buses. Nevertheless, its share of all the energy consumed in the transportation sector actually declined over four decades, from 4.0 percent in 1973 to 2.9 percent in 2013.[60]

There are two main options for using natural gas as a transportation fuel. One is to use it directly in the form of either compressed natural gas (CNG) or liquefied natural gas (LNG) in properly designed internal combustion engines. The other is to convert it into methanol, which, like ethanol, can be blended with gasoline and used in modified gasoline-powered engines.

A big advantage of natural gas is that it is already widely available. Thus, the main additional costs of using CNG on a large scale would be manufacturing vehicles that can run on it and building the necessary refueling infrastructure, primarily in the form of compressing facilities. CNG-powered cars are already widely used in several countries, including Iran, Pakistan, and Argentina; and most gasoline engines can be modified relatively inexpensively to use natural gas. Instead, the principal cost—and disadvantage—associated with CNG-powered LDVs is its high-pressure storage tank, which takes up more room than a typical gas tank but provides only roughly half the range. Recently CNG passenger cars, such as the Honda Civic GX, have sold for roughly $4,000 more than gasoline-powered versions do.[61] Meanwhile, building an adequate refueling infrastructure is likely to cost several billion dollars, assuming that the cost would be similar to that of deploying a comparable infrastructure for E85 or hydrogen (see the next section). If each new CNG vehicle replaced a gasoline-powered car that used roughly 400 gallons per year (10,000 miles per year divided by 25 mpg), then

40 million CNG vehicles would be required to reduce US gasoline consumption by 1 mb/d. Although the vehicle price differential is likely to decline over time with growing production volumes, the cost of a full government subsidy for achieving this goal could be on the order of $100 billion. Alternatively, similar to the fuel economy mandate contained in the CAFE standards, the federal government could require that automakers produce a certain number of CNG vehicles each year.

Because of the higher cost of natural gas–powered vehicles, they are most cost-effective when the average vehicle is used extensively, especially when the price of natural gas is relatively low compared with that of petroleum products. In addition, natural gas engines burn cleaner and tend to require less maintenance. Thus, some companies with numerous delivery vehicles, such as FedEx, are experimenting with the use of CNG in their fleets.

Even greater potential for replacing oil lies with the use of natural gas in heavy (class 7 and 8) freight trucks, especially those involved in long-haul traffic. In 2012 those trucks accounted for 17.2 percent of transportation energy use and 27.9 billion gallons of fuel consumption.[62] The EIA projects that in 2040 they will be responsible for 26.4 percent of all energy used in the sector.[63] In the case of long-haul trucks, however, most attention is focused on the use of LNG, which because of its greater energy density does not sacrifice range.

The challenge with this approach is that LNG-powered trucks and their necessary refueling structure will have to be built largely from scratch, and both will be expensive. According to various estimates, the additional cost of outfitting a long-haul truck to use LNG is about $50,000 to $70,000.[64] In addition, LNG refueling stations can cost up to several million dollars. These high up-front costs have not prevented businesses from finding the LNG market attractive, however. Several companies are building LNG plants and refueling stations, and at least four major truck manufacturers are introducing optimally sized LNG engines.[65] As a result, in 2013 the EIA projected that natural gas use in heavy trucks will increase to 1 trillion cubic feet in 2040, displacing about 0.5 mb/d of liquid fuels per day.[66]

Obviously, this process could be accelerated and broadened if the federal government were to provide financial incentives for purchasing LNG-powered vehicles and constructing LNG refueling stations. In 2011, for example, bills were introduced in Congress that would have provided an income tax credit of $64,000 for heavy trucks and a refueling infrastructure tax credit of up to $100,000 for an LNG station.[67] Given the fluidity of the situation, it is difficult to estimate how much, if any, support would be needed to make large-scale use of LNG self-sustaining. But assuming tax credits of $50,000 for the first 100,000 long-haul trucks and $100,000 for the first 1,000 refueling stations, the total cost to the government would be about $5 billion. And if these steps, in combination with sustained low natural gas prices, led to a 50 percent share of the long-haul trucking market by 2035, the total savings in oil consumption would amount to roughly 15 billion gallons per year, or about 1 mb/d.

As noted previously, natural gas can also be converted into methanol, a liquid fuel, which can be substituted for gasoline. At recent natural gas prices, methanol can be produced with existing technology at a cost that is comparable to that of gasoline on an energy-equivalent basis.[68] Like ethanol, however, methanol is more corrosive than gasoline and absorbs water; thus, its use requires modest changes to engines and the fueling infrastructure. Methanol could be used in tri-flexible-fuel vehicles that operate on any combination of methanol, ethanol, and gasoline.

Federal policies intended to promote methanol's use in the transportation sector would look similar to those for ethanol. They might include setting an open fuel standard, paying subsidies for producing and converting vehicles to run on methanol and for building methanol refueling structures, and including natural gas–derived methanol in the renewable fuel standard. Providing a methanol capability to an FFV in new LDVs would cost an additional $100 to $200 per vehicle.[69] Because the technology for producing methanol from natural gas is well developed, including methanol in the RFS could possibly compensate for the difficulties encountered with developing cellulosic ethanol. However, because its energy content is only half that of gasoline, thus further limiting the range of vehicles with standard-sized fuel tanks, the demand for methanol would be diminished.[70]

HYDROGEN

Some have pinned their hopes for reducing oil consumption on the use of hydrogen to power vehicles. The George W. Bush administration placed particular emphasis on hydrogen as an alternative transportation fuel, and the 2005 EPACT contained nearly $4 billion for research, demonstration projects, and transition programs involving hydrogen and fuel cells. Another attraction of using hydrogen is that, depending on how it is produced, it could substantially reduce carbon dioxide emissions.

The obstacles that hydrogen faces, however, are greater than those for biofuels and natural gas, because its large-scale use would require major advances in all three areas: production, distribution, and vehicle design. The most efficient use of hydrogen would be in fuel cells that power electric motors, but hydrogen fuel-cell vehicles (HFCVs) are still only in the development stage. Also, as with natural gas, hydrogen's costs are increased by the need for high-pressure storage tanks. But unlike natural gas, large-scale production of hydrogen would require an entirely new delivery system. Hydrogen fueling stations alone would cost on the order of $1 million to $2 million apiece, depending on their size.[71]

Nevertheless, according to a 2012 analysis, HFCVs have the potential to be cheaper than battery-powered vehicles, and estimates of the long-run costs of hydrogen are as low as $2.50 per gallon of gasoline equivalent.[72] Thus, a 2008 National Research Council study found that even with a relatively modest investment by the federal government, HFCVs could become economically competitive on a life-cycle basis with conventional LDVs and constitute some 60 million of the vehicles on the road by 2035. As a result, liquid fuel use could be reduced by nearly 25 percent by 2035 and by as much as 70 percent by 2050.[73] To achieve this positive outcome, the government would need to contribute about $5 billion for research and development and half the total cost of building and operating the hydrogen supply infrastructure (another $8 billion). In addition, it would have to subsidize the incremental cost of HFCVs relative to conventional gasoline vehicles ($40 billion), for a total outlay of about $55 billion over fifteen years.[74] As high as this figure might seem, it compares favorably with the annual cost of the ethanol excise tax credit—about $6 billion per year—at the time it was phased out in 2011.

Electrifying the Transportation Fleet

The final principal option for reducing petroleum consumption is through the electrification of the transportation fleet. This approach might also offer some potential for "fuel switching" in an emergency through extensively deploying vehicles that can be powered both by liquid fuels and by energy drawn from the electric power grid. Like biofuels, electricity will increasingly substitute for petroleum as a source of transportation energy with the introduction of all-electric vehicles (EVs) or battery-electric vehicles (BEVs). Likewise, hybrid-electric vehicles (HEV), which combine internal combustion engines and electric motors, and, increasingly, micro hybrids—vehicles with electrically powered auxiliary systems that allow an internal combustion engine to be turned off when the vehicle is idling or coasting but do not use batteries to provide propulsion—will play leading roles in achieving higher fuel economy. For example, the EIA has projected that micro hybrids could account for as much as 46 percent of new LDV sales in 2035 as a result of the new, higher CAFE standards.[75]

The key to fuel flexibility, however, is the combination of the hybrids' propulsion systems and the electric vehicles' plug-in capability and large battery capacity. Plug-in hybrid electric vehicles (PHEVs) allow consumers to vary substantially the amount of liquid fuel they use by relying more or less on their batteries' stored electricity, which can be replenished from the grid as necessary. Thus, when oil prices are low, PHEVs can be driven as traditional hybrids, relying mainly on gasoline. When oil prices are high, as during an oil supply disruption, PHEVs can be used exclusively as electric vehicles, recharging their batteries from the electrical power grid as needed.

The realization of this fuel-switching potential depends in turn on the widespread penetration of plug-in hybrids into the transportation fleet. The first plug-in hybrids were put on the market only in 2010 (model year 2011), and sales reached 97,100 vehicles in 2013.[76] In 2008 and 2009 Congress approved a federal tax credit of up to $7,500 per vehicle (depending on battery capacity), but the credit phased out after a manufacturer had produced 200,000 qualifying vehicles.[77] Because of their redundant features and large batteries, plug-in hybrids are relatively expensive—on the order of $10,000 more than comparable gasoline-powered vehicles—so a large tax credit was important for stimulating initial sales.[78]

How quickly the price of PHEVs can come down to the point where they are competitive with other vehicles is uncertain. Three main technological challenges still need to be addressed: battery capacity, battery life, and recharging time. Thus, in 2015 the EIA projected that PHEVs will account for only 2 percent of LDV sales in 2040. In the event of breakthroughs in battery technologies that substantially lower the costs, however, sales of plug-in hybrids could reach 6 percent of total vehicle sales in 2035, or roughly 1 million per year, according to the EIA. Assuming that the fuel economy of PHEVs is about average for hybrid vehicles, it could represent a non-negligible fuel-switching capability, depending on how much they are run on gasoline. Sales of non-plug-in hybrid electrics and all-electric vehicles would also benefit from such technological advances, enabling them to account for another 19 percent of the light vehicle market in 2035. Altogether the more rapid penetration of electric vehicles could reduce liquid fuel consumption by an additional 5 percent by 2035, or nearly 1 mb/d.[79]

To realize the potential of PHEVs (and BEVs), what other obstacles will have to be overcome? The US electrical-generating capacity should be sufficient to meet the needs of a growing number of plug-in vehicles for many years, especially if they are charged at night.[80] Instead, the most immediate impediments, other than battery cost, are the limited infrastructure currently available for recharging batteries. Residential recharging is potentially available in about only 40 percent of American dwellings, and the number of public recharging stations (less than 10,000 in mid-2015) is minuscule in comparison with the 160,000 or so gasoline refueling stations.[81] Thus, a substantial increase in recharging infrastructure will be necessary to ensure the full exploitation of declining vehicle costs.

The federal government has played and could continue to play a role in accelerating the electrification of the transportation fleet. In addition to the tax credits for electric vehicles noted earlier, the 2009 stimulus package (American Recovery and Reinvestment Act) included $2 billion in grants for US manufacturers to produce highly efficient batteries and other components for electric vehicles and $400 million to demonstrate and evaluate EV technologies. In addition, in 2012 the Department of Energy reported that it was on track to demonstrate a substantial reduction in the cost of producing lithium ion batteries to $300 per kilowatt hour by 2015, exceeding the goal of $405 contained in the high-technology battery breakthrough scenario described previously, and more recent reports indicate that costs have already dropped even lower.[82] Thus, the potential for additional federal government spending to help reduce the cost of electric vehicles (PHEVs as well as HEVs and EVs) would seem to be substantial.

Indeed, a 2010 National Research Council study found that as many as 40 million PHEVs (out of a total of 300 million LDVs) could be on the road by 2030 and 240 million by 2050, assuming strong policy intervention. The cost to the government could range from $40 billion to $400 billion, depending on the price of oil, which shapes market incentives, and how much — and how quickly — battery costs can be reduced. Depending on the battery range of the PHEVs, liquid fuel consumption could be cut 40–55 percent by 2050, and according to a 2009 estimate, PHEVs could potentially displace the equivalent of 6.5 mb/d in gasoline consumption.[83] To be sure, many of these savings could be attained simply through the large-scale deployment of HEVs purchased to meet higher fuel economy standards, reducing the unique contribution of the plug-in capability to only 7–23 percent.[84] Nevertheless, even this more modest differential could represent a substantial fuel-switching capability, on the order of up to several million barrels per day of liquid fuel, depending on the relative prices and convenience of using electricity and gasoline prior to an oil price shock.[85]

Summary

Clearly the federal government has numerous options for substantially reducing oil use in the transportation sector. It is already pursuing some of these options through rising fuel economy standards and the renewable fuel standard. Determining what precise mix of policies would make the most sense, however, would require much more extensive analysis, which is beyond the scope of this chapter. Given the complicated interactions among them, as a general rule, the adoption of one approach tends to limit the potential contributions of other approaches to reducing US oil consumption. Indeed, improving fuel economy is already complicating the task of incorporating increasing volumes of biofuels into the transportation fuel supply. But it is equally clear that substantial additional reductions in oil consumption, on the order of half of all remaining gasoline and diesel use through 2050, could be purchased with policies costing the government in the range of $100 billion to $200 billion. The various measures and their potential benefits and costs are summarized in table 7.2.

International Policy Extensions

Through the measures discussed, the United States could substantially reduce the amount of oil that it consumes and the amount that it imports, thereby reducing proportionately the potential economic costs of a future oil supply disruption. It could also diminish the impact of a supply disruption on oil prices by releasing oil from the Strategic Petroleum Reserve to compensate for losses elsewhere and by encouraging the proliferation of vehicles that can run on liquid fuels, on electricity, and, to a lesser extent, on combinations of petroleum products and biofuels, thereby quickly reducing demand for petroleum in a crisis.

The United States can do only so much by itself, however, to bring down the baseline world price of oil through various supply- and demand-side measures and, perhaps more important, to stabilize the price of oil in the event of an oil supply disruption by quickly increasing supply or reducing demand. Success in these areas will also depend on efforts by and developments in other countries. In principle, then, it would be useful, if not essential, for the United States to promote similar policies in other consumer states. What measures can it take in this regard, and what are their prospects for success? This section explores some of the most promising options, organized according to whether they fall on the supply or demand side of the ledger.

Supply Side

On the supply side, it is once again useful to distinguish between increasing oil production and production capacity, on the one hand, and increasing strategic stocks of crude oil and petroleum products, on the other. The United States has long promoted oil exploration and development, both by the private sector and state-owned enterprises, outside the Persian Gulf in places such as the Caspian Sea region, West Africa, and Latin America.[86] Thus, what more the government could do in this regard is unclear. There do not appear to be substantial amounts of easily accessible oil reserves outside the Persian Gulf whose exploitation could fundamentally alter the world market. Indeed, the EIA projects that the Persian Gulf's share of petroleum production will actually grow from less than 28 percent in 2010 to more than 32 percent in 2040.[87]

Table 7.2. Summary of possible demand-side solutions

Policy measure	Oil consumption reduction potential[a]			Cost to government	Fuel-switching potential in crisis
	2025	2035	2050		
Reducing oil consumption					
Feebates ($120/gal/1,000 miles)[b]	1.2–1.8 mb/d	2.4–3.6 mb/d		Several billion dollars	No
2012 CAFE standards[c]	1.7 mb/d	3.6 mb/d		Minimal	No
Taxes on gasoline, diesel[d]	1.5 mb/d	3 mb/d		Minimal	No
Alternative fuels and energy sources					
Biofuels (chiefly ethanol)[e]	1.6 mb/d	1.6 mb/d	3.3 mb/d	Minimal	Up to 1 mb/d
2007 renewable fuel standard				Minimal	
Open fuel standard				$10 billion–$20 billion	
FFV subsidies (100 million LDVs)				$3 billion	
Infrastructure subsidies					
Natural gas[f]					
CNG (40 million LDVs)	0.5 mb/d	1.0 mb/d		Up to $100 billion	No
LNG (100,000 trucks/1,000 stations)	0.5 mb/d	1.0 mb/d		$5 billion	No
Methanol	0.5 mb/d	1.0 mb/d			Less than 1 mb/d
Hydrogen[g]		3.0 mb/d	7.0 mb/d	$55 billion	No
Electric vehicles (PHEVs)[h]	0.5 mb/d	2.2 mb/d	4.1–5.6 mb/d	$40 billion–$400 billion	Up to 3–5 mb/d

a. Estimates are not additive, as most assume that limited additional measures are taken.

b. Assumes that feebates reduce projected gasoline and diesel consumption by 20–30 percent over twenty years.

c. Estimate is for total reduction in liquid fuels.

d. Assumes implementation of a 50 percent tax on gasoline and diesel over ten to twenty years, eventually resulting in a 25 percent reduction in projected gasoline and diesel consumption of 12 mb/d in 2035. EIA, *Annual Energy Outlook 2012*, 153.

e. Assumes full implementation of the 2007 RFS by 2022.

f. Assumes half of 2035 estimate is achieved by 2025.

g. Assumes gasoline contains up to 10 percent ethanol and implementation of 2007 fuel economy standards. See NRC, *Focus on Hydrogen*, 76 and 83.

h. NRC, *Plug-in Hybrid Electric Vehicles*, is based on the same reference case as is NRC, *A Focus on Hydrogen*. Assumes linear growth in EV market penetration between 2015 and 2035.

The United States might have more to offer with regard to the more technologically challenging process of producing unconventional forms of oil, such as
oil (tar) sands, extra-heavy oil, tight oil, and liquids from coal and natural gas, but
the potential here too seems highly limited. For example, the EIA has projected
that total unconventional liquids production (excluding biofuels) will reach
8.4 mb/d, or less than 9 percent of conventional oil production, in 2035. The Persian Gulf's share of the production of all liquid fuels will rise from around 27 percent to 31 percent over the same period. Even in the event that oil prices were
to rise to $200 (in 2009 dollars), production of unconventional liquids (again
excluding biofuels) would reach only 13 mb/d. The Paris-based IEA is more
optimistic in its projection of unconventional oil production, which it expects to
surpass 15 percent of total world oil production in 2035 in its central scenario,
but it also projects the share of output from the Persian Gulf to increase to more
than 34 percent. Thus, even if US policy were able to promote greater production
of unconventional liquids abroad, the resulting additional volumes would likely
be insufficient to reduce the Persian Gulf's role in the world oil market.[88]

In the EIA scenarios, half or more of the production of unconventional liquids (excluding biofuels) would take place in Canada. This observation raises
the question of what energy security benefits the United States might obtain
by building additional pipelines, such as the controversial Keystone XL pipeline, linking Canadian oil sands to the US market. Insofar as oil from Canada is
refined at inland refineries with excess capacity and cannot be readily exported
to third countries, the oil will sell at a discount in comparison with world prices.
But part of the Keystone XL project connects the pipelines bringing oil from
Canada to the Gulf of Mexico, so the Canadian oil will become part of the world
supply and command the same price as comparable grades from other regions.
It could also be argued that Canada represents a more secure source of oil, but
the United States now imports only about 10 percent of the oil it uses from the
Persian Gulf.[89]

It follows that the United States also could do little to increase the world's
secure spare oil production capacity. Since the 1970s, the world's spare capacity
has been concentrated in the Persian Gulf, reflecting the relatively low cost of
producing oil in the region.[90] Unless heavily subsidized to do otherwise, producers of more expensive oil will want to maximize output, and any oil production
that is withheld from the market will tend to push world oil prices higher unless
higher levels of production from the Persian Gulf compensate for it.

Efforts to increase the world's strategic oil reserves then would seem more
promising. Currently the members of the IEA are required to maintain oil stocks
equivalent to no less than ninety days of net imports, and the twenty-six mem-

bers that are net oil importers hold an average of seventy-four days of imports in government-held stocks and a hundred days in commercial stocks.[91] In recent years, these combined stocks amounted to more than 4 billion barrels of crude oil and petroleum products, although government-controlled stocks consisted of only 1.5 billion barrels and the actual availability of some commercial stocks has been questionable.[92] The IEA also maintains an emergency mechanism for sharing oil stocks in the event of a major supply disruption.

As the developing world's share of global oil consumption has grown—from 28 percent in 1974, the year the IEA was founded, to 48 percent in 2011—however, the IEA stockpiling program has become increasingly inadequate to stabilize world oil prices by itself in the event of a supply disruption. Instead, it may be necessary for developing countries, especially major consumers such as China and India, to create substantial stocks of their own. China is, in fact, well into the process of developing a government-controlled reserve of 475 million barrels, with an expected completion date of 2020. China also plans to require industry to maintain additional reserves of more than 200 million barrels. India is much further behind, with plans to create a reserve holding only 37.4 million barrels.[93] What the United States could do to promote this stock-building process is unclear; however, one area in which it could exercise leadership would be in developing mechanisms to coordinate the release of IEA and other stocks in the event of a crisis.

Demand Side

What about the demand side of the equation? Here too the greatest potential for reductions in other countries would appear to lie in the transportation sector. Globally transportation accounted for 55 percent of all liquid fuel consumption in 2010. The EIA projects that share will grow to more than 58 percent—and that total consumption will increase by nearly 50 percent in absolute terms—by 2040 owing to the rapid motorization of many developing counties. Transportation's closest competitor is industry, whose share of consumption is projected to remain around 30 percent. All other uses—residential, commercial, and electric power—will account for a small and declining share of liquid fuel consumption.[94]

In addition, the use of energy in transportation will shift steadily from the United States and other member countries of the Organization for Economic Cooperation and Development (OECD) to the developing world. The EIA projects that the OECD's share of liquid fuel consumption for transportation will drop from 59 percent in 2010 to 37 percent in 2040. The biggest increases will occur in the developing (non-OECD) regions of Asia, especially China and India, which will see their combined share increase from 11 percent in 2010 to

24 percent in 2040. In absolute terms, liquid fuel consumption for transportation in developing countries will more than double.[95]

What can the United States do to promote less oil consumption in the transportation sector in other countries? The United States has made tremendous strides in the area of raising its fuel economy standards for LDVs in recent years; however, it has lagged behind the other biggest automobile markets—the European Union, Japan, and China—in this regard.[96] Thus, it is not clear what US policy could offer to these other major consumers, although opportunities might exist in those developing countries where fuel economy standards have not yet been put in place. Also, the United States could assume a leadership role in promoting fuel economy standards for the road freight sector, where only it and Japan have taken action.[97]

Although the United States has also emerged as the world leader in biofuels production, the principal process it currently uses—converting corn to ethanol—is increasingly regarded as environmentally and economically problematic. Although corn is a renewable feedstock, the process of creating corn ethanol requires almost as much energy as it produces, and if the process uses other fossil fuels, such as natural gas, then substituting ethanol for gasoline results in little or no net reduction in greenhouse gas emissions. Thus, the long-term potential for biofuels hinges on the development and widespread deployment of more environmentally friendly means, such as sugarcane-based and cellulosic ethanol, which have much more favorable energy balances.

What is the global potential for advanced biofuels production? A 2008 Department of Energy study projected that world production of ethanol-equivalent biofuels would reach 54 billion gallons in 2020 and 83 billion gallons in 2030, with 30 billion gallons and 54 billion gallons, respectively, being produced outside the United States. Thus, the non-US production would amount to the energy equivalent of about only 2.5 mb/d of petroleum. In addition, the two biggest non-US sources of ethanol-equivalent biofuels are expected to be Brazil and possibly Western Europe; together, even in 2030, they would account for more than half of the non-US supply.[98] These producers, however, are already the two most advanced biofuel markets outside the United States, so what the United States could offer them to increase their output is not clear. Thus, the main question is whether the US government can play a role in fostering the spread of technologies for making cellulosic biofuels to other potential biofuel-producing areas, such as China and India, once those technologies are sufficiently mature to be applied commercially on a large scale.

Even greater uncertainty would seem to attend what the United States could do to promote the electrification of transportation in other countries, given the limited progress that has occurred so far in the United States, as well as the relative immaturity of US policy in this area. The United States has undertaken an electric vehicle initiative with China, involving the joint development of standards, demonstration projects, and data sharing.[99] But given the relatively high cost of BEVs and PHEVs, advances are likely to lag behind those in the areas of fuel economy and biofuels. Clearly the potential for progress also will depend on the extent and capacity of the electric power systems in other countries. Where the United States might be able to help most is not necessarily in the markets where PHEVs will be built and sold but in promoting access to the relatively scarce raw materials, such as lithium and various rare earth metals, that are needed to fashion advanced batteries and other components of electric vehicles.

Conclusion

This chapter has examined what steps the United States might take to reduce the economic costs of a future oil supply disruption originating in the Persian Gulf. It has identified a number of measures that the United States might implement, or has already begun to implement, both on the supply side and on the demand side. The analysis has found that the most promising opportunities are at home, because it is unclear how much the United States might be able to contribute to the adoption of similar policies in other major oil-consuming countries.

In terms of measures intended to affect the overall supply-demand balance over the long term, the most promising ones would seem to lie on the demand side. Indeed, a substantial reduction in petroleum demand can be achieved simply through implementing existing policies for raising the fuel economy standards and the amount of biofuels in the transportation fuel supply. Together, if fully implemented, they could cut petroleum consumption by light-duty vehicles roughly in half, and total US petroleum consumption by roughly a quarter, through 2035. A sufficient tax on petroleum-based fuels and government efforts to promote the use of natural gas–, hydrogen-, or electricity-powered vehicles could yield even deeper reductions (see table 7.2).

These approaches, however, usually have negative interaction effects. For example, a rising fuel economy will tend to reduce the amount of biofuels that can be absorbed in the fuel supply, while a higher percentage of biofuels will limit the impact of greater fuel economy on petroleum demand. Nevertheless, such demand-side measures have the potential to reduce US petroleum consumption to a much greater extent than the US government could increase petroleum production by relaxing current restrictions on exploration and development in the Arctic National Wildlife Refuge and the outer continental shelf. In addition, increasing domestic production, while reducing net outlays for imports, would do little to reduce the increased amounts that US consumers would have to pay for oil should a major supply disruption elsewhere cause a sudden jump in oil prices.

As for short-term measures designed to mitigate the impact of supply disruptions, ideally by preventing or limiting oil price increases, here the greatest potential appears to be on the supply side with the maintenance of the Strategic Petroleum Reserve and its possible expansion. The current SPR, by itself and especially when used in conjunction with the strategic reserves held by other countries, could neutralize the negative consequences of a range of small to medium-sized disruptions totaling as much as 1.5 billion barrels of lost production.[100] Nevertheless, without considerable expansion, it would be of limited effectiveness in the event of a large-scale and/or extended supply disruption, such as a months-long closure of the Strait of Hormuz or a prolonged loss of Saudi Arabian oil production. In addition, compared to demand-reduction measures, a smaller percentage of the SPR benefits on the supply side would accrue to the United States, because all consumers would benefit from the release of US reserves. Thus, from an energy security perspective, the United States should examine what else it could do to accelerate the penetration of plug-in hybrid electric vehicles and perhaps even to introduce standby rationing plans, which were last developed at the end of the Carter administration.

This analysis suffers from some important limitations. In some cases, it has not tried—or been able—to quantify the economic costs of these measures, but that step would be a necessary component of a thorough cost-benefit analysis. Nor has it sought to identify or evaluate potential externalities of these measures, especially the potential environmental consequences of a greater use of alternative fuels and electricity to power the transportation fleet.

Nevertheless, the analysis suggests that the United States could substantially reduce—and, indeed, is in the process of reducing to a significant extent—the economic costs of a future oil supply disruption through a combination of realistic and affordable supply- and demand-side measures. That possibility, in turn, raises questions about the continued necessity of using diplomacy and costly military preparations to influence the flow of oil from the Persian Gulf. A principal caveat to concluding that the United States could reduce its role in the region concerns the continued dependence of other parts of the world on Persian Gulf oil. A future oil supply disruption in the region might still have a devastating impact on the economies of other countries with which the United States is tightly integrated economically. While US oil consumption may stagnate or decline, that of the rest of the world is projected to continue to increase, and the Persian Gulf is expected to provide a growing share of the total. In particular, Asian countries, such as China and India, which will play ever-larger roles in the world economy, are also becoming increasingly dependent on Persian Gulf oil. If their economies were ever to be hit hard by an oil supply disruption, the effects would soon be felt in the United States as well. Given these potential indirect effects, whether the United States could ever afford to allow a major disruption to occur bears further analysis.

Notes

1. US Energy Information Administration (EIA), *Annual Energy Review, 2011* (Washington DC: EIA, 2012), 127.

2. John S. Duffield, *Over a Barrel: The Costs of U.S. Foreign Oil Dependence* (Stanford: Stanford University Press, 2008). See also Kenneth R. Vincent's chapter 3 in this volume.

3. EIA, *Annual Energy Review*, 123.

4. Ibid., 121, 139.

5. EIA, *Annual Energy Outlook, 2015* (Washington DC: EIA, 2015), C-9, D-9.

6. Ibid., A-23. These figures assume the implementation of some of the policies to reduce US oil consumption that are described in the section on demand-side solutions.

7. EIA, *Annual Energy Review*, 121.

8. Organization for Economic Cooperation and Development (OECD), *Inventory of Estimated Budgetary Support and Tax Expenditures for Fossil Fuels, 2013* (Paris: OECD Publishing, 2012), 429.

9. EIA, *Analysis of Crude Oil Production in the Arctic National Wildlife Refuge* (Washington DC: EIA, 2008).

10. EIA, *Annual Energy Outlook, 2009* (Washington DC: EIA, 2009), 35–37.

11. Michael Levi, *The Power Surge: Energy, Opportunity, and the Battle for America's Future* (New York: Oxford University Press, 2013).

12. EIA, *Analysis of Crude Oil Production*, 11.

13. Levi, *Power Surge*, 69–70.

14. Duffield, *Over a Barrel*, 81–82; and EIA, *Annual Energy Review, 2011*, 157. In 2011, 30 million barrels were sold as part of a coordinated release in response to oil supply disruptions in Libya and elsewhere, leaving a total of less than 700 million barrels in the SPR.

15. US Government Accountability Office (GAO), *Strategic Petroleum Reserve: Available Oil Can Provide Significant Benefits, but Many Factors Should Influence Future Decisions about Fill, Use, and Expansion* (Washington DC: GAO, 2006), 25.

16. Ibid.

17. See US Department of Energy (DOE), "Strategic Petroleum Reserve—Profile," http://energy.gov/fe/services/petroleum-reserves/strategic-petroleum-reserve.

18. The buildup of the SPR was accompanied by a decline in privately held stocks of crude oil and petroleum products in the United States. See EIA, *Annual Energy Review, 2011*, 157.

19. GAO, *Strategic Petroleum Reserve: The Cost Effectiveness of Filling the Reserve* (Washington DC: GAO, 2008), 2.

20. The 18.0 mb/d figure comes from estimated consumption of liquid fuels less renewable fuels in EIA, *Monthly Energy Review* (May 2015), 45.

21. EIA, *Annual Energy Outlook, 2015*, A-23. These figures assume the increased fuel economy standards adopted in 2007 and 2009 and the renewable fuel standard (RFS) adopted in 2007 are implemented.

22. Ibid.

23. EIA, *Monthly Energy Review* (May 2015), 35.

24. National Research Council (NRC), *Transitions to Alternative Transportation Technologies: A Focus on Hydrogen* (Washington DC: National Academies Press, 2008), 15.

25. EIA, *Annual Energy Outlook, 2008* (Washington DC: EIA, 2008), 129.

26. Robert L. Bamberger, "Energy Policy: The Continuing Debate and Omnibus Energy Legislation," Congressional Research Service (CRS) Issue Brief for Congress (Washington DC: CRS, 2004), 11.

27. Jay Hakes, *A Declaration of Energy Independence* (Hoboken NJ: John Wiley & Sons, 2008), 87–88; and Fred Sissine, "Energy Independence and Security Act of 2007: A Summary of Major Provisions," CRS Report for Congress (Washington DC: CRS, 2007).

28. According to Christopher R. Knittel, "Reducing Petroleum Consumption from Transportation," *Journal of Economic Perspectives* 26, no. 1 (2012): 99, the effective increase will be to 34.1 mpg.

29. EIA, *Annual Energy Outlook, 2012* (Washington DC: EIA, 2012), 146.

30. Nancy Pelosi, *A New Direction for Energy Security: A Detailed Summary* (Washington DC: US House of Representatives, 2007); Edmund L. Andrews, "Senate Adopts Energy Bill Raising Mileage for Cars," *New York Times*, June 22, 2007; and EIA, *Annual Energy Outlook, 2008*, 3.

31. Bill Vlasic, "US Sets Higher Fuel Efficiency Standard," *New York Times*, August 28, 2012.

32. EIA, *Annual Energy Outlook, 2012*, 30, 146; and EIA, *Annual Energy Outlook, 2015*, A-16.

33. EIA, *Annual Energy Outlook, 2015*, A-17.

34. Duffield, *Over a Barrel*.

35. Andrew Kleit, "Impacts of Long-Range Increases in the Fuel Economy (CAFE) Standard," *Economic Inquiry* 42, no. 2 (2004): 279–94; David Austin and Terry Dinan, "Clearing the Air: The Costs and Consequences of Higher CAFE Standards and Increased Gasoline Taxes," *Journal of Environmental Economics and Management* 50 (2005): 562–82; Keith Crane et al., *Imported Oil and U.S. National Security* (Santa Monica: RAND, 2009), 87; Eduardo Porter, "Taxes Show One Way to Save Fuel," *New York Times*, September 11, 2012; and Valerie J. Karplus et al., "Should a Vehicle Fuel Economy Standard Be Combined with an Economy-Wide Greenhouse Gas Emissions Constraint? Implications for Energy and Climate Policy in the United States," *Energy Economics* 36 (2013): 322–33.

36. Stacy C. Davis, Susan W. Diegel, and Robert G. Boundy, *Transportation Energy Data Book: Edition 33* (Oak Ridge TN: Oak Ridge National Laboratory, 2014), 10-1.

37. Duffield, *Over a Barrel*, 64–65.

38. Steven E. Plotkin and David L. Greene, "Prospects for Improving the Fuel Economy of Light-Duty Vehicles," *Energy* 25 (14–15): 1179–88; Congressional Budget Office (CBO), *Reducing Gasoline Consumption: Three Options* (Washington DC: CBO, 2002); and Louis Uchitelle and Megan Thee, "Americans Are Cautiously Open to Gas Tax Rise," *New York Times*, February 28, 2006.

39. Sarah E. West and Robert C. Williams III, "Empirical Estimates for Environmental Policy Making in a Second-Best Setting," National Bureau of Economic Research (NBER) Working Papers (Cambridge MA: NBER, 2004); Christopher W. Evans, "Putting Policy in Drive: Coordinating Measures to Reduce Fuel Use and Greenhouse Gas Emissions from US Light-Duty Vehicles" (Cambridge MA: Massachusetts Institute of Technology [MIT], Engineering Systems, 2008); Lucas W. Davis and Lutz Killian, "Estimating the Effects of a Gasoline Tax on Carbon Emissions," NBER Working Paper (Cambridge MA: NBER, 2009); and John Heywood et al., "An Action Plan for Cars: The Policies Needed to Reduce US Petroleum Consumption and Greenhouse Gas Emissions," MIT Energy Initiative Report (Cambridge MA: MIT, 2009).

40. Terry Dinan and David Austin, "Fuel Economy Standards Versus a Gasoline Tax," Economic and Budget Issue Brief (Washington DC: CBO, 2004); and Robert N. Stavins, "A Tale of Two Taxes, a Challenge to Hill," *The Environmental Forum* 21, no. 6 (November–December 2004): 12.

41. For example, Heywood et al., "An Action Plan for Cars," 3.

42. Ibid., 3, 7.

43. Ibid., 8. See also David L. Greene et al., "Feebates, Rebates and Gas-Guzzler Taxes: A Study of Incentives for Increased Fuel Economy," *Energy Policy* 33 (2005): 757–75.

44. Heywood et al., "An Action Plan for Cars," 8.

45. From an economic standpoint, alternative liquid fuels can be regarded as having an effect similar to that of an increase in the supply of oil rather than a reduction in oil consumption.

46. Heywood et al., "An Action Plan for Cars," 4.

47. Duffield, *Over a Barrel*, 74–75; and EIA, *Annual Energy Review, 2011*, 44.

48. Sissine, "Energy Independence"; and Randy Schnepf and Brent D. Yacobucci, "Renewable Fuel Standard (RFS): Overview and Issues," CRS Report for Congress (Washington DC: CRS, 2012).

49. Sandia National Laboratories, "90-Billion Gallon Biofuel Deployment Study: Executive Summary" (Lincoln NE: DOE, February 2009), http://digitalcommons.unl .edu/cgi/viewcontent.cgi?article=1083&content=usdoepub; Gal Luft and Anne Korin, *Turning Oil into Salt: Energy Independence through Fuel Choice* (Charleston SC: BookSurge Publishing, 2009), 85; and NRC, *A Focus on Hydrogen*, 15. A gallon of ethanol contains only about 68 percent as much energy as does a gallon of gasoline.

50. EIA, *Annual Energy Outlook, 2012*, 97, 153.

51. EIA, *Annual Energy Outlook, 2015*, A-23.

52. Ibid., A-23.

53. Davis, Diegel, and Boundy, *Transportation Energy Data Book*, 2-5, 6-3.

54. Ibid., 6-10, 4-19. See also the statement of Howard Gruenspecht, deputy administrator of the Energy Information Administration, before the Subcommittee on Energy and Power, Committee on Energy and Commerce, US House of Representatives, July 17, 2012, 8, http://energycommerce.house.gov/sites/republicans.energy commerce.house.gov/files/Hearings/EP/20120717/HHRG-112-IF03-WState -GruenspechtH-20120717.pdf.

55. Henry Fountain, "Corn Ethanol Makers Weigh Switch to Butanol," *New York Times*, October 23, 2012.

56. Luft and Korin, *Turning Oil into Salt*, 58–59. See also the testimony of Don Althoff, CEO of Flex Fuel US, before the Energy and Commerce Committee of the US House of Representatives, July 10, 2012, http://energycommerce.house.gov/sites/republicans .energycommerce.house.gov/files/Hearings/EP/20120710/HHRG-112-IF03-WState -AlthoffD-20120710.pdf.

57. Alternative Fuels Data Center, "Energy Policy Act of 2005," http://www.afdc .energy.gov/laws/epact_2005.

58. EIA, *Annual Energy Outlook, 2014* (Washington DC: EIA, 2014), MT-15.

59. BP, *BP Statistical Review of World Energy, 2012*; and EIA, *International Energy Outlook, 2011* (Washington DC: EIA, 2011), 244.

60. Davis, Diegel, and Boundy, *Transportation Energy Data Book*, 2-7, 2-4.

61. Knittel, "Reducing Petroleum Consumption," 104.

62. Davis, Diegel, and Boundy, *Transportation Energy Data Book*, 2-7, 5-3.

63. EIA, *Annual Energy Outlook, 2015*, A-16.

64. MIT, *The Future of Natural Gas: An Interdisciplinary MIT Study* (Cambridge MA: MIT, 2011), 26; and Bob Tita, "Slow Going for Natural-Gas Powered Trucks," *Wall Street Journal*, August 25, 2014.

65. Josie Garthwaite, "The New Truck Stop: Filling Up with Natural Gas for the Long-Haul," *National Geographic Daily News*, 2013, http://news.nationalgeographic.com /news/energy/2013/03/130318-natural-gas-truck-stops/.

66. EIA, *Annual Energy Outlook, 2013* (Washington DC: EIA, 2013), 36.

67. See Natural Gas Vehicles for America, 2011, http://www.ngvamerica.org/pdfs /2011_NatGas_SidebySide_111511.pdf.

68. Methanol Institute, "Methanol: The Clear Alternative for Transportation: Methanol Fuel and FFV Technology" (Arlington VA: Methanol Institute, April 2011), http:// www.methanol.org/energy/resources/alternative-fuel/methanol-flexible-fuel-vehicles .aspx.

69. MIT, *Future of Natural Gas*, 125–27; and Knittel, "Reducing Petroleum Consumption," 103.

70. L. Bromberg and W. K. Cheng, "Methanol as an Alternative Transportation Fuel in the US: Options for Sustainable and/or Energy-Secure Transportation" (Cambridge MA:

Sloan Automotive Laboratory, MIT, November 2010), 3–4, http://www.afdc.energy
.gov/pdfs/mit_methanol_white_paper.pdf.

71. Luft and Korin, *Turning Oil Into Salt*, 51; and California Fuel Partnership, *A California Roadmap: Bringing Hydrogen Electric Fuel Cell Vehicles to the Golden State* (West Sacramento: California Fuel Partnership, 2012), 24.

72. Knittel, "Reducing Petroleum Consumption," 109.

73. The NRC analysis was based on the CAFE standard increases contained in the 2007 Energy Independence and Security Act. The potential reductions in liquid fuel use are not as great under the fuel economy standards adopted in 2012.

74. NRC, *A Focus on Hydrogen*.

75. Statement of Howard Gruenspecht.

76. Davis, Diegel, and Boundy, *Transportation Energy Data Book*, 6-9.

77. Bengt Halvoson, "Federal Tax Credits for Plug-in Hybrids, Electric Cars: What You Need to Know," *Washington Post*, August 20, 2104, http://www.washingtonpost.com/cars/federal-tax-credits-for-plug-in-hybrids-electric-cars-what-you-need-to-know/2014/08/20/0ae02718-2886-11e4-8b10-7db129976abb_story.html.

78. EIA, *Annual Energy Outlook, 2012*, 32.

79. Ibid., 33–35; and EIA, *Annual Energy Outlook, 2015*, 10.

80. Luft and Korin, *Turning Oil into Salt*, 73–74; and NRC, *Transitions to Alternative Transportation*, 5.

81. *Alternative Fuels Data Center*, available at afdc.energy.gov.

82. EIA, *Annual Energy Outlook, 2012*, 33; and Stephen Edelstein, "Electric-Car Battery Costs Already Cheaper Than 2020 Predictions: Study," *Green Car Reports*, March 26, 2015, http://www.greencarreports.com/news/1097446_electric-car-battery-costs-already-cheaper-than-2020-predictions-study. See also written statement of Dr. Kathleen Hogan, deputy assistant secretary for energy efficiency, before the Subcommittee on Energy and Power, Committee on Energy and Commerce, US House of Representatives, July 17, 2012, http://energycommerce.house.gov/sites/republicans.energycommerce.house.gov/files/Hearings/EP/20120717/HHRG-112-IF03-WState-HoganK-20120717.pdf.

83. Luft and Korin, *Turning Oil into Salt*, 73.

84. NRC, *Transitions to Alternative Transportation Technologies: Plug-in Hybrid Electric Vehicles* (Washington DC: National Academies Press, 2010), 2, 23, 28–30.

85. The upper-end estimate assumes a per vehicle average annual mileage of twelve thousand miles and fuel economy of 50 mpg when using gasoline and that all vehicles switch from gasoline to electricity in response to an oil price shock.

86. For an overview, see Duffield, *Over a Barrel*.

87. EIA, *International Energy Outlook, 2013* (Washington DC: EIA, 2013), 248.

88. EIA, *International Energy Outlook, 2011*, 229, 232, 236; and International Energy Agency (IEA), *World Energy Outlook, 2013* (Paris: IEA, 2013), 458, 484.

89. EIA, *Monthly Energy Review* (May 2015), 49.

90. IEA, *World Energy Outlook, 2013*, 454.

91. See IEA, "Closing Oil Stock Levels in Days of Net Imports," available at http://www.iea.org/netimports (accessed June 16, 2015).

92. See EIA, *International Petroleum Monthly* (October 2010), table 4.5; and EIA, "International Energy Data and Analysis: Total Petroleum and Other Liquids Production," http://www.eia.gov/beta/international/ (accessed March 20, 2013).

93. See Javier Blas, "China Stops Filling Strategic Oil Reserve," *Financial Times*, November 23, 2012, http://www.ft.com/intl/cms/s/0/c7090954-347d-11e2-8b86-00144feabdc0.html#axzz3vw18XDwm; and Rakesh Sharma, "India Unveils Strategic Oil Stockpile Plans," *Wall Street Journal*, December 21, 2011, http://www.wsj.com/articles/SB10001424052970204464404577111893998225190.

94. EIA, *International Energy Outlook, 2014* (Washington DC: EIA, 2014), 30.

95. Ibid., 27–30.

96. Feng An, Robert Earley, and Lucia Green-Weiskel, *Global Overview on Fuel Efficiency and Motor Vehicle Emission Standards: Policy Options and Perspectives for International Cooperation* (New York: Commission on Sustainable Development, 2011), 18.

97. IEA, *World Energy Outlook, 2012* (Paris: IEA, 2012), 89.

98. DOE, *World Biofuels Production Potential* (Washington DC: DOE, 2008), 34; and EIA, *International Energy Outlook, 2011*, 232, 236.

99. DOE, *US-China Clean Energy Cooperation: A Progress Report by the US Department of Energy* (Washington DC: DOE, 2011).

100. GAO, *Strategic Petroleum Reserve* (2006), 27.

PART III

Conclusions and Policy Options

CHAPTER 8

Should the United States Stay in the Gulf?

Charles L. Glaser and Rosemary A. Kelanic

This chapter and chapter 9 by Caitlin Talmadge offer major policy alternatives to the current US strategy in the Persian Gulf. Our chapter focuses on the basic grand strategy question, *should the United States continue to rely on military force to preserve the flow of Persian Gulf oil?* While the answer is complicated, several factors suggest the United States could possibly end its military commitment by 2025 by investing in measures that increase its economic resilience to oil shocks if no significant new threats emerge. Even so, we envision the United States remaining in the Gulf while these investments are made; it raises the question of what the US military posture should be in the interim. It is also possible, given the many uncertainties involved in our analysis, that the situation ten years hence could evolve in ways that militate against exiting the Gulf. For these reasons, considering alternative force postures for US forces that remain in the Gulf on an interim basis or longer is crucial. Talmadge's chapter examines potential shifts in US posture if the United States were to stay in the Gulf.

Although the United States has a variety of interests in the Persian Gulf, including nonproliferation and antiterrorism, historically oil has been the defining reason for the grand strategic commitment of the United States to the region. Thus, while our analysis is not comprehensive, we believe it offers compelling insights on what is arguably the most important determinant of American strategy in the Gulf. Ending the US military commitment to protect the flow of oil would entail significant changes, including no longer sizing US military forces to fight a major theater contingency in the Gulf, no longer deploying troops or maintaining permanent bases in the region, and no longer routinely stationing an aircraft carrier in or near the Gulf. Furthermore, because the United States would no longer be committed to reacting to Persian Gulf contingencies with large-scale military force, its military planning would no longer emphasize the ability to deploy to the region quickly, particularly in circumstances where US troops were already involved in a regional contingency elsewhere. Of course, the United States would still have options for military engagement, including using special operations forces and military trainers, as it does elsewhere across the globe.

Whether the United States should end its military commitment to protect the flow of Gulf oil depends on a wide variety of factors, including the type and magnitude of damage that the United States would suffer from various possible disruptions of Persian Gulf oil, the probability of these disruptions and the amount that the US military commitment reduces them, the availability of alternative approaches for reducing the probability of disruptions or the damage that the United States would suffer if disruptions should occur, and the amount that the United States spends on its military forces and operations for protecting the flow of Gulf oil that could be directed toward other purposes if the United States ended its military commitment to the Gulf. The core of this volume—chapters 3 through 7—sheds light on these key factors. This chapter pulls together the insights that the earlier chapters offer and embeds them in an overall assessment of the US commitment to the Gulf. Many of these findings are characterized by large uncertainties. As a result, simple, clear-cut policy conclusions are not easily available. We grapple with this challenge in the final section of this chapter.

We conclude that the case for changing US grand strategy is much stronger than suggested by the conventional wisdom, which holds that US oil interests in the Persian Gulf are so large and threatened that the United States must dedicate large military capabilities to their defense. In contrast, our analysis suggests that a fundamental shift in US grand strategy to eliminate the American military commitment may be within reach. Change deserves serious consideration because many of the dangers that were crucial in shaping current policies have disappeared or declined since the underlying conventional wisdom originally gelled. First, although a large sustained disruption would still inflict significant damage on the US economy, that damage would be much milder than it was in the past. In a thirty-year trend that is widely expected to continue, the oil intensity of the US economy—defined as the amount of oil consumed to produce each dollar of gross domestic product (GDP)—has decreased steadily at a rate of about 2 percent per year. As a result, total US economic output today is about 60 percent less reliant on oil than it was in 1980, thus providing a level of resilience that the United States lacked during the oil shocks of the 1970s.[1] At the same time, the United States and its International Energy Agency (IEA) partners have amassed extensive strategic petroleum reserves (SPRs) to cushion the economic impact of shocks. Second, the probability of a major, long-lasting oil disruption appears to be arguably a great deal lower than it was during much of the Cold War. Third, efficiency gains and the reasonable prospect of future technological advances have opened the possibility that the US transportation sector could dramatically reduce its consumption of oil over the coming decades, particularly if the government invests in research and development (R&D), energy distribution infrastructure, and market incentives. Finally, we need to factor in that the United States spends a large sum each year to meet its military commitment to the Gulf; ending that commitment would make these resources available for other valuable purposes.

All things considered, we argue that further reductions in US vulnerability, achieved by moderate investments in domestic and international policies through 2025, could potentially reduce the danger of oil disruptions enough to permit the United States to end its military commitment to the Persian Gulf. Ultimately, however, the decision will depend on Gulf politics. Although the Iran nuclear deal of 2015 brings some hope of increasing stability in the region, the future nevertheless remains difficult to predict because of upheaval in the region. The emerging relationship between the United States and China might also influence the US decision about its military role in the Gulf.

The Pieces of the Grand Strategy Puzzle

Although unrestricted access to Persian Gulf oil has frequently been described as a vital US national security interest, it is no longer the case. Geopolitical changes have transformed the nature of US interests. During the Cold War, the United States required reliable access to Persian Gulf oil to ensure its ability to fight a long war against the Soviet Union in Europe. In contrast, today in the post–Cold War era, the United States continues to have large prosperity interests but not fundamental security interests in the Gulf. Current US security interests are limited and are not generated directly by US concern about the reliable flow of oil.

Appreciating that the US interest in Gulf oil is not a security interest but "only" an economic interest has potentially large implications for US policy. Security interests are often considered to be so large that policies accepting any risk are ill advised. At a minimum, putting a value on security is exceedingly challenging and makes potential trade-offs with other possible uses of US resources difficult. In contrast, while economic interests can also be large, defending them typically receives somewhat lower priority. Optimal policies for protecting economic interests sometimes provide less insurance, accept a higher probability of losses, and require smaller US investments. Where to strike this balance depends, of course, on the magnitude and probability of suffering economic damage, as well as on how economic prosperity is weighed against human costs. Normatively speaking, protecting US national security, as opposed to achieving economic interests, may be a more palatable reason for putting American soldiers in harm's way.

In chapter 3, Kenneth Vincent addresses the magnitude of the economic losses that would be inflicted by oil supply disruptions and finds that expert predictions vary quite substantially. While part of this variation reflects the differences in the size and duration of the hypothesized disruptions, much of it is attributable to large uncertainties about the price elasticity of supply and demand and the price elasticity of US GDP. Vincent identifies an overall price elasticity of approximately −0.12 as representative of the best current estimates. (Thus, a 1 percent reduction in supply can result in approximately an 8 percent increase in the price.) He warns, however, that because the world has never experienced a very large disruption—for example, on the scale of a complete loss of Saudi exports or an Iranian action in the Strait of Hormuz that halved the regular flow of oil from the Gulf—uncertainty about the price impact of this scale of disruption unavoidably increases. If this elasticity does apply to large disruptions, then the complete loss of Saudi oil exports—or approximately 8.5 million barrels a day (mb/d)—would roughly double global oil prices. Cutting the flow of oil through the Strait of Hormuz by half would produce a similar result.

The price elasticity of GDP also spans a wide range, going from −0.05 to −0.01; Vincent conjectures that the middle of this range, or −0.03, is likely most relevant for our project's analysis. (This figure means that a 100 percent increase in the price of oil would result in a 3 percent reduction in GDP.) Using this elasticity, he estimates that the US GDP loss from a disruption that doubled the price of oil would be approximately $500 billion.[2] Given the uncertainties noted earlier, the results could be smaller or larger. Nevertheless, to ground our discussion, we will use this number as a point of comparison for the cost of a very large disruption and return later to policy implications of this uncertainty. Of course, smaller disruptions would result in smaller losses, and the most catastrophic disruption—a long, complete closing of the Strait of Hormuz—would cause larger economic losses.

An important factor that many of these models do not capture but we think changes the ball game significantly is the potentially large impact of strategic petroleum reserves. Models that do not include the possibility that the United States and other countries will use their SPRs and private oil reserves to offset the shortfall that a major disruption would create almost certainly exaggerate the cost of disruptions, especially disruptions that are shorter than a few months. The IEA member countries now have reserves that exceed 4 billion barrels, or enough to replace the oil from a complete disruption of oil through the Strait of Hormuz for eight months.[3] (In 2013 17 mb/d, or around 20 percent of global oil production, passed through the Strait of Hormuz, making it a critical choke point.[4]) Actual replacement would be limited by maximum drawdown rates and the states' access to private reserves. In addition to the approximately 4.5 mb/d that the United States can release from its SPR, the other IEA countries can release approximately 8.5 mb/d during the first month of a crisis; however, these rates would decrease in following months.[5] In addition, China, which is not an IEA member, is creating a large strategic reserve with the capacity to replace ninety days of its oil imports.[6] A coordinated international release of reserves would therefore initially be able to replace the vast majority of the daily loss of oil if the Strait of Hormuz were completely blocked.[7] As John Duffield explains in chapter 7, major disruptions that continue for very long periods would eventually exceed the capacity of strategic and private reserves. However, in all but the worst-case scenarios, reserves would provide a substantial buffer to the damage done by disruptions.[8]

Moreover, because an Iranian effort to close the Strait of Hormuz would be unlikely to entirely shut down the flow of oil, states holding strategic reserves would be still better able to replace lost oil and for a proportionally longer period.[9] Although one reasonable measure of a policy is against the worst case—in this situation, a complete closure—we need to keep in mind that such a scenario is exceedingly unlikely. In more plausible, albeit still unlikely scenarios, the cushion created by strategic reserves would last much longer.

The substantial buffer that strategic reserves provide can greatly reduce, if not entirely eliminate, the economic damage that would otherwise be generated by very large disruptions lasting less than three months. Reserves could be even more effective in reducing the costs of smaller and shorter disruptions. It is true that we cannot determine the ability of strategic reserves to moderate fully the costs of a disruption simply by imagining that withdrawals would directly replace lost oil. Various other factors—including market psychology, uncertainty about the duration of an oil disruption, and failures to manage and coordinate the releases effectively—could reduce the positive impact of reserves. Nevertheless, even taking these additional factors into consideration, domestic and global reserves should significantly reduce the probability that the United States will suffer an oil disruption that greatly harms its economy and should ensure that any disruptions that do occur will be less damaging.[10]

Whether the United States and other major oil-consuming states should invest in further increasing the size and capability of their strategic reserves is addressed in chapter 7. The point to appreciate here is that the strategic reserves that the developed countries have built since the 1970s, and that China is in the process of building, already provide significant insurance against the risks of major oil disruptions. As a result, estimates of the damage that would result from oil disruptions need to factor in the potential of strategic reserves. Estimates that do not include this buffer almost certainly significantly overestimate the negative impacts and should be understood as providing a type of very pessimistic upper bound.

Ending the US military commitment to the Persian Gulf, of course, would not necessarily result in a major disruption of Gulf oil. Thus, we need to consider how likely these disruptions would be if the United States withdrew from the Gulf, as well as how likely they are now. The analyses in chapters 4 and 5 address these issues and find only one potentially grave threat to the flow of Gulf oil—that is, Iran's blocking the Strait of Hormuz. Thomas Lippman's chapter on Saudi Arabia finds the domestic threats to the export of Saudi oil are limited. Although they could result in partial and relatively short-lived disruptions, there is little prospect that any sabotage by al-Qaeda, the takeover of the Saudi government by a radical regime, or a civil war would result in massive reductions in the flow of Saudi oil for an extended period. Moreover, the most valuable contributions that the United States makes to Saudi domestic security, including training its internal security forces and sharing intelligence, could continue unchanged even if the United States ended its direct military commitment to defending the Gulf.

Joshua Rovner's chapter explores the three key ways in which analysts typically envision a regional conflict posing a major threat to the flow of Persian Gulf oil: conquest enables a country to achieve regional hegemony, which provides the capability to control such a large fraction of Gulf oil that the victor can dramatically manipulate global oil prices; war between regional powers extensively damages the Gulf's oil infrastructure or makes shipping too risky, thereby greatly reducing the export of oil for an extended period; and closure of the Strait of Hormuz, most likely by Iran, blocks a critical choke point, providing Iran with the ability to coerce the United States and other countries. Rovner finds that of this standard list of threats to the flow of Gulf oil, only the closing of the Strait of Hormuz by Iran is sufficiently likely (albeit still unlikely) that it should influence US oil policy in the region. The Gulf states that might possibly pose a hegemonic threat—Iraq, Iran, and Saudi Arabia—have been weakened by war, US invasion, sanctions, and internal threats; moreover, Saudi Arabia has shown no interest in power projection, having bought forces that emphasize deterrence and denial. A damaging war between regional powers is unlikely for largely the same reasons and because of the underlying difficulty of waging successful offensive campaigns.

In contrast, Iran has the capability to significantly interrupt, if not fully shut down, tanker traffic through the Strait and might have incentives to do so. Estimates of the probability of an Iranian decision to close the Strait are unavoidably subjective. Although Iran has shown little inclination to try to close the Strait, even during the Iran-Iraq War, terminating the US military commitment would so significantly change the regional environment that Iran's past behavior might provide little information about its future behavior.[11] As Rovner emphasizes in his chapter, the prospect of US intervention is a highly credible deterrent to Iranian disruption of the flow of oil. Thus, we have to expect that removing this deterrent would increase the probability of an Iranian effort to close the Strait.

How much it would increase, and how large it is to start with, is difficult to surmise. One major source of Iranian restraint is that closing Hormuz not only would block others' oil exports but also would interfere with its own oil exports. Thus, military action in the Strait would cost the long-struggling Iranian economy a critical source of income. Given the dire economic consequences of a closure, Iran is unlikely to attempt it except in extraordinary circumstances. What might motivate Tehran to make such a costly move? Analysts point to only a few reasons.

First, and potentially the most likely scenario, Iran might retaliate against the Strait to punish any attack on its nuclear program. A full-scale American attack would likely destroy Iran's capability for blocking the Strait, thereby eliminating its option to retaliate, but a more limited attack would not. The Iran nuclear deal likely reduces the probability of this scenario, although its effects cut in two potential directions. On the one hand, the agreement probably makes an Iranian attempt to build nuclear weapons less likely overall, thus reducing the chances of a US or Israeli attack that could prompt Iranian retaliation against the Strait. On the other hand, if Iran cheats on the agreement—not only moving closer to making a bomb but also breaking its promise to Washington—then the United States might feel pressure to penalize Iran more harshly than it would have if no deal had been reached. Thus, if Iran takes further steps to weaponize its nuclear program in contravention to the agreement, the United States might be more likely to attack, providing Iran with a plausible reason for closing the Strait. Compounding the uncertainty, the deal begins to loosen restraints on Iranian nuclear development after ten years, and that could lead to increased concerns about Iran's nuclear program further down the road. Some advocates of the deal suggest it might improve US-Iran relations enough that Iran might lose interest in proliferation or that a nuclear Iran would be less threatening a decade from now. Ultimately the scenario of a military strike that provokes Iran to close the Strait seems less likely after finalizing the nuclear deal, but it cannot be definitively dismissed.

Second, if engaged in a major war with one of its neighbors, Iran might block the Strait to open a second front that would divert its adversary or punish it.[12] However, based upon Rovner's finding that the probability of large interstate wars in the region is small, this type of situation deserves little weight in guiding US policy. Another possibility is that Iran could close the Strait to punish the West for enforcing sanctions against its oil exports, but experience suggests it is improbable. In late 2011 Iran threatened to close the Strait of Hormuz if the United States and its European allies imposed sanctions that severely reduced Iran's oil revenue.[13] It turned out to be a bluff. Iran suffered under these sanctions, having its exports cut from 2.5 mb/d to 1.1 mb/d, but it did not move against the Strait.[14] Admittedly this scenario might have played out differently if the US military threat had not existed. The nuclear deal will loosen and eventually eliminate the sanctions that the United States and the United Nations have imposed on Iran. The possibility that sanctions could be instituted on other grounds means that this path is not eliminated but certainly less likely because, among other reasons, renewed severe sanctions on oil could lead Iran to withdraw from the nuclear agreement.

If Iran were eventually to acquire nuclear weapons, the deterrent value of maintaining the US military commitment would likely be larger. A common fear is that having nuclear weapons would embolden Iran and enable it to pursue more assertive policies in the Persian Gulf region, including closing the Strait of Hormuz.[15] Without local US military capabilities to counter Iran's, Iran might believe that it faced little risk in attempting to close the Strait. By reducing the risk of Iranian proliferation, the nuclear deal also decreases this danger.

Pulling these arguments together, in rough and simplified terms, the United States faces the following situation. Ending the US military commitment to the Gulf appears unlikely to increase the probability of major sustained disruptions of Persian Gulf oil, with the potential exception of an Iranian attempt to close the Strait of Hormuz. The nuclear deal mitigates against this possibility but does not eliminate it. Smaller disruptions are likely to continue to occur, as they have since the 1980s, and possibly will become more frequent. However, the combination of flexible oil markets and, for more significant disruptions, the availability of large petroleum reserves promises to limit their economic damage. The real danger is in a near-worst-case scenario, a disruption that lasts long enough to greatly deplete global strategic reserves. As noted earlier, such a historically unprecedented disruption could result in a doubling of the price of oil, which would in turn reduce US GDP by $500 billion, or about 3 percent. Unfortunately, we have no reliable way of estimating the increased probability that Iran would inflict a very large, long oil disruption if the United States left the Gulf.

Given these risks, conducting an assessment of US policy requires knowing how much the United States spends to defend its oil interests in the Persian Gulf. Resources spent on protecting the Gulf could be directed to other purposes, whether protecting different regions of the globe or investing at home in the United States. If the value of defending the Gulf is smaller, then the case for spending US resources on other purposes increases.

In chapter 6, Eugene Gholz addresses this spending question, exploring how much the United States spends to defend its oil interests in the Persian Gulf. He finds that how much the United States could reduce its spending would depend on whether it decides to revise US force planning requirements. Since the end of the Cold War, US plans have called for being able to deter and defeat two regional aggressors in different theaters in overlapping time frames.[16] One of these planning scenarios typically includes a major regional contingency (MRC) in the Persian Gulf. A key rationale for the two-war readiness standard is to deter opportunistic aggression—to prevent the possibility that a hostile state would feel confident in launching a regional conflict because the United States was fighting in a different theater and therefore unable to intervene in the second war. If the United States decides that it no longer needs to size its forces for a major contingency in the Gulf, it would have two broad options. The first would be to maintain its current planning criteria, thus continuing to plan to prevail against two aggressors by elevating a new regional theater or scenario to replace the Gulf. The second would be to reduce its planning criteria and shift to a one-MRC requirement. Given the long-standing position of the Persian Gulf in the two-MRC construct, our judgment is that ending the US commitment to protecting the flow of Persian Gulf oil should enable the United States to adopt the latter route.

Gholz shows that if the United States chooses the former approach—retaining its two-MRC requirement—then it will save only a modest $5 billion per year, not counting the increased costs of operations during crises and wars.[17] In contrast, if the United States moves to a one-MRC requirement, or being able to fight two major wars sequentially, then terminating the US military commitment to the Gulf could save roughly $75 billion dollars a year, or about 15 percent of the US defense budget.[18] According to this estimate, the United States would be able to cut two aircraft carrier strike groups, two US Army divisions, and a few hundred Air Force fighters and bombers.

US Policy Options

Where does this leave us with respect to the grand strategy question of whether the United States should end its military commitment to preserving the reliable flow of Persian Gulf oil? Given the potentially grave economic damage that a very large, sustained disruption could inflict, current US policy is not clearly out of line. Hedging against low-probability, high-cost events is often appropriate, especially when faced with large uncertainties about both the probabilities and costs, as is the case in the Gulf.

That said, we nevertheless conclude the case for significantly revising US military policy toward the Gulf is substantially stronger than the conventional wisdom suggests. The conventional wisdom has long held that US oil interests in the Gulf are so large and threatened that the United States has no option other than actively defending them with large military capabilities. The Gulf is the one geographical area that the debate over US grand strategy has not seriously questioned. Experts on US energy requirements similarly continue to see an ongoing US military commitment to the Gulf as essential.[19]

In contrast, our analysis so far supports the possibility that a fundamental change in its grand strategy may be the best option for the United States. This conclusion partly reflects the reduction in the number of threats that could cause potentially extremely costly disruptions in the Gulf. The dissolution of the Soviet Union, for example, removed the danger of a major power that could threaten the Gulf.[20] In addition, the possibility that a regional hegemon could gain control of the majority of Persian Gulf oil has been essentially eliminated for the foreseeable future. As Rovner explains in chapter 5, the US wars with Iraq have greatly reduced Iraq's military capabilities and eliminated a regime that might have harbored hegemonic ambitions; furthermore, violent turmoil since the 2011 departure of US forces and the 2014 invasion by the Islamic State have further weakened Iraq. In addition, the Iranian nuclear deal reduces the prospect of Iran's using nuclear weapons to expand its regional influence. Moreover, as Lippman lays out in chapter 4, although the Arab Spring uprisings have shaken the region, the key oil state in the Persian Gulf—Saudi Arabia—appears to be quite stable. The possibility of ending the US commitment also reflects the effective cushion that the US SPR, in combination with other global reserves, provides against all but the most severe and sustained disruptions. Finally, the attraction of ending the US military commitment to the Gulf lies in the opportunity to redirect the large amount that the United States spends annually on military forces that play a role in protecting the Gulf.

The next step in evaluating the possibility of severing the US military commitment to the Gulf is asking what policies the United States could pursue that would further reduce the impact of large oil disruptions. If available, investments in these alternative approaches would reduce the risk of a US shift away from its military commitment to the Gulf. As John Duffield lays out in chapter 7, the United States has a wide range of complementary supply-side and demand-side options for reducing the costs of a major supply disruption. Moreover, he finds that the annual investment in an appropriate mix of these options would amount to a small fraction of what the United States currently spends to defend the Gulf.

On the supply side, the United States could improve its ability to replace blocked oil for an extended period by increasing the size of its SPR. From 2005 to 2015, oil prices fluctuated between a low of about $35 per barrel to a high of about $115 per barrel (in 2014 dollars). Assuming prices stay in this broad range, increasing the SPR by 50 percent, or about 350 million barrels, would cost anywhere between $10 billion and $40 billion and would extend the country's ability to offset its "share" of a major oil disruption by several months.[21] This increase, especially if matched by other countries, would add significantly to the insurance policy that the IEA countries and China have already built. In addition, changes in how the United States manages its SPR—including the development of procedures for expediting IEA decisions—could increase its potential to reduce the impact of disruptions.[22]

On the demand side, the United States has already implemented some effective measures, especially in requiring higher fuel efficiency for cars and light trucks, and it could pursue a range of other options that would contribute to reductions in US oil consumption, including further regulations on transportation, higher taxes and related incentives, and greater investments in R&D and energy infrastructure. Reduced consumption, in turn, would mitigate the economic damage that price increases would inflict, because if the US economy depends less on oil, it is less sensitive to changes in its price. Continuing investments in transportation efficiency and alternative fuels would further reduce the impact of oil disruptions. A variety of taxes could reduce US oil consumption and thereby diminish the economic impact of oil disruptions that, either because of the SPR's inability to offset the lost oil or because of market psychology, result in increased oil prices. These taxes would cost the US government very little, although consumers would face higher total prices for oil. Assessing the optimal mix of approaches and investments remains challenging and is beyond the scope of this analysis. Some of the investments—especially in R&D—would have uncertain returns, but overall they appear promising and are eventually likely to partially offset the higher price of oil to consumers. Duffield estimates that an investment of approximately $100 billion to $200 billion could reduce US oil consumption by approximately half by 2035.

In sum, then, an overall US oil policy that combined a large increase in the size of the SPR, new taxes, and increased investments in alternative fuels and fuel efficiency would likely require the US government to invest roughly $100 billion dollars over a single decade. Although certainly a large amount, the annual investment of $10 billion would be about 13 percent of the $75 billion that the

United States currently spends to defend the Gulf. This policy would provide a larger cushion against supply disruptions that would also last longer because US oil consumption would be quite significantly reduced.

To complement these domestic policies, the United States could pursue a range of international policies. An important possibility is for the United States to encourage the Gulf states to reduce their vulnerability to the Strait's closure by increasing the capacity of their bypass pipelines to divert oil from passing through the Strait of Hormuz. As of November 2014, Saudi Arabia and the United Arab Emirates (UAE) had bypass pipelines capable of carrying about 6.6 mb/d directly to the Red Sea or the Gulf of Oman. Only 2.9 mb/d of this capacity was then in use, leaving a spare capacity of 3.7 mb/d, or enough to quickly replace more than 20 percent of the oil transported through the Strait of Hormuz.[23] When used in combination with strategic reserves during a disruption, this pipeline capability could reduce required withdrawal rates and extend the period over which strategic reserves could continue to help meet unmet demand.

Given the central role that the Strait of Hormuz plays in possibilities for large disruptions, the United States should encourage and pressure the major Gulf oil producers to further increase their bypass pipeline capacity by building new ones, refurbishing old ones, and increasing the throughput capacity of existing pipelines. Further increases in Saudi capability would likely be most valuable, but other countries, including Iraq, could make worthwhile efforts.[24] The cost of pipelines varies, depending on a variety of factors.[25] The UAE pipeline built in 2012 with a capacity of 1.5 mb/d cost about $3.5 billion and is approximately 250 miles long.[26] Saudi Arabian pipelines from the Persian Gulf to the Red Sea need to be essentially three times as long. A rough estimate therefore suggests that the Saudis could build such a pipeline for approximately $10 billion. Thus, although new pipelines are expensive, their costs are dwarfed by the value of oil exports, and major oil producers can definitely afford them.[27] In addition, much less expensive approaches—using chemical agents—might be capable of significantly increasing the capacity of existing pipelines during a crisis in the Strait.[28] Given the vastly larger sums that the United States invests to ensure the flow of Gulf oil, the United States should reasonably expect the oil-exporting countries of the Gulf to provide this dimension of insurance.

A question that naturally arises is whether Iran could destroy these pipelines or the Saudi oil production and export capability more broadly. The key potential threat would be missile attacks. Analysis shows that the Saudi complex is not highly vulnerable to possible Iranian missile attacks, although significant improvements in missile accuracy would increase the Iranian threat. In addition, the weak link in the complex is the Saudi stabilization plants, not its pipelines.[29]

Consequently, even when considered in these strategic terms, increased bypass pipeline capacity would be a good investment.

A second component of US international efforts could focus on strategic reserves. If the United States decides to expand its SPR, it should work to convince other IEA members, as well as the major developing country importers, to make comparable increases in their capabilities. Otherwise, the United States will be left trying to cushion more than its share of a massive supply disruption, and that will greatly reduce the effectiveness of its investments.

Pulling these strands together, and recognizing that US policy must be contingent on the evolution of both regional and global politics, we recommend a dual-pronged approach that would better position the United States to terminate its military commitment to the Gulf. First, over the course of a couple of decades, the United States should invest in further reducing its vulnerability to oil shocks by pursuing both supply- and demand-side approaches. Depending on the specific mix of investments, substantial gains could be achieved within a decade, especially via a larger SPR but also via continued improvements in transportation efficiency. The United States could make this investment on top of its defense spending, which might be offset by modest reductions to US forces and operations committed to the Gulf, as laid out in chapter 9. If after a decade or so the United States could then terminate its Gulf commitments, the investment would, in effect, be repaid quickly. During the same period, the United States should cooperate with other major oil importers to ensure that their strategic reserves are comparable to, and well coordinated with, US reserves and to reduce the oil intensity of their economies. The United States should also work with Saudi Arabia and other key exporters to further increase their pipeline capacity bypassing the Strait of Hormuz.

Second, the United States should continue to evaluate the risks in the Gulf, particularly those posed by Iran. The recent nuclear deal raises the possibility that the Iranian threat will diminish down the road. No longer facing sanctions on its oil exports, Iran would likely pose a smaller danger as its incentives for keeping oil flowing would be that much greater. And the higher probability of a nonnuclear Iran, both during the period of the agreement and afterward, reduces the prospect that Iran would be emboldened with a nuclear deterrent to menace the Strait of Hormuz. Moreover, even in this worst case, improved bypass pipelines would significantly curtail the impact of a closure and thereby shrink this danger, which would be further reduced by instituting policies designed to cushion the impact of oil disruptions. If Iran becomes less threatening, then the United States would be well positioned to leave the Gulf. If it becomes more threatening, however, the United States would confront a more complicated choice. Being much better insulated from even worst-case disruptions, the United States might still withdraw, incurring the increased probability of oil disruptions and the accompanying damage to its GDP but gaining the opportunity to reallocate substantial resources to other purposes. Alternatively, the United States might decide that its best option is to maintain its military commitment to the Gulf, benefiting from a reduced sensitivity to large disruptions but nevertheless continuing to spend large sums to protect the flow of Gulf oil.

The possibility that a combination of US policies and world events could sufficiently protect American oil interests to enable the United States to end its military commitment to Gulf security raises a final provocative question: If the United States withdrew its military commitment from the region, would another country—perhaps China—step in to replace it? After all, one or another great power has possessed a sphere of influence in the Persian Gulf for most of the past hundred years. From the early twentieth century until 1971, that power was Great Britain. Attracted initially by the Gulf's proximity to colonial India—and later by its unparalleled petroleum resources—the British established a significant military foothold in the region that maintained local stability and kept rival great powers out. Scarcely a decade after Britain formally divested of its Gulf responsibilities, the United States moved in to prevent the region from falling into Soviet hands. If the United States signaled an intention to close its security umbrella, some experts warn, then Gulf nations might start "cozying up with others."[30] Some observers believe the regional clamoring for security partnerships with China has already begun.[31]

In the short to mid-term, a US decision to end its commitment to Gulf security would not create a military opening for China, which lacks the wherewithal to adopt the role of regional security provider anytime soon, even if it had the desire to do so. In fact, some argue an American withdrawal would hurt China in the short run because, perhaps more than any other country, it benefits substantially from free riding on the public good of US Persian Gulf security commitments.[32] Lacking global power projection capabilities, China currently could not provide tanker traffic with nearly as much security as it enjoys free of charge, courtesy of Uncle Sam.[33]

However, in a couple or more decades, China's economic growth and military expansion could conceivably position it to project power into the region. Whether this posture would favor or endanger the United States is open to debate. On the one hand, those who argue that a US-China strategic antagonism is inevitable would view China's entry into the Gulf with alarm. Some experts already anticipate that the emerging rivalry between the United States and China in Asia could spread to include security competition in the Persian Gulf.[34] On the other hand, the United States might benefit from an expanded Chinese role in the region. Given its large and increasing oil consumption, China has a growing stake in Gulf stability; the United States could gain from China's security efforts while avoiding the costs.

Our conclusion is that US policy should proceed without waiting to know how all of the imponderables will play out; taking one step at a time makes sense in this case. Further reducing its vulnerability to disruptions, through both supply- and demand-side measures, will be valuable even if the United States decides later to maintain its military commitment to the Gulf. Moreover, there appears to be a reasonable chance that the regional and global politics will play out in ways that enable this bet to pay off handsomely. And, of course, the risks are small because the United States will retain the option of maintaining its military commitment and, in turn, its grand strategic commitment to the Persian Gulf.

Still more broadly, we conclude that the analysis presented in this book demonstrates that the US grand strategic commitment to the Persian Gulf should not simply be taken for granted, as it has been for decades. While the US presence in the Gulf reflects many interests—not only oil but also nonproliferation and counterterrorism—oil is arguably the American interest that has driven its commitment to the region the most. US policies designed to reduce further its vulnerability to oil disruptions have a reasonable prospect of allowing the United States to change its grand strategy in future decades.

Notes

1. Adam Sieminski, "Energy and the Economy," presentation at US Energy Information Administration (EIA) and Johns Hopkins University School of Advanced International Studies 2010 Energy Conference: Short-Term Stresses, Long-Term Change, Washington DC, April 6, 2010, 5; and US EIA), *Annual Energy Outlook, 2015* (Washington DC: Department of Energy, 2015), 16–17. Observers generally attribute this trend to efficiency gains and the restructuring of the US economy away from highly energy-intensive manufacturing in favor of less energy-intensive services.

2. US GDP in 2015 was roughly $17 trillion in current dollars.

3. International Energy Agency (IEA), *Energy Supply Security, 2014* (Paris: IEA 2014), 23; and William Komiss and LaVar Huntzinger, "The Economic Implications of Disruptions of Maritime Oil Chokepoints" (Arlington VA: CNA, March 2011), 21.

4. EIA, *World Oil Transit Chokepoints* (November 10, 2014), 2, http://www.eia.gov/beta/international/analysis_includes/special_topics/World_Oil_Transit_Choke points/wotc.pdf.

5. US Government Accountability Office (GAO), *Strategic Petroleum Reserve: Available Oil Can Provide Significant Benefits, but Many Factors Should Influence Future Decisions about Fill, Use, and Expansion* (Washington DC: GAO, 2006), 25. The release capabilities

of states would decline as a large disruption continued, because the amount of oil that can be released decreases as reserves are drained.

6. China has plans to build a petroleum reserve capable of holding at least 500 million barrels by 2020. However, the extent of its progress thus far is uncertain because the Chinese government rarely comments on the status of its reserves. Industry experts estimate that as of May 2015, China had a storage capacity of 140 million to 180 million barrels and an actual SPR stockpile of 130 million barrels. In addition, China has about 350 million barrels of oil in commercial reserves. See EIA, *China*, updated May 14, 2015, 14–15, http://www.eia.gov/beta/international/analysis_includes/countries_long/China/china.pdf. We should note that because even a major Persian Gulf disruption would not eliminate all global oil exports, China still would be able to continue to import oil; therefore, its reserves would last longer.

7. Because China is not an IEA member, it does not have a treaty obligation to participate in a coordinated release of strategic reserves; however, China and the United States took steps toward cooperation on strategic reserves in July 2014. See Judy Hua and Chen Aizhu, "Update 1: China, U.S. to Cooperate on Strategic Reserves," Reuters, July 11, 2014, http://uk.reuters.com/article/china-usa-oil-idUKL4N0PM3IE20140711.

8. In *Strategic Petroleum Reserve*, the GAO identifies in its range of illustrative scenarios one exception, a two-year complete disruption of Saudi oil. In that case, reserves are not large enough to protect against a large percentage of the total damage.

9. Eugene Gholz and Daryl G. Press, "Protecting 'The Prize': Oil and the U.S. National Interest," *Security Studies*, 19, no. 3 (2010): 478–81, argue that Iran could not "seriously disrupt shipping for an extended period" even in the absence of US military intervention.

10. GAO, *Strategic Petroleum Reserve*.

11. Caitlin Talmadge, "Closing Time: Assessing the Iranian Threat to the Strait of Hormuz," *International Security* 33, no. 1 (Summer 2008): 87–88.

12. On these possibilities, see Talmadge, "Closing Time," 87–88.

13. David E. Sanger and Annie Lowrey, "Iran Threatens to Choke Route of Oil Shipments," *New York Times*, December 28, 2011, 1. For background on US and UN sanctions against Iran, see Kenneth Katzman, *Iran Sanctions* (Washington DC: Congressional Research Service, January 10, 2013).

14. EIA, "Iran's Oil Exports Not Expected to Increase Significantly despite Recent Negotiations" December 10, 2013, www.eia.gov/todayinenergy/detail.cfm?id=14111. Analysts projected that losses to government revenue would surpass $50 billion for 2013. Katzman, *Iran Sanctions*, 54.

15. See, for example, Scott D. Sagan, "How to Keep the Bomb from Iran," *Foreign Affairs* 85, no. 5 (September–October 2006): 45–59.

16. US Department of Defense, "Quadrennial Defense Review Report" (Washington DC: Department of Defense, February 2010), vi, 41–42.

17. Gholz contends that the costs of future oil-related military operations in the Gulf are virtually impossible to estimate because they hinge so strongly on the distribution of future scenarios. The range of possibilities is wide, and the costs could be substantial. Re-

flagging Kuwaiti tankers during the Iran-Iraq War was a relatively cheap mission, costing only $500 million in 2013 dollars. At the other end of the spectrum, the 2003 Iraq War and its aftermath cost nearly $1 trillion, with some estimates being much higher. See Joseph E. Stiglitz and Linda J. Bilmes, *The Three Trillion Dollar War: The True Cost of the Iraq Conflict* (New York: W. W. Norton, 2008).

18. For a range of estimates, see Keith Crane et al., *Imported Oil and U.S. National Security* (Santa Monica: RAND, 2009), 59–75.

19. See for example, Jan H. Kalicki and David L. Goldwyn, *Energy & Security: Strategies for a World in Transition* (Baltimore: Johns Hopkins University Press, 2013).

20. There was debate during the Cold War over whether the Soviet Union actually posed a serious threat. See, for example, Joshua M. Epstein, *Strategy and Force Planning: The Case of the Persian Gulf* (Washington DC: Brookings, 1987).

21. BP, *BP Statistical Review of World Energy, June 2015*, 15, https://www.bp.com/content/dam/bp/pdf/energy-economics/statistical-review-2015/bp-statistical-review-of-world-energy-2015-full-report.pdf. The actual length of the extension would depend on the size of the disruption, whether other countries increased their reserves in parallel with US increases, and whether other countries released oil in coordination with the United States. If we assume that the United States needs to replace its "share," or roughly 15 percent, of total imports and if we hypothesize a disruption of 8mb/d—approximately half the flow of oil through the Strait of Hormuz—then a 50 percent increase in the US SPR would extend the country's ability to replace its share of lost oil for almost ten months. Of course, if the United States bore more of the burden of replacement because other IEA countries, or China, failed to pitch in their share of reserves to the global market, then the extension would be smaller.

22. Michelle Billig Patron and David L. Goldwyn, "Managing Strategic Reserves," in Kalicki and Goldwyn, *Energy & Security*.

23. EIA, *World Oil Transit Chokepoints*.

24. Dagobert Brito and Amy Myers Jaffe, "Reducing Vulnerability to the Strait of Hormuz," in *Getting Ready for a Nuclear-Ready Iran*, ed. Henry Sokolski and Patrick Clawson (Carlisle PA: Strategic Studies Institute, October 2005), 217–19. Kuwait studied the possibility of building a bypass pipeline but decided against it in 2013 because it was too expensive. To further complicate this project, the pipeline would have to run across a neighboring state. "Kuwait Drops Idea of Hormuz Bypass Oil Pipeline," *Arab News*, September 18, 2013, www.arabnews.com/news/464928.

25. On pipeline costs, see Christopher E. Smith, "Worldwide Pipeline Construction: Crude, Product Plans Push 2013 Construction Sharply Higher," *Oil & Gas Journal*, February 4, 2013, 1–13, http://www.ogj.com/articles/print/volume-111/issue-02/special-report--worldwide-pipeline-construction-crude-products.html.

26. Javier Blas, "Pipelines Bypassing Hormuz Open," *Financial Times*, July 15, 2012; and "Abu Dhabi Ships First Crude outside Strait of Hormuz," *Platts Oilgram News*, July 17, 2012.

27. Of course, whether their expected value exceeds these costs is a different issue

because, among other reasons, disruptions are uncertain and occur with low probability. For an assessment of the expect value, see M. Webster Ewell Jr., Dagobert Brito, and John Noer, "An Alternative Pipeline Strategy for the Persian Gulf" (Houston: James A. Baker III Institute for Public Policy, the Center for International Political Economy, and the Office of the Secretary of Defense, April 1997). They find that the investment is not clearly financially attractive. This conclusion raises the possibility that the United States should consider subsidizing a portion of the cost of the enhanced bypass capability.

28. On the potential of drag-reducing agents, see Dagobert L. Brito, "Revisiting Alternatives to the Strait of Hormuz" (Houston: James A. Baker III Institute for Public Policy, Rice University, January 26, 2012).

29. Joshua R. Itzkowitz Shifrinson and Miranda Priebe, "A Crude Threat: The Limits of an Iranian Missile Campaign against Saudi Arabian Oil," *International Security* 36, no. 1 (Summer 2011): 67–201.

30. Michael A. Levi, "The False Promise of Energy Independence," *New York Times*, December 21, 2012.

31. Emile Hokayem, "Looking East: A Gulf Vision or a Reality?," in *China and the Persian Gulf: Implications for the United States*, ed. Bryce Wakefield and Susan L. Levenstein (Washington DC: Woodrow Wilson International Center for Scholars, 2011), 38, 41–42.

32. "German Intelligence Report Examines Global Impact of U.S. Energy Independence," *BBC Monitoring Europe*, January 18, 2013.

33. US dominance actually cuts both ways. On the negative side, China and the rest of the world are at the mercy of US policy concerning the Gulf, and it is not always strategically sound. Many grumble that the Iraq War created a "public bad" insofar as it caused regional instability that possibly contributed to high oil prices. Thus, even while other nations benefit when American policies are sound, the significant downside is they cannot avoid collective suffering from bad US policies. On perceptions of US strategic mismanagement in the Gulf, see Jon B. Alterman, "The Vital Triangle," in Wakefield and Levenstein, *China and the Persian Gulf*, 30, 34.

34. John J. Mearsheimer, "The Gathering Storm: China's Challenge to U.S. Power in Asia," *Chinese Journal of International Politics* 3, no. 4 (Winter 2010): 391–92.

CHAPTER 9

The Future of US Force Posture in the Gulf: The Case for a Residual Forward Presence

Caitlin Talmadge

For the first time in many years, the United States is in a position to consider anew the appropriate size, shape, and purpose of its military presence in the Gulf. Much of this volume has addressed the question of whether the American security commitment to protect Gulf oil remains necessary given the present-day threat environment, which differs substantially from the initial conditions that prompted direct US involvement in the 1970s.[1] Although the answer regarding strategy is not clear cut, virtually no one argues that the United States should repeat the force posture experience of 1991–2011, when the presence of large, permanent, and highly visible US military forces was a fact of life in the Gulf. Especially as the United States initiates its so-called pivot toward Asia, the question for those favoring a continued commitment to the Gulf is not whether the US footprint in the Middle East should be reduced but to what extent and in what ways to do so while still securing core US interests, including the free flow of affordable oil.[2]

In chapter 8, Charles Glaser and Rosemary Kelanic explore that oil-based rationale for the current US grand strategic commitment to the Gulf. They conclude that the case is weaker than generally appreciated and that policies dedicated to further reducing the US economy's vulnerability to disruptions of Persian Gulf oil could lay the foundation for ending the US commitment. At best, however, such a break is a decade or more away, and even then it is far from inevitable. Consequently, this chapter assumes that the United States retains it commitment to protecting the free flow of Persian Gulf oil and explores US military requirements for achieving this goal.

This chapter develops what I call a residual forward presence (RFP) option for US posture in the Gulf, under the assumption that the United States retains its commitment to protecting the steady flow of oil. As its name implies, the RFP posture would maintain a forward military presence in the Gulf but keep much of this presence offshore, leaving only a carefully tailored, minimal footprint on land. Specifically, it would keep a few thousand soldiers in Kuwait, along with prepositioned equipment to support larger forces if needed; one air wing each at low-visibility bases in the United Arab Emirates (UAE) and Qatar, as well as command facilities at the latter; and the Fifth Fleet headquarters ashore in Bahrain. Afloat, this approach would maintain a robust forward presence of smaller US ships well suited to operating in the Gulf, but US carriers would mostly remain in the Indian Ocean. The analysis shows that this RFP option could offer substantial military and political advantages both over the highly visible, ground-heavy presence of the period 1991–2011, as well as over the other major posture alternative discussed in the open-source literature that advocates a nearly complete withdrawal of US forces to an over-the-horizon (OTH) stance.

The chapter advances the argument in four main parts. It begins by establishing a framework for evaluating US military posture in the Gulf, one designed to be useful even for those who believe that RFP is not the right option. The framework outlines key assumptions about US goals, particularly related to maintaining the flow of oil. It then identifies six subsidiary questions that any posture seeking to secure those goals has to address. I argue that most of the posture debate stems from reasonable disagreements on these underlying issues and what weight to assign them in formulating policy.

Drawing on this framework, the second section briefly reviews US posture from 1991 to 2011. I describe this posture as heavy forward presence (HFP) and explain its basic parameters and the assumptions it embodied with respect to those six subsidiary issues identified in the framework. The third section repeats this procedure with respect to a posture that would withdraw US military forces from the region, one I refer to as the OTH option.[3]

The chapter's fourth section then advocates a middle way, or residual forward presence, explaining where and why its assumptions differ and the implications for future US presence. Rather than inventing the specifics of the posture from whole cloth, however, the chapter develops them simply by outlining current US land, air, and naval forces in the region and asking what the consequences of withdrawing these forces might be for the objectives identified in the framework from the first section, if the aforementioned assumptions are correct.[4] This approach makes clear that US forces in the Gulf are already smaller and less locally controversial than OTH advocates often assume, suggesting that the political price tag of any operational advantages they afford is small. This is good news, because these operational advantages, as well as the broader political benefits to maintaining an

RFP, are more substantial than withdrawal proponents have sometimes acknowledged. Nevertheless, the analysis shows that some components of the current US presence can and should leave the Gulf.

A Framework for Analyzing Posture in the Gulf

Multiple goals underlie US policy decisions in the Gulf, including maintaining the flow of affordable oil, containing and deterring Iran, protecting Israel, and preventing terrorism.[5] These objectives are irreducible, in the sense that each is viewed as a distinct end worth pursuing in and of itself, even though they are interrelated.[6] In keeping with the goal of this volume, the chapter does not attempt to examine comprehensively all considerations relevant to US posture in the Gulf; instead, it disaggregates one of the big rationales, oil, and generates a set of minimal requirements for securing it. After all, even advocates of a more selective or restrained US grand strategy acknowledge maintenance of the free flow of Gulf oil as a core interest.[7]

Given this scope, what are the most likely threats to the flow of affordable Gulf oil? Three have garnered the most attention. First, many analysts worry about the possibility of an Iranian attempt to close the Strait of Hormuz, the narrow waterway through which roughly one-fifth of world oil passes on a daily basis. In chapter 5, Joshua Rovner identified this scenario as the most serious potential threat to stable oil prices, though he views the scenario as unlikely. But even those who believe Iran lacks the motivation or ability to sustain a true closure of the Strait—through a blockade or, more likely, through the use of mines, missiles, and small boat attacks against tankers—acknowledge that naval conflict in the area could send prices skyrocketing.[8]

Second, observers fear that Iran or non-state actors could engage in attacks on critical oil infrastructure in the region, such as the Saudi stabilization plant at Abqaiq or ports at Ras Tanura and Ras al-Juaymah. If such nodes were successfully hit, either by terrorist bombs or Iranian missiles, the consequences for global oil production could rival those resulting from a closure of the Strait of Hormuz.[9] Most notably, Saudi Arabia would be unable to deliver some significant portion of its oil to market, and prices would rise dramatically. Such a situation may be unlikely, as Rovner argues, but it remains a relevant consideration for American force planners who must consider worst-case scenarios.

Last, civil conflict within the major oil-producing states constitutes another potential threat to the flow of affordable oil. The world has had a taste of this problem with the wars in Iraq and Libya, both of which disrupted oil production, but other producers, notably Saudi Arabia, were able to compensate for the loss

Table 9.1. Summary of threats to the free flow of oil from the Gulf

Threat	Actor/locus
1. Closure of the Strait of Hormuz	Iran
2. Attacks on oil infrastructure	Iran or non-state actors
3. Civil conflict in oil-producing states	Non-state actors, such as Islamic State in Iraq
	Local populace, especially in Saudi Arabia

of those supplies.[10] Even today in Iraq, where some observers have made much of the Islamic State's efforts to control some oil sites such as the refinery at Baiji, oil production has continued to climb throughout the turmoil. This increased production is partly a result of the different factions in the country's conflict wanting to capture oil resources for their own use.[11]

Nevertheless, internal disorder in oil-producing states could disrupt oil production in a number of ways in the future—for example, through strikes by oil workers or attacks on pipelines, refineries, or ports. The biggest nightmare would be civil conflict in Saudi Arabia. It is especially concerning that many of Saudi Arabia's most unhappy citizens, the Shia minority, live in the Eastern Province, where much of the oil production network is located.[12] While Thomas Lippman in chapter 4 offers reasons for optimism about internal Saudi stability, and the Saudi regime has taken a number of steps to insulate itself from nearby revolutions and the threat from the Islamic State, upheaval in the kingdom would be of grave concern to world oil markets.[13]

Simply identifying threats offers little guidance for posture, however, absent additional information about the environment in which the posture is intended to operate. At least six additional questions must be answered to come to some conclusion about which sorts of military capabilities and political conditions would be most useful for combating those threats:

- What are the nature and likely future trajectory of the military capabilities of regional opponents?
- How important is operational speed in responding to threats in the region and in deterring their emergence in the first place?
- How does a physical US presence affect the host nation's stability and legitimacy? In other words, what are the local political effects of US forward deployment?
- How does a physical US presence affect the host nation's military capabilities? In other words, does it augment local capacities or incentivize counterproductive free riding?

- How important is a physical US presence for ensuring that potential allies and partners balance against US adversaries rather than bandwagon with them? For example, would a US withdrawal lead the smaller states in the region to develop closer ties to Iran? Would it decrease the willingness of Gulf Cooperation Council (GCC) countries to share intelligence with the United States and allow US operational access in times of crisis or war?[14]
- To what extent does a US military presence in the Gulf motivate anti-American terrorism? For example, is it central or peripheral to al-Qaeda or Islamic State recruiting?

Different answers to these questions, or different weightings of the issues involved, generate different subsidiary assumptions and, logically, different preferences about US posture. The rest of this chapter discusses how one set of answers to these questions shaped US posture in the 1990s and 2000s, and how different answers today might lead to the adoption of various alternatives. Table 9.2 previews these contrasts.

Heavy US Forward Presence in the Gulf, 1991–2011

Though often attributed to the attacks of September 11, 2001, the US heavy forward presence in the Gulf actually traces its origins to the 1991 Gulf War and the policy of dual containment that followed. Introduced by the Bill Clinton administration in 1993, dual containment reflected American frustration with past attempts to rely on regional allies—first Iran under the shah and then Iraq during the 1980s—to maintain a balance of power in the region.[15] Under dual containment, the United States took it upon itself to block aggression directly by either Iraq or Iran, using its forward presence to enforce sanctions, build the military strength and political cohesion of the GCC countries, and, in the Iraqi case, patrol no-fly and no-drive zones.[16]

At its core, dual containment simply kept in place many of the forces that had come to the region for the 1991 Gulf War. Welcomed by the region's monarchs, the US Army established a permanent presence of five thousand troops in Kuwait, along with prepositioned heavy equipment, more than fifty tanks, and two dozen combat aircraft. It also prepositioned substantial heavy equipment, including armor, in Qatar, the UAE, and Oman. The US Air Force also enjoyed regional access to a large base outside Doha, Qatar, known as Al Udeid, as well as to Saudi bases, which came to house a squadron of combat aircraft and more than five thousand air force personnel. In addition, the naval presence grew from three or four small ships homeported in Bahrain to fifteen vessels, including a carrier

Table 9.2. Comparing the underlying assumptions of different postures

Assumptions about . . .	Heavy forward presence (HFP)	Residual forward presence (RFP)	Over-the-horizon (OTH)
Opponent capabilities	Very threatening (Iran, Iraq)	Threatening, growing incrementally (Iran)	Relatively weak and static (Iran)
Need for speed	Very important	Very important	Not that important
Local political effects of US presence	Categorically positive	Positive if footprint kept minimal	Categorically negative
Local military effects of US presence	Positive: builds partner capacity, interoperability	Positive: builds partner capacity, interoperability	Negative: encourages free riding
Preventing bandwagoning	Robust physical presence essential	Some physical presence useful	Physical presence irrelevant at best
Motivations for anti-US terrorism	Forward presence largely irrelevant	Forward presence relevant but not central	Forward presence highly significant

and its associated combat aircraft, on station at any given time. In addition to the ten thousand service personnel typically afloat in the area, the US Navy acquired a larger headquarters ashore in Bahrain and rechristened the forces there as the Fifth Fleet in 1995.[17]

Maintaining a constant and visible military presence in the region was intended to provide a highly credible signal of the willingness and ability of the United States to reverse any regional aggression immediately, thereby making it unlikely such aggression would ever occur.[18] Forward deployment positioned the United States from a posture of strength, both militarily and politically, to counter any attempts to revise the status quo. Relevant forces would be nearby, familiar with their operating environment, and have all needed access prearranged. In addition, the United States would have strong relationships with regional allies, who likely also would provide needed intelligence, possibly contribute military capabilities, and add legitimacy to any operations.

Dual containment also was said to enhance overall regional stability in other ways that helped to ensure the affordable flow of oil. Most notably, the US presence arguably helped to alleviate security dilemmas that otherwise would have arisen.[19] As analyst Ken Pollack has noted, "One of the dirty little secrets of the Persian Gulf is that GCC unity is a fiction: the Qataris want American military bases not to shield them from Iran or Iraq but to deter Saudi Arabia. Likewise, Bahrain wants powerful missiles not to make it an effective member of the Peninsula Shield Force but so that it can strike Qatar if it ever feels the need."[20] In short, American troops provided a security guarantee for its allies, not only versus Iran and Iraq, but against one another. This reassurance, in turn, was intended to improve cooperation among the Gulf states on their common objectives of containing Iraq and Iran or at least on supporting the United States as it did so.

As is well known, the forces originally stationed in the region to pursue dual containment became the nucleus of US operations in Afghanistan starting in 2001 and in Iraq from 2003 to 2011.[21] Although the term "dual containment" disappeared (along with one of the regimes that inspired it), the policy's political and military remnants persisted. The primary military task of US forces in the region shifted to occupying and pacifying Iraq and to supporting such efforts in landlocked Afghanistan. Yet even after the 2011 withdrawal from Iraq and before the rapid rise of the Islamic State in Iraq and Syria, US military commanders and diplomats emphasized the importance of a forward presence in the region. Notably the 2012 US Defense Strategic Guidance stressed that "*the United States will continue to place a premium on U.S. and allied military presence in—and support of—partner nations in and around this region.*"[22]

Part of this emphasis may have stemmed from the fact that whatever the actual benefits of retaining a heavy presence in the region, transitioning to any alternative could prove difficult. In this view, efforts to downsize the US presence in the region, even if reasonable from a purely military perspective, could significantly damage US credibility not only with regional allies but worldwide. The long-standing US presence in the region has engendered expectations for a continued presence, and any deviation from that commitment could be politically unsettling.

To return to the six questions mentioned earlier, then, HFP has typically assumed a highly threatening regional environment, one in which both Iraqi and Iranian military capabilities have generally been growing (Iraq in the 1990s, Iran in the 2000s). Conventional capabilities have posed as much of a concern as potential nuclear proliferation. It bears noting, for example, that the concern about nuclear programs in both countries has had as much or more to do with the belief that such weapons would shield their owners' *nonnuclear* aggression, thereby neutralizing US conventional superiority.[23]

In addition, HFP has placed a premium on reacting extremely quickly to threats in the region so as to deter them from ever arising. It takes an optimistic view of the political and military implications of a highly visible US presence for the domestic politics of partners and allies, the development of their military capabilities, and the incentives that such a presence creates for their alignment choices in the region. Last, it has reflected the general assumption that a large, standing US presence in the region either does not aid in terrorist recruitment and motivation or that this cost is worth bearing given the posture's other benefits.

In short, HFP has made a series of fairly strong assumptions: The environment is highly threatening, operational speed is very important in that environment, the effects of a US presence are almost entirely positive, and a presence must be very robust to achieve said effects. As we will see, the proposed RFP alternative ratchets back the strength of most of these assumptions considerably, though it does not reject them outright, as advocates of withdrawal generally do.

Going over the Horizon

Some analysts suggest that the United States should simply get its forces out of the Gulf, withdrawing all permanent military forces and distancing itself politically from the region's monarchies. Two of the most prominent advocates of this approach, Eugene Gholz and Daryl Press, describe their favored posture as essentially a return to the Jimmy Carter and Ronald Reagan years: "The U.S. military pre-positioned equipment and built base infrastructure, but it did not station

American troops in the region during peacetime."[24] Instead, the bulk of US fighting power was located over the horizon: in the Indian Ocean, at Diego Garcia, or even in the United States or Europe. Although poised to flow forces into the theater quickly in the event of a crisis, the United States did not maintain a large day-to-day footprint.

Gholz and Press's OTH posture is quite different from the argument that Glaser and Kelanic offer in chapter 8. The latter argue that the United States should prepare to eventually end its grand strategic commitment to the Gulf. In contrast, Gholz and Press assume that the United States retains its commitment to defend the free flow of oil from the Gulf, but they find that a much different force posture is better suited to achieving US objectives.

Gholz and Press argue that a version of this OTH posture would be even more appropriate today, given that conventional cross-border threats to the flow of oil are less menacing than they were during the Cold War. As they explain, "A U.S. force stationed over-the-horizon could thwart any invasion as effectively as a locally deployed force could. . . . An over-the-horizon force of long-range bombers, naval aviation, and ships and submarines armed with cruise missiles would pose as formidable a bulwark against cross-border invasion as the current in-theater force."[25]

Furthermore, in their view, an OTH posture would be well suited to dealing with any potential naval threat from Iran, which they rate as relatively minor.[26] Gholz and Press explain, "The U.S. military could respond if Iran harassed tanker traffic in the Gulf, but even strong action would not depend on having a peacetime forward presence in the region. Naval forces operating in the Indian Ocean would be ideally positioned to counter Iranian attacks. . . . The U.S. Navy could prosecute all of these missions with over-the-horizon forces. Ground-based airpower could also fly to the Gulf in a crisis."[27]

Presumably, a similar logic would apply with respect to protecting the region's oil infrastructure from Iranian attacks: US forces would not need to be physically in the region to deter such aggression. The United States might want to continue naval patrols in the region and maintain remote special operations bases, but OTH advocates see little need for a larger permanent presence.[28]

In addition, Gholz and Press argue that the OTH posture would reduce the risk of two other threats identified earlier: civil unrest in major oil-producing states, especially Saudi Arabia, and terrorism. They note that rather than stabilizing the region, the heavy, post-1991 US footprint has been a rallying call for extremists. Other experts agree.[29] Robert Pape has gone so far as to quantify the impact, noting that "although there may well have been excellent reasons for their presence, the stationing of tens of thousands of American combat troops on the Arabian Peninsula from 1990 to 2001 most likely made al Qaeda suicide attacks against Americans, including the atrocities committed on September 11, 2001, from ten to twenty times more likely."[30] In this view, withdrawing highly visible, forward-deployed US forces "would remove a critical irritant and a useful recruiting theme."[31] It also would reduce the number of potential US targets.[32]

In fact, adopting an OTH posture ultimately would shore up the legitimacy and stability of the Gulf monarchies, according to this logic. The US presence in the region provides few internal security benefits to the region's leaders, but it does emasculate them, making them appear as though they cannot defend their own people.[33] Going over the horizon is therefore the strategic equivalent of "less is more," according to Gholz and Press.[34]

Last, an OTH posture possibly could have further benefits over the long term. For example, the heavy US presence in the region has created a moral hazard for oil-producing countries. Why should they invest in more reliable alternative means of export, such as pipelines, when they know that the United States will massively subsidize the potential military costs of continuing to export oil through the Strait of Hormuz?[35] In other words, whatever their purported benefits, the robust forward presence of the US military and the close political relationships between the United States and the Gulf states insulate the latter from the incentives they otherwise would face to secure oil on their own. An OTH posture might lessen this dependence and the perverse behaviors it has engendered, ultimately making both the United States and the Gulf states better off.[36]

As these recommendations indicate, the OTH posture stems from a distinct set of assumptions: The threat environment is relatively benign; the premium on operational speed in responding to such threats is lower; the regional political and military effects of a US presence are almost categorically negative, especially when it comes to terrorism; and a physical US presence on the ground is at best unnecessary for securing US goals and is often counterproductive.

A Middle Way: Residual Forward Presence in the Gulf

Not only would the RFP posture maintain more forward presence in the Gulf than many critics of recent US policy might prefer, but it also would eschew the highly visible, ground-heavy footprint that characterized US posture from 1991 to 2011. The notion of an RFP begins with a different assumption about the threat environment: Iran is likely to remain a capable actor opposed to most US regional objectives but not one whose conventional or nuclear capabilities are likely to dramatically increase in the next five to ten years. On the conventional side, the posture assumes both that Iran's capabilities in areas relevant to littoral and unconventional warfare, especially rockets and missiles, are growing but only incrementally, and that Iran neither possesses a full suite of anti-access, area-denial capabilities (akin to those attributed to China) nor likely will acquire them in the near term.[37] On the nuclear side, the posture rests on the expectation that the US and Israeli governments will not allow Iran to proliferate.[38] As a result, the posture views the future threat environment with caution but not alarm.

The posture also takes a circumspect view of the political and military effects of US presence in the region. For reasons discussed later, it concurs that speed is very important in responding to threats to the flow of oil—and in deterring such threats from emerging in the first place—but it also recognizes that a forward presence can foment negative domestic political effects in host countries, reduce the incentives for those countries to engage in military burden sharing, and provide a rallying point for anti-American terrorism under some conditions. That said, the posture acknowledges significant benefits to some forward deployment, arguing that a physical presence is required to build the useful partner capacities that are crucial for responding quickly to regional aggression and that the US presence plays an important role in encouraging these states to balance effectively against Iran.

What would such a posture look like? In brief, an RFP would reduce the overall size of US forces both ashore and afloat. Key capabilities would remain forward deployed: most notably, command and control facilities; intelligence, surveillance, and reconnaissance (ISR) assets; some land-based tactical airpower; the logistical skeleton needed to return large land forces rapidly to the region if needed; mine countermeasure ships, coastal patrol craft, and the smaller ships that today patrol Gulf waters as part of carrier strike groups; and, on occasion, a carrier itself. Although US forces would not withdraw, they would be made relatively invisible on a day-to-day basis. In short, the posture seeks to achieve many of the political and military benefits of forward presence in the region without paying many of the costs.

As mentioned, American forces in the region are already smaller than they have been at almost any time since the mid-1990s—even given the 2015 surge of approximately 3,500 American advisers to Iraq to combat the Islamic State.[39] As of December 2012, for example, American officials publicly stated that US military personnel in the region numbered approximately 50,000, as compared with a high of 234,851 in December 2008.[40] More recent open-source estimates are even smaller, suggesting a presence of around 35,000 US military personnel.[41] By examining where these forces are now, their current and potential functions, and their political profile, it is possible to discern what a residual forward presence focused primarily on securing the affordable flow of oil might look like.

The Army

The US Army already has its smallest footprint in the Gulf since 1990, amounting to what is often described as a "brigade plus," though it can often vary from as little as 7,000 soldiers to as many as 13,500.[42] Small contingents of soldiers operate Patriot missile batteries at various spots in the region, but other than the advisers in Iraq, the bulk of US Army forces are in Kuwait, where the Third Army, also known as Army Central (ARCENT), has had a permanent presence since Operation Desert Storm.[43]

The Third Army would be the first to acknowledge that its presence in Kuwait is the legacy of a time when the primary threat to the flow of oil was a cross-border conventional war. Its original function was to manage the rapid flow of much larger forces to the region during a crisis, and it performed this massive logistical endeavor successfully both in 1991 and 2003 and in reverse during the 2011 Iraq drawdown. Today the army remains the nucleus of any effort to surge land forces to the Gulf and would be vital to securing US bases and installations throughout the region in the event of a crisis or war. It continues to oversee a significant stock of prepositioned weapons and matériel, which former chief of staff of the army Gen. Ray Odierno has noted is unlikely to go away any time in the next decade.[44]

That said, the Third Army currently conducts a wide variety of other missions in Central Command's (CENTCOM's) area of responsibility, which encompasses numerous non-Gulf states, ranging from Egypt in the west to Pakistan in the east, as well as the Levant and Central Asia. Thus, many of the Third Army's activities now have little direct connection to the mission of maintaining the flow of affordable oil from the Gulf. Instead, the presence in Kuwait, which includes a string of bases and training ranges, functions as a "lily pad" from which the Third Army can conduct operations throughout the region. For example, the Third Army provides military adviser teams that help develop local security forces. Given that ground forces are the dominant service component of virtually all of the region's militaries, these military-to-military contacts are an important aspect of US bilateral relations with many of the states both inside and outside the Arabian Peninsula. They also surely provide an important source of general intelligence about the region.

Still the connection between these activities and oil-related objectives— deterring and countering Iranian action in the Strait of Hormuz, protecting Gulf oil infrastructure, and preventing internal disorder in the major oil-producing states—is indirect at best. With Soviet ground forces dissolved, the Iraqi army neutered, and Iranian conventional land forces dysfunctional, the oil-related rationale for permanently stationing the Third Army in the region is much weaker than it was in the 1990s. Although the Third Army has evolved to serve other valuable functions in a broader regional security strategy, particularly given the growing threat from the Islamic State, the case for keeping a brigade-plus in Kuwait as part of a minimal forward presence is difficult to sustain on the basis of oil security concerns. Even from a logistics perspective, the other services are relatively self-contained and do not need the US Army to underwrite their operations in the region.

That being said, it is important to examine the politics surrounding US presence in Kuwait and any potential withdrawal. In fact, the army's enduring presence is largely uncontroversial in Kuwait, where the US military still wears the halo of 1991. Though the two allies do experience some friction, there are few if any voices clamoring for the US military's withdrawal. Indeed, many Kuwaitis view the Third Army as a bulwark against the violence and chaos of southern Iraq and against potential Iranian coercion. No doubt a US presence in Kuwait reassures the Saudis for the same reasons while conveniently keeping US forces off their soil.

Furthermore, while most Kuwaitis are aware that some US forces remain in their country, these forces are not visible on a daily basis to the average person. US bases are located away from Kuwait City, where most Kuwaitis live. US military vehicles generally do not travel on civilian roads, especially during daylight. American soldiers mix with the local population only rarely and never in uniform. Notably, for instance, in more than twenty years of US basing in Kuwait, US military personnel have never been involved in the type of criminal incidents that have made a US presence in Japan and Korea unpopular.

Nor have there been the kind of terrorist attacks that happened in Saudi Arabia in 1995 and 1996, though there have been some foiled al-Qaeda plots in Kuwait.[45] Violent Islamic extremists would undoubtedly cheer a US withdrawal from Kuwait and the Gulf as a whole, but the presence of US troops in these areas is now in many ways peripheral to the extremists' broader agenda. Al-Qaeda, with its focus on the "far enemy" of the United States, has largely been eclipsed by the Islamic State, which is much more focused on the "near enemy" of apostate governments in the Middle East, especially in Syria and Iraq.[46] The rallying cry is not about foreign presence but about illegitimate local regimes. More broadly, the US military's presence in the Middle East is low on the list of complaints about US foreign policy as expressed in polling of average people in the region.[47]

Furthermore, it is far from clear that even al-Qaeda's grievances are only about US boots on the ground. Osama bin Laden's successors object even to US political support for the Gulf monarchies, as well as to lower-profile activities such as intelligence sharing or training for foreign internal defense.[48] Hence while it may be true that the US military's presence in the region remains a loose rallying call for the country's enemies, it also seems that no American grand strategy besides extreme isolationism could completely solve the problem. The question then becomes one of mitigation, keeping the US presence as low profile as possible and accepting trade-offs. Even a low-profile presence will be a residual irritant but perhaps one worth managing if it delivers important benefits.

In short, although the connection between the continuing US Army presence in Kuwait and the free flow of oil has weakened, little evidence suggests that US presence has engendered the problems that withdrawal advocates emphasize or that US withdrawal would truly solve these problems any better than the alternatives would. US presence in Kuwait does not seem to be politically costly, nor is it financially expensive given that Kuwait covers most basing costs. In fact, Kuwaitis likely would react with alarm were the Third Army to depart. For these reasons, the United States would do well to keep prepositioned equipment and a "brigade-minus" in Kuwait, amounting to a few thousand troops sufficient for maintaining a surge capability.

The Air Force

The United States maintains substantial land-based airpower in the Gulf. As with the US Army, however, the current Air Force footprint is already lighter than it once was and is deliberately designed to be low profile despite the capability it provides. Its potential relevance to oil-related missions is also clear.

As mentioned, much of land-based airpower of the United States was once based in Saudi Arabia, but precisely because of concerns about its role as a rallying cry for al-Qaeda, almost all of it moved elsewhere, especially after 2003.[49] Notably, Air Force Central (AFCENT) forward headquarters is now located at the aforementioned Al Udeid Air Base in Qatar.[50] This base—which is owned by Qatar, not the United States—also houses the Combined Air and Space Operations Center (CAOC), which functions as the command hub for all US air operations in the region. Approximately eleven thousand American service personnel are stationed there at any given time, though the base can accommodate nearly twice that number in austere conditions.

AFCENT commands multiple expeditionary wings, including at least one still in Afghanistan. Four wings are on the Arabian Peninsula (see table 9.3). The first wing, based at Al Udeid, performs multiple missions with more than a hundred

Table 9.3. US Air Force assets on the Arabian Peninsula

Wing	Based in	Missions	Primary aircraft
3379th	Qatar	Airlift, refueling, aeromedical evacuation, ISR, combat, airborne command and control	KC-135 Stratotanker, B-1B Lancer, C-130 Hercules, E-8C Joint STARS, RC-135U Combat Sent, and RC-135V/W Rivet Joint
380th	UAE, Oman, Djibouti	Refueling, high-altitude ISR, airborne command and control, combat	RQ-4 Global Hawk, EQ-4 Global Hawk, U-2S Dragon Lady, KC-10 Extender, E-3 Sentry (AWACS), F-15E Strike Eagle, F-22 Raptor[a]
386th	Kuwait	Airlift, electronic warfare	C-130 Hercules, EC-130H Compass Call, C-17 Globemaster, MQ-1B Predator
332nd	Probably Kuwait	ISR, combat	F-16 Fighting Falcon, A-10 II Thunderbolt, MQ-1 Predator, C-130 Hercules, HH-60G Pave Hawk[b]
432nd	Nevada	ISR, combat[c]	MQ-1B Predator, MQ-9 Reaper

Note: Except where otherwise noted, data taken from US Air Force Central Command, "AFCENT Mission," http://www.afcent.af.mil/AboutUs.aspx, accessed on August 25, 2015.

a. See endnote 52; and AFCENT, "380th Air Expeditionary Wing," April 12, 2013, http://www.afcent.af.mil/Units/380thAirExpeditionaryWing/FactSheets/Display/tabid/324/Article/445043/380th-air-expeditionary-wing.aspx.

b. See endnote 53.

c. Data taken from the unit description page, "432nd Wing, 432nd Air Expeditionary Wing," May 16, 2013, http://www.creech.af.mil/library/factsheets/factsheet.asp?id=12878.

aircraft: airlift and aerial refueling, close air support, ISR, and airborne command and control.[51] A second wing, based primarily at Al Dhafra in the UAE with additional assets located in Oman and Djibouti, provides persistent high-altitude surveillance, airborne command and control, transport, and aerial refueling. It also has recently hosted a deployment of F-22s and acquired a squadron of F-15E Strike Eagles relocated from Afghanistan.[52]

A third wing is housed at Ahmed Al Jaber Air Base in Kuwait, where it focuses on airlift and electronic warfare, both missions in heavy demand during Operation Iraqi Freedom. A fourth wing, most likely based in Kuwait at Ali Al Salem Air Base, is primarily a combat wing and probably operates fighter-bombers and unmanned aerial vehicles with ISR and strike capabilities.[53] A fifth wing, located at Creech Air Force Base in Nevada and consisting entirely of unmanned aircraft, also contributes both ISR and strike capabilities to AFCENT.

Does the forward deployment of these forces substantially contribute to the objective of maintaining the free flow of oil? In other words, does keeping these forces in the region enable the United States to perform missions relevant to defending the Strait of Hormuz, preventing attacks on key oil nodes, or stabilizing Gulf states? While land-based airpower is probably of little relevance to the last mission, such forces do afford the United States significant advantages in dealing with the first two.

Chief among these advantages is high-altitude persistent ISR in the Gulf. The real value of peacetime forward-deployed airpower does not come solely or even mostly from the likes of the B-1 Lancer and F-22 Raptor; more ground-based combat aircraft can always flow rapidly to the theater in the event of a crisis or war. The value comes from ISR platforms that make it less likely combat aircraft will ever be needed in the first place. Stationing ISR assets in the region reminds potential aggressors that any offensives will be detected quickly, reducing the temptation to try. Although the navy also has ISR assets, as discussed in the following section, the MQ-1 Predator and RQ-4 Global Hawk can provide much greater sustained coverage.

Furthermore, even if a forward ISR presence does not deter aggression in the region, early detection facilitates stopping aggression in the least costly and escalatory manner. For example, defending the Strait becomes significantly more difficult for the United States the more mines Iran is able to lay without detection. While the United States ultimately could reopen the Strait even if Iran laid thousands of mines, the task would clearly be much simpler if the United States intervened on day 2 of an Iranian campaign rather than on day 20.

This sort of warning is exactly what the 379th, 380th, 332nd, and 432nd air wings can provide. They are well positioned to regularly monitor Iranian mine depots, cruise missile sites, and submarine pens, all of which would likely display notable changes in the run-up to an Iranian attempt to mine the Strait or major Gulf ports. Early detection, in turn, could limit the total number of mines laid, greatly reduce the time involved in any mine clearance efforts, and decrease the length and severity of any price shocks. Again communicating the existence of such monitoring to the Iranians could also help deter such aggression in the first place.

Failing that, however, if a crisis or war did start, it is unlikely that the United States would regret having forward deployed the air force assets currently based at Al Udeid and Al Dhafra. Again, the key capabilities are not necessarily combat assets per se, because carriers can provide a floating base for such aircraft in the Indian Ocean. Rather, the "enablers"—especially tankers, as well as reconnaissance and airborne command and control—matter most. Without these land-based helpers, the range, sortie generation rate, and survivability of naval aircraft would be much more limited than in previous US operations.

Enablers do not necessarily have to be forward deployed in peacetime, but from a purely military perspective, doing so certainly presents an advantage. For example, Al Udeid is one of the few places in the region that a full KC-135 Stratotanker can reliably operate year-round; the region's hot weather lowers the performance of heavily loaded jet aircraft, requiring additional space for take-off. A peacetime forward deployment at Al Udeid helps ensure wartime access to its critical 12,500-foot runway. Forward presence at Al Udeid also enables the United States to maintain an established in-theater headquarters (the aforementioned CAOC) from which to manage any multiservice air operations in the event of a crisis or war. Admittedly the United States could always attempt to gain access to or establish such a headquarters after the fact, but an ad hoc approach takes time that the United States may not wish to spare during a crisis. To be sure, some of the combat aircraft and lift capability currently in the region, especially in Kuwait, could be redeployed after the United States withdraws from Afghanistan. But in purely military terms, there is little reason to redeploy the air force's tanker and ISR assets, or the CAOC, outside the Gulf.

Fortunately, the political costs of forward deployment seem small. The air force's regional profile is already surprisingly low. Air bases are deliberately located well outside of populated areas. The one exception, Al Udeid, is located on the outskirts of Doha, but it is still not easily visible from the main roads out of the city. Furthermore, the Qataris still own the base, control all access to it, and use it extensively for their own training and operations, so little about it appears American from the outside. Indeed, it is not a coincidence that Al Udeid houses mostly "enabling" aircraft—tankers, reconnaissance, and airborne command and control—rather than the potentially more controversial combat platforms, such as drones or fighter-bombers.[54] Predators, MQ-9 Reapers, and F-22s do not operate out of Al Udeid, only out of the more remote Al Dhafra.

In addition, US aircraft taking off from or landing at Al Udeid follow flight paths that avoid travel over Doha. The vast majority of service personnel who serve a tour at Al Udeid never leave the base. The few who venture into Doha travel in civilian clothing. In short, Qatar's close relationship with the US military is not a secret, but it is not especially visible to the average Qatari either. Notably, the US military's presence there has not been subject to attack.

A similar state of affairs prevails with respect to US air bases in Kuwait and the UAE. It no doubt helps that the United States normally refers to wings stationed in these countries as being deployed "in Southwest Asia" rather than in specific countries. On the one hand, this vague terminology, along with the other efforts to reduce the visibility of a US forward presence, suggests that US bases can still inflame local political sensitivities. On the other hand, that the Qatari, Kuwaiti, and Emirati governments continue to welcome the US presence suggests they believe this potential liability has been minimized. For example, Qatar has the ability to deny the United States permission to use Al Udeid at any time, but Qatar instead continues to encourage a long-term American presence. For all of these reasons, it seems reasonable to maintain the wings at Al Udeid and Al Dhafra (along with ample stocks of equipment, advanced munitions, and fuel) as a residual forward presence in the region.

The Navy, Marines, and Coast Guard

In contrast to the army and air force, the US naval presence in the region has increased rather than decreased since the US withdrawal from Iraq in 2011. Ashore, the centerpiece is the Fifth Fleet/US Naval Forces Central Command (NAVCENT), headquartered in Manama, the capital of the small island kingdom of Bahrain. The forward headquarters of the US Marine Corps Forces Central Command (MARCENT) is also located there.[55] Estimates of current total personnel ashore in Bahrain vary, ranging from fifteen hundred to twenty-four hundred people, but are still small in absolute terms.[56]

NAVCENT and MARCENT provide command and control to each of their respective forces operating throughout the CENTCOM area of responsibility, and they coordinate with allied forces in the region. Both headquarters have grown substantially in recent years, especially NAVCENT. Although the US Navy has been in Bahrain in some form since at least the 1950s, observers report that its current presence is nearly an order of magnitude larger than it was in the early 2000s, and it is still growing.[57] Still, most of this presence is staff. Other than some land-based airpower — notably the P-3 Orion maritime patrol aircraft and EP-3 signals reconnaissance version of the Orion — most of the navy and marine presence is, unsurprisingly, offshore.

Indeed, the US naval presence afloat has been growing and now accounts for approximately fifteen thousand additional American personnel in the region at any given time. Prior to 1991, finding naval officers who argued for routine US carrier visits to the Gulf would have been difficult. After all, carriers are designed for blue waters, not a shallow, enclosed environment like the Gulf. Yet for most of the ten years following the US invasion of Iraq in 2003, the United States had an average of nearly two carrier strike groups in or near the Gulf at any given time. Reports indicate that CENTCOM commander Gen. James Mattis had even requested a third in early 2012.[58] Carrier presence has recently dipped as sequestration forced the Pentagon to cancel the deployment of a second carrier to the region and eventually led it to accept some intervals in which no carriers would be present in the Gulf at all. Still, there has been no strategically driven decision to permanently reduce carrier presence in the Gulf.[59]

Each carrier when under way houses approximately five thousand people, roughly divided between those who run the ship itself and those associated with the air wing. No two carriers have identically configured wings, but typically one would expect to see about seventy to seventy-five associated aircraft, including dozens of fighter-bombers, as well as platforms for electronic warfare, airborne early warning, antisubmarine warfare, and mine hunting (see table 9.4).

Despite this immense offensive potential, however, carriers have few organic defenses and must rely on the other components of their strike group to travel safely through contested areas. For this reason, a strike group always includes an Aegis cruiser, as well as destroyers and frigates, and often submarines, in addition to logistics ships and a supply ship. All told, another twenty-five hundred personnel typically serve in a carrier strike group on some vessel besides the carrier.

Notably, US carriers have never been permanently stationed in the Gulf the way that carriers are homeported in Japan as part of Seventh Fleet. Rather, US-based carriers rotate in and out of the Gulf as needed, making stops at the two appropriately sized regional ports of Manama (thanks to an enormous pier that the Bahrainis built in the last decade) and Jebel Ali in Dubai.

Among the only US Navy ships permanently stationed in the Gulf are the small four *Avenger*-class mine countermeasure (MCM) ships in Bahrain, though four more have recently been sent to the region.[60] To function effectively, these ships rely on a subsurface mine-hunting sonar system that has to be towed by MH-53 helicopters, of which there are also currently four in the region. These

Table 9.4. Typical carrier air wing

Mission(s)	Aircraft	Quantity
Combat	F/A-18 Hornets or F/A-18 Super Hornets	4 squadrons, ~12 aircraft per squadron
Electronic warfare	EA-6B Prowlers or EA-18G Growlers	~4–6
Airborne early warning	E-2C Hawkeyes	~2–4
Small cargo aircraft	C-2 Greyhound (land based)	2
Antisubmarine warfare, mine hunting, others	Variants of MH-60 Seahawk	~6–8

helicopters operate from ships with large decks, such as carriers and amphibious assault ships, making the latter's presence an important enabler of US mine clearance capability.

In addition, at least one amphibious assault ship almost always stays in the Gulf. These Marine Corps vessels house an entire marine expeditionary unit of more than two thousand marines. By anything but American standards, a marine expeditionary unit is a floating army, capable of rapidly deploying integrated air and ground forces wherever needed and typically including tanks, armored vehicles, amphibious assault vehicles, a variety of rotary-wing aircraft, and logistical support.

In 2012, the United States also deployed its first afloat forward staging base in the region. Essentially a retrofitted old warship, this ship currently provides an additional platform for mine countermeasure operations. Helicopters can use its deck, underwater dive teams can conduct their work from its base, and it delivers fuel and maintenance to the dedicated MCM vessels.[61]

The US Coast Guard also maintains a substantial forward presence in the region in the form of cutters and other patrol vessels. The US Navy permanently bases eight coastal patrol vessels in Bahrain as well.[62] These vessels and the smaller ships in the carrier strike groups participate regularly in training and exercises with the GCC navies, as well as with British, Japanese, and Australian forces. These foreign navies supply additional minesweepers: four British, four Saudi, and two Emirati.

What purpose does this substantial forward-deployed US naval presence serve? Clearly some of these forces are unrelated to the narrow mission of maintaining the flow of affordable oil. For example, at least half of the US carrier presence in or near the Gulf typically has supported Operation Enduring Freedom. The presence of amphibious assault ships and the buildup of the US forces ashore in Bahrain also have little operational relevance to patrolling the Strait, protecting Gulf oil networks, or maintaining internal stability in Saudi Arabia. Observers in the region instead interpret these aspects of the US posture as having been tied more directly to the possibility of a conflict with Iran over its nuclear program, especially prior to the recent nuclear deal. The increased staff in Bahrain was likely responsible for contingency planning and crisis response related to conflict over Iran's nuclear program, and amphibious assault ships held the forces that might have been used had such a conflict escalated. Most recently these forces also have played a significant role in the fight against the Islamic State.

That being said, much of the other US naval presence in the Gulf does relate directly to the oil missions. This point is most clear with respect to the MCM ships. These vessels move slowly, at about eight knots an hour; thus, from Bahrain they already would need roughly four days to reach the Strait in the event of mine detection. Unfit for loitering on the open ocean, MCM vessels would probably relocate to Diego Garcia to accommodate an OTH posture. But given the MCM ships' slow speed and the vast distance to the Gulf, a heavy-lift ship would have to transport the Diego Garcia–based MCM ships to the region. Unfortunately the heavy-lift ship also moves slowly and lacks the ability to operate in a contested environment, which is presumably what the Gulf would be if forces were called in from over the horizon.

In short, keeping MCM capabilities anywhere but the Gulf makes little sense. Forward deploying them contributes significantly to both the feasibility and speed of any potential US response to mines in the Gulf. It also affords the United States the opportunity to train and exercise with other nations whose MCM assets could be quite valuable in a crisis or war. Historically the United States has almost always worked multilaterally in the MCM mission. At a time when US MCM technology is aging—and is unlikely to be replaced rapidly because of delays in the littoral combat ship, the US Navy's future platform for countermine operations—the ability to partner with other nations on this mission is valuable. But it would also be hard to do from the middle of the Indian Ocean and without some command presence ashore in Bahrain.

The forward presence of coastal patrol vessels, cruisers, destroyers, and frigates also contributes to the oil missions in ways that would be difficult to replicate from over the horizon. These ships assist local navies in securing their ports and other maritime infrastructure, and they also patrol the waters of the Gulf.[63] Some can even launch and recover their own small unmanned aerial vehicles, such as the ScanEagle. These activities enable the United States to discern anything that differs from the normal "pattern of life" in the area and help deter threats from emerging in the first place. US personnel report near-daily contact with Iranian naval forces, reinforcing US red lines about maintaining freedom of navigation in the Strait. The missile defense capabilities of Aegis cruisers and destroyers also perform an important deterrent function.

That said, the United States should reconsider the utility of routinely operating carriers inside the Gulf. The navy has little operational reason to sail such valuable targets through these waters when virtually all of their deterrent and combat power would remain intact in the Indian Ocean, perhaps augmented by an occasional patrol or exercise inside the Gulf. The smaller ships—the MCM and coastal patrol vessels, as well as the cruisers and destroyers, which already regularly conduct operations untethered from their carriers—actually provide the most insurance against possible Iranian mine-laying operations and the highest likelihood of early visual warning of attacks on traffic in the Strait or on maritime infrastructure relevant to oil production. These smaller ships are also the most appropriately proportioned partners for allied training and exercises.

Furthermore, the United States appears to pay a low political price for its offshore presence. Virtually by definition, US ships are not visible to the region's publics unless the United States wants them to be. Interestingly, the US Navy's long-standing presence in Bahrain is so accepted that the base is located quite centrally in Manama. Unlike in Kuwait or Qatar, where the US Army and Air Force have taken pains to remain out of sight and out of mind, any Bahraini cab driver can drop his passenger at the front gate of NAVCENT headquarters without needing directions. American service personnel live among Bahrainis, shop at their markets, and eat in their homes. Precisely because Bahrainis know that the real combat power is afloat—and destined to remain there—little local allergy seems to have developed regarding the US presence ashore, which is still small in absolute terms.

This consensus seems to be holding despite the immense political tumult in Bahrain since 2011.[64] Historically even the Bahraini Shia have seen the US presence in their country as a necessary bulwark against Iran, and the US presence has not been one of their core grievances with the ruling Al Khalifa family. If anything, having Americans in Manama has probably restrained the regime from dealing with the opposition even more harshly. That said, popular attitudes toward the US presence might change if the United States appears increasingly complicit with the regime's repression, and the status of the Fifth Fleet's presence ashore could grow more tenuous were the Khalifas to fall from power.[65] Or the regime could stay in power but feel the need to distance itself from the United States, limiting US access, though that possibility seems less likely.

This fluid situation requires close monitoring, but even the loss of US headquarters in Bahrain, though not ideal, would not be the end of the world. The navy and marines are used to commanding forces afloat and routinely practice the ability to do so, not necessarily because the Bahraini government will evict them, but because their base could someday be the target of missile or terrorist attacks. In fact, one could imagine the United States using this fact to pressure the current regime into moderating its behavior toward the opposition and engaging in a genuine reconciliation process. Particularly given the economic benefits that the US presence provides, Manama may need Washington more than the other way around. The Fifth Fleet's presence ashore is a helpful luxury from a military standpoint, especially as it provides greater bandwidth to US military operations than would be available from a command based entirely at sea, but it is not operationally essential and could be eliminated were it to become politically untenable.[66]

The bigger political question surrounds how the United States can transition forces deemed operationally unnecessary out of the region without alarming GCC allies. For example, rather than continue to emphasize the symbolism and importance of its carrier presence, the United States ought to be quietly conveying the facts of life about these ships' vulnerability and the utility of keeping them farther rather than closer to Iran's shores. By the same token, the United States should privately emphasize the utility of the other, lower-profile forces that are kept on land and at sea in the region and the US ability to surge more if needed. Recent US emphasis on the AirSea Battle operational concept, now known as the Joint Concept for Access and Maneuver in the Global Commons, and the procurement of the littoral combat ship, which is designed to work in close-in environments such as the Persian Gulf, already have laid some of the groundwork for credibly explaining that this shift is about finding a sustainable US commitment to the Gulf allies rather than abandoning them.[67]

Implications and Conclusions

Whatever the advantages accrued, the United States has paid a high price for the permanent forward deployment of highly visible, land-based forces in the Gulf in the pursuit of oil security. The willingness of American policymakers to absorb these costs has stemmed from the fact that the United States has had and will continue to have significant interests at stake in the region. But although the 1991–2011 period represented one extreme, Washington should not flee to the other after the wars in Iraq and Afghanistan. The United States does have a viable option between heavy forward presence and total withdrawal; in fact, a residual forward presence could provide many of the political and military benefits of a heavy forward presence while avoiding many potential pitfalls.

An RFP cannot eliminate every oil-related threat, of course. Although the posture substantially reduces the likelihood of threats to the Strait of Hormuz or to oil infrastructure, for example, it does remarkably little to reduce the prospect of civil conflict in Saudi Arabia, one of the other major oil security dangers identified at the outset. Still a residual forward presence neither makes the problem worse nor precludes the United States from using other, more appropriate tools of grand strategy to address it. The United States also may want to insert additional forces in the region to pursue other objectives, such as the fight against the Islamic State, but not for reasons related to oil security.

That said, the framework developed here does provide some guidance as to when a residual forward presence might be too much or, conversely, not enough. To give just one example, major changes in the threat environment concerning oil security—or a disagreement with the way this chapter has characterized the present threat environment—would render the posture infeasible. Were Iranian nuclear or conventional capabilities to grow rapidly, for instance, US posture would have to adjust accordingly. In particular, were Iran in the future to acquire significant anti-access, area-denial capabilities on a par with those China is developing today, the United States would have to reconsider the design of its entire forward engagement strategy in the region.[68] Similarly, were China to develop a power projection capability that could keep the United States out of the Gulf, the United States would have to reconsider its posture.[69] Interestingly, it is not clear that either scenario would actually be a reason to forward deploy more forces to the region—potentially quite the opposite. The United States also might need to reconsider its posture if Islamic State forces appeared poised to capture or destroy significant oil resources in southern Iraq or in Saudi Arabia.

Nevertheless, over the short to medium term, these more pessimistic assumptions seem unwarranted. Certainly, this is a judgment call, and as the chapter has demonstrated, different judgments lead to different preferences regarding the US military's posture in the region. But that is exactly the point: Whatever one's assumptions, the United States currently has one of those rare opportunities to air estimates explicitly and adjust posture in the region accordingly. If the past is any guide, such a chance will not soon come again.

Notes

The author gratefully acknowledges guidance and feedback on this research from the other contributors to this volume, as well as from Nathan Brown, Owen Cote, Michael Eisenstadt, Amb. Edward "Skip" Gnehm, Brendan Green, Marc Lynch, Colin Kahl, Michael O'Hanlon, and Ken Pollack; participants in workshops and conference panels at the American Political Science Association, Massachusetts Institute of Technology, George Washington University, and University of Texas–Austin; and US military officers, defense officials, and regional contacts who wished to remain anonymous. Field research was funded in part by a grant from the SOAR program at the Elliott School for International Affairs.

1. For more background on these conditions, see Joshua Rovner and Caitlin Talmadge, "Hegemony, Force Posture, and the Provision of Public Goods: The Once and Future Role of Outside Powers in Securing Persian Gulf Oil," *Security Studies* 23, no. 3 (Fall 2014): 548–81; and Joshua Rovner and Caitlin Talmadge, "Less Is More: The Future of the U.S. Military in the Persian Gulf," *The Washington Quarterly* 37, no. 3 (Fall 2014): 47–60.

2. This consensus is described nicely in Michele Flournoy and Janine Davidson, "Obama's New Global Posture: The Logic of Foreign Deployments," *Foreign Affairs*, July–August 2012, especially 60–62.

3. This posture is sometimes also called offshore balancing, though I avoid this term.

As the analysis shows, the distinction between forces on- and offshore is in many ways less important than the distinction between forces in the Gulf (forward) and outside of it (over the horizon).

4. Except where otherwise noted, the chapter draws its information from interviews with senior US diplomats and military officers in the Persian Gulf region and in Washington, conducted by the author, February–April 2012.

5. Daniel Byman in chapter 2 of this volume provides a comprehensive review of American interests, including those beyond oil.

6. For an example of how these goals interrelate in practice, see "In Obama We Trust?," *Jerusalem Post*, May 31, 2012. Unfortunately, postures that are optimal along one of these dimensions may be problematic along another. For example, a posture that robustly protects Israel might be provocative to Iran, which in turn might engage in actions that raise the price of oil, such as harassing tanker traffic in the Strait of Hormuz or attacking oil infrastructure on the Saudi coast.

7. See, for example, Eugene Gholz, Daryl Press, and Harvey Sapolsky, "Come Home, America: The Strategy of Restraint in the Face of Temptation," *International Security* 21, no. 4 (Spring 1997): 25–26; and Robert J. Art, "Selective Engagement in the Era of Austerity," in *America's Path: Grand Strategy for the Next Administration*, eds. Richard Fontaine and Kristin Lord (Washington DC: Center for a New American Security, 2012), 17.

8. Caitlin Talmadge, "Closing Time: Assessing the Iranian Threat to the Strait of Hormuz," *International Security* 33, no. 1 (Summer 2008): 82–117. For a range of estimates on how a Hormuz closure might affect oil prices and the US economy, see Kenneth R. Vincent's chapter 3 in this volume.

9. Joshua Itzkowitz Shifrinson and Miranda Priebe, "A Crude Threat: The Limits of an Iranian Missile Campaign against Saudi Arabian Oil," *International Security* 36, no. 1 (Summer 2011): 167–201.

10. Clifford Krauss, "Why the Disruption of Libyan Oil Has Led to a Price Spike," *New York Times*, February 23, 2011; and Ayesha Daya, "Saudi Arabia Can Raise Output 25% if Needed, Says Naimi," Bloomberg.com, March 20, 2012.

11. Such groups being able to generate oil revenue is still highly problematic from a counterterrorism perspective, but it does suggest that preventing US loss of oil access should not be a primary driver of US policy in this area. Hugh Naylor, "The Islamic State Threatens to Capture Massive Iraqi Oil Refinery," *Washington Post*, May 15, 2015.

12. Simon Henderson, "The Other Threat to Oil Supplies: Shiite Tensions in Saudi Arabia and Bahrain," Policy Alert (Washington DC: Washington Institute for Near East Policy, July 16, 2012).

13. Rachel Bronson, "Could the Next Mideast Uprising Happen in Saudi Arabia?," *Washington Post*, February 25, 2011; and "Saudi Arabia 'Arrests 93 Members of Islamic State Cells,'" BBC News, April 28, 2015.

14. For more on the distinction between balancing and bandwagoning, see Kenneth M. Waltz, *Theory of International Politics* (New York: Random House, 1979); and Stephen Walt, *The Origins of Alliances* (Ithaca: Cornell University Press, 1990).

15. For background on the policy, see Anthony Lake, "Confronting Backlash States," *Foreign Affairs* 73, no. 2 (March–April 1994): 45–55; and F. Gregory Gause III, "The Illogic of Dual Containment," *Foreign Affairs* 73, no. 2 (March–April 1994): 56–66.

16. The GCC includes Saudi Arabia, Kuwait, Bahrain, Qatar, the UAE, and Oman.

17. F. Gregory Gause III, *The International Relations of the Persian Gulf* (New York: Cambridge University Press, 2010), 127–28.

18. For a broader discussion on the determinants of credibility, see Daryl Press, *Calculating Credibility: How Leaders Assess Military Threats* (Ithaca: Cornell University Press, 2005); and Thomas Schelling, *The Strategy of Conflict* (Cambridge MA: Harvard University Press, 1960).

19. On the security dilemma, see Robert Jervis, "Cooperation under the Security Dilemma," *World Politics* 30, no. 2 (January 1978): 167–214.

20. Ken Pollack, "Securing the Gulf," *Foreign Affairs* 82, no. 4 (July–August 2003): 15.

21. Gause, *International Relations*, 134–35.

22. Emphasis in original. US Department of Defense, "Sustaining U.S. Global Leadership: Priorities for 21st Century Defense" (Washington DC: Department of Defense, January 2012), http://archive.defense.gov/news/Defense_Strategic_Guidance.pdf.

23. This basic logic appears in Matthew Kroenig, "Exporting the Bomb: Why States Provide Sensitive Nuclear Assistance," *American Political Science Review*, February 2009, 113–33.

24. Eugene Gholz and Daryl Press, "Footprints in the Sand," *The American Interest* 5, no. 4 (March 1, 2010): 59. The OTH approach is also discussed in Ken Pollack, "Securing the Gulf," *Foreign Affairs* 82, no. 4 (July–August 2003): 10.

25. Gholz and Press, "Footprints in the Sand," 60–61.

26. Eugene Gholz and Daryl Press, "Protecting 'The Prize': Oil and the U.S. National Interest," *Security Studies* 19, no. 3 (2010): 476–80.

27. Ibid., 480–81.

28. On naval patrols, see ibid., 484; and on remote special operations bases, see Gholz and Press, "Footprints in the Sand," 67.

29. Gause, *International Relations*, 128–29; and Anthony Cordesman, *Saudi Arabia, the U.S., and the Structure of Gulf Alliances* (Washington DC: Center for Strategic and International Studies, February 25, 1999), 41–43.

30. Robert Pape, *Dying to Win: The Strategic Logic of Suicide Terrorism* (New York: Random House, 2005), 242.

31. Gholz and Press, "Footprints in the Sand," 65.

32. Ibid.

33. Ibid., 481.

34. Ibid., 62; and Gholz and Press, "Protecting 'The Prize,'" 484.

35. The Saudis have only one non-Gulf port, at Yanbu on the Red Sea, and the UAE has recently completed construction of a pipeline linking its Habshan oil fields to the port of Fujairah in the Gulf of Oman. The capacity of both pipelines is small. "First Oil Flows through UAE's Hormuz Bypass," *Reuters*, June 21, 2012.

36. Barry Posen, *Restraint: A New Foundation for U.S. Grand Strategy* (Ithaca: Cornell University Press, 2014).

37. Iran and China are the two countries whose anti-access, area-denial capabilities were most often cited as motivating the development of the US AirSea Battle operational concept. Mark Gunzinger, *Outside-In: Operating from Range to Defeat Iran's Anti-Access and Area-Denial Threats*, with Chris Dougherty (Washington DC: Center for Strategic and Budgetary Assessments, 2011).

38. American and Israeli leaders have made strong public commitments to this effect, making it a reasonable assumption of regional analysis. For a review of the US statements, as well as an assessment of how US policy might evolve should Iran manage to go nuclear despite US efforts at prevention, see Colin Kahl, *If All Else Fails: The Challenges of Containing a Nuclear-Armed Iran* (Washington DC: Center for a New American Security, May 2013).

39. Michael Gordon and Julie Hirschfeld Davis, "In Shift, U.S. Will Send 450 Advisers to Help Iraq Fight ISIS," *New York Times*, June 20, 2015.

40. Leon Panetta, quoted in "U.S. Arms to Gulf Allies Hint of Strategy," *Washington Times*, December 16, 2012; and Amy Belasco, *Troop Levels in the Afghan and Iraq Wars, FY2001–FY2012: Cost and Other Potential Issues*, Congressional Research Service (CRS) Report (Washington DC: CRS, July 2, 2009), 6. The current number fluctuates slightly as forces rotate in and out of the region.

41. Karen DeYoung and Juliet Eilperin, "Persian Gulf Leaders to Press Obama to Strengthen U.S. Security Relationship," *Washington Post*, May 11, 2015.

42. "U.S. Arms to Gulf Allies Hint of Strategy," *Washington Times*, December 16, 2012.

43. Camp Arifjan in Kuwait is the Third Army's forward command post; its main command post is Shaw Air Force Base in South Carolina.

44. Ray Odierno, "Building a Flexible Force in a Time of Transition," *Foreign Affairs*, May–June 2012.

45. Although the targets of these attacks were not civilian, the US government classifies the incidents as terrorism because the military forces were not engaged in combat at the time. After the 1995 attack on a US training mission attached to the Saudi National Guard in Riyadh and the 1996 bombing of the Khobar Towers apartment complex in the Eastern Province, personnel for Operation Southern Watch were moved to the more isolated Prince Sultan Air Base, which sits in the desert outside Riyadh. Eventually most of these forces then moved to Al Udeid in Qatar. Gause, *International Relations*, 128.

46. J. M. Berger, "The Islamic State vs. al Qaeda: Who's Winning the War to Become the Jihadi Superpower?," *Foreign Policy*, September 2, 2014.

47. Polling data from Egypt, Jordan, Morocco, Lebanon, and the UAE shows that average people seem to share this view. When asked, "What two steps by the United States would improve your views of the United States the most?," respondents consistently identified "Israel-Palestine peace agreement" (55 percent) and "stopping aid to Israel" (42 percent) as their top answers. Although "withdrawal from Arabian Peninsula" (29 percent) and "with-

drawal from Iraq" (26 percent) also scored high, these answers suggest that the US presence in the Gulf is only one of several issues affecting views of the United States and any possible motivations for terrorism. Shibley Telhami, *Annual Arab Public Opinion Survey*, conducted October 2011, slide 28, http://www.brookings.edu/~media/events/2011/11/21%20arab%20public%20opinion/20111121_arab_public_opinion.pdf.

48. Daniel Byman, "A U.S. Military Withdrawal from the Greater Middle East: Impact on Terrorism," in *The Prudent Use of Power in American National Security Strategy*, eds. Stephen Van Evera and Sidharth Shah (Cambridge MA: Tobin Project, 2010), 157–65.

49. The US Air Force does retain a very small security forces group in Saudi Arabia to protect American personnel training the Saudi military.

50. Like ARCENT, the air force also has a headquarters at Shaw Air Force Base in South Carolina.

51. Data taken from 379th Air Expeditionary Wing, "Fact Sheet," August 27, 2014, http://www.afcent.af.mil/Units/379thAirExpeditionaryWing/FactSheets/Display/tabid/320/Article/501479/379th-air-expeditionary-wing-fact-sheet.aspx.

52. Amy Butler, "UAE-Based F-22s a Signal to Iran," *Aviation Week*, April, 26, 2012; Ladane Nasseri, "Iran Condemns U.S. F-22 Fighter Deployment to the Gulf, Fars Reports," *Bloomberg*, April 30, 2012; and Rajiv Chandrasekaran, "In the UAE, the United States Has a Quiet, Potent Ally Nicknamed 'Little Sparta,'" *Washington Post*, November 9, 2014.

53. This wing was deactivated in 2012 and reactivated in November 2014. Information is taken from interviews based on previously known functions and location of the wing, though they may have changed. Currently the wing is officially listed only as being located in "Southwest Asia"—another clue that it likely is responsible for sensitive missions. Tech. Sgt. Jared Marquis, "332nd Air Expeditionary Group Reactivates," U.S. Air Forces Central Command, November 25, 2014, http://www.afcent.af.mil/Units/386thAirExpeditionaryWing/News/Display/tabid/311/Article/554925/332nd-air-expeditionary-group-reactivates.aspx.

54. Al Udeid does host B-1s, but they were used primarily for close air support in Afghanistan, not to conduct long-range strategic bombing.

55. Rear headquarters are at MacDill AFB in Tampa, Florida.

56. Gunzinger with Doughtery, *Outside-In*, 13.

57. Hendrick Simoes, "Bahrain Expansion Latest Signal of Continued U.S. Presence," *Stars and Stripes*, December 13, 2013.

58. The Obama administration denied this request. Eli Lake, "As Obama Preaches Patience, U.S. Prepares for War with Iran," *The Daily Beast*, May 21, 2012; and Julian Pecquet, "Report: White House Scrapped CentCom's Request for Third Carrier Group off Iran Coast," *The Hill*, May 25, 2012.

59. Jeremy Herb, "Pentagon's Carrier Cancellation Heats Up Sequester Fight as Cuts Take Effect," *The Hill*, March 3, 2013; and "Navy to Pull Carrier from Central Command This Fall," *Navy Times*, June 5, 2015.

60. Thus, almost all of the US military's worldwide MCM capabilities are concen-

trated in the Gulf. Sydney J. Freedburg Jr., "Iran Mine Threat Scares Navy; CNO Scrambles to Fix Decades of Neglect," AOL Defense, May 4, 2012.

61. The afloat forward staging base also provides an obvious potential launching point for special operations forces. Thom Shanker, "Floating Base Gives U.S. New Footing in the Persian Gulf," *New York Times*, July 11, 2012.

62. Christopher P. Cavas, "Navy Boosts Arabian Gulf Patrol Craft Force," NavyTimes .com, July 3, 2013.

63. US submarines also perform this mission. Their role is not discussed in detail here because submarines are essentially invisible in the region.

64. Brian Murphy and Reem Khalifa, "U.S. Slammed from Both Sides of Bahrain's Divide," Associated Press, May 28, 2012, http://news.yahoo.com/us-slammed-both -sides-bahrains-divide-160528666.html.

65. Paul Richter, "Another Setback in Bahrain for the U.S.," *Los Angeles Times*, September 8, 2012, 8.

66. For a more pessimistic view about what would happen if the United States left Bahrain, see Richard McDaniel, "No 'Plan B': U.S. Strategic Access in the Middle East and the Question of Bahrain," Brookings Foreign Policy Paper (Washington DC: Brookings, June 2013), especially ch. 5.

67. On AirSea Battle, see Adm. Jonathan W. Greenert and Gen. Norton A. Schwartz, "Air-Sea Battle: Promoting Stability in an Era of Uncertainty," *The American Interest*, February 20, 2012, http://www.the-american-interest.com/2012/02/20/air-sea-battle. On the Joint Concept for Access and Maneuver in the Global Commons, see "Pentagon Drops Air Sea Battle Name, Concept Lives On," *U.S. Naval Institute News*, January 20, 2015. For a detailed treatment of how US posture in the Gulf would need to change in the event Iran acquired anti-access/area-denial capabilities comparable to those of China, see Gunzinger, *Outside-In*.

68. This possibility and a resulting posture option are developed in detail in ibid. Iran already regularly makes threats to this effect regarding the targeting of US military installations in the region, though little evidence yet suggests that its missiles have the accuracy needed to make good on these threats. Marcus George, "Iran Says Can Destroy U.S. Bases 'Minutes after Attack,'" *Reuters*, July 4, 2012; and Shifrinson and Priebe, "Crude Threat."

69. Such a scenario is examined in Lt. Col. Eduardo A. Abisellan, "CENTCOM's China Challenge: Anti-Access and Area Denial in the Middle East," 21st Century Defense Initiative Policy Paper (Washington DC: Brookings, June 28, 2012).

CONTRIBUTORS

Daniel Byman is a professor in the Security Studies Program at Georgetown University's School of Foreign Service and a senior associate dean for undergraduate affairs. He is also the research director of the Center for Middle East Policy at the Brookings Institution. Dr. Byman is the lead faculty member for Georgetown's "Terrorism and Counterterrorism" Massive Open Online Course, with 20,000 students enrolled. At Brookings, Dr. Byman is also the foreign policy editor of the *Lawfare* blog. He has served as a professional staff member with both the National Commission on Terrorist Attacks on the United States (the 9/11 Commission) and the Joint 9/11 Inquiry Staff of the House and Senate Intelligence Committees. He has also worked as the research director of the Center for Middle East Public Policy at the RAND Corporation and as an analyst of the Middle East for the US intelligence community. Dr. Byman has written widely on a range of topics related to terrorism, international security, and the Middle East. His publications have appeared in the *New York Times, The Atlantic, Wall Street Journal, Foreign Affairs, International Security,* and numerous other scholarly, policy, and popular journals. His latest books are *Al Qaeda, the Islamic State, and the Global Jihadist Movement: What Everyone Needs to Know* (Oxford University Press, 2015) and *A High Price: The Triumphs and Failures of Israeli Counterterrorism* (Oxford University Press, 2011). Dr. Byman received his BA in religion from Amherst College and his PhD in political science from the Massachusetts Institute of Technology (MIT).

John S. Duffield is a professor of political science and the director of academic assessment at Georgia State University in Atlanta. He earned a BA from Williams College in 1980 and a PhD from Princeton University in 1989. Duffield is the author of *Fuels Paradise: Seeking Energy Security in Europe, Japan, and the United States* (Johns Hopkins University Press, 2015); *Over a Barrel: The Costs of U.S. Foreign Oil Dependence* (Stanford University Press, 2008); *World Power Forsaken:*

Political Culture, International Institutions, and German Security Policy after Unification (Stanford University Press, 1998); and *Power Rules: The Evolution of NATO's Conventional Force Posture* (Stanford University Press, 1995), as well as numerous articles, book chapters, and book reviews on international security and energy policy. He is also coeditor of *Balance Sheet: The Iraq War and U.S. National Security* (Stanford University Press, 2009) and *Toward a Common European Union Energy Policy: Problems, Progress, and Prospects* (Palgrave Macmillan, 2011). His research focuses on the politics of energy and climate change in the United States and other industrialized countries.

Eugene Gholz is an associate professor of public affairs at the Lyndon B. Johnson (LBJ) School of Public Affairs at the University of Texas–Austin. From 2010 to 2012 he served in the US Department of Defense as a senior adviser to the deputy assistant secretary for manufacturing and industrial base policy. From 2007 to 2010, he was the director of the LBJ School's master's program in global policy studies. Gholz received BS degrees in political science and in materials engineering in 1992 and a PhD in political science in 2000, all from MIT. Before joining the LBJ School, he was an assistant professor at the University of Kentucky's Patterson School of Diplomacy and International Commerce. Gholz is a research associate at MIT's Security Studies Program, a life member of the Council on Foreign Relations, and an adjunct scholar in the Cato Institute's Defense and Foreign Policy Department.

An expert on the aerospace and defense industries, Gholz has authored and coauthored numerous articles, book chapters, and op-ed columns on innovation, business-government relations, defense management, and US foreign military policy. He is the coauthor of *Buying Military Transformation: Technological Innovation and the Defense Industry* (Columbia University Press, 2006) and *US Defense Politics: The Origins of Security Policy* (Routledge, 2008; second edition, 2014; Chinese edition, 2016). Gholz has also worked extensively on US grand strategy and energy security. A key recent publication (with Daryl Press) is "Protecting 'The Prize': Oil in American Grand Strategy," *Security Studies* (2010).

Charles L. Glaser is a professor of political science and international affairs at George Washington University and is the director of the Elliott School's Institute for Security and Conflict Studies. Glaser holds a PhD (1983) and an MA in public policy (1981) from the Kennedy School of Government at Harvard University, an MA in physics from Harvard (1983), and a BS in physics from MIT (1977). Before joining George Washington University, Glaser was the Emmett Dedmon Professor of Public Policy and the deputy dean at the Harris School of

Public Policy at the University of Chicago. He has also taught political science at the University of Michigan, was a fellow at the Wilson Center and a visiting fellow at the Center for International Security and Cooperation at Stanford, served on the Joint Staff in the Pentagon, was a Peace Fellow at the United States Institute of Peace, and was a research associate at MIT's Center of International Studies.

His publications on international relations theory include *Rational Theory of International Politics: The Logic of Competition and Cooperation* (Princeton University Press, 2010); "When Are Arms Races Dangerous?," *International Security* (2004); "The Security Dilemma Revisited," *World Politics* (1997); and "Realists as Optimists: Cooperation as Self-Help," *International Security* (1994/95). His security policy publications include *Analyzing Strategic Nuclear Policy* (Princeton University Press, 1990); "Counterforce Revisited" (with Steve Fetter), *International Security* (2005); "How Oil Influences U.S. National Security," *International Security* (2013); and "A U.S.-China Grand Bargain? The Hard Choice between Military Competition and Accommodation," *International Security* (2015).

Rosemary A. Kelanic is an assistant professor of political science at Williams College. From 2011 to 2013, Kelanic was an associate director of the Institute for Security and Conflict Studies and a research instructor in international affairs at the Elliott School of International Affairs at George Washington University. She received her PhD in political science from the University of Chicago in 2012; an MA in international relations, with honors, from the University of Chicago (2003); and a BA in political science, summa cum laude, from Bryn Mawr College (2002).

Her research focuses on energy security and international relations theory, and her work has appeared in *Security Studies,* the Council on Foreign Relations' Energy Reports series, *The National Interest* (online), and *H-Diplo* (online). Her book manuscript, *Black Gold and Blackmail: The Politics of International Oil Coercion,* examines whether countries can use the threat of oil disruption to coerce political concessions from their adversaries. Kelanic has received fellowships from the Belfer Center for Science and International Affairs at the Harvard Kennedy School, the Chicago Energy Initiative, and the Chicago Project on Security and Terrorism.

Thomas W. Lippman is an award-winning author and journalist who has written about Middle Eastern affairs and US foreign policy for more than three decades, specializing in Saudi Arabian affairs, US-Saudi relations, and relations between the West and Islam. He is a former Middle East bureau chief of the *Washington Post* and has served as that newspaper's oil and energy reporter. Throughout the

1990s, he covered foreign policy and national security for the *Post*, traveling frequently to Saudi Arabia and other countries in the Middle East. In 2003 he was the principal writer on the war in Iraq for Washingtonpost.com. Prior to his work in the Middle East, he covered the Vietnam War as the paper's bureau chief in Saigon.

Lippman is the author of numerous magazine articles, book reviews, and op-ed columns about Mideast affairs and has written seven books: *Understanding Islam: An Introduction to the Muslim World* (New American Library, 1982; third revised edition, 2002); *Egypt after Nasser: Sadat, Peace, and the Mirage of Prosperity* (Paragon House, 1989); *Madeleine Albright and the New American Diplomacy* (Westview Press, 2000); *Inside the Mirage: America's Fragile Partnership with Saudi Arabia* (Westview Press, 2004); *Arabian Knight: Colonel Bill Eddy USMC and the Rise of American Power in the Middle East* (Selwa Press, 2008); *Saudi Arabia on the Edge: The Uncertain Future of an American Ally* (Potomac Books, 2011); and, most recently, *Hero of the Crossing: How Anwar Sadat and the 1973 War Changed the World* (Potomac Books, 2016). *Arabian Knight* won a Benjamin Franklin Award from the Independent Book Publishers Association as best biography of 2008.

Joshua Rovner is the Tower Distinguished Chair in International Politics and National Security Policy and an associate professor of political science at Southern Methodist University. He is the author of *Fixing the Facts: National Security and the Politics of Intelligence* (Cornell University Press, 2011), which won the International Studies Association Best Book Award for security studies. He has also published articles on intelligence reform, politics and strategy, nuclear proliferation, and deterrence. Rovner is reviews editor for the *Journal of Strategic Studies*. Rovner holds a PhD in political science from MIT.

Caitlin Talmadge is an assistant professor of political science and international affairs at George Washington University, where her research and teaching focus is on US defense policy, civil-military relations, military effectiveness, nuclear strategy, and Persian Gulf security issues. During the 2014–15 academic year, she was also a Stanton Nuclear Security Fellow at the Council on Foreign Relations. Dr. Talmadge is the author of *The Dictator's Army: Battlefield Effectiveness in Authoritarian Regimes* (Cornell University Press, 2015) and coauthor of *U.S. Defense Politics: The Origins of Security Policy* (Routledge, 2014). Her other writings have appeared in *International Security, Security Studies, The Nonproliferation Review, The Journal of Conflict Resolution, The Washington Quarterly, New York Times,* and *Washington Post,* among other publications. Dr. Talmadge previously worked at the Center for Strategic and International Studies and the Brookings Institution, and as a consultant to the Office of Net Assessment at the US Department of Defense. She holds a BA in government from Harvard College, summa cum laude, and a PhD in political science from the Massachusetts Institute of Technology.

Kenneth R. Vincent is a PhD candidate in the Department of Political Science at George Washington University. He also serves as an economist for the Office of Petroleum Reserves in the US Department of Energy. In this position, he oversees major program planning and economic studies for the Strategic Petroleum Reserve, conducts petroleum market and policy analysis, and executes the program's international activities. Previously he worked as an industry economist at the US Energy Information Administration. Before entering federal service, Vincent was the assistant director of the Scowcroft Institute of International Affairs at Texas A&M University. He holds a BA in foreign affairs from the University of Virginia and a master of international affairs degree from Texas A&M University. His dissertation is titled "The Strategic Determinants of Oil Stockpiling Behavior."

Salim Yaqub is an associate professor of history at the University of California, Santa Barbara, and director of UCSB's Center for Cold War Studies and International History. He specializes in the history of US foreign relations, with a particular focus on US involvement in the Middle East in the postwar era. Yaqub is the author of *Containing Arab Nationalism: The Eisenhower Doctrine and the Middle East* (University of North Carolina Press, 2004) and of numerous book chapters and journal articles on US relations with the Middle East. His second book, *Imperfect Strangers: Americans and Arabs in the 1970s,* will be published by Cornell University Press in 2016.

INDEX

Figures, maps, notes, and tables are indicated by f, m, n, and t following the page number. Surnames starting with "al-" are alphabetized by the subsequent part of the name.

Abdullah (king), 149

Abisellan, Eduardo A., 279n67

Abqaiq refinery, 120–21, 123, 124, 138n25

acts of sabotage as threats. *See* sabotage

Adelman, Morris: "International Oil Agreements," 88

Aden (British colony), 29–30

adjustment (allocation) costs to oil supply disruption, 94, 97–98, 99, 102, 110n75, 199

Afghanistan, 34–35, 41, 63, 182, 194n58, 257, 264–65

AIOC (Anglo-Iranian Oil Company), 25–26, 44n10

Air Force's (US) military role: cost of, 179, 181, 185, 186, 188n7, 190n24, 241; heavy US forward presence of, 255; residual forward presence of, 264–68, 265t; in Saudi Arabia, 24, 38, 133, 278n49; in Strait of Hormuz, 174, 190n24; in UAE, 24, 38

AirSea Battle operational concept, 273

Alexander, Keith B., 119

Algeria, 68, 131

all-electric vehicles (EVs), 215, 216

al-Qaeda: acts of sabotage by, 120–22; current strength of, 56; democratization inciting, 57–58; as Israel's foe, 72n1; Saudi Arabian insurgency (2003–2007), 125, 126, 129, 148; terrorism acts and threats by, 55–56,

74n26, 260, 263, 264; US military presence inciting, 61, 66; US military strategy against, 176; US security arrangements, impact on, 61

al-Qaeda in the Arabian Peninsula (AQAP), 148

alternative fuels and energy resources, 208–18; biofuels, 209–12, 227n45; electrification of transportation fleet, 10, 215–17; future implications for, 217–18; hydrogen, 214–15; natural gas, 212–14; overview, 83, 208–9; renewable, 117; US military options based on, 242–43

Al Udeid Air Base, 255, 264, 267–68

American Recovery and Reinvestment Act of 2009, 217

Anglo-Iranian Oil Company (AIOC), 25–26, 44n10

anti-access/area-denial (A2/AD) challenge, 178, 181, 192n44, 261, 277n37

anti-American sentiment: democratization and, 58; US foreign policy creating, 263, 277–78n47; US military presence creating, 40, 61, 68, 69, 76n52, 260, 261; US-Saudi relations creating, 42, 132, 133, 134, 136

anti-Saudi sentiment, 42

ANWR (Arctic National Wildlife Refuge), 201, 202

al-Anzi, Abdel Aziz: "The Religious Rule on
Targeting Oil Interests," 120–21
AQAP (al-Qaeda in the Arabian Peninsula),
148
Arabian American Oil Company. *See* Aramco
Arab-Israeli War (1967), 31, 32–33
Arab nationalism, 25, 29, 39, 126, 152, 155,
174
Arab oil embargoes. *See* oil embargoes
Arab Spring (2011): al-Qaeda and, 56; democratization and, 57, 58, 59, 70; oil security
and, 4, 43, 52–53; Saudi Arabia and, 125,
126, 130, 149; US policy on intervening
with, 58–59, 134, 242
Aramco (Arabian American Oil Company):
accidental refinery explosion, 120, 138n25;
act of sabotage on, 121, 122, 123; China,
relations with, 4; cyber attacks on, 118–19;
history of, 25, 130; modernization of Saudi
Arabia and, 44n9; protection from attacks,
124; US oil imports from, 137n2
Arctic National Wildlife Refuge (ANWR),
201, 202
Army's (US) military role: in East Asian scenarios, 179–80, 192nn43–44, 192–93n47;
heavy forward presence of, 255; reduction
of, 5, 180, 185, 186, 188n7, 195n68; residual forward presence of, 262–64; in Saudi
Arabia, 180
al-Assad, Bashar, 4
al-Assaf, Ibrahim, 139n43

Ba'ath regime, 133, 143–44, 146
Baghdad Pact, 26–27
Bahrain: democratization and, 57, 59; dual
containment and, 255–56; heavy forward
military presence in, 255–56; instability in,
52, 53, 135; possible US departure from,
279n66; Qatar-Bahrain relations, 257;
residual forward military position in, 252,
268, 269, 270, 272; Shia majority in, 130;
US military presence in, 25, 61, 63, 121,
134–35, 159, 161, 176, 180, 193n52

ballistic missile defense (BMD) facilities, 66
Barsky, Robert, 91
Base Force Review (1991) on fighting two
regional wars simultaneously, 169
Base Realignment and Closure (BRAC) pro-
cess, 171, 189n9, 189n12
battery-electric vehicles (BEVs), 215, 216
Bernanke, Benjamin, 96
Biafra secession (1967–70), 131
Bilmes, Linda, 194n60
bin Laden, Osama, 40–41, 42, 56, 121, 129, 133
bin Nayef, Muhammad (prince), 123
biodiesel, 83, 209
biofuels, 83, 209–12, 222
Bleek, Philipp, 54
Bolsheviks, 131
Bottom-Up Review (1993) on fighting two
wars simultaneously, 169
BP, 106n2, 115–16
BRAC (Base Realignment and Closure) pro-
cess, 171, 189n9, 189n12
Brazil, 114, 222
Brezhnev Doctrine, 59
Britain: imperialism of, 21; military power of,
41, 44n2, 161, 246; as oil-producing nation,
99; security relationships of, 10, 23–31,
44n10, 60, 147, 246; transportation fuel
taxes in, 207
Bronson, Rachel: *Thicker than Oil*, 76n52; on
US-Saudi relations, 133
budgetary issues. *See* defense budget (US)
Budget Control Act (2011), 5, 184, 191n37
Bush, George H. W., 38
Bush, George W.: on alternative transportation
fuel, 214; on fuel economy, 205; Middle
East policies of, 41, 42, 57, 58, 173; on SPR
capacity, 202, 203; on terrorism, 55; visit to
Riyadh (2008), 122
butanol, 210
Byman, Daniel, 11

CAFE (Corporate Average Fuel Economy)
standards, 205, 215, 229n73

Canada, 82, 99, 114, 220

Carter, Ashton, 162n16

Carter, Jimmy, 1, 34–36, 202

Carter Doctrine, 1, 34, 35, 36

Cattaneo, Claudia: "Will Tight Oil Change the World?," 72n3

Central Command (CENTCOM), 1, 60, 63, 176–77, 180, 188n7, 190n24, 262, 268

China: alternative energy policies of, 222, 223; anti-access/area-denial capabilities of, 261, 277n37; Aramco relations with, 4; on nuclear proliferation in Iran, 42; oil demand by, 4, 50, 72, 92, 129, 135, 221–22; oil reserves in, 14, 203, 221, 237–38, 248nn6–7; oil shock response by, 99; Persian Gulf stability and, 43, 246–47, 250n33, 274; US military posture toward, 169, 178–79, 192n41

civil wars: Iraq, 41, 144–46, 148, 154; terrorist backing of, 55, 56; as threats to oil production and distribution, 50, 51, 52–53, 127, 128, 253–54; as threat to Saudi Arabian oil, 130–31, 134, 139n40, 174, 238

Clayton, Blake, 118, 137n15

Clinton, Bill, 39, 255

Clinton, Hillary, 152

Coast Guard's (US) military role, 270

Cold War: anti-Iraq resolutions and, 46n44; influence on US policies, 22; Soviet Union threat in Persian Gulf, 3–4, 15, 25–26, 235, 242, 249n20; US defense budget for, 168, 188n3

USS *Cole* attack (2000), 122

communism and anti-communism, 27, 28, 29, 34

compressed natural gas (CNG) vehicles, 212–13

Congressional Budget Office on transportation fuel taxes, 207

Cordesman, Anthony, 144

Corporate Average Fuel Economy (CAFE) standards, 205, 213, 215, 229n73

Council of Economic Advisers on economic impact of oil shocks, 97

counterterrorism and terrorism: cyber attacks as, 118–20, 137–38nn15–16, 138n18, 138n21, 175, 191n32; democratization effect on, 55–56, 57, 58, 70; Iran's use of terrorism, 52, 54; on oil infrastructure, 253; in Saudi Arabia, 64, 148, 277n45; US military strategy for, 65–66, 68, 175–76, 191n33, 261; US priority of counterterrorism, 55–57, 61. *See also* al-Qaeda; Islamic State; sabotage as threat to Saudi Arabian oil

Cutting Sword of Justice on Saudi Arabian cyber attack, 118, 138n16

cyber attacks, 118–20, 137–38nn15–16, 138n18, 138n21, 175, 191n32

Dammam mosque bombing (2015), 148

Davidson, Janine, 274n2

defense budget (US), 167–95, 240–43; analytical challenges of, 168–72, 188n3, 188n7, 189n9, 189n11; future implications for, 187, 240–41, 248–49n17; military options and, 242–43; overview, 167–68, 187–88n2; Persian Gulf operations and, 172–77, 190n20, 190n24, 191n23, 191nn37–38; two-MRC strategy and cutbacks, 184–87; two-MRC strategy and potential savings, 177–84

Delucchi, Mark A., 189n9, 195n62

demand oil shocks. *See* supply and demand oil shocks

demand-side solutions, 200t, 204–18, 243; alternative fuels and energy resources as, 208–15; biofuels as, 209–12; electrification of transportation fleet, 10, 215–17; fuel demand reductions, 204–8; fuel economy increases, 205–6; fuel taxes as, 206–8; future implications for, 217–18; hydrogen as, 214–15; international policy extensions as, 221–23; natural gas as, 212–14; overview, 219t; as strategy alternatives, 243

democratization: counterterrorism and, 55–56, 57, 58, 70; military presence effect on, 68; US policies on, 11, 57–59, 70, 72n1

Department of Defense (DOD): on cyber attacks, 119; on oil security threat, 168. *See also* defense budget

Department of Energy: on electrification of transportation fleet, 217; on global biofuel production, 222; on oil security, 122, 203; on transportation fuel taxes, 207

Diego Garcia Base, 1, 66, 271

dimaj officers, 145

DOD. *See* Department of Defense

dual containment policy, 255–56, 257

Duffield, John S., 13, 14, 171–72, 189n14, 237, 242–43

Dugan, Regina E., 119

Dulles, John Foster, 26

economic costs of supply disruptions, 50–51, 79–112, 132–34, 198–99; continuity and change in petroleum market, 82–85, 83f; demand vs. supply shocks, 50, 72n3, 84, 87–88, 89, 90t, 91–93; energy security alternatives and, 198–99; estimating impact, 100–104, 103t, 112nn91–92; harm of oil shocks, 91–92; historical overview, 96–98; international impacts of, 98–100; lessons learned and future trends, 104–6; literature review, 88–100; maintaining Strategic Petroleum Reserve, 203–4; Middle East, importance of, 85–87, 86f, 86t; monetary policy and, 95–96; oil shocks, defined, 89–91; overview, 79–82; price fluctuations, 87–88, 236; reduced supply due to oil shocks, 93–95; Saudi Arabian oil and, 132–34, 136n1; Strait of Hormuz blockade scenario, 51–52, 158

economic sanctions: against Iran, 5, 26, 42, 144, 151, 155, 240; against Iraq, 34, 39, 40; against Soviet Union, 34

Egypt: democratization stance of, 57, 59, 68, 70; economic climate in, 127; as Israel's foe, 72n1; military presence and, 68; oil security and, 28–29; reactive proliferation potential by, 54; revolution in, 125; Suez

Canal Company crisis, 27; on Western imperialism, 26

EIA. *See* Energy Information Administration

Eisenhower, Dwight D., 26, 27, 28

Eisenhower Doctrine, 27–28

elasticities of oil price fluctuations, 100–101, 110–11n77, 111n79

electric vehicles (EVs), 215, 216

electrification of transportation fleet, 10, 83, 204–5, 215–17, 222–23

energy consumption (US), 82–85, 83–84f

energy efficient vehicles. *See* fuel economy

Energy Independence and Security Act of 2007 (EISA), 205, 209

Energy Information Administration (EIA; US): on biofuel, 210; on electrification of transportation fleet, 215, 216; on energy markets, 79, 106n2; on fuel consumption, 221–22; on fuel economy, 205, 206; on GDP responses to oil shocks, 112n91; on natural gas vehicles, 213; on oil consumption, 204, 226nn20–21; on oil imports, 114, 136–37n2; on oil production, 200–201, 218, 220; on oil reserves, 201, 202; on Saudi Arabia's oil and gas future, 116; on supply shocks, 101

Energy Policy Act of 2005 (EPACT), 203, 209, 211, 214

energy security alternatives (US), 197–230; alternative fuels and energy sources, 208–15; biofuels, 209–12; demand-side solutions, 204–18, 221–23; electrification of transportation fleet, 10, 215–17; future implications for, 217–18; hydrogen, 214–15; increasing fuel economy, 205–6; increasing Strategic Petroleum Reserve, 202–4; increasing US oil production, 200–202; international policy extensions, 218–23; natural gas, 212–14; oil supply disruptions and, 198–99, 200t; overview, 197–98; as policy strategy option, 243; reducing oil demand, 204–8; supply-side solutions, 199–204, 218–21; taxes, 206–8

Enhanced Carrier Presence plan, 191n37
EPACT. *See* Energy Policy Act of 2005
ethanol, 83, 209–12, 222
EVs (electric vehicles), 215, 216
external threats to oil security, 118–36, 253–55, 254t; acts of sabotage, 52, 54, 120–24, 135, 139n41, 151, 157–59, 253; civil wars, 51, 52–53, 130–31, 134, 139n40, 253–54; as consideration for military presence, 238; cyber attacks, 118–20, 137–38nn15–16, 138n18, 138n21, 175, 191n32; over-the-horizon military posture and, 258–60; role of US and, 52, 131–36, 254–55. *See also* hostile takeover threats; Strait of Hormuz

Facilities Security Force (Saudi Arabia), 123, 124
Fahd (king), 133
al-Faisal, Turki (prince), 123
al-Falih, Khalid, 4, 116
feebate, 208
Fifth Fleet, 38. *See also* Navy's (US) military role
Financial Times on Saudi Arabian cyber attack, 118–19
flex-fuel vehicles (FFVs), 210–11
Flournoy, Michele, 274n2
forward presence posture: costs of, 181–82; heavy US forward military presence (HFP) posture, 255–58; naval forces and, 176–77, 191n37, 255–56; residual forward presence (RFP) posture, 15, 251–53, 260–73
fracking, 6–7, 200, 212
France, 27, 55, 143, 147, 207
fuel economy, 204–6, 222, 226n28, 243
fuel subsidies, 99, 117

G-7 countries, 98–99
GDP. *See* gross domestic product (GDP) as measurement of oil price shocks
geography as regional war deterrence, 154–56, 160
Germany, 44n2, 207
Gertler, Mark, 96

Gfoeller, Michael, 122
Gholz, Eugene, 12–13, 50, 67, 158, 241, 248–49n17, 258–60
Glaser, Charles L., 1, 13, 251, 259
Goldstone, Jack, 125
Government Accountability Office (GAO) study (2006) on SPR capacity, 112n91, 202–3, 204, 248n8
Great Britain. *See* Britain
Green Revolution (2009), 59, 152
gross domestic product (GDP) as measurement of oil price shocks: asymmetry of, 98; in China, 99; energy alternatives to effects on, 199; for estimating economic impact of oil disruption, 100; oil intensity definition and, 234–35; oil price elasticities and, 102–4, 103t, 236; reliability of, 11, 81–82, 91–92, 97; US military presence and, 239–40
Gulf Cooperation Council (GCC): countries on, 276n16; on Iran's nuclear program, 136; on military coordination, 156–57, 255, 257, 270; on Saudi Arabian oil security, 114
Gulf War (1991): costs of, 67, 128, 183, 195n62; military posture policy due to, 37, 38–39, 40, 144, 169, 173–74, 255–56; oil security and, 1, 15

Halliday, Fred, 40
Hamilton, James, 91–92
Hammond, Andrew, 126
Hashemite dynasty and regime of Iraq, 26, 28, 143
heavy US forward military presence (HFP) posture, 255–58
hegemony. *See* regional hegemony
Hegghammer, Thomas, 148
Heiss, Mary Ann: *Empire and Nationhood: The United States, Great Britain, and Iranian Oil, 1950–1954*, 44n10
Heritage Foundation: on civil war threat, 134; on Saudi Arabian oil, 113
Hezbollah, 39, 56, 57

HFCVs (hydrogen fuel-cell vehicles), 214–15
horizontal drilling, 200, 212
hostile takeover threats: by Iran, 151–52,
239–40; by Islamic State, 254, 275n11;
possible scenarios of, 50–51, 124–30; US
military presence as deterrence to, 67,
132–33, 135–36
Houthi rebels, 133, 147, 163n20
human rights issues, 70
Huntington, Hillard G: "Economic Consequences," 112n92
Huntzinger, LaVar: "The Economic Implications of Disruptions to Maritime Oil
Chokepoints," 136n1
Hussein, Saddam: Gulf War (1991), 38, 39,
60, 64, 133, 172; invasion of Kuwait, 1, 10,
144, 146; Iraq War (2003) and, 4, 40–41,
61; as Israel's foe, 72n1; post–Iran-Iraq War,
37; post–Iraq War (2003), 51; US alliance
with, 22, 36
hybrid-electric vehicles, 204–5, 217
hydrogen fuel-cell vehicles (HFCVs), 214–15

imperialism, 26–27, 28–29
India, 23, 54, 72n3, 221–22, 225, 246
insurgencies, 29, 32, 41, 53–54, 55. *See also*
al-Qaeda; counterterrorism and terrorism;
cyber attacks; sabotage as threat to Saudi
Arabian oil
Integrated Air and Missile Defense Center, 63
International Energy Agency (IEA): China
and, 248n7; on oil production, 5, 114, 220;
on oil reserve distribution, 104, 186, 243,
249; on oil reserve stockpiles, 14, 101–2,
203, 220–21, 234, 236–37; on US energy
self-sufficiency, 79–80, 106n2
international impacts: demand side, 221–23;
of economic costs of supply disruptions,
98–100; sanctions against Iraq, 144; strategy alternatives and, 244–47; supply side,
87–88, 218–21
International Institute of Strategic Studies: on
Iraqi military forces, 144; on Saudi Arabian
military forces, 147

interstate oil disruptions, 141–65; future
implications for preventing, 160–61; oil
shipping risks and, 157–60; overview,
141–42; regional hegemony and, 142–53;
by regional war possibility, 153–57
intrastate oil disruptions, 118–40; by acts of
sabotage, 120–24; by civil war, 130–31; by
cyber attacks, 118–20; by radical, hostile
group takeover, 124–30; US role in preventing, 131–36. *See also specific countries*
Iran: anti-access/area-denial capabilities of,
261, 277n37; Baghdad Pact and, 26, 27;
civil unrest in, 22, 33–34, 52; Cold War
crisis involving, 25; on communism, 29;
counterterrorism in, 56–57; economic climate in, 151; Green Revolution (2009), 59,
152; as Israel's foe, 72n1; military power
of, 142–43, 147, 149–53, 156, 160–61,
163n29, 164n41, 173, 238, 242, 279n68;
military presence to counter, 65–67, 69,
70–71, 257–61; nationalization of oil
production in, 25–26; nuclear negotiations
with, 4, 5, 239–40; nuclear proliferation
risks from, 4, 42, 53–54, 136, 152–53,
164n41, 175, 245–46; oil security and,
51–52, 114, 118–19, 122–23, 133, 239–40,
253; oil shipping risks and, 157–60; plot
to overthrow Syria, 27; political climate in,
151, 152; post–Arab-Israeli War (1967),
31–33; regional hegemony of, 21–22,
149–53; sanctions against, 5, 26, 42, 144,
151, 155, 240; security relationships in past
with US, 60; Shiite protests in Saudi Arabia
and, 148; Strait of Hormuz blockades and
scenarios, 51–52, 136n1, 151, 157–60, 174,
237–40, 244, 253; US military aid to, 29;
war deterrence and offense-defense balance
in, 154, 155; World War II and, 23–24
Iran hostage situation (1979), 34
Iran-Iraq War (1980–1988), 30, 36–37, 144, 146
Iraq: Baghdad Pact, 26–27; civil war in,
52, 148; counterterrorism in, 191n33;
Eisenhower Doctrine and, 28; Islamic
State and, 160–61; as Israel's foe, 72n1;

military power of, 22, 142, 143–46, 162n3, 162nn14–16, 163n18, 173, 238, 242; military presence against, 69, 257–58; Nasserism and, 28; oil security and, 51, 114, 253–54; post–Arab-Israeli War (1967), 32; regional war deterrence in, 154, 155, 156; sanctions against, 34, 39, 40; terrorism and, 55, 56; US alliance with, 35–36; US security arrangements and, 60–61, 64, 69, 133. *See also* Gulf War (1991); Iraq War (2003)

Iraq War (2003): anti-American sentiment and, 42, 68; cost of, 182, 183, 194n58, 194n60, 195n62, 249n17; oil security and, 1, 15, 172; US military policy after, 37, 41, 173–74

Islamic Republic of Iran. *See* Iran

Islamic Revolution (1979), 57, 60, 150

Islamic State: air strikes against, 4; current strength of, 56; in Iraq, 65, 145; as military power, 160–61; oil security and, 114, 160–61, 254; terrorism threat of, 55, 148; US military strategy against, 65, 176

Israel: anti-American sentiment associated with, 277–78n47; democratization and, 58; on JCPOA, 53–54; security support for, 72n1; Suez Canal crisis, 27

al-Jabri, Saad, 122

Jadwa Investment group on Saudi Arabian domestic consumption of oil, 116

Japan, 222

Jebel Ali port, 63, 269

Jervis, Robert: "Cooperation under the Security Dilemma," 164n42; on nuclear proliferation, 53

jihadist movements. *See* counterterrorism and terrorism

Johnson, Lyndon B., 29

Joint Commission on Infrastructure and Border Protection, 122–23

Joint Comprehensive Plan of Action (JCPOA), 53–54

Joint Concept for Access and Maneuver in the Global Commons, 273

Jones, Toby Craig, 44n9

Jordan: anti-American sentiment in, 58, 68; fragile status of, 132; military power of, 133; US military presence in, 28

Kapur, Paul, 54

al-Kayyal, Fahad, 121–22

Kazakhstan, 114

Kelanic, Rosemary A., 1, 13, 251, 259

Kelberer, John J., 120

Kennedy, John F., 28–29

Kenya, 35

Khobar Towers bombing (1966), 277n45

Khomeini, Ruhollah, 34

Kilian, Lutz, 91–93, 99

Kirkuk, 145

Kissinger, Henry, 33

Knittel, Christopher R., 226n28

Komiss, William: "The Economic Implications of Disruptions to Maritime Oil Chokepoints," 136n1

Kosovo War (1998–99), 190n24

Krepinevich, Andrew, 119

Kurdish population as political class, 32, 36, 38, 143, 145–46, 160–61

Kurdish Regional Government, 145–46

Kuwait: attacks on US presence in, 263, 277n45; BMD systems in, 66; hostile takeover possibilities, 51; invasion of, 37–38, 60, 142, 144, 156; military power of, 156; oil disruption in, 128; pipeline possibility for, 249n24; security arrangements with, 61, 63; US military presence in, 37, 68–69, 172, 182–83, 255, 262–65, 267; US residual forward military position in, 252

Labs, Eric, 191n36

Lebanon, 28, 39, 56, 57

Leiby, Paul, 175, 191n28

Lend-Lease assistance, 23–24

Lenin, Vladimir, 131

Levi, Michael: *The Power Surge: Energy, Opportunity, and the Battle for America's Future*, 112n94

Libya, 50, 52, 56, 57, 70, 87, 253

Lippman, Thomas W., 12, 81, 138n25, 238, 242, 254

liquefied natural gas (LNG) vehicles, 212, 213–14

Macmillan, Harold, 28

Macris, Jeffrey R., 35

al-Majed, Saad, 123

major regional contingency (MRC) strategy: defense budget and, 169, 188n7; defined, 169, 188n5; future implications for, 187, 241; Persian Gulf missions of, 172–77, 190n20, 190n24; two-MRC strategy cutbacks, 184–87; two-MRC strategy possible savings, 177–84

al-Maliki, Nouri, 145, 155, 162n15

Manama (Bahrain), 272

Marines' military role, 186, 187, 270

Mattis, James, 268

Maugeri, Leonardo: "Oil: The Next Revolution," 72n3

McNaugher, Thomas L., 190n26

methanol, 212, 214

Middle East: exceptionalism of democracy in, 57; importance of, 85–87, 86*f*, 86*t*; nuclear proliferation in, 53–55, 152–53; oil production in, 50–53; regional war as possibility in, 153–57; trade relationships with, 65; US security arrangements in, 61–65. *See also* military presence and posture (US); United States policies; *specific countries*

Middle East Force (MIDEASTFOR), 25, 28, 29, 35, 36–37

Middle East War (1973–1974), 128–29

military presence and posture (US), 65–71, 141–65, 251–79; after 9/11, 61; base network, 61, 62*m*, 194n55, 264–68, 265*t*; during Carter administration, 34–36; Coast Guard, 270; comparing, 256*t*; costs and risks of, 67–69, 194n53, 194n55, 194nn57–58; counterterrorism argument against, 56; direct power of (1990 to pres-

ent), 37–43; Eisenhower Doctrine and, 28; expansion of, 69; framework for analyzing posture of, 253–55; future implications for, 160–61, 273–74; heavy forward presence, 69, 255–58; history of, 22; after Kuwait invasion (1990), 60–61; light but visible forward presence, 70–71, 141–42; Marines, 186, 187, 270; oil shipping risks and, 157–60; options for, 241–47; over-the-horizon presence, 258–60; recommendations, 258–60; regional hegemony and, 142–53, 164n41; regional war as possibility, 153–57; residual forward presence (middle way), 251–53, 260–73; security arrangements for, 60–65; trade-offs for, 65–69; withdrawal of forces, 258–60. *See also* Air Force's (US) military role; Army's (US) military role; defense budget (US); Navy's (US) military role; *specific countries*

monetary policy, 95–96

Mossadeq, Mohammed, 25–26

MRC. *See* major regional contingency (MRC) strategy

Mubarak, Hosni, 57, 70

Mujahedeen-e-Khalq, 152

al-Muqrin, Abdul Aziz, 121

Murphy, James J., 189n9

al-Naimi, Ali, 107n20

Nasser, Gamal Abdel, 26–29, 72n1, 126

nationalism (Arab), 25, 29, 39, 126, 152, 155, 174

nationalization, 25–26, 27

National Research Council: on fuel economy gains (2008), 204–5; on hybrid fuel vehicles, 215, 229n73; on plug-in hybrid electric vehicles (2010), 217

National Security Strategy on fighting simultaneous wars, 169

natural gas, 83, 200, 212–14

Navy's (US) military role: cost of, 185, 188n7, 190n24, 193n52; in East Asian scenarios, 179, 180, 193n49; Enhanced Carrier Presence plan of, 191n37; Fifth Fleet and, 38, 63, 66, 121, 135, 159, 252, 257, 268, 272; heavy forward presence of, 61, 63, 75n35, 122, 133, 176–77, 191n37, 255–56; during Iran-Iraq War, 37; post–Gulf War, 38–39; post–WWII, 24, 25; residual forward presence of, 268–73, 269t; for Strait of Hormuz protection, 159, 174, 180, 193n49

New York Times on Saudi Arabian cyber attack, 118

Nigeria, 131

Nixon, Richard M., 31–32

Nixon Doctrine, 31–32, 35

non-OECD countries, 4, 92, 99–100, 110n75, 221–22

North Korea, 179–80, 192n42, 192–93n47

nuclear proliferation: assessing for strategy alternatives, 245–46; in Iran, 42, 53–54, 136, 152–53, 164n41, 175, 245–46; Iranian negotiations on, 4, 5, 239–40; military presence preventing, 65–66, 69; residual forward military posture and, 260–61; US military strategy and, 175, 176; US policies on, 53–55, 72n1

Obama, Barack: alternative energy policies of, 205–6; on Bahrain uprising, 135; on commitment to security arrangements, 64; on democratization, 58; on fuel economy, 205–6, 226n28; GCC states' leaders meeting (2015), 136; on Iran's nuclear proliferation possibility, 42, 43; Middle East policy of, 43, 64, 114, 132, 136, 172–73, 190n20; on military action against Islamic State, 132; on oil security, 18n14; on terrorism, 55

Oberwetter, James, 122

OECD countries, 4, 98–100, 221–22

offense-defense balance and theory, 154–56, 164n42

offshore production of crude oil, 200, 274–75n3

oil as economic interest, 235–36

oil embargoes, 31, 33, 90, 202

oil intensity, defined, 234–35

oil price shocks, 87–104; alternative energy sources and, 198–99, 200t, 202, 211, 217, 229n85; with blockage of Strait of Hormuz, 51; defined, 89–91, 92t; as demand and supply shocks, 72n3, 84–85, 90t, 91–94, 97, 108n26, 112n94; economic impacts of, 79, 91–95; energy security alternatives to prevent, 198–99; external threats creating, 51; focusing on, 87–88; global market and, 6; history of, 96–98; international impact of, 98–100; monetary policy and, 95–96; MRC missions and, 174, 190n26; oil embargoes and, 33–34; overview, 88–89, 89f; Persian Gulf supply disruption, effect on, 100–104, 112n91; Saudi Arabia's mitigation of, 50. *See also* economic costs of supply disruptions; supply and demand oil shocks

oil production and reserves: in North America, 82, 85, 87; oil shocks and, 89–90; in Persian Gulf, 85–87, 86t; outside Persian Gulf, 218; reserves of oil for, 85–87, 86f, 116; as supply-side solution, 199, 200–202. *See also* Strategic Petroleum Reserves (SPR); tight oil production

oil security as US interest: defense budget and, 180, 192–93n47; oil shocks and, 87–88; threats to, 50–53, 66; US policy and, 1–4, 6, 235; WWII and early postwar years, 24–25. *See also* economic costs of supply disruptions; energy security alternatives (US); interstate oil disruptions; intrastate oil disruptions; military presence and posture (US); Saudi Arabian oil; strategy alternatives

oil shocks, effect of. *See* economic costs of supply disruptions; oil price shocks; supply and demand oil shocks

Oman: Britain and, 29–30; civil war in, 32; post–Arab-Israeli War (1967), 32; US military presence in, 35, 255; US security arrangements with, 61, 63, 75n35

OPEC (Organization of the Petroleum Export-
ing Countries), 33, 84, 87, 114, 174
Operation Earnest Will (1988) costs, 182–83,
249n17
Operation Iraqi Freedom (2003), 265
Operation Praying Mantis (1988), 65
Operations Desert Shield and Desert Storm
(1990–91), 128, 144, 172
Operations Southern Watch (1990s), 183
Operation Vigilant Warrior costs (1994), 183
Optimized Fleet Response Plan (2014), 177,
191n37
Organization for Economic Cooperation and
Development. *See* OECD countries
Organization of the Petroleum Exporting
Countries. *See* OPEC
over-the-horizon (OTH) posture, 258–60

Pacific operations, 178–79, 180–81
Pahlavi, Mohammad Reza Shah, 21–22, 30, 60
Pakistan, 26, 34, 54
Palestinian territories, 68
Panetta, Leon, 56
Pape, Robert, 259–60
Paris terrorist attack (2015), 55
peak oil theory, 85
People's Democratic Republic of Yemen, 30
People's Liberation Army (China), 178
Persian Corridor, 23
Persian Gulf: China possible military presence
in, 246–47; counterterrorism and terrorism
in, 55–57; economic costs of oil disruption
in, 79–112, 112n91; oil production in,
85–87, 86*f*, 86*t*; regional hegemony in,
142–53; regional war as possibility in, 153–
57; severing US military commitments to,
effects of, 141–65; share of oil production,
218, 220; US basing network in, 61, 62*m*,
69, 70–71, 159, 174, 181–82, 194n55, 252,
265*t*; US defense budget for operations
in, 172–77; US residual forward military
presence in, 251–53, 260–74; US security
arrangements in, 60–65; war as possibility,

153–57, 238. *See also* military presence
and posture (US); oil price shocks; *specific
countries and wars*
Persian Gulf War. *See* Gulf War (1991)
pipelines, 131, 157, 220, 244, 249n24,
249–50n27, 260, 276n35
plug-in hybrid electric vehicles (PHEVs),
215–16
political reform. *See* democratization
Pollack, Kenneth, 155, 257
Press, Daryl, 50, 258–60
price fluctuations: economic costs of supply
disruptions, 87–88, 236; elasticities
of, 100–101, 110–11n77, 111n79. *See
also* gross domestic product (GDP) as
measurement of oil price shocks; oil price
shocks

Qaddafi, Muammar, 52, 57, 130
Qatar: BMD systems in, 66; cyber attack on,
119; military power of, 156; protection
from Saudi Arabia, 257; US military presence in, 61, 63, 255; US residual forward
military position in, 252
Quadrennial Defense Review: on fighting two
wars simultaneously, 169; on Gulf War
(1991), 173

RAND Corporation on defense budget reductions, 170–71, 181–82, 186–87, 194n55,
195n68
Rapid Deployment Joint Task Force (US), 1,
60, 172, 189n15
RasGas, 119
reactive proliferation, 54–55, 65
Reagan, Ronald, 36, 37
rebound effect, 206
recessions (US), connection to oil prices, 88,
89*f*, 92–93, 95–96
regional contingency strategies. *See* major
regional contingency (MRC) strategy
regional hegemony, 142–53, 238, 242; Iran,
21–22, 149–53; Iraq, 143–46; overview,

142–43, 238; Saudi Arabia, 146–49; US
   military options for, 242
regional proxies, 30–37
renewable energy resources, 117
renewable fuel standard (RFS), 209–10
reserves. *See* oil production and reserves;
   Strategic Petroleum Reserves; tight oil
   production
residual forward presence (RFP) posture,
   251–53, 260–73; Air Force role in, 264–68;
   Army role in, 262–64; defined, 252; future
   implications for, 273–74; Navy, Marines,
   and Coast Guard role in, 268–73; overview,
   251–53, 260–62
revolutions. *See* hostile takeover threats
RFP. *See* residual forward presence (RFP)
   posture
Riedel, Bruce, 59
al-Rodhan, Khalid R., 131
Rovner, Joshua, 12, 72, 72n5, 81, 238, 239,
   242, 253
Royal Dutch, 137n2
Royal Saudi Land Forces, 147
Russia, 4, 42, 179, 192n43, 192–93n47. *See also*
   Soviet Union

sabotage as threat to Saudi Arabian oil: by Iran,
   52, 54, 151, 157–59, 253; risk assessment
   of, 120–24, 135, 139n41
Salih, Ali Abdullah, 57
Salman (king), 124, 127, 132
San Bernardino (California) terrorist attack, 55
sanctions: against Iran, 5, 26, 42, 144, 151, 155,
   240; against Iraq, 34, 39, 40; against Soviet
   Union, 34
Sandia National Laboratory on evaluation of
   sabotage threats, 122
al-Saud family, 125, 126, 149
Saudi Arabia: attacks on US presence in, 263,
   277n45; Bahrain intervention by, 53, 135;
   British-Saudi relations, 26–27; counterterrorism and, 55; on democratization, 59, 70;
   deterrence for regional war and, 153–54,

155–56; domestic security training by
   US, 238; economic climate in, 127, 129,
   139n43, 146; Houthi rebels and, 147;
   infrastructure development in, 25, 44n9;
   instability concerns in, 53; on JCPOA,
   53–54; loyalty of military and security
   forces, 127; military power of, 22, 142–43,
   146–49, 151–52, 161, 163n20, 173, 238;
   military presence in, 61, 68–69, 255; on
   Nasserism, 29; National Guard training
   mission (1995), 277n45; oil policies
   of, 115–17, 129–30, 137n12, 140n46;
   pipelines bypassing Strait of Hormuz, 244;
   political climate in, 125–27; post–Arab-
   Israeli War (1967), 32–33; problems
   facing, 124–25; Qatar-Saudi relations,
   257; reactive proliferation potential by, 54;
   religion in, 125–27; security arrangements
   with US, 29, 60, 61, 64, 65, 67, 75n35,
   76n47, 87, 172; Strait of Hormuz and, 159,
   160, 253; terrorism in, 55, 56, 64, 148,
   277n45; US military equipment sales to,
   64; US military presence in, 61, 131–36;
   US-Saudi trade relations, 65; welfare
   improvement projects in, 127, 129, 130,
   140n47, 146, 149; World War II and, 24;
   Yemen-Saudi relations, 127–28. *See also*
   Saudi Arabian oil
Saudi Arabian oil, 113–40; civil war threat and,
   130–31, 134, 139n40, 254; cyber attacks
   and, 118–20, 137–38nn15–16, 138n18,
   138n21; hostile takeover threat and, 51, 67,
   124–30, 132–33, 135–36, 151–52; overview, 113–15; rising domestic demand and
   dwindling resources of, 23, 115–18, 116t,
   146; sabotage threat to, 52, 54, 120–24,
   135, 139n41, 151, 157–59; spare oil capacity of, 50; US role in, 131–36, 253
Saudi Aramco. *See* Aramco
Saudi-Iran Cold War, 157, 165n51
al-Saud regime, 118, 128, 130, 134, 135
Sectarianism, 55, 68, 145, 152, 155, 157, 169,
   191

security arrangements and relationships (US), 60–68; current, 61–65; defense budget for, 172–77; free riding on, 67–68; past, 60–61; with Saudi Arabia, 121–24, 133, 146–48. *See also* military presence and posture (US); *specific countries*

Segal, Adam, 118, 137n15

September 11, 2011, terrorist attacks, 37, 40, 42, 61, 260

sequestration, 184, 195n63

Seventh Fleet, 269. *See also* Navy's (US) military role

Shatt al-'Arab (river), 32, 155

Shell, 131, 137n2

Shia population: Bahrain, 135, 272; Iran, 34, 155; Iraq, 38, 41, 52, 145, 155, 161; possible radicalization of, 130–31; Saudi Arabia, 121, 125, 130–31, 148, 156, 254

shipping risks, 157–60. *See also* Strait of Hormuz

al-Sistani, Ali, 145

Smith, James L.: "World Oil," 111n77

Sony Pictures Entertainment cyber attack (2014), 119

South Korea, 179–80, 192n42, 192–93n47

South Yemen, 29, 32

Soviet Union: Afghanistan invasion by, 22, 34–35; as Cold War threat to oil security, 1, 3, 7, 15, 24–25, 242, 249n20; Eisenhower Doctrine and, 27–28; Iran-Soviet relations, 32; Iraq-Soviet relations, 46n44, 143; as Israel's foe, 72n1; as oil exporter, 131; sanctions against, 34; US policies affected by, 60, 242; World War II and, 23–24, 44n2. *See also* Russia

spare oil capacity, defined, 85–87, 107n20

SPR. *See* Strategic Petroleum Reserves

stability-instability paradox for nuclear proliferation, 53

stagflation, 93

Stern, Roger J.: "United States Cost of Military Force Projection in the Persian Gulf, 1976-2007," 188n7, 191n36

Stiglitz, Joseph, 194n60

Strait of Hormuz: blockade scenarios, 51–52, 157–60, 174, 237–40, 244, 253, 275n8; economic impact of full closure, 136n1; MRC strategy and, 174, 190n24; nuclear proliferation and, 54; as security risk, 157–58; threatened closure during Iran-Iraq War, 37

Strategic Guidance 2012 (DoD), 172, 184, 195n63

Strategic Petroleum Reserve (GAO), 112n91, 248n8

Strategic Petroleum Reserves (SPR): as economic buffer during disruption, 236–38, 248n8; economic impact of, 101–2; increasing size of, 202–4, 220–21; as strategy alternative, 185–86, 236–38, 243, 245; as supply-side solution, 31, 199–200, 202–4, 225n18

strategy alternatives, 185–86, 233–50; defense budget and, 240–41; demand-side, 243; future implications for, 247; international policies as, 244–47; military reduction and, 242–43; options, 241–47; overview, 233–35; SPRs as, 185–86, 236–38, 243, 245; to Strait of Hormuz, 238–40; supply-side, 243; view of oil as economic interest only, 235–36

Stuxnet cyber attack, 118, 175

subsidies: for alternative transportation fuel and vehicles, 210–11, 213, 214, 215; for domestic oil production, 201, 220; by Gulf states for US military presence, 67; OECD country fuel subsidies, 99; for pipelines, 249–50n27, 260; Saudi Arabia fuel subsidies for domestic consumers, 116–17; Saudi Arabia using to preempt unrest, 149

Suez Crisis (1956), 27, 45n13, 202

sunk costs, 12–13, 171–72, 180, 189n13

Sunni population: Iran, 42, 152, 154; Iraq, 41, 145, 148; radicals, 145; Saudi Arabia, 130, 133

supply and demand oil shocks: defined, 91; differences between, 92–93; external threats creating, 50, 72n3; moderating, 84–86; oil disruption and estimation of, 100–104,